STUDIES IN
THE INTELLECTUAL HISTORY OF
TOKUGAWA JAPAN

STUDIES IN
THE INTELLECTUAL HISTORY OF
TOKUGAWA JAPAN

MASAO MARUYAMA

translated by MIKISO HANE

PRINCETON UNIVERSITY PRESS
UNIVERSITY OF TOKYO PRESS
1974

Copublished by
Princeton University Press
    and
University of Tokyo Press
Library of Congress Catalog Card Number:
    70-90954
ISBN: 0-691-07566-2

CONTENTS

TRANSLATOR'S PREFACE

The author, Masao Maruyama, is one of the most brilliant and influential thinkers to emerge in modern Japan. His incisive and original analyses mark him as the leading theorist of Japanese modes of thought and behavior. One observer compared his emergence in postwar Japan to the appearance of a comet, a bright spark that illuminated the darkened skies of a nation that had just suffered a devastating defeat. Just as Ogyū Sorai, the central figure of this work, is seen by the author as the "discoverer of politics" in Japan, he himself can be regarded as the founder of "modern" political science and intellectual history in Japan. His rare analytical faculties allow him to cut through masses of unstructured external material and to extract what is essential, while delineating configurations that remain undetected to less discerning eyes.

Professor Maruyama is wholly committed to scholarly and intellectual excellence and remains an uncompromising perfectionist and an unrelenting purist. Hence, he refuses to publish anything unless he has meticulously examined the evidence, deliberated upon the problems under study until he is thoroughly satisfied, and has concluded that he has something unique and worthwhile to say. As a result the body of his published works is not voluminous, although over the years he has produced a considerable number of highly original and profoundly perceptive treatises.

The chronological range of the subjects he has examined extends from antiquity to the present. His first major work, the treatises included here, dealt with Tokugawa thought. He then proceeded to examine the Meiji thinkers, such as Fukuzawa Yukichi, modern nationalism, contemporary political thought and behavior, and the Japanese mode of thinking in general. Recently he has turned his attention to the early roots of Japanese thought, going as far back as the *Kojiki*, discerning in the "ancient substra [*kosō*] certain patterns that have persisted to the present."[1] He has also returned to the study of Ogyū Sorai and has been making meticulous textual analyses of his writings.

Not only is Professor Maruyama steeped in classical Chinese and Japanese learning, but he is also deeply grounded in Western scholarship, especially in the works of the German idealists (Hegel in particular), German sociologists, and Western positivists. He once stated that his early intellectual life had been the object of a tug of war between German idealism and Western positivism; ultimately he settled somewhere in between German historicism and English empiricism, that is, in the scholarship represented by men like Max Weber, Hermann Heller, and Karl Mannheim.[2]

As a college student he was exposed to Marxism, but he did not embrace the ideology that came to hold such fascination for so many Japanese students and intellectuals of the pre- and postwar years. He ascribes his inability to commit himself to Marxism to "my inbred scepticism of any 'grand theory' as well as my belief in the force of ideas operating in human history."[3] He has continued to eschew all forms of dogmatism and has remained a rationalist and a pragmatist and a sympathetic but stern critic of Marxism.

The dogma that Professor Maruyama had to confront and combat early in his life was the ideological complex that supported the Emperor system. His early interest in Marxism led him into confrontations with the special higher police (*tokkō*), the formidable foe of intellectual freedom and handmaiden of the sys-

---

[1] Cf. citations in author's introduction.

[2] Masao Maruyama, *Thought and Behaviour in Modern Japanese Politics* (London: Oxford University Press, 1963), p. xvi.

[3] Ibid.

tem, who held him suspect and even abused him physically. As the author explains in his introduction, the current work was a form of protest against the authoritarian ideology. In the postwar years, after the collapse of the Emperor system, Professor Maruyama turned his attention to the examination of the mode of thinking that had sustained the system. He was convinced that a new world outlook would not emerge in Japan without thorough exposition and understanding of the mode of thinking and behavior that contributed to the rise of fascistic ideology. The result of his studies was the publication of *Gendai seiji no shisō to kodō*.[4] He continued his examination of the Japanese mode of thinking in a series of treatises, several of which were collected and published in his *Nihon no shisō*.[5] The thesis of one of the key essays is the absence in Japan of an axial intellectual system comparable to Christianity in the West. This left the Japanese, when they were exposed to Western thought in the nineteenth century, without the frame of reference necessary to properly sift, adopt, adapt, and assimilate Western ideas. Consequently, all sorts of theories and concepts were indiscriminately imported and allowed to jostle each other in a helter skelter fashion. In addition, Japanese intellectual life lacked the tradition of individuals, as independent subjects, or autonomous minds, confronting the objective world, and through a logical process extracting from it significant concepts that could be raised to the level of transcendent ideas.

The task facing the Japanese, in Professor Maruyama's opinion, is the creation of an autonomous mind that can function as an intermediary between reality and ideas. It would seek to objectify reality and, on the basis of a fixed standard of values, bring order to the complexities of the external world by a process of conceptualization and abstraction. Such a mind (subject), because of its sensitivity to the process by which ideas are abstracted from reality, would not turn them into fetishes and worship them as absolute dogmas. On the other hand, it would not rely upon non-conceptualized, felt, or immediately apprehended truth as the

[4] 2 vols., Tokyo: Miraisha, 1956–57. About half the essays were translated into English and published in the West in 1963, as *Thought and Behaviour in Modern Japanese Politics, op. cit.* revised edition, 1969.

[5] Tokyo: Iwanami, 1961.

guidepost of life, a tendency that is widespread in Japan. The task that the author has set for himself then is to work for the creation of this independent subject in Japan.

The treatises included here constitute a milestone in the study of Tokugawa thought. They comprise the first systematic, in-depth analysis of the mode of thinking of the Tokugawa scholars, a methodical examination of changes occurring in the basic assumptions of Tokugawa thought. These essays, in particular the first two, have become the reference points for all subsequent studies of Tokugawa thought. Since they appeared, scholars have either sought to build upon them or to challenge the author's theses. Among many others, Professor Albert Craig of Harvard believes that "all who write on Tokugawa thought must at some point ask themselves how their work relates to Maruyama Masao's brilliant elucidation of the development of the school of Ancient Learning in his *Nihon seiji shisōshi kenkyū*."[6]

In these studies Professor Maruyama traces the disintegration of the Chu Hsi hegemony in Tokugawa thought and reveals emergent strains of modern consciousness. In the first essay he sees Chu Hsi philosophy with its all-embracing *li* (Principle), which linked together all aspects of the universe, being challenged by the emergence of the school of Ancient Learning. The central figure in this confrontation was Ogyū Sorai who ultimately separated the Neo-Confucian natural and moral laws as well as private (moral) and public (political) aspects of life, thus seriously undermining its continuative mode of thinking. The examination of Sorai's challenge to Chu Hsi philosophy is continued in the second treatise. Here Sorai is seen as rejecting the Chu Hsi concept of the natural order. The Way of the Sages, upon which all institutions and values were founded, Sorai argued, was not part of the natural order but was invented by the sages. In both essays the author sees Sorai's mode of thinking influencing in a significant way the scholars of National Learning as well as other Tokugawa thinkers.

The author also discusses the relationship between the disintegration of the orthodox worldview and the deterioration of the

---

[6] Marius B. Jansen, ed., *Changing Japanese Attitudes Toward Modernization* (Princeton: Princeton University Press, 1965), p. 155.

feudal sociopolitical system itself. His studies show that Tokugawa thought was not static and fixed, as is generally assumed, but underwent subtle but dynamic changes that prepared the ground for the adoption of modern (Western) concepts and intellectual systems during the Meiji period. Another understanding that emerges from the author's investigations is that, contrary to conventional opinion, Tokugawa thinkers were not merely uncritical purveyors of Chinese Confucian concepts. There were, in fact, a number of independent-minded, "original" thinkers. Chief among them was Ogyū Sorai, a seminal mind in Professor Maruyama's opinion. The author not only provides a succinct exposition of Chu Hsi philosophy but, in analyzing the changes in Tokugawa thought, also draws a parallel to the intellectual changes that had taken place in Europe from Aquinas to Descartes.

As Professor Maruyama points out in his Introduction, he had to abandon his original plan of examining in the last essay the rise of nationalism after the Meiji Restoration and limit his study to the closing years of the Tokugawa period. Modern nationalism, he concludes, failed to develop in Tokugawa Japan because the society was divided basically into two classes, the ruling and the ruled. But he does discern the emergence of premodern nationalism, stimulated by the arrival of the Western powers to Japanese shores. This sentiment fused with the *sonnō* (reverence for the Emperor) movement and found expression in the movement to "enrich the nation and strengthen the military," but it failed to develop beyond this stage because it excluded the common people from its thinking.

Because work on this translation was spread over many years and underwent several transformations, some inconsistencies in translation as well as editorial policy may have slipped in. For example, the citation of sources in Part III is different from that in Parts I and II. This resulted partly from the fact that we changed our policy regarding the many source references found in the main body of the text in Part III. Initially we decided to leave them out, but after the galleys were returned we decided to retain them. Consequently, some are placed at the foot of the page while others are incorporated into the text. Also these citations are not always followed by English translations as is the case with those in the earlier parts. However, all the works cited by the author—with English translations—can be found in the index.

The emphases indicated by italics in the passages quoted by the author and in his own writing were placed there by him. In transcribing Japanese names we have followed the practice of giving the surname first. Tokugawa figures, however, are usually identified by their given names.

We tried to keep the translation as close as possible to the original but in some cases liberties were taken for the sake of clarity and for stylistic reasons. Also in some instances Professor Maruyama amplified the original passages.

I started translating this work over a decade ago and received help of numerous persons, some of whom remain unknown to me. I am unable to acknowledge my debt to everyone but I must thank Mr. Shigeo Minowa, Director of the University of Tokyo Press, for his patience and determination to see this translation completed and published. I am also grateful to Ms. R. Miriam Brokaw of Princeton University Press for her encouragement during the early stages of this translation. Of the many editorial assistants at the University of Tokyo Press I must give special thanks to Ms. Linda Glass for seeing the manuscript safely through the galley and page proof stages. Mr. Toshirō Oka checked the early version of the translation for accuracy. Above all, I am deeply indebted to Mr. Benjamin Brewster for going over the translation meticulously, making extensive stylistic improvements as well as catching lapses in translation. I am also grateful to Professors Marius B. Jansen and Ronald P. Dore for examining the translation and facilitating its publication. In addition, Professor Dore kindly translated the author's introduction for us. Most importantly, I am enormously indebted to Professor Maruyama. Not only has translating his work been a stimulating and challenging intellectual experience, but he also expended an enormous amount of time and energy patiently checking over the translation with me.

I am also thankful to the Associated Colleges of the Midwest and Knox College for the assistance extended to me over the years, and to my colleagues at Knox for responding patiently to my incessant queries about proper English phraseology. To my wife, Rose, I owe much more than the fact that she typed and retyped the manuscript with great patience and skill.

Galesburg, Illinois   Mikiso Hane
October, 1974

AUTHOR'S INTRODUCTION
TO ENGLISH EDITION*

I

The three parts that make up this book were originally published as independent essays in the *Kokka Gakkai Zasshi*[1]. The first essay appeared in 1940, and the last just thirty years ago, in 1944. The intervening three decades have seen a vast outpouring of publications on the topics which are the main concern of this book—the Tokugawa Confucianism and its intellectual adversaries. Moreover, in terms of approaches to the history of ideas, the Japanese academic world is incomparably richer today than it was then. Thirty years is enough in any branch of scholarship to make a work out of date. What makes this book something of a curiosity, therefore, is the fact that it has not been neglected by influential postwar scholars of Tokugawa intellectual history, or treated as a mere relic of the past, but is still considered, even today, as a work that is still "in active service." In their different ways, students of Tokugawa thought—including those concerned with rejecting its approach to intellectual history or with refuting its interpretations of Neo-Confucianism or of Sorai's ideas or of National Learning or its view of semantics—have recognized it as a "point of departure."

---

* The translation of this introduction was prepared by Prof. Ronald P. Dore.
[1] A journal the inspiration of which is best indicated by translating its title as the "Journal of the Association of Staatswissenschaften"—the association founded by Ito Hirobumi following the promulgation of the Imperial Constitution.

For the author this is at once a great honor and a source of some embarrassment, for my present views, both on the broader questions of the writing of intellectual history and, more narrowly, on the other currents of Tokugawa thought with which this book chiefly deals, have shifted in many important respects over the last thirty years. It would, indeed, be an admission of intellectual stagnation if this were not so. On the other hand, among the postwar criticisms of my methodology and interpretations there are some that seem to me to be mistaken or to misread my intentions and to which it would be possible to mount a rebuttal, even in terms of the position I had taken thirty years ago. Hence to bring this work up to date would require a simultaneous battle on two fronts: with my critics and with my own youthful self. Rather than undertake such a complex task, I would find it easier to write a new book. It is for this reason that I still allow the original Japanese edition to continue to be reprinted as it stands.

For this same reason I shall not attempt in this introduction to develop in any positive, detailed fashion my present views on the subject matter of this book. Instead, it might be a better contribution to the English reader's understanding if I try to give some idea of the atmosphere of the Japanese academic world at the time I wrote these essays and of the studies which preceded them —of the intellectual heritage on which they were built and by which their approach was conditioned.

II

It is no easy task to convey a convincing picture of the spiritual atmosphere that surrounded those who devoted themselves to the study of *Japanese* thought in those days of the so-called dark valley of Japanese history. It is even difficult to convey it to the younger generation brought up in postwar Japan, let alone to the Western reader from a quite different cultural environment. It is not enough simply to express abstractly things that everyone knows—the severity of government censorship or the taboos surrounding such concepts as "the national polity." Perhaps the best way to give the reader a feeling for the mental climate in which Japanese intellectuals lived in the thirties and early forties—including the inhabitants of ivory towers—is to recount one or two episodes that occurred at the time I was writing these essays.

The essay that makes up Part I of this book appeared in four successive numbers of the *Kokka Gakkai Zasshi* between January and April 1940. When the first one came out I soon became aware of a grave misprint. In discussing the arrival of Confucianism to Japan (see p. 7 below) I referred to Emperor Ōjin's reign. But for *jin* the character 仁 (benevolence) was used instead of 神 (god). The late Professor Muraoka Tsunetsugu (1884–1946) who was lecturing on Japanese thought at both Tokyo and Tōhoku Imperial Universities made a point of coming round to my room at the university to advise me to put an immediate correction in the next issue. He told me then that Dr. Inoue Tetsujiro (1854–1944) had once made exactly the same mistake[2] and had been fiercely attacked for it by right-wing nationalists. "A nice irony, when you come to think of it," he added, "Dr. Inoue who had long been famous for attacking other scholars and men of religion like Uchimura Kanzō [1861–1930], accusing them of harboring ideas and theories contrary to the national polity, and there was the same Inoue, being accused of lèse majesté for a simple slip." At any rate, in Imperial Japan, there was no question about it: to get the name of any one of Japan's long succession of Emperors wrong was not a matter that could be simply excused as a mere printing error or slip of the pen. I put an errata table in the next issue. For other errors I merely paired the mistakes and corrections, but when it came to Emperor Ōjin I felt compelled to include a special phrase: "I *reverently* make this correction" (*Tsutsushinde teisei suru*). A modern Japanese student, finding such a portentous phrase in an academic article, would doubtless roar with laughter; thirty years ago it was far from being a laughing matter.

My second memory is not of a misprint, but of an amendment I made in the manuscript before it went to the printers. On page 18 appears the phrase "Motoori Norinaga's philosophy, a phi-

---

[2] Japanese are likely to make this mistake for two reasons. (1) The Emperor Ōjin 応神 was succeeded by the Emperor Nintoku 仁徳 The character 仁 is pronounced in Japanese both as *jin* and as *nin*. (2) One of the greatest civil wars in Japan is called *Ōnin no Ran*, which began in the first year of Ōnin 応仁 (1467 A.D.) and brought about vast destruction in Kyoto.

losophy that inherited Sorai's mode of thought but completely transformed it." What I had originally written was "For Norinaga, Sorai's mode of thinking was truth standing on its head. In the sense that he turned it back the right way up, Norinaga can be seen as inheriting Sorai's thought." I had in mind, of course, the analogy of Marx's relation to Hegel. The change was due to my tutor, the late Professor Nanbara.[3] It was not, of course, that he thought that I was being in any way subversive. However, he knew that I was at the time under the surveillance of our "thought police" (tokkō), and he was concerned to warn me, in the kindest way possible, that the use of this phrase from Marx's criticism of Hegel's dialectic in the preface to the second edition of *Das Kapital* would raise a provocative echo in the ears of the authorities and of conservative professors. I must admit that I thought he was being a little over-sensitive, even given the reactionary political situation, but from gratitude for his concern if for no other reason I decided to accept his advice and changed the original expression. Such was the care one needed to exercise even in choosing one's metaphors and even when writing about philosophers two centuries dead in an academic journal.

III

So much for the mental climate of the time. Let me say a little, now, about the scholarly antecedents of my essays and try to give, in chronological order, a typology of the main approaches to the history of Japanese thought in earlier academic works. For the reader who has the patience to follow this book's complex—and it will probably seem to him almost scholastic—analysis of Tokugawa Confucianism, National Learning, and other intellectual currents, it may be helpful in understanding the background to have a brief catalogue[4] of the intellectual heritage which was this book's starting point, even if my categories have, of necessity, to be somewhat Procrustean.

In the first category come studies that can be grouped under

---

[3] Nanbara Shigeru (1889–1974), a liberal political philosopher and postwar president of the University of Tokyo.

[4] Not intended, of course, as a comprehensive bibibliography of the book's sources.

the rubric *kokumin dōtoku-ron* (theories of the national morality). *Kokumin dōtoku* translated straight as "national morals" may seem a difficult concept to comprehend given the assumption—an assumption nowadays common in many other cultural areas besides the Christian—that morality is basically a matter of conscience and hence a matter for the individual. In Imperial Japan, however, it was a word which began to be used with distinct ideological connotations by politicians and educators around the turn of the century, but which persisted and retained those same connotations among conservative groups through the First World War and right into the period of "Taishō democracy." The most generous interpretation is to say that it was, in a Japan overwhelmed by the tide of Westernization after the Meiji Restoration, an expression in the moral sphere of the desperate effort to establish a national identity. There was, it was frequently asserted, an urgent need to establish a new morality to guide the Emperor's subjects, something that would suitably combine both the non-Western teachings of Confucianism, Buddhism, and Shinto and also those elements of Western morals that were not subversive for the new Imperial Japan but rather supplied what were seen as deficiencies in the traditional teachings—for example, what came to be known as "civic morality." Since it was morality that was in question it was natural that the emphasis, among traditional ideologies, should be placed on Confucianism. The earnest exponents of such ideas among scholars and educators were known as "theorists of the National Morality." Dr. Inoue Tetsujirō, the Professor of Ethics at Tokyo Imperial University mentioned above, was a representative figure in this group. His numerous books and articles on the National Morality, strident as they were in their exhortatory tone, had little scholarly value, though his three-volume study[5] of Tokugawa Confucianism, in which he employed the categories of the Western philosophy that he had studied in Europe, remains a milestone in the modern study of Tokugawa Confucianism. It was the first work to break from the long tradi-

---

[5] *Nihon yōmeigaku-ha no tetsugaku* [The philosophy of the Japanese Wang Yang-ming school], Tokyo, 1900; *Nihon kogaku-ha no tetsugaku* [The philosophy of the Japanese school of Ancient Learning], Tokyo, 1902; and *Nihon Shushigaku-ha no tetsugaku* [The philosophy of the Japanese Chu Hsi school], Tokyo, 1905.

tion of scholarship confined to exegetical commentary on the Chinese classics and to treat the history of Japanese Confucianism as the history of "thought." Even if one discounts his insistence on forcing every single Confucian scholar or Confucian-influenced thinker into one or another of his three "schools," and for the mechanical way in which he forced his interpretation into the categories of European philosophy, his work has still not outlived its usefulness. Other works that come in the same category are Iwabashi Junsei's *Dai-Nihon rinri-shisō hattatsu-shi* [History of the development of ethical thought in great Japan, 2 vols., 1915] and Kiyohara Sadao's *Kokutai-ron-shi* [History of the theory of the National Polity, 1920].

In the first decade of the century new trends appeared in reaction to this approach to the study of Japanese thought. The first one might tentatively be labeled as "the history of thought as cultural history." The source of inspiration for these writers lay in the *Kulturgeschichte* of nineteenth-century Germany from the *Philologie* of which August Böckh (1785–1867) was a representative exponent, to the *Geistesgeschichte* of Wilhelm Dilthey (1833–1911). To give a concrete example of a work that is even now recognized as a classic in the study of "National Learning," Muraoka Tsunetsugu's *Motoori Norinaga* (1911) is written on the assumption that the underlying method of Norinaga's ancient learning and study of the ancient way conformed precisely to the principles of Böckh's *Philologie*—"the re-cognition of that which was once cognized" ("*Erkennen des Erkannten*"). Muraoka later applied this method not only to National Learning, but also to Confucianism and Shinto and the whole field of the history of Japanese thought, producing a number of valuable works.

Another leading scholar who, though he differed in his concerns from Muraoka was also heavily influenced by the methods of German cultural history, was Watsuji Tetsurō. Watsuji's methodological inclination was toward hermeneutics, and, although he was in this regard more influenced in his later years by Martin Heidegger than by Dilthey, the influence of Diltheyesque *Geistesgeschichte* is clear in the title of the first collection of essays in which he developed his many-sided view of Japanese culture, *Nihon seishin-shi kenkyū* [Studies in the history of the human spirit in Japan, vol. 1, 1926; vol. 2, 1935]. As such, his emphasis naturally lay less in the field of political and social thought than in literature, drama (for example, the Kabuki), and the formal arts. From the 1930s on, Watsuji began to apply his own characteristic ethical theory to the history of Japanese thought and to emphasize reverence for the Emperor (*sonnō*) as the continuing core of the Japanese tradition. As a historian of Japanese ethical thought, therefore, his work came to overlap subtly with that of the first category mentioned above, though Watsuji himself never ceased until the end to display open hostility to the exponents of the Theory of the National Morality. Fundamental to Watsuji's approach was a concept of culture (*Kultur*), which was—as was typical of the intellectuals of the 1910s and the early 1920s—apolitical if not anti-political. We can say that he left his mark in the scholarly world by setting his view of the Japanese tradition as conceived in this light against, on the one hand, the theory of the National Morality of Inoue and his lesser followers and, on the other, the historical materialist view of ideas and doctrines as a mere function of the class war. It is worth remarking in passing that because of the origins of the concept in Dilthey's work the Japanese words *Nihon seishin-shi* have a dual meaning: the one, "the history of the human spirit in Japan," and the other, "the history of the Japanese spirit." Those who used it in the latter sense—with the implication that there is some substantive entity called "the Japanese spirit" that develops through the centuries manifesting itself from time to time in a variety of historical guises—had their heyday in the militaristic period of the 1930s and clearly belong, genealogically, to the National Morality school. In contrast, the study of Japanese culture and thought to which the influence of Dilthey and Böckh gave birth was infused with the flavor of historical relativism.

Yet another reaction against the National Morality school, almost contemporary with, but different from, that of Watsuji or Muraoka is the distinctive position adopted by Tsuda Sōkichi (1873–1961). His most outstanding contribution to the history of Japanese thought was his *Bungaku ni arawaretaru waga kokumin shisō no kenkyū* [The study of thought in our country as revealed in literature, 4 vols. 1916–1921].[6] This great overview of Japanese thought from the ancient beginnings to the Tokugawa period still stands, together with his work on Japanese myths and the ancient history of Japan, as a luminous landmark in the history of the subject. It is hard to summarize Tsuda's methodology in any simple manner. Essentially he sought to grasp not just the "doctrines" or the "schools" of Japanese thought, but what he called the *jisseikatsu*—the texture of life as it was lived; he tried, in other words, to elucidate the main ideological currents of each period in relation to the everyday life attitudes of the classes that played a dominant role in the development of Japanese culture—the court nobles of the Heian period, the warriors of the early, the commoners of the later feudal period—classifying them under such headings as "views of nature," "views of human existence," "views of love," and "views of politics." For Tsuda, the theories of most Confucian and Buddhist scholars were the products of bookish knowledge and armchair speculation, having little to do with the real daily life, the *jisseikatsu*, of the people. As such he treated them as of little importance, while he made extensive use of popular stories, satirical poems, and other materials hitherto neglected by historians of Japanese thought to elucidate the currents of thought that they episodically revealed. He liberated the history of thought from the biographical study of "thinkers," and directed attention to the ways of thought of the nameless masses and to the manifold forms in which their consciousness was expressed. And therein lay his great contribution. Marxist historians were later to claim him as the pioneer of studies rooted in "the theory of ideology," but this is to judge from historical consequences rather than from intentions. In fact, Tsuda's approach too was formed in the first decades of the century within the stream of "cultural history" studies; it was just that he differed from Muraoka and Watsuji in seeking to understand culture in close relation with its social and political context. He was later to say that it was a reading of Georg Brandes' *Main Currents in the Literature of*

---

[6] When the work was reprinted after the war, the word "*waga*"—"our country"—disappeared from the title, and the contents were largely revised in a more conservative, traditionalist direction.

the Nineteenth Century [Original Danish ed., 6 vols. 1870–1890] that inspired him to try this method of tracing currents of thought through Japanese history. But from Brandes he got only the germ of the idea; the structure of Tsuda's work in its entirety is wholly Tsuda's own creation.

In the second half of the twenties came Marxism, sweeping through the Japanese intelligentsia like a whirlwind and drawing the academic world, too, into its turbulence. Hence there naturally appeared a third category of studies of the history of Japanese thought differing from the other two, studies rooted in the Marxist materialist view of history. The impact of Marxist methodology in the field of intellectual history in Japan was in a curious way ambivalent.[7] The relevant aspect of Marxism, of course, to which the modern reader needs no introduction, was the theory of ideology—the assumption that the religious doctrines, ethical teachings, and metaphysical systems of every historical period— not to speak of political, economic, and social ideas—were a superstructure built on the economic foundations of society, not something that developed autonomously. Even if some kind of two-way interrelation between ideologies and their social infra- structure be admitted, changes in the former are "ultimately" conditioned by the latter. For historians dominated by such a view of history, therefore, it was to the economic system and the class structure or the concrete stage of the class struggle that primary attention had to be directed; the historical development of ideas and philosophies seemed at most as of secondary importance, "reflections" of these basic driving forces. And in fact the over- whelming majority of Marxist studies of Japanese history were concentrated in the fields of economic history or the history of class conflict.

In this the Japanese academic world was hardly exceptional. On the other hand, one should not overlook another, at first sight contrary, aspect of the influence of Marxism on Japanese histori- ography and social science. For members of the Japanese intel- ligensia who still retained in some remote corner of their conscious-

---

[7] See my *Nihon no shiso* (Tokyo: Iwanami Shoten, 1961), for a discussion of the striking influence of Marxism over wide fields of Japanese scholarship and literature and of the reasons for this influence.

ness the sediment of an animistic view of the universe inherited from ancient times, but who had also been trained in the *specialized* fields of higher academic learning imported directly from Europe, Marxist methodology presented a startling freshness of vision as an integrating, systematic science that offered to unite the specialized sciences in a comprehensive *Weltanschauung*. Paradoxically enough, Marxism as a grand theory of modern idealism, *which bore the name materialism*, performed for the Japanese academic world the role that the subjectivist stream of epistemology from Descartes to Kant had played in Europe. The early translation of the philosophical writings of the young Marx, and the popularity in the early thirties of the epistemological works of such Marxist writers as Georg Lukacs or Karl Korsch, who were heavily influenced by German idealism, have to be understood in relation to these special characteristics of the Japanese intellectual climate.

As a consequence, there was, in Japan, a curiously more mature aspect to the scholarly understanding of Marxism as compared with the Anglo-Saxon world. For example, the view of historical materialism widely diffused in the thirties in Britain and America —as simply a kind of economic determinism—seemed at the time to any young Japanese student with the least pretentions to a concern with philosophy far too naive. This background helps to explain why I myself, though I could hardly even then be called a Marxist, when I came to try and trace the development of thought in Tokugawa Japan, received a great many methodological hints and stimuli from such a work as *Der Übergang vom feudalen zum bürgerlichen Weltbild* by Franz Borkenau, one of the foremost scholars of the group of Marxist social scientists who gathered at the Frankfurt Institut für Sozialforschung in Weimar Germany. What appealed to me was the fact that, in sharp contrast to the simplistic way in which orthodox Soviet Marxists frequently attempted to see debates of even the most metaphysical questions as direct reflections of class struggle, Borkenau never lost sight of the internal structural interrelations between basic categories of thought—of "nature," "reason," and "law"—in his attempt to trace the subtle transformation of world views from the mediaeval period to the Renaissance.

It was not, however, until after 1934, when Japan was already sliding down an ever more steeply inclined plane toward disastrous militarism that Marxist scholars began to publish in the field of the history of Japanese thought proper, as opposed to economic or social history. The studies of "traditional" ideology —Confucianism, National Learning, and Shinto—by Nagata Hiroshi, Torii Hiroo, Saegusa Hiroto, Hani Gorō and so on— belong to this time. For them, the main antagonists were *not* the writers influenced by European "bourgeois" historiography but none other than the ideologues of the "Japanese spirit." Given the social and political circumstances of the time they were forced into a defensive posture. The tighter thought control became the more they had to stress the scientific requirements of universalism and objectivity, rather than the partisan (*parteilich*) character of any study. (By contrast—an ironic contrast—those other Marxists who converted from Marxism to Japanism simply replaced their assertion of the class conditionings on thought and doctrine by equal emphasis on the national and geopolitical conditionings.) For example, Nagata Hiroshi had the following to say in the preface to his *Nihon tetsugaku shisōshi* [History of Japanese philosophical thought, 1938], one of the representative works of this camp:

> What is essential in writing the history of ideas is to elucidate the various significant currents of thought of the past in historical relation with those of the present day, particularly with those which hold promise for the future. *It is not to choose and select from among them in accordance with one's own subjective preferences.* It is to be regretted that most of the studies in the history of ideas published in this country have been overwhelmingly influenced by the *moral prejudices* of the writer. (My italics)

This claim to freedom from value judgement comes from none other than a Marxist scholar! His reference to work in the history of ideas "overwhelmingly influenced by the moral prejudices of the writer" refers to those, from the theorists of the National Morality to the philosophers of the Imperial Way, who wrote in celebration of the virtues of the National Polity. (He chose to refer to them in this indirect manner, of course, in deference to the censors.) That a Marxist scholar, whom one would expect to expose the false pretence of "objectivity" in bourgeois historiography, should adopt such a position, is, of course, an indication of the desperate straits to which Marxists were driven in their contemporary situation. At the same time, it illustrates most vividly the paradoxical role played by Marxism in the prewar Japanese intellectual scene.

IV

When I began my academic career as a student of the development of Japanese political thought, I derived, of course, a great deal of benefit from the legacy of these previous writings on the history of ideas in Japan—as well as from the much longer tradition of *Keigaku* (studies in the Confucian classics). But I do not think I got more from them than specific interpretations of the writings of particular individual scholars. As far as concerned the method and approach to be used in analyzing "trends" of thought in the Tokugawa period I was, frankly speaking, feeling my way in the dark. Methodologically I was not prepared to give my allegiance to any one of the "schools" summarized above.

To begin with, as a young man, I felt an almost physical revulsion toward the ethical and political dogma that infused the writings—even the relatively less fanatical writings—of the National Morality writers and those of their decendants who were developing the then-fashionable "Theory of the Japanese Spirit" and whose works made up the greater part of the current output. The second group of "cultural history" writers was generally far superior in academic value, but I had already had enough of a baptism in Marxism to be unable any longer to treat "culture" and "philosophy" as self-sufficient entities, divorced from their social-historical context or from the society's class structure. On the other hand, I did not find satisfaction in the writings of the Marxists themselves. As I have already said, Japanese Marxism of the thirties had passed beyond the stage of naively categorizing all ideology as a mere expression of class interest or a mechanical reflection of production relations, but it still had not shown how, concretely, one could relate, on the one hand, those developments and ideas that can be attributed to the autonomous working-out of their own internal logic to, on the other, changes in the social base and in class relations. For some it was still not impersonal thought categories but individual thinkers who were the focus of attention, and in that sense they had not broken out of the tradition of biographical studies. Others, despairing of the conscious thought—particularly political thought—of intellectuals in pre-modern Japan, both for its monotonic uniformity and for its lack of all but the rarest flash of any anti-authoritarian sentiment, had looked to the records of peasant rebellion for signs of the burgeoning of an anti-feudal, revolutionary ideology. Neither group seemed to me satisfactory. As far as the study of thinkers was concerned, to seek merely to separate out the "progressive" sides and the "reactionary" sides of such men as Sorai and Norinaga, when both aspects were organically interrelated within the personalities of single individuals, seemed to me to fail to grasp their ideas in their proper integrity. And the more populist students of peasant rebellions seemed to me, working as they did at such a low level of abstraction, to have no persuasive answer to the question of how far one could be sure that the records of historical events that they relied on really told one anything about the "thought" of the mass of the people.

Of course it would be unfair to pass judgement on these Marxists without taking into account the handicaps under which they labored, in the circumstances already described, when they began to direct their attention to the field of Japanese thought. One had to give them credit for the way in which they sought to preserve their scholarly conscience, even to the point of retreating to the bastions of bourgeois ideas—universalism, scientific objectivity, or the Enlightenment's belief in progress. To that extent I did, to be sure, feel a sympathy with them. But the other aspect of that retreat was a dilution of all that was uniquely characteristic of Marxist ideology—which much reduced the freshness of their appeal to me and their relevance to my work.

There was one thing that I felt I could cling to in my struggle to find some way of combining the study "from the inside" of the logical development of ideas with the study "from the outside" of their social function, and that, drowning man's straw though it may have been, was Karl Mannheim's sociology of knowledge. I realized later what a great help it would have been to me if I had been able to see at the time the prefatory "Preliminary Approach to the Problem" that appears in the English edition of his *Ideology and Utopia*. But, alas, the original German edition (*Ideologie und Utopie*, 1929) lacked this simple and comprehensive preface, and it was from that difficult text with its densely compressed style that I had to work. But it gave me some valuable ideas, notably Mannheim's concepts of what he called *Aspektstruktur*— or perspectives—and *Denkmodellen*—thought models, or as we should now say paradigms—which he saw as playing an intermediary role between the social base and individual social or political ideas, and, also, his ideas on the distinction between what he called "the total and the particular conceptions of ideology." It was under the inspiration of Mannheim that I attempted in Part I of this book—albeit with indifferent success—to treat early Tokugawa Neo-Confucianism not as the doctrines of individual Confucianists, but rather, on an impersonal level, as a "Neo-Confucian mode of thought" and to try to trace through the historical vicissitudes of that mode of thought the disintegration of the "orthodox" world view of the Tokugawa period. The idea was attractive enough in its conception, but the actual labor of trying to bridge the gap between Mannheim's abstract methodology and the embarrassingly rich historical material on Tokugawa Confucianism and National Learning was far from easy.

I have already mentioned that I also found Borkenau's work an illuminating illustration of how to go about linking the internal logical and the external sociological perspectives on the history of ideas. The argument of Part I—that the twin related concepts of "norm" and "nature" that characterized Neo-Confucianism split apart later in the development of Confucian thought and that it was this split which prepared the ground for the mode of thought of the scholars of the National Learning—got many hints from Borkenau's description of the historical development of Thomas Aquinas' concept of "natural law" and its various categories.[8]

---

[8] Quite by chance Naramoto Tatsuya also published a study of the dissolution of the Neo-Confucian concept of natural law at almost the same time—also much influenced by Borkenau's method of analysis. (See his *Nihon hōken shakai-shi-ron* [Historical treatises on Japanese feudal society], 1948, in which it is included.) One can also find other attempts to tackle intellectual history with chief attention to impersonal thought categories in the wartime work of Ienaga Saburō (*Nihon shisōshi ni okeru hitei*

As for the leitomotiv of Part II—the transition from the idea of a natural to that of an artificial social order—I cannot think of any obvious influence under which it was written although I did receive some occasional hints from writers like Ferdinand Tönnies, Max Weber, and Ernst Troeltsch whom I cite in the notes. Part II, in point of fact, was written as a sort of supplement to the first part. I was, after all, destined for a post as a lecturer in the history of Japanese *political* thought. Although I could claim my own justification for doing so, having concentrated in my maiden publication (i.e., Part I of this book) on the philosophical categories of the Confucianists and the apolitical literary theories of the Scholars of National Learning, thus leaving aside the direct response of these thinkers to their social and political environment, I felt it was necessary to supplement this with something that explicitly shifted attention to political ideology in its narrow sense. And yet, in terms of overt political doctrines the two and a half Tokugawa centuries were really a barren, impoverished period. There was not even a trace of the mediaeval European theory of the *right* of resistance, let alone any hint of a social contract theory or notions of popular sovereignty. If one excepts the "forgotten thinker"[9] Andō Shōeki, right up to the end of the period there was not a trace of any fundamental ideological rejection of the class structure of Tokugawa society itself—as distinct from those ideas that simply challenged the authority of the central Tokugawa government or the various fief governments. Even the "realism" of the commoner philosophers (Hiraga Gennai, Shiba Kōkan, Kaiho Seiryō), with their jeering attacks on the empty theories of the "rotten Confucians" (*kusare jyusha*), implied a realistic approval of the existing "reign of peace and order." And the "revere the Emperor" theorists were not actually as anti-Tokugawa as subsequent traditionalists and National Polity ideologists have tried to make out, let alone being anti-feudal. (Hayashi Razan who served loyally as Ieyasu's Chief Secretary

---

no ronri no hattatsu [Development of the logic of negation in the history of Japanese thought], 1940, and *Nihon ni okeru shūkyōteki shizenkan no tenkai* [The development of a religious view of "nature" in Japan], 1944).

[9] To use the title of the Japanese translation of the late E. H. Norman's study of Andō Shōeki.

was already stressing the tradition of reverence for the Emperor!)
What I wanted to do in Part II, therefore, was to show how the
basis for a modern consciousness had emerged as an "unintended
consequence," in the same way as in Part I, but at a more explicitly political level. The approach that emerged from my rather
desperate efforts in this direction was to show how a new and
different ideological underpinning could be created for the *same*
sociopolitical order.[10] But, the present-day reader may ask, why
this stubborn preoccupation with seeing the history of Tokugawa
thought in terms of the emergence of modern consciousness? The
answer to *that* question must again take us outside the sphere of
scholastic methodology, back to the atmosphere of the time that
I have referred to above.

The word "modern" (*kindai*) has long since held a very special
significance, a very particular nuance in Japan—as witness Ōsugi
Sakae's choice of *Modern Thought* as the title of his anarchist
magazine in 1912. (This prewar background was, incidentally,
one source of the misunderstandings that arose between Japanese
and Anglo-Saxon scholars over the concept "modernization" during the series of seminars on the modernization of Japan held in
the early sixties.) I wrote these articles at a time when, in Japanese
intellectual circles, one constant topic of debate was *kindai no
chōkoku*—"overcoming modernity." The "modernity" to be "overcome" was a complex concept; it meant the scholarship, art,
literature as well as the technology, industry, and political institutions of Europe from, in the broadest definition, the Renaissance, in the narrowest from the Industrial Revolution and the
French Revolution, to the present day. The common perspective
of these "We shall overcome" theorists was that a great turning
point in world history had been reached; the whole world of
modernity which had been created by the "advanced nations"
of the West and the global supremacy of these nations were now
collapsing loudly about their ears. A completely new civilization
was about to be born. The intellectuals who held this view were

---

[10] Thus, both parts are attempts at "Problemgeschichte" from a particular viewpoint, not comprehensive histories. Hence even some important scholars like Arai
Hakuseki and Muro Kyūsō are not dealt with because they were not relevant to that
perspective.

not by any means all fascists and militarists; to me, too, at the
time, some of these ideas seemed plausible. However, in the atmosphere of the early 1940s the subtleties of this position tended
to get lost as the voices of the "overcomers" were engulfed in the
swelling chorus of denuciation proclaiming that the mission of the
intellectual was to hasten the demise of "outmoded" European
liberalism and to cooperate in the glorious task of constructing
the New World Order that Japan, Germany, and Italy were
seeking to build. The chorus was led, not only by the militarists,
"reformist" bureaucrats, and politicians, but also by former liberals and leftist intellectuals who had converted to Japanism. It
was, moreover, part and parcel of this view that the disease of
"modernity" had seeped into every sphere of Japanese life since
the Meiji Restoration and that nowhere were the inroads of path-
ological decay more apparent than in the intellectual world.
Hence the problem was not merely one of international conflict
between the Axis and the Allies, but at the same time one of
internal ideological division that cried out for definitive *Gleich-
schaltung*. Hence modernity became the universal scapegoat, and
any intellectual or scholar who reacted strongly against these
"overcome modernity" theorists and the background currents of
totalitarian ideas that sustained them was bound to feel a duty,
each in his own field, to defend it. Those who went against the
contemporary ideological tides, both liberals and Marxists, stood
together on this intellectual battleground on the side of "modernity." Thus the position adopted by one group of Marxists that was
described above; their reaffirmation of the bourgeois-liberal
academic ideals of objectivity and freedom from value judgement.

In the field of history, including the history of ideas, this intellectual confrontation revolved around two intimately interrelated questions. How true, in the first place, was the ultra-na-
tionalists' assumption that Japan had already been thoroughly
modernized in the period since the Meiji Restoration and, indeed,
that all the greatest ills of contemporary Japanese society are
nothing but the toxic effects of overabsorption of modern Western
culture and institutions? Second, what historical foundation was
there for their assertion that "before its purity was sullied by
'modernity,' Japanese culture exhibited a perfect harmonious

fusion between its Ancient Faith and the 'Oriental Spirit,' such as Confucianism and Buddhism derived from the Continent, a tradition which in all fields—culture, society, the polity—had been firmly maintained, withstanding the erosion of history"? Or that, as it followed, Japan's great contribution to the establishment of the New World Order should be to purge this glorious tradition of our ancestors and free it from the impurities of "modernity"?

Thus, as the reader will by now have gathered, underlying my own choice of theme in the first two of these essays—the maturing of "modern" modes of thought in the Tokugawa period and the attempts to measure the degree of such maturity—lay the extra-academic motive of combating the "overcome modernity" theorists in my own professional field. Briefly, what I was trying to show was that (1)—in response to the first assumption—contemporary Japan was still not so modernized that the "overcoming of modernity" could conceivably be the greatest problem on the agenda; *vide* the fact that the technological capacity to produce first-class battleships coexisted with, was mutually supportive with, the national myth, the *pre*-twentieth-century myth, that Japan's rulers had been designated in perpetuity by edict of the Sun-Goddess Amaterasu. But, on the other hand, (2)—and this in response to their second theme—even before the Restoration it was not true, as the glorifiers of tradition would have it, that there was an Oriental Spirit, quite alien to all concepts of "modernity," which was maintained intact and impervious to the vicissitudes of history. Even Tokugawa ideas, if one looked at the "deep currents," could be seen as developing unceasingly toward modernity. It was the desire to document these two themes, responses to the two contentions of the "overcomers," that constituted the nonrational mainspring of my work. The first theme does not appear directly in the first two parts of this book, but it had been my original intention to tackle one aspect of it in the essay that forms Part III, of which I have not yet spoken. This was to deal with the periods since the Restoration. That it finally ended up in its present form was due to certain personal circumstances.

Part III was originally commissioned by the editor of the *Kokka*

Gakkai Zasshi, Professor Oka Yoshitake, who had planned to run a special issue in 1944 entitled "The Emergence of Modern Japan" (this initiative itself was intended as a covert act of protest). That this essay, compared with the other two, is closer to conventional academic history of political ideas and by the same token provides, for better or worse, less scope for methodological innovation on my part, is largely explained by the fact that it was my "allotted share" in the work for this special issue. My original design was to trace the development of nationalism since the Restoration in terms of a transition from modern—democratic—nationalism to bureaucratic statism. So I had originally entitled the essay "The Emergence of the Theory of Nationalism." However, early in July 1944, as I was still in the middle of writing the Tokugawa section which was intended only as the prelude, I was suddenly drafted into the army and sent off to Pyongyang to receive my basic military training. That is why the exposition stops short at the end of the Tokugawa period. Between getting the papers and taking the train from Shinjuku station I had exactly one week, and that whole week, until literally the last minute before leaving the house, I concentrated on tidying up my manuscript. I can still remember, the memory as vivid as yesterday, seeing through the window, as I sat writing, my mother and the wife I had married just three months earlier bringing out the pots of ceremonial red-bean rice to feast the neighbors as they arrived with their Rising Sun flags for the ritual "send-off to battle." If that essay strikes an occasionally pathetic note, the circumstances of its writing may help to provide the explanation. July 1944 was, after all, a time when there were plenty of reasons for supposing that my chances of ever returning to academic life were very small. I left it behind as something of a last testament.

V

I have tried, I fear at somewhat excessive length, to give the reader some idea of the (even in the context of Japanese history somewhat exceptional) social and political circumstances in which, and the intellectual background against which, this book was written. I have hoped thereby to help his understanding, not in the least to excuse or to justify my conclusions or my choice of themes. The gulf between my present views and this product of my late twenties is so large that I would not know where to begin if I were to try, in any summary form, to chart it. Each essay, for better or for worse, fits organically into the total structure, so that any partial amendment might well bring the whole edifice crumbling down. I believe that such a study as this one—unlike, for example, a general textbook history—can, as an attempt to elucidate the subject from a very particular angle, have a continuing raison d'etre even though the author himself might subsequently change his views. There are, however, two particular points which I cannot conscientiously leave without amendment and on which I must add a brief commentary.

The first concerns the assumption, common to the first two essays, that what I called the "Neo-Confucian" mode of thought had achieved a general social ascendancy in the early Tokugawa period, and that the universality of its acceptance began to crumble subsequently in the late seventeenth and early eighteenth centuries, as it was subjected to the calculated challenge of the rising School of Ancient Learning. Not only is this assumption too mechanical a reflection of historical evolutionism, but it also does not correspond with the ascertainable facts. Leaving out the details and presenting only the broad outlines one can say this: it is certainly true that the Tokugawa government and that of the fiefs did realize the usefulness of Confucianism (concretely, for the most part Chu Hsi's Neo-Confucianism) in their attempts to stabilize the turbulent social situation of a Japan emerging from the feudal wars by a policy of "rule through the civil, rather than the military, arts." But, it was not really until the late seventeenth century that the Confucian classics and the authoritative commentaries on them came to be printed and circulated, and the doctrines of Confucianism *as an ideology* came to penetrate the society in general. It was, for example, in 1655 that Yamazaki Ansai, who played a great part in creating the national vogue for Chu Hsi's Neo-Confucianism, started to lecture on what he claimed to be the *pure* version of those doctrines in Kyoto. But the publication of Yamaga Sokō's *Seikyō yōroku* [Essential teachings of the sages], the work which boldly challenged the whole Chu

Hsi school, dates from 1666, and Itō Jinsai completed the manuscript of his highly original *Rongo kogi* [Ancient meanings of the Confucian Analects] and *Mōshi kogi* [Ancient meanings of Mencius] in 1663. In short, the diffusion of Neo-Confucianism as an ideology and the School of Ancient Learning's challenge to it developed almost contemporaneously. Moreover, if one asks not just about *scholarly* Confucianism but about the basic thought categories of Confucianism that constituted the *Aspektstruktur* of Tokugawa society, then one can argue that they tenaciously retained a currency until the very last instant of the Tokugawa regime. In short, from the perspective of the present day, there is room for a good deal of doubt how far the evolutionary schema implicit in the first two essays—of a universal spread of Chu Hsi type Neo-Confucian mode of thought followed by its gradual disintergration, or of a transition in emphasis from "nature" to "invention"—will actually stand up to the historical evidence. However, I like immodestly to think that even if one totally discards that whole schema, several of the individual pieces of analysis—for example, of the internal structure of Sorai's system or of the significance of the split between the private and the public or of the connection between Sorai and the National Learning School as lying in the latter's development of the former's "private" sphere—that these still have a value as providing a basis for further research.

The second serious defect of the book is my assumption that early Tokugawa Confucianism "was as unadulterated as if it had just arrived from China" (cf. p. 26, n. 14 below), thus overlooking the genuinely *Japanese* characteristics of Tokugawa Neo-Confucianism. It is, of course, true that Yamazaki Ansai and his school *claimed* a fierce orothodoxy in their exposition of Chu Hsi's doctrines, and to avoid any danger of distortion and misinterpretation filled their books with lengthy extracts from his work. But whether or not their own outlook, or their choice of texts or of emphasis, coincided *objectively* with those of Chu Hsi is an entirely different matter. For all their subjective intentions one might, ironically, see the Ansai school precisely as a characteristic illustration of the distance between Japanese Neo-Confucianism and that of China. To be sure, a comparison of Confucianism in the two countries was outside the scope of the book, and I did not omit to make reservations on this point, including an admission of my own lack of the knowledge to tackle it (see p. 20, n. 3 and p. 26, n. 14). However, if one starts by bringing out much more clearly how much not only Ansai's Confucianism, but also that of Hayashi Razan who stands right at the very point of departure of Tokugawa Confucianism, rested on essentially revisionist interpretations, one would arrive at a version of Tokugawa intellectual history rather considerably different from the perspective of this book.[11]

While on the subject of comparions, it is worth adding that no study of Tokugawa Confucianism can possibly neglect to consider the Neo-Confucianism of Li-dynasty Korea, and particularly the scholarship and ideas of Yi Hwang (T'oegye) 李滉 (退溪). The tendency to belittle the intellectual history of Korea and to limit scholarly attention chiefly to Japan and China is, I fear, quite apart from all the excuses that one might offer about the availability of materials, a genuine blind spot, and one that I shared by and large with most students of traditional intellectual history in Japan.

Finally, I must express my deepest appreciation of the work of Professor Mikiso Hane who embarked on the English translation of this book more than ten years ago as, he says, a private study exercise. The many passages from original historical sources alone make it an extraordinarily difficult book to translate, and I have nothing but admiration for the effort and patience with which he has, single-handedly, brought the project to a publishable conclusion. Thanks are also due to Mr. Benjamin Brewster for editorial help and to Professor Ronald Dore who appeared in Tokyo as I was finishing this Introduction, just in time to cheer me on my last spurt and to offer to translate the introduction, thus calling to mind all kinds of proverbial cliches, both Confucian and Anglo-Saxon, about friends in need, coming joyously from a distance, etc. And, to conclude with a confession: the fact that

---

[11] I have tackled one aspect of this in a recent article, "Rekishi ishiki no kosō" ["The ancient layers of historical consciousness"], published as a commentary on the works in that collection, in *Rekishi shisō-shu* [Collected writings on the philosophy of history], Tokyo: Chikuma-shobō, 1972).

the publication of this book has been delayed two or three years beyond the completion of the manuscript is solely due to my own dilatory postponement of the task of writing this Introduction. To the translator, and to the Tokyo and Princeton Presses, I would like to express my apologies and my thanks for their untiring patience.

Tokyo   Masao Maruyama
August, 1974

PART I

THE SORAI SCHOOL:
ITS ROLE IN THE DISINTEGRATION OF TOKUGAWA CONFUCIANISM AND ITS IMPACT ON NATIONAL LEARNING

CHAPTER I

INTRODUCTION:
THE FORMATION OF TOKUGAWA
CONFUCIANISM

The Static Character of Chinese History and Confucianism. Confucianism in Japan. The Objective Conditions
for the Formation of Tokugawa Confucianism. The Subjective Conditions. Why Trace the Development of
Tokugawa Confucianism.

I

In his *Reason in History* Hegel described the specificity of the
Chinese empire in the following terms:

The Chinese and Mongol Empire is the empire of theocratic despotism. Underlying it is the patriarchal condition. A father stands at the
summit and controls even what we would subordinate to conscience.
In China, this patriarchal principle has been organized into a State.
. . . In China, there is a single despot at the summit who leads a
systematically constructed government via the many levels of the
hierarchy beneath him. Here religious relations as well as family
matters are regulated by State laws. The individual is morally self-
less.[1]

Needless to say, Hegel is here thinking in terms of the pattern
of his philosophy of history, which begins in the Oriental world,
passes through the Greco-Roman stages, and culminates in the
German world. Because he describes the development of the
world spirit in terms of the rise and fall of the peoples who have
served as its bearers, historical stages come to coincide with a

---

[1] G. W. F. Hegel: *Die Vernunft in der Geschichte*, ed. G. Lasson (Leipzig, 1930), pp.
236–37.

certain geographical classification. A positivist historian would
see this schema as somewhat arbitrary. Although there may be
differences in degree, the characteristics Hegel ascribed to the
Chinese, or Oriental, stage can also be discerned at some point in
the historical development of practically any nation. But what is
significant is the fact that in China these characteristics did not
constitute only one phase; they are constantly reproduced. This
is what is called the static nature of Chinese history. Here, too,
Hegel's insight did not fail him. He writes:

> Thus, what exists first of all is the state in which the Subject has not
> yet attained its rights, but in which an immediate lawless ethic
> [*Sittlichkeit*] prevails: the childhood of history. This form is divided
> into two aspects. The first is the state as it is founded upon family
> relationships, a state of fatherly care, which holds the whole society
> together by exhortation and punishment. It is a prosaic empire be-
> cause there is still no opposition or ideality. At the same time, it is an
> empire of duration; it cannot change from within. This is the form of
> the Far East, essentially that of the Chinese Empire. In the other
> aspect, the Form of Time stands in contrast to this spatial duration.
> States do not change in themselves or in their principles, but are
> constantly changing their position towards each other. They are in
> an endless conflict which prepares the ground for their rapid decline.
> . . . This decline is thus not a true decline because no progress results
> from all these restless changes. The new which replaces the fallen also
> sinks into decline. No progress takes place. This agitation is an un-
> historical history.[2]

Hegel's observations about the specificity of imperial China can
only be appreciated if this cyclical nature of Chinese history is
taken into account. The closed family society under the absolute
authority of the patriarch constituted the unit of social relations.
The state structure was built hierarchically upon this basis, and
at its summit was the despot with his "fatherly care." Because this
social structure was very firmly established in imperial China, the
subject (the individual) failed to attain his own rights and, not
giving birth to any internal opposition, remained an unmediated
unity. In consequence, China remained an "empire of duration."

[2] Ibid., pp. 234–35.

But precisely because opposition did not emerge from within, it arose from outside this rigidly fixed state structure. In Hegel's words, "On the one hand, we find duration and stability, but on the other, self-destructive arbitrariness. . . . Thus the magnificent edifice of the single power, from which nothing can be removed and in whose presence nothing independent can form, is linked with unbounded arbitrariness."[3] As a result, an apparently invincible dynasty easily collapses from external shocks such as invasions by "barbarian" forces. But the new dynasty that replaces the old one is constructed upon exactly the same foundation and is organized in exactly the same way as its predecessor. In consequence, it, too, is destined to undergo the same fate. With characteristic acumen, Hegel's interpretation strikes to the root of the matter: Chinese history remained "unhistorical" despite frequent dynastic changes, not because of internal dissension but precisely because it lacked such dissension.

There is surely a close relationship between this and the place Confucianism held in Chinese history. The origin of Confucianism is a question for specialists, but we can note that Confucianism as we know it today was gradually systematized through the disputes of the "hundred philosophers" of the Warring States period and obtained its exclusive place as the official philosophy simultaneously with the establishment of a unified political order under Wu Ti (140–87 B.C.) in the Former Han period after the Ch'in Dynasty (221–206 B.C.). Confucian ethics made the subordination of the son to the father the basis of its moral code and compared the specific human relationships between lord and subject, husband and wife, elder brother and younger brother, to that of father and son. After linking them together into relationships of high and low, noble and base, it taught the necessity of maintaining these distinctions rigidly.[4] This ideological system was no doubt most

[3] Ibid., p. 238.

[4] Of the so-called five relationships, that between friends is the only one that involves equals. But this relationship is mentioned the least. Moreover, the relationship between friends is also discussed in terms of "the proper order of friends," i.e., as a relationship between a superior and an inferior. In addition we should note that in Confucian thinking there is no code of conduct that applies to the public at large, i.e., to people who are not even friends. This unique characteristic of Confucian ethics was recognized even by a comparatively conservative moral philosopher of the Meiji period, Nishimura Shigeki (1828–1902), who said: "Confucianism is advantageous to the

appropriate for the magnificent Han empire, which was founded on "the paternal care on the part of the emperor, and the spirit of his subjects—who like children do not advance beyond the ethical principle of the family circle and can gain for themselves no independent and civil freedom."[5] After the Former Han period, many dynasties rose and fell, but, despite slight variations in its fortunes, Confucianism was always recognized as the orthodox philosophy by each succeeding dynasty.[6] This must be closely related to the fact that Chinese social relations, the precondition for the formation of Confucian morality, were repeatedly reconstituted. As a result, a system of thought capable of competing successfully with Confucianism failed to develop until the Ch'ing period. If we set aside religious thought, it would not be wrong to say that the development of thought in China unfolded entirely within Confucian doctrine. The Chinese intellectual world, like the Chinese empire, did not experience any real ideological confrontation. Only in recent years, after modern bourgeois elements had gradually infiltrated Chinese society under international pressure, did Confucianism finally encounter a social philosophy with an entirely different system of thought, namely, the Three People's Principles of Sun Yat-sen.

---

people of superior status and disadvantageous to the inferior. It seems as if the superior has only rights and no duties, while the inferior has only duties but no rights. Although this may be necessary for the preservation of order, it does seem a rather burdensome evil." Nishimura Shigeki: *Nihon dōtokuron* [A discussion of Japanese morality] (Tokyo, 1935), p. 29.

[5] G. W. F. Hegel: *Philosophie der Geschichte,* in *Samtliche Werke,* ed. H. Glockner (Stuttgart, 1927ff.), XI, p. 172. English translation by J. Sibree: *The Philosophy of History* (New York, 1956), p. 123.

[6] We cannot ignore the fact that in the course of its development from the Warring States period (c. 403–222 B.C.) to the Ch'in and Han periods, Confucianism underwent changes that made it better qualified to become the orthodox philosophy. In the period of the Warring States when the princes were in constant conflict, the Confucian Way of the Early Kings was an ideal that had to be turned into a reality. For this reason, Confucian precepts took on the characteristics of protest, and their political, activist aspects were prominent. It is not surprising therefore that, after the Han period, when Confucianism found it necessary to make its premises harmonize with an absolutist imperial authority, it lost these "protestant" qualities and became a kind of *Rechtfertigungslehre* (apologetic doctrine). But this transformation occurred through the development of certain moments inherent in it from the outset, such as the exaltation of decorum in order to uphold the hierarchical structure, the foundation of imperial authority on the will of heaven, and so on.

II

It is generally believed that Confucianism was first introduced into Japan around the end of the fourth century A.D., during Emperor Ōjin's reign, when Wani of Paekche (in Korea) brought the Confucian Analects and the *Thousand Character Classic* to Japan with him. Some authorities date its entry even earlier. Be that as it may, Confucianism undeniably has a long history in Japan. There are, however, two conflicting views as to the extent of Confucian influence on Japanese society and culture. Of course the content of Confucian morality cannot be considered apart from the characteristics of the Chinese empire that we have just discussed, but all modes of thought that are more than guides or programs for action in specific situations contain within them the possibility of universality. Confucianism is no exception, and that is why it was accepted in Japan. However, when an ideology like Confucianism, profoundly marked by the peculiar conditions of the society that produces it, is universalized and applied to another country with a different historical and social structure, it is apt to become highly abstract, in extreme cases retaining no more than the original terminology. Differences of opinion about whether or not Confucianism was suitable for Japan stem from disagreements over the extent of this abstraction. This study is not intended to examine such major problems.

However, even those scholars who are most skeptical about the Confucian influence in Japan acknowledge one period in which it suited the existing social conditions.[7] This was the Tokugawa period (1603–1868), the golden age of Confucianism in Japan. This period in the nation's history saw the most rapid development of Confucianism. Why was this? One reason is that the social and political structures of Tokugawa feudal society were comparable with those on which Confucianism was based in the Chinese empire. This made it easy to apply Confucian ideas in Tokugawa Japan. The other reason is that Confucianism underwent radical

[7] Even Dr. Tsuda Sōkichi, who takes a very negative view of the Confucian influence on Japanese culture, agrees that Confucianism had some effect on Tokugawa feudal society. See Tsuda Sōkichi: *Bungaku ni arawaretaru waga kokumin shisō no kenkyū* [A study of Japanese thought as manifested in literature] (Tokyo, 1916–21), II, pp. 585ff.

changes during the early Tokugawa period. I shall now examine concretely these two factors, one objective and the other subjective, that contributed to the rise of Confucianism during this period.

Tokugawa feudalism emerged during the Sengoku era in the sixteenth century. It differed from the feudal society of the middle ages (c. twelfth to sixteenth centuries) because of the changes in warfare that resulted from the introduction of firearms and from Hideyoshi's policy of tying the peasantry to the soil, depriving them of the right to bear swords.[8] These changes made the distinction between the samurai and the peasant a very rigid one. At the same time, they severed the samurai's immediate ties with the soil, concentrating them in the castle-towns, where they constituted a hierarchical group of vassals beneath a feudal lord. This process came to completion in the Tokugawa period, when there was an inflexible class distinction between the samurai on the one hand and the peasants, artisans, and merchants on the other, and within the samurai class itself a minutely differentiated social hierarchy. According to Fukuzawa Yukichi, the Meiji period educator and advocate of Western liberalism, there were over one hundred different levels of distinction in the Nakatsu *han* (a small domain in Kyushu), although it had only fifteen hundred samurai. This status structure of the samurai, ranging from the shogun and daimyo at the top to lowly servitors (*wakatō* and *nakama*) at the bottom, and insisting on the absolute superiority of the samurai over the common people, had close affinities with the Confucian ideal: the feudal system[9] of the Chou period in China with its hierarchy of emperor, feudal princes, chief ministers, high officials, gentlemen-scholars,[10] and commoners. It was appropriate, therefore, to use the Confucian moral code as an ideological foundation

---

[8] Toyotomi Hideyoshi (1536–98) subdued the contending feudal lords by 1590 and ruled as a military dictator. In 1588 he prohibited the peasants from possessing swords or other arms. (Translator's note.)

[9] The term "feudal" as applied to the Chou period refers only to the political system in which the emperor allotted fiefs to his barons. It does not refer to social or economic feudalism and hence does not correspond precisely to the historical usage of the term. Tokugawa and Chou societies are not identical in this latter sense, but insofar as political feudalism is concerned, there are certain common characteristics. In this respect, the Tokugawa Confucians were not mistaken in comparing their society with Chou society and labeling it "feudal."

[10] *Shi*, or the Chinese *shih*, gentleman-scholar. (Translator's note.)

for the Tokugawa system of social relations.[11] For example, when the period of strife ended and peace was achieved, the raison d'être of the samurai, who had severed their ties with rural life and become a class living off the commoners' labor, quite naturally came into question. Yamaga Sokō (1622–85) begins his exposition of "The Way of the Samurai" with these words of self-criticism: "The samurai eats without tilling the soil, consumes without producing anything, and gains profits without engaging in any business. Why is this so?. . . He must have duties to perform as a samurai. If he were to satisfy his hunger and other needs without working, he should be labeled a loafer."[12] Attempts were made to justify this dominance of the samurai by quoting the classical texts of Confucianism. The efforts of the Chu Hsi scholar Amenomori Hōshū (1668–1755) are typical. He wrote:

> There are four classes of men: samurai, peasants, artisans, and merchants. The samurai use their minds, the peasants and those below them use their muscles. Those who use their minds are superior; those who use their muscles are inferior. Those who use their minds have broad visions, high ideals, and profound wisdom. The peasants and those of lower estate labor only to sustain themselves. If these positions were reversed, there would be, at best, discontent in the land and, at worst, chaos.[13]

Formerly the master-servant relationship within the samurai class had been limited to a relatively small number of vassals and had been founded upon comparatively minor benefices; it was sus-

[11] The term "ideological" is used here because the Chinese social relations that were the basis for Confucian ethics were not in content the same as those of the Tokugawa period. A moment's consideration of the difference between the Chinese *shih* (gentleman-scholar) and the Japanese *bushi* (warrior) shows this. It is not our purpose here, however, to consider these differences of content and to decide whether or not it was fitting that the Confucian ethical system was applied to Tokugawa social relations. Instead, we are concerned with the role that the Confucian ethical system actually played during this period.

[12] *Yamaga gorui* [The works of Yamaga Sokō], Book XXI; in *Nihon rinri ihen* [Collection of works on Japanese ethics], ed. Inoue Tetsujirō and Kaninoe Yoshimaru (Tokyo, 1901–3), IV, p. 34.

[13] Ibid., VII, p. 320 (*Kissō sawa*, Book I). Needless to say, this is based on Mencius's statement that "Some men use their minds while others use their muscles. He who uses his mind governs others, while he who uses his muscles is governed by others. He who is governed by others has a duty to feed others, while he who governs others is fed by them. This is the principle of the world."

tained psychologically by such concepts as "compassion" (*nasake*) and "vow" (*chigiri*). But these ideals could no longer be preserved in the relationship between a feudal lord and his many feudal followers when they congregated in the castle-town. In consequence, an objective ethical code not founded merely upon human sentiments was needed as an ideological aid for the control of the vassals. It is easy to see that the master-servant ethic of Confucianism readily met this need. Often it was elevated even into a legal form.[14] Tokugawa society was thus a feudal political system that froze life, deplored all innovations and made rigid distinctions within a very complex hierarchy of status divisions among retainers based on differentiations of clothing, modes of address, and means of transportation.[15] As such it resembled the static and

[14] Of course, when the Tokugawa Bakufu was first established, there was still a possibility that armed conflicts would occur. The daimyo of the outlying regions were not yet really under the control of the bakufu. The bakufu was therefore organized in such a manner that it could be transformed immediately into a military organization whenever an extraordinary situation arose. The laws issued by the bakufu had strong strains of militarism in them. It was unavoidable that Legalist rather than Confucian tendencies predominated. (The Legalist school, *Fa Chia,* flourished during the third century B.C., particularly in the state of Ch'in. It emphasized state power, statecraft, and strict enforcement of the law. The philosopher who synthesized Legalist thought was Han Fei-tzu, who died in 233 B.C.) For example, Article 3 of the first Buke Hatto (Laws governing the military households), issued in 1615, states: "Offenders against the law should not be harbored or hidden in any domain. Law is the basis of social order. Reason may be violated in the name of law, but law may not be violated in the name of reason. Those who break the law deserve heavy punishment." Article 13 states: "The lords of the domains should select officials with a capacity for public administration. Good government depends on getting the right men. Due attention should be given to their merits and faults; rewards and punishments must be properly meted out" (*Sources of the Japanese Tradition*, comp. Ryusaku Tsunoda, Wm. Theodore de Bary, and Donald Keene [New York, 1958], pp. 336 and 338). These articles clearly reveal a Legalist ideology. But these provisions disappeared after the Shoshi Hatto of 1629, and the Buke Hatto of 1635 begins with this statement: "Loyalty to the lord and filial piety must be encouraged, and proper conduct be maintained. Attention must be given to learning and to the military arts. Just principles must be stressed and purity of customs and manners be preserved." The Buke Hatto of 1683, issued by Shogun Tsunayoshi, states: "Encourage learning, the military arts, loyalty and filial piety, and maintain proper conduct." This replaced the provision in the earlier versions: "Learning, and the military arts of archery and horsemanship must be emphasized and practiced by all." See *Ofuregaki kampō shūsei* [Laws of the bakufu compiled in the Kampō era], ed. Takayanagi Shinzō and Ishii Ryōsuke, for the Buke Hatto.

[15] For instance, the Buke Hatto of 1635 states: "Dress materials must not be used indiscriminately. White twill may be worn only by those above the status of chief minister [*kyō*], white wadded silk only by those above the rank of high official [*taibu*]. Purple kimono, and garments with purple lining, of glossed silk, or of crestless wadded silk must not be worn indiscriminately. It is contrary to traditional practice to permit retainers and warriors of various domains to wear garments of twill, brocades or embroi-

elaborate system in China, which was rationalized by Confucianism with its concept of *li* (*rei* in Japanese), or "decorum."[16] Aside from his rights as parent and husband, the head of the samurai family did not have any special patriarchal legal authority. But because the family system was dependent upon the politico-economic relationship of the feudal stipend, the real power of the head of the family over its members was very great, and the latter could hardly ever assert their individuality against the paternal and conjugal authority of the former. (Since the age of retirement was seventy, it was unusual for two different individuals to exercise parental authority and the authority of the head of the family.) Here, too, Confucian family ethics were highly appropriate to the Tokugawa family system.[17]

Thus far we have been discussing the correspondence between Confucian ethics and the internal structure of the samurai class and the structure of the relation of domination between the samurai and the common people. But in a *Standesgesellschaft* (society of estates) the social relations of the upper stratum usually become

---

deries. These practices must be prohibited by law." It also states: "Those who are allowed to ride palanquins are restricted to dignitaries of the Tokugawa clan, lords of domains, lords of castles, sons of retainers receiving over 10,000 *koku,* sons of daimyo, heirs of lords of castles and of those with the status of chamberlain and above. Those above the age of fifty, and invalids under the care of doctors and practitioners of the art of *yin-yang* are exempt from this prohibition. Others are prohibited from enjoying privileges reserved for those of higher rank. However, those with special permission are exempt. Each military household may exercise the right to permit certain people to ride palanquins within its domain. Court nobles, heads of monasteries and temples, and monks are exempted from this regulation."

[16] In his *Shunkanshō* [Excerpts from a vernal mirror], the founder of the official Tokugawa philosophy, Hayashi Razan, explains the concept of *li* (*rei*) as follows: "Among the subjects, depending on a person's official rank, there must be differences in the vehicles to be ridden and in the apparel to be worn. When sitting in a room, men of high rank must sit at the head of the room and those of lower rank must sit at the lower end of the room. These rules of behavior are what constitute *li*" (*Zoku-zoku gunsho ruijū* [Classified collection of historical sources, 3rd Series] [Tokyo, 1906–9], X, p. 53).

[17] Fukuzawa Yukichi describes the situation in the samurai family as follows: "Since feudal Japan was dominated by the samurai, by examining the conditions of the samurai family we will be able to gain insight into the spirit that prevailed in the society as a whole. The head of the family was like an autocratic dictator and held the entire family authority in his hands. He dealt with the members of his family with stern dignity. In his presence, women and children, from his wife downwards, had to behave as if they were his servants or maids and show proper deference. The rigid distinction in status between husband and wife resembled the relationship between lord and servant rather than that between male and female" (*Zoku Fukuzawa zenshū* [Collected works of Fukuzawa, 2nd Series] [Tokyo, 1932], V, pp. 631–32).

the model for the social relations of the lower strata (witness the master-servant relationship that prevailed between the master and the apprentice among artisans—*oyakata* and *totei*—and among merchants—*shujin* and *detchi*). The general law that in a *Standesgesellschaft* the forms of consciousness also permeate from the upper to the lower layers of society held true for Tokugawa society,[18] and Confucian ethics were adopted with only slight modifications for social relations among the common people. At any rate, the correspondence between the social structure of Tokugawa feudal society and the ideological structure of Confucian ethics was the objective precondition that enabled Tokugawa Confucianism to attain a commanding position in the ideological realm as the predominant social ethos.[19]

But Tokugawa Confucianism would not have triumphed without the presence of a subjective factor also. This was the ideological transformation of Confucianism itself. What distinguishes the sub-

---

[18] For the formative principles of a *Standesgesellschaft,* cf. Hans Freyer: *Soziologie als Wirklichkeitswissenschaft* (Leipzig and Berlin, 1930), especially pp. 268–85. According to Freyer, in modern bourgeois society, the pattern moves from bottom to top. The typical class is the proletariat. "The townsfolk [*das Bürgertum*]," he writes, "were made into the 'bourgeoisie' from below" (p. 285). In contrast, in earlier *Standesgesellschaften,* the estate of authentic significance was the ruling estate (the aristocracy). "Estate thought filtered downwards from the top of the social structure, finally permeating the entire society" (ibid.). Eventually, the formative principles of the lower estates deviate from those of the ruling class. In the famous words of the Abbé Sieyès, when the Third Estate was no longer content with its "portion" and demanded the "whole," it was no longer possible to preserve the estate system.

[19] It is possible to understand the historical reasons why Confucianism became the general target of attack for so many bourgeois thinkers after new forms of social relations had been established with the Meiji Restoration only if we recognize the ideological role it had played in Tokugawa feudal society. Typical examples of such criticism can be found in Fukuzawa Yukichi's *Bunmeiron no gairyaku* [Outline of civilization], *Gakumon no susume* [Encouragement of learning], *Onna daigaku hyōron* [Criticism of Ekken's onna daigaku], and other essays too numerous to cite. The laudatory remarks of the "decadent Confucians" about the feudal system are also attacked in all those early Meiji works intended for public enlightenment.

On the other hand, there were many examples of reactionary protest against the Restoration's "equalization of the four classes" relying on a theory of moral obligations (*meibunron*). Shimazu Hisamitsu, the de facto lord of Satsuma, vehemently opposed the process of "civilization" that set in after the Restoration, arguing that "there is a danger of falling into the evil ways of republican government under the present form of government." He insisted that "it is necessary to clarify the distinctions between the nobility and the common people," and demanded that "promiscuous behavior be strictly prohibited and the sexes clearly separated." These positions were typical of the reactionary viewpoint. *Cf. Fukuchi Genjirō, Hisamitsukōki* [A record of the prince Hisamitsu] (Tokyo, 1887), p. 218.

stantive pattern of Tokugawa Confucianism from that of earlier Confucianism is the fact that while early Confucianism had been a science of scholarly exegesis practiced at the imperial court by learned scholar families (*hakase*) in the tradition of Han and T'ang Confucianism and among the people only the object of private dilettante research by Buddhist monks, Tokugawa Confucianism gained significance as a preeminently educational discipline, and its studies were no longer confined to a narrow circle of scholars but to some extent were opened to the public by independent Confucians.[20] This ideological transformation was made possible by the emergence of Sung philosophy.

Sung or Neo-Confucian philosophy had already been imported into Japan in the Kamakura period (1185–1333) by Zen monks and was the traditional preserve of the monks of the Five Zen Monasteries,[21] but they naturally made Sung philosophy conform to Buddhist doctrines, particularly Zen concepts, and expounded upon the unity of Confucianism and Buddhism. For example, the Chu Hsi concept of "investigating the principles of particulars to comprehend the principles of the universe" was equated with the Buddhist concept of "attaining Buddhahood after comprehending the nature of reality," and "holding fast to seriousness"[22] with sitting quietly in *zazen* (Zen meditation). The men who liberated Sung philosophy, especially Chu Hsi philosophy, from this total subjugation to Buddhism and laid the foundation for the development of Tokugawa Confucianism were Fujiwara Seika (1561–1619) and his principal disciple, Hayashi Razan (1583–1657).

[20] The *Tokugawa jikki* clearly states: "Since the ancient period, succeeding generations of scholars in Japan have taught the classics in terms of the interpretations made by the Han and T'ang scholars. Moreover, many scholars dealt with trivial verses. Seika was the first scholar to adopt the teachings of the Sung philosophers and emphasize the practical application of the classics. As his teachings began to spread widely, people began to appreciate the correctness and usefulness of Sung philosophy" (*Shintei zōho kokushi taikei* [Collection of Japanese historical classics, revised and enlarged edition] [Tokyo, 1874–1946], XXXVIII, pp. 339–40).

[21] During the Kamakura and Muromachi (1336–1573) periods, certain Zen monasteries were given special status by being officially designated as belonging to this category. The third Ashikaga shogun, Yoshimitsu (1358–1408), designated five in Kyoto and five in Kamakura. (Translator's note.)

[22] *Ching,* a state of mind that is similar to the Buddhist calmness of mind, but in Sung philosophy (Neo-Confucianism) an effort at handling affairs is also stressed. It is variously translated as "attentiveness," "concentration," "composure," "prudence," and "seriousness." (Translator's note.)

Both of these men were born into families of Buddhist priests but foresook Buddhism and became followers of Sung philosophy, and, as Confucians, came to criticize Buddhism as an escapist philosophy.[23] The path they pursued is very similar to the path of independence followed by Confucianism itself.

The attempt to establish Chu Hsi philosophy as a discipline for popular dissemination conflicted with the Confucian tradition in Japan. It is very easy to understand why it encountered impassioned opposition from the old circles of Confucian scholars, particularly from high-ranking professorial families linked to the imperial court. If the rising Confucian school had not succeeded in gaining sufficient political support to counteract the court nobles' opposition, its prospects would have been dim. But it did acquire important political support. This was provided by the founder of the Edo Bakufu (military government), Tokugawa Ieyasu (1542–1616).[24]

[23] The following passage from the *Sentetsu sōdan* (a work consisting of biographical sketches of seventy-two Confucian scholars from the Muromachi period—1336–1573—to the beginning of the nineteenth century, written by a Confucian scholar, Hara Masaru, 1760–1820) throws light on Seika's decision to abandon Buddhism and become a Confucian. "Shaku Shōtai (1548–1607) and Reizan were both confident of their learning. They admonished Seika, saying, 'You had at first embraced Buddhism but have now become a Confucian. You have abandoned the truth and have returned to worldly ways. Why is it that you fail to understand this?' Seika replied, 'The two paths of the supramundane and mundane ways is a theory expounded by you Buddhist monks. You label things as mundane arbitrarily. But this conflicts with the principle of Heaven, and ignores principles of proper human relationships. How can this be called the true way?' The two monks were unable to reply" (*Sentetsu sōdan*, Vol. I, *Dai Nihon bunko* [Tokyo, 1936]). And Razan writes in his *Seika sensei gyōjō* [The conduct of Master Seika]: "Our master was a disciple of Buddhism for quite some time, but his mind was not free of doubts. Then he read the writings of the Confucian sages and was convinced without any sense of misgiving. This is where the Way lies. The Way cannot consist of anything but proper human relationships. Buddhism eliminates the source of benevolence and abandons righteousness. That is why it is a pagan philosophy" (*Razan sensei bunshū* [A collection of the writings of Master Razan], ed. Kyoto Shisekikai [Kyoto, 1918–19], II, p. 20). However, Hayashi Razan went furthest in these anti-Buddhist positions. But the anti-Buddhist arguments of the Chu Hsi scholars were not always logically sound. This was because Sung philosophy itself had developed by assimilating Buddhist concepts, especially the *Kegon* (*Hua-yen*) philosophy, which arose during the T'ang period (the Kegon sect emphasized the concept of Buddha as the cosmic soul).

[24] The *Tokugawa jikki* records the following episode: "One year Dōshun [Razan's Buddhist name] gathered his students and lectured on the *Analects* of Confucius, using Chu Hsi's commentaries on the text. People flocked from all over Japan to hear him and the front of his gate was as crowded as a market place. Kiyowara Hidetaka advised the Imperial Court that traditionally no one had been allowed to lecture in the city on his own initiative. Moreover, Dōshun was not adhering to the interpretations of the

Ieyasu had shown interest in Confucianism even before he established the Tokugawa Bakufu. According to Razan's *The Conduct of Master Seika* (*Seika sensei gyōjō*), Ieyasu invited Seika to Edo as early as 1593 and asked him to lecture on "The Essence of the Political Views of the T'ang Emperor T'ai Tsung."[25] Even after his victory in the battle of Sekigahara in 1600 (which in effect established the Tokugawa Bakufu), Ieyasu frequently attended Seika's lectures in Kyoto. Seika did not become Ieyasu's retainer, but in 1607 his disciple Razan was made a political adviser to the bakufu and gained Ieyasu's trust and confidence. It was said that "he gained such favor that during the founding of the government he made proposals on government policies and drafted laws and ordinances. All important government documents passed through his hands."[26] He made the Hayashi family the custodian of the official philosophy of the regime. Why was Ieyasu so interested in Confucianism? On this point, the *Tokugawa jikki*[27] states:

Ieyasu had conquered the nation on horseback, but being an enlightened and wise man, realized early that the land could not be governed from a horse. He had always respected and believed in the way of the sages. He wisely decided that in order to govern the land and follow the path proper to man, he must pursue the path of learning. Therefore, from the beginning he encouraged learning. As

Han and T'ang scholars, but was employing the new theories of the Sung sholars. His crime was not a trifling one. Opinion varied on how to deal with the case, and no agreement could be reached. In consequence, the Court asked the opinion of the military. Upon hearing this, Ieyasu expressed the opinion that the Way of the Sages must be studied by everyone. Individual scholars should be allowed to choose between old and new interpretations. Hidetaka's attempt to prevent this stemmed from his narrow-minded attitude and from jealousy. His behavior was indeed reprehensible. As a result, Hidetaka's complaint was rejected by the Court" (*Zōho kokushi taikei*, op. cit., XXXVIII, pp. 340–41). In another section of the same chronicle (*Tōshōgū jikki* [A true record of Ieyasu], Vol. VII), a similar account is given. It concluded with the comment: "From this time on, Nobukatsu [Razan] was able to lecture in Kyoto on the Confucian classics using Chu Hsi's interpretations without any interference. Thus, he was the first to teach the Chu Hsi philosophy in Japan" (p. 100).

[25] T'ai Tsung, the second T'ang emperor, was instrumental in establishing the T'ang dynasty and reigned from A.D. 627–50. (Translator's note.)

[26] *Sentetsu sōdan*, op. cit., I, p. 8.

[27] The official history of the Tokugawa regime, begun in 1809 and completed in 1849. It covers the period from the first shogun, Ieyasu, to the tenth shogun, Ieharu. (Translator's note.)

a result, people mistakenly considered him to be a lover of literature, a person who indulged in elegant and refined literary activities.[28]

It is doubtful that Ieyasu had such a high opinion of Confucianism as a political philosophy that he believed there was no other alternative. On the contrary, there was a strong strain of militarism in the early bakufu policies. But it is understandable that Ieyasu, who had gained political power by military force, should feel compelled to encourage learning and turn the people's minds away from violence and warfare in order to strengthen the foundations of his government. Among the Confucian Classics, Ieyasu was particularly fond of the Book of Mencius. It was said that he remarked, "He who desires to become the ruler of the land must become familiar with the Four Books of the Confucian Classics.[29] If it is not possible to study all four, he should familiarize himself thoroughly with one of them, the Book of Mencius."[30] In March, 1612, Ieyasu held a discussion with Razan at Shizuoka about Emperor T'ang, the founder of the Shang dynasty (c. 1766–1122 B.C.), and his dethroning of the tyrant Chieh, the last of the Hsia emperors. Razan firmly upheld T'ang's action, stating that "T'ang Wu overthrew Chieh Chou in accordance with the command of Heaven and the wishes of the people. He did not do so in order to further his own interests. From the beginning, his intention was to eliminate evil from the land and save the people. Hence we cannot condemn him in the least." Ieyasu is reported to have commented: "This opinion is just and brilliant."[31] Ieyasu's statement may indicate that he not only saw in Confucianism an instrument of indoctrination but was also seeking a position of legitimacy for the Edo Bakufu. At any rate, it is obvious that Ie-

[28] Zōho kokushi taikei, op. cit., XXXVIII, p. 339.
[29] The Confucian Analects, the Book of Mencius, the Great Learning, and the Doctrine of the Mean. (Translator's note.)
[30] Zōho kokushi taikei, op. cit., XXXVIII, p. 339.
[31] Ibid., pp. 344–45. A similar account is given in Razan Hayashi sensei bunshū, op. cit., Vol. XXXI. Moreover, if the Tōshōgū ikun (Ieyasu's testament) is actually based on Ieyasu's words, he clearly sought to rationalize the transfer of power to the military government by referring to the "Way of Heaven." The issue is not whether it was proper to equate the status of the Japanese military leaders with that of the Chinese feudal lords, given their different natures. Nor is it whether the commonly held conception of the Way of Heaven was similar to the Confucian Will of Heaven. The point to consider is the ideological significance of the use of such an explanation by Ieyasu.

yasu was interested in Confucianism because of its fundamental moral principles and its concepts of political legitimacy, not because of its literary or exegetic values. It was natural, therefore, that he patronized Sung philosophy, especially Chu Hsi philosophy, for this school, in contrast to those that favored exegetic studies of the Chinese classics, claimed to have inherited the orthodox doctrines of the sage-kings of ancient China, Yao, Shun, and Yu.[32]

Given these favorable subjective and objective conditions, Tokugawa Confucianism dominated the intellectual world throughout the Tokugawa period, and its first stage was the Chu Hsi school. What effect did the fact that the intellectual development of Tokugawa Confucianism began with the Chu Hsi school have on the development of the other schools that emerged later? Did the development of Confucianism in Japan merely follow the same path that Confucianism took in China? If this were true, then the Tokugawa intellectual world, like the intellectual world of imperial China, would not have experienced any real ideological opposition and would not have undergone any real intellectual growth. But just as Tokugawa feudal society was not an "empire of duration," so the development of Tokugawa Confucianism was not just an internal development of Confucian thought. This development, from the rise of the Chu Hsi school via the Wang Yang-ming school to the school of Ancient Learning (*kogaku*), which rejected Sung philosophy in favor of a return to fundamental Confucianism, is superficially similar to the Chinese pattern, with the rise of the Chu Hsi school in the Sung period, the Wang Yang-ming school in the Ming period, and the school favoring "investigation based on evidence"[33] in the Ch'ing period. But these developments were totally different in their intellectual significance. In Tokugawa Japan, Confucianism disintegrated into completely heterogeneous elements because of developments within its own structure. Throughout the Tokugawa period, Japanese Confucianism certainly did fail to free itself, where its political

[32] Legendary rulers of ancient China who, it is said, ruled during the second half of the third millennium B.C. They were all enlightened, virtuous, model rulers. (Translator's note.)

[33] *K'ao-cheng-hsueh* or *kōshōgaku*. (Translator's note.)

thought in the narrow sense is concerned, from the kind of feudal limitations described above. These limitations affected not only Confucianism, but also its rival, the school of National Learning (*kokugaku*). But beneath the superficial political discourse a revolutionary change was gradually taking place deep in the mode of thought itself. Our task is to trace this process up to the time of Ogyū Sorai and to ascertain how it laid the groundwork for Motoori Norinaga's philosophy, a philosophy that inherited Sorai's mode of thought but completely transformed it.

To appreciate the historical significance of the fact that Tokugawa Confucianism began with Chu Hsi philosophy, we must first review the philosophical principles specific to the Chu Hsi school. After that we shall examine the growth of the antithesis to the Chu Hsi school, or rather the antithesis to the Chu Hsi school mode of thought, a movement that reached its climax with the Sorai school.

CHAPTER II

THE CHU HSI MODE OF THOUGHT
AND ITS DISSOLUTION

The Structure of Chu Hsi Philosophy. The Specificity of the Chu Hsi Mode of Thought. How This Specificity Is Reflected in the Intellectual World of the Early Tokugawa Period. The Zenith of the Chu Hsi Method. Rapid Changes in Intellectual Trends from the Kambun to the Kyōhō Eras. The Disintegration of the Chu Hsi Method of Thought—Yamaga Sokō, Itō Jinsai, and Kaibara Ekken.

I

Sung philosophy originated with Chou Lien-hsi and was developed further by the Ch'eng brothers, Ch'eng Ming-tao and Ch'eng I-ch'uan.[1] The Chu Hsi school inherited this tradition and elaborated it. It differed from Han and T'ang Confucianism in the following ways: (1) It rejected exegetical practices that consisted solely of making philological studies of the classics and emphasized the importance of the propagation of the Way of the Sages. Hence it reduced the emphasis on the Five Classics (the books of History, Odes, Rites, and Changes, and the Spring and Autumn Annals) in favor of the Four Books (the Analects of Confucius, the Book of Mencius, the Great Learning, and the Doctrine of the Mean), in order to become a philosophy of justice

[1] The term Chu Hsi philosophy, or school, is used here to refer not only to the ideas of Chu Hsi himself but also as a general term for the intellectual system descending from Chou Lien-hsi to Chu Hsi. It is generally referred to as the Ch'eng-Chu school (after Ch'eng I and Chu Hsi) or as the Tao Hsueh (Study of the Tao) and is also widely known as the Sung school or Sung philosophy. However, Sung philosophy contains another section, the school of Lu Chiu-yuan (better known as Lu Hsiang-shan, 1139–93), which branched off from Ch'eng Ming-tao (the high point of this school came with Wang Yang-ming, 1472–1529, in the Ming period). To avoid confusing the two branches, the term Chu Hsi philosophy, or school, will be used henceforth. (Chou Lien-hsi [1017–73] is also known as Chou Tun-i, Ch'eng Ming-tao [1032–85] as Ch'eng Hao, and Ch'eng I-ch'uan [1033–1107] as Ch'eng I. Translator's note.)

and righteousness, embodying the spirit of Confucius, Mencius, Tseng Tzu, and Tzu-ssu.[2] (2) In order to strengthen the theoretical aspect of Confucianism, hitherto its weak point, it formulated a metaphysics encompassing both the universe and man. These two moments in close conjunction produced a comprehensive system of thought ranging from the rules of everyday behavior to problems of global ontology. It was the first, and probably the last, large-scale theoretical system which that essentially practical philosophy, Confucianism, has ever produced (the Wang Yang-ming school cannot hope to compete in magnitude). Chu Hsi philosophy is so systematic that its whole structure collapses if a single element is disturbed. As we shall see, this precisely structured character is a natural result of the specificity of the Chu Hsi mode of thought. In comparison with the Wang Yang-ming school, let alone the school of Ancient Learning, the Tokugawa Chu Hsi scholars show a marked lack of theoretical originality. But this does not necessarily mean that they were incompetent. Rather it is a result of the closed character (*Geschlossenheit*) of Chu Hsi philosophy.

There is a need for an examination of the intellectual structure of the Chu Hsi system in all its ramifications, but it is not the task of the present author or the direct object of this book to present a comprehensive picture of this philosophy. I shall give merely an outline of its metaphysics (its theory of the universe), of its theory of human nature, and of its practical ethics, in order to explain the decline of the Chu Hsi mode of thought within Confucianism in general.[3]

Chou Lien-hsi's *Diagram of the Supreme Ultimate* (*T'ai chi t'u shou*) is the foundation stone of Chu Hsi metaphysics. According to the

[2] Tseng Tzu (505–c.436 B.C.) was Confucius's disciple and was famous for filial piety. Tzu-ssu was Confucius's grandson. (Translator's note.)

[3] My knowledge of Sung philosophy is based on the Tokugawa Confucian scholars' understanding of it, and also on the works of contemporary Confucian scholars, rather than on a study of the original texts. Nor have I made any attempt to analyze the genealogy of Sung philosophy; that is, I do not attempt to examine such problems as how Taoist thought or Buddhist philosophy, which developed during the T'ang period, was assimilated into Sung philosophy, partly because these things are beyond my competence, but also because they are not relevant to the problem at hand, namely, the role that Chu Hsi philosophy played in molding the mental structure of Tokugawa society. Among contemporary Confucian scholars I am particularly indebted to Professors Takeuchi Yoshio and Nishi Shin'ichirō and to Dr. Morohashi Tetsuji.

Book of Changes, "In the *I* (change), there is the Supreme Ultimate which produced the two forms (*yin* and *yang*). These two
forms produced the four emblems (major and minor *yin* and *yang*),
and the four emblems produced the eight trigrams."[4] This was
used in conjunction with the theory of the five elements to explain
the origin of everything in the universe. Briefly, the theory holds
that "*yin* and *yang* are produced by the Supreme Ultimate, the
ultimate source of nature and man. By the transfiguration of the
yang and the *yin*, water, fire, wood, metal, and earth are produced.
These five elements become diffused in harmonious order, and the
four seasons proceed in their course. *Yin* and *yang*, as female and
male elements, interact to produce all things. It is man alone,
however, who receives all these in their highest excellence, and
hence is the most intelligent of all beings. The sage, in particular, is
in unity with Heaven and Earth. The object of human morality,
therefore, is to attain the state achieved by the sage."[5] The laws of
the universe and human morality are regarded as governed by the
same basic principles. This ideology is known as the unity of
heaven and man, and it is more or less current in all Chinese
thought, but especially so in Sung philosophy. It acquires its most
concise presentation in the *Diagram of the Supreme Ultimate*.

Chu Hsi (1130–1200) adopted Ch'eng I's interpretation that
"the Supreme Ultimate is the principle of all things in Heaven
and Earth." He reduced the emanatory tendencies still strong in
the *Diagram of the Supreme Ultimate* and established a kind of rationalist philosophy.[6] According to Chu Hsi, the Supreme Ultimate
is the *li* (Principle) that makes the *ch'i* (Ether)[7] of *yin* and *yang* and

---

[4] Eight combinations of long and short lines, viz.:

☰ ☷ ☳ ☶ ☵ ☲ ☶ ☱

In the order presented, they stand for: heaven and father; earth and mother; thunder
and eldest son; wood, rain, and eldest daughter; water, moon, and second son; fire,
sun, and second daughter; mountain and youngest son; marsh and youngest daughter.
Cf. Fung Yu-lan: *A History of Chinese Philosophy*, trans. Dirk Bodde (Princeton, N.J.,
1952), I, p. 382. (Translator's note.)

[5] The translation of this passage is based partly on Dirk Bodde's translation of Fung
Yu-lan, ibid., II, p. 437. (Translator's note.)

[6] The sentence is qualified with the term "a kind of" because Chu Hsi's rationalism
is essentially different in nature from modern rationalism. How it differs should become clear in the course of our discussion.

[7] On *ch'i*, Wing-tsit Chan writes: "Every student of Chinese thought knows that

of the five elements what it is. Thus it is the ultimate source, transcending everything in heaven and earth. "Before there was Heaven and Earth, there was Principle (*li*). Heaven and Earth exist because of Principle. Without Principle neither Heaven nor Earth can exist." On the other hand, *li*, along with *ch'i*, is inherent in each individual thing, and together they constitute the nature of all things. Because in Chu Hsi's philosophy Principle is inherent in all individual things and yet transcends them all, retaining its monistic character, Chu Hsi philosophy has been interpreted variously as monistic (based on Principle alone), dualistic (based on Principle and Ether), or pluralistic.

Fundamentally, however, it does not contain the "either-or" (*Entweder-oder*) category found in the Diagram of the Supreme Ultimate, which says: "*Speaking in terms of the whole*, the Supreme Ultimate encompasses all things. *But speaking of individual things*, each thing has its own Supreme Ultimate." Chu Hsi said: "Principle and Ether are two different things," and "the two things can exist *as separate entities*." By referring to Principle as a "thing" (*wu*), he seems to have been ascribing a material character to it, but at the same time he made it the source of the authority of the Ether. For this reason, the frequent modern comparisons of Chu Hsi's philosophy with philosophies such as German idealism (Dr. Inoue Tetsujirō's,[8] for example) are questionable. Would it not be more proper to say that the uniqueness of Chu Hsi philosophy lies in the fact that transcendence and immanence, materialism and idealism, were immediately unified in themselves (*an sich*) in it?

According to Chu Hsi philosophy, all things in heaven and earth consist of metaphysical Principle and physical Ether. Principle determines the nature of a thing and Ether its form. Insofar as all things originate from the same source, Principle, they are equal. "The nature of all things is the same," says the *Diagram of*

---

ch'i as opposed to *li* (Principle) means both energy and matter, a distinction not made in Chinese philosophy." A literal translation would thus be "matter-energy," but this lacks an adjectival form, so Chan settles for the term "material force." Wing-tsit Chan: *A Source Book of Chinese Philosophy* (Princeton, N.J., 1963), p. 784. Although this should be borne in mind, I shall continue to use the term "Ether" (used by Dirk Bodde in his translation of Fung's history) for the sake of brevity. (Translator's note.)

[8] Inoue Tetsujirō (1855–1944) was an authority on German idealism, but later in his life he turned to the study of Confucian thought. (Translator's note.)

the Supreme Ultimate. But they acquire different characteristics because of Ether. Man and other things in nature are endowed with the same Principle, but man is superior to all other things because he is endowed with the highest Ether. However, this relationship of equality and distinction exists not only between man in general and other things, but also between one man and another. Thus, Chu Hsi's cosmology is directly related to his theory of human nature.

The Supreme Ultimate, that is, Principle, resides in man as his nature. This gives the "Original Nature," or "innate character" (*honzen no sei*), endowed upon every human being at birth. Ether (ch'i) on the other hand determines whether a person is wise or foolish. When ch'i is endowed on a man, it becomes the ch'i specific to him (*kishitsu no sei*).[9] There are differences of purity and impurity, clarity and turbidity, in the nature of this Specific Ether. The Specific Ether of a sage is completely pure and clear, so his Original Nature appears in its entirety. But an ordinary person has a more or less turbid Specific Ether, giving rise to the various human desires. These desires conceal and obstruct the Original Nature and produce human evil. But the good in human nature is more deeply rooted than the evil. That is to say, Original Nature, based on Principle (absolute good), is more deeply rooted than Specific Ether, based on Ether (relative good and evil). Anyone who can remove the impure and turbid tendencies from his Specific Ether will be able to restore his Original Nature.[10] Hence

---

[9] Commenting on Chu Hsi's cosmogony, Fung Yu-lan writes of *kishitsu*, or *ch'i-chih*: "*Ch'i* or Ether . . . is the basic material from which concrete things are produced, and to which *li* or Principle supplies the pattern or form. This 'material' is equivalent to what Plato and Aristotle term matter, whereas *chih* (corporeal matter) is this same 'material' when it appears in more solid and tangible form" (Fung Yu-lan, op. cit., II, p. 547). Henceforth, for convenience sake, I shall use the Japanese term *kishitsu*, or "Specific Ether." (Translator's note.)

[10] "Heaven, in creating man, endowed him with *li* [Principle] in the form of benevolence, righteousness, propriety, and wisdom. But when things in the universe are brought forth, *ch'i* [Ether] is bound to cooperate with *li* in putting together various elements in one thing and in determining its form and character [*chih*]. Now, the *ch'i* that is endowed upon things is not the same in purity and clarity in all things. Those who receive clear and pure Ether and are free from desires become sages. Those who are endowed with Ether that is not perfectly clear and pure and have some traces of desire can become worthies [*hsien*] if they succeed in overcoming their desires. Those who receive impure and turbid Ether and are consumed with desires become obtuse and degenerate. All this is caused by Ether and desire. The good in human nature has always been the same" (Chu Hsi Yu-shan: *Lectures*).

the question of the way this is to be achieved. This is the starting point of Chu Hsi philosophy's practical ethics.

The classical texts that Chu Hsi philosophy turned to for its practical ethics were the Doctrine of the Mean and the Great Learning. The Doctrine of the Mean states that "a gentleman [*chun tzu*] prizes virtuous nature and pursues the path of inquiry and learning." Chu Hsi took these two points (first, to prize virtuous nature, and second, to pusue the path of inquiry and learning) and made them the fundamental principles of the moral cultivation that would enable a person to free himself from human desires and return to the Principle of Heaven. The first referred to moral cultivation in the strict sense, while the second signified intellectual investigation. We can call the former a subjective, the latter an objective, approach. The subjective approach may be described as "preserving the heart." The phrases "preserving the heart and holding fast to seriousness" and "maintaining quiescence and adhering to seriousness"[11] were the Chu Hsi school's most typical maxims of practical conduct. "Preserving the heart" is purely subjective introspection, since "preserving the heart *does not mean that a person's heart is preserved by any particular thing*." By this subjective introspection, a person is able to perceive intuitively the Original Nature within him. As a result, "the Principle of Heaven will constantly be clear, and human desires will naturally be suppressed and disappear of themselves."

The second approach, that is, the objective method, was "the extension of knowledge through the investigation of things"[12] as stated in the Great Learning. Originally, the Great Learning, together with the Doctrine of the Mean, constituted an obscure section of the *Li chi* (Book of Rites), but Chu Hsi extracted it, described it as "the gateway to virtue for the student beginner," and made it the basic introductory text for those interested in studying Confucian philosophy. He held it in such high regard that he wrote commentaries on it until his death. The section on "the extension of knowledge through the investigation of things" is especially famous for his addenda to the original text.

We saw earlier that in Chu Hsi's philosophy Principle had a

---

[11] *Ts'un-hsin ch'ih-ching; shou-ching chü-ching.* (Translator's note.)
[12] *Ko-wu chih-chih.* (Translator's note.)

transcendent character, unifying everything, but was at the same time immanent in each individual thing. This Principle, when endowed upon man, constitutes his Original Nature. Hence by investigating the Principle in each individual object, we should be able to understand our own Original Nature better. "If a person devotes his energies to the investigation of Principle for a long time and finally understands it in a sudden flash of illumination, he will be able to comprehend the external and the internal, the minute and the broad aspects of all things. Thus the whole structure and function of our spirit will become perfectly clear." This is the meaning of "the extension of knowledge through the investigation of things." Whereas "maintaining quiescence and holding fast to seriousness" involves the direct intuition of the individual's nature by introspection, "the investigation of things and extension of knowledge" is an attempt to reach the Principle of the subject conceptually via the mediation of objective things. However, here, too, rational understanding ends with the leap of a "sudden flash of illumination."

Thus anyone can become a sage if by "preserving the heart" and "investigating the Principle," and by using the subjective and objective methods, he succeeds internally in eliminating all human desires and returning to his Original Nature, and externally, in fusing with the law of the world. This is the ultimate objective of man's moral endeavors. And this individual moral effort is an absolute precondition for the realization of all political and social values. "The extension of knowledge consists in the investigation of things. When things are investigated, knowledge is extended; when knowledge is extended, the will becomes sincere; when the will is sincere, the mind is rectified; when the mind is rectified, personal life is cultivated; when personal life is cultivated, the family will be regulated; when the family is regulated, the state will be in order; and when the state is in order, there will be peace in the world. From the Son of Heaven down to the common people, all must regard the cultivation of personal life as the root or foundation. There is never a case when the root is in disorder and yet the branches are in order."[13] These opening words of the

[13] The translation of this passage is based on Wing Tsit-chan: *A Source Book of Chinese Philosophy,* op. cit., pp. 86–87. (Translator's note.)

Great Learning constitute the last word of the entire Chu Hsi philosophical system.

What special characteristics can we discern in the Chu Hsi philosophical system as briefly and basically outlined above?[14] The first point to consider is the nature of its basic notion, "Principle" (*li*). Principle is inherent in all things; it is the principle that governs movement and stillness, transformation and unity. Hence it is the law of nature. But it is also a principle inherent in man, his Original Nature. Hence it is the normative standard for human conduct. In other words, Principle in Chu Hsi philosophy is a moral as well as a physical law. Chu Hsi philosophy links natural law with moral norms. I shall discuss the nature of this connection later, noting here only that this relationship is not an equal one but a hierarchical one. Physical principle is subordinate to moral principle, and natural law to moral standards. They are not placed on the same level.

It is normal to discuss a philosophical system's theories of human nature and practical ethics in terms of their metaphysical foundations, and this is what I have done with Chu Hsi's philosophy. But Chu Hsi's metaphysics cannot be granted the status of a "first philosophy" in the Aristotelian sense. Chu Hsi's cosmology, or ontology, only has the position of a "reflection" of his theory of human nature. Chou Lien-hsi's *Diagram of the Supreme Ultimate* deduced its theory of human nature from its ontology, although it did so in the manner of a doctrine of emanation. "The Supreme Ultimate through movement produces the *yang*. This movement,

---

[14] The characteristics to be discussed below are not limited to Chu Hsi philosophy. Some were inherent in Confucian thought in general but became more pronounced in Chu Hsi's philosophy. Generally speaking, all intellectual systems are potentially self-sufficient and potentially contain within them all intellectual tendencies. The intellectual characteristics extracted from a system depend upon individual personality and social environment. Hence the variety and complexity of intellectual developments. Especially with a system like Chu Hsi philosophy, which directly links together all sorts of contradictory elements, it is possible, exaggerating slightly, to extract from it any tendency or characteristic at will. Needless to say, we are concerned here with the Chu Hsi philosophy that became dominant in the early Tokugawa period and later became the object of the criticisms of the school of Ancient Learning. Since the Japanese Chu Hsi philosophy of the early Tokugawa period was as unadulterated as if it had just arrived from China, we cannot go far wrong in searching there for the basic features of that philosophy.

having reached its limit, is followed by quiescence, and by this quiescence it produces the *yin*. When quiescence has reached its limit, there is a return to movement. Thus, movement and quiescence, in alternation, become each the source of the other. The distinction between *yin* and *yang* is determined, and their Two Forms [*liang yi*] stand revealed."[15] However, in annotating this first cosmological point, Chu Hsi wrote: "The Supreme Ultimate's motion and quiescence constitute the Will of Heaven. The alternation between *yin* and *yang* constitutes the Way. *Sincerity constitutes the foundation of a sage, and is the beginning and end of all things.* It is the Way of the Will of Heaven. *When the Supreme Ultimate is in motion, sincerity emanates.* This is followed by goodness, which is the basis and origin of all things. *When the Supreme Ultimate is quiescent, sincerity flows back to it.* The [essential] nature of things is fixed by this process. All things are rectified by their immanent nature." Thus, Chu Hsi was quickly able to introduce the concept of "sincerity" (*ch'eng*). Because the Doctrine of the Mean states that "sincerity is absolute truth and the basis of the Principle of Heaven," Chu Hsi sought to conceive the Supreme Ultimate (*li*) in terms of "sincerity," which is essentially an ethical category. And he did not subordinate nature alone to morality but also history.

Abstract and rationalistic systems of thought tend to view the complexity of historical development in terms of a single rational standard, failing to perceive the individual features in history. But because his standard of measurement, Principle, was essentially ethical in nature, Chu Hsi's "rationalism" has an absolutely unique historical outlook, exemplified in his *T'ung-chien kang-mu* [Outline and digest of the general mirror].[16] Here, history is seen above all as a moral lesson, a mirror, a way of "maintaining proper relationships between people of different statuses." Judging by these standards, Chu Hsi did not recognize the independent value of historical fact. I shall discuss later how Ogyū Sorai and Motoori Norinaga completely rejected this historical outlook. Here it is enough to note that the basic characteristic of Chu Hsi ratio-

---

[15] The translation is based on Dirk Bodde's translation of Fung Yu-lan: *A History of Chinese Philosophy,* op. cit., II, pp. 436–37. (Translator's note.)

[16] An abridged version of Ssu-ma Kuang's history, completed in 1084. (Translator's note.)

nalism, or intellectualism, is its subordination of everything to do with nature, history, and culture to morality. Only by keeping this moralistic limitation in mind can we understand why Chu Hsi rationalism necessarily gave rise to the nonrationalism of the philosophies of Sorai and Norinaga, and why the process that, at first glance, seems to involve an intellectual inversion, from rationalism to nonrationalism, was in reality a necessary stage in the formation of modern rationalism.

In spite of this highly moralistic strain in Chu Hsi philosophy, its theory of human nature is not ethically imperative or idealistic in form, because its moral principle is also a physical principle, that is, because its ethics is a continuation of nature. Instead, a naturalistic optimism predominates. Both the sage and the ordinary person are endowed with Original Nature. Evil arises merely because impure and turbid Ether obstructs it. As soon as the obstruction is removed, goodness, which is inherent in man, will be clearly revealed. This mode of thought is certainly optimistic; its standard of morality is not a transcendent concept but an intrinsic characteristic of man. The statement that "everyone can become a sage" reflects this optimism. It also gives rise to the belief that "as long as a person has faith and works strenuously, difficulties can be overcome and the Principle of Heaven realized."

But we cannot overlook the fact that this optimism contains an element of harsh rigorism. The standard to be realized is a natural one, but because ordinary human sensory experience and emotions are under the restrictions of the Specific Ether, which is a mixture of good and evil, *concretely and practically* the Principle of Heaven loses all its natural foundations and confronts human desires as an absolute moral imperative. Thus, because a naturalistic optimism and a self-denying rigorism coexisted in the Chu Hsi theory of human nature (one as an abstract theoretical system, the other as a concrete code of conduct) they moved in two separate directions as the Chu Hsi mode of thought began to disintegrate. One sought to purify Confucian normative principles by liberating them from their naturalistic limitations, while the other came to tolerate human desires as natural. I shall discuss the specific forms these two movements took later.

The optimistic constitution of the Chu Hsi theory of human

nature arose from the fact that normative principles and nature were linked together in this way. This continuative mode of thought is also an important characteristic of Chu Hsi philosophy. As we saw in the Chu Hsi cosmology, Principle (*li*) unites transcendence and immanence, substance and principle (*genri*). This is one manifestation of this continuative mode of thought. Similarly, the Principle of Heaven and human nature, the Ether and human desires, laws and normative standards, things and human beings, ordinary men and sages, intellect (exhaustive pursuit of Principle by the investigation of things) and virtue, virtue (cultivation of personal life and regulation of the family) and government (order in the state and peace in the world) are all directly linked together. And all these links are arranged in a perfectly orderly fashion beneath the above-mentioned sovereignty of morality (the equation of Principle and sincerity).[17] In this sense, we may say that optimism was a characteristic not only of the Chu Hsi theory of human nature but of the entire Chu Hsi system. As soon as this optimism could no longer be preserved, the various links fell apart. A more modern consciousness, Hegel's "divided consciousness," imperceptibly took its place.

As the final characteristic of Chu Hsi philosophy we must mention its tendency towards quiescence and meditation. Chou Lien-hsi's *Diagram of the Supreme Ultimate* classified movement with yang and quiescence with yin. But the Supreme Ultimate, which is an absolute entity transcending both movement and quiescence, was still strongly marked by absolute quiescence: "The sage in settling any affair relies on the principles of the mean, rectitude, benevolence, and righteousness. And he considers *quiescence (due to an absence of human desire) to be the primary principle. In this manner he establishes man's ultimate standard.*" This quiescent element inherent in all Sung philosophy was fully developed in Chu Hsi's philosophy. Commenting on the above statement from the *Diagram of the Supreme Ultimate*, Chu Hsi noted that "this means that the sage,

[17] "If in one's daily life the Principle of Heaven prevails, all things—such as the relationship between the ruler and the subject, father and son, husband and wife, elder and younger brothers, and when one is visiting, drinking, eating, seeing, and listening —will be in accord with Principle and nothing will be in disorder. If even one thing falls into disorder, the Principle of Heaven will vanish" (*Chu Hsi wen-chi* [Collection of Chu Hsi's works] [1532 ed.], Vol. XLV).

having perfected the virtue of movement and quiescence, always *founds virtue upon quiescence.*" "When a person is quiescent, sincerity will return to him and his true nature will prevail. *Unless the heart is calm, without desire, and quiescent,* it cannot withstand the transformation of things and bring unity into the motions of the world. Thus the sage . . . *even in moving, subjects himself to quiescense.*" Hence Chu Hsi laid great stress on the value of quiescence. This is a logical consequence of the fabric of his theory of human nature. In Chu Hsi philosophy, Original Nature is placid and motionless, and all movements of the heart are regarded as feelings under the control of the Ether. Hence benevolence (*jen*), righteousness (*i*), propriety (*li*), and wisdom (*chih*) are classified, as a priori factors, as [human] nature (*hsing*), but the four beginnings (*ssu-tuan*), the senses of commiseration, shame, compliance, and moral judgement, which the above four characteristics produce, are not considered to be a part of nature. They are classified as feelings (*ch'ing*). Thus benevolence (*jen*) is distinguished from love (*ai*) and is considered to be the "principle of love." Only this thoroughly quiescent characteristic of Original Nature explains the importance of the concepts of "maintaining quiescence and holding fast to seriousness" and "adhering to seriousness and remaining quiescent" in Chu Hsi's practical ethics. However much practical significance is read into "the exhaustive pursuit of Principle by the investigation of things," when compared to the practical ethical position of men like Itō Jinsai (see section IV below), its contemplative character clearly stands out. But this emphasis on quiescence over movement and meditation over action[18] derives, in the final analysis, from the continuative mode of thought; it is one more manifestation of the optimism of the Chu Hsi system.

[18] Of course, this does not mean that the Chu Hsi school gave little weight to practical ethics. That would be impossible for any school of Confucian philosophy. As opposed to the Wang Yang-ming school's theory of the unity of knowledge and action, the Chu Hsi school is identified with the slogan "First knowledge, then action." But Chu Hsi said, "Knowledge and action always require each other. Without legs the eyes cannot move forward. Without eyes the legs cannot see. With respect to the order of things, knowledge comes first, and with respect to relative importance, action comes first" (*Chu Hsi yu-lei,* Book IX). Thus, placing knowledge before action is merely a matter of logical sequence—in value terms, action is given great emphasis. But our concern here is with the content of practical ethics.

From the vast Chu Hsi philosophical system I have distilled such characteristics as a moralistic rationalism, a naturalism incorporating moral rigorism, a continuative mode of thought, and a propensity to quiescence and contemplation. I have also found that an optimistic strain ran through all these characteristics. These unique attributes of Chu Hsi philosophy provide the best explanation of its monopolistic position in the intellectual world of the early Tokugawa period. The optimistic character of Chu Hsi philosophy was a mental attitude (*Geisteshaltung*) ideally suited to a stable society and one that itself contributed to the stabilization of that society. The Tokugawa period followed the turbulent years of the Sengoku era, the period of "the country at war," a period of disorder and confusion, but also one of new movements and developments in all areas of life. This was transformed by the emergence of Tokugawa feudal society, based on a stable social structure and mental outlook. In this situation, the quiescent optimism of the Chu Hsi school of thought was well suited to become the universal attitude. But since the Tokugawa feudal system was not an empire of duration, national life could not long remain immobile. As a result, the universal optimism of Chu Hsi philosophy was bound to reach the limits of its effectiveness. A time came when the Chu Hsi continuative mode of thought was no longer satisfactory. Was the Principle of Heaven really Original Nature? Could or should human desires be eliminated? Was the Principle powerful enough to govern all things? Could mastery of the Principle be completely equated with ethical practice? Could all men really become sages? Would "cultivation of personal life and regulation of the family" ipso facto result in "order in the state and peace in the world"? One uncertainty led to another, and the links in the Chu Hsi system of thought were severed one by one. We are now in a position to examine concretely this process of dissolution.[19]

[19] The Wang Yang-ming school originated with Lu Chiu-yuan in the Sung period and reached its high point with Wang Yang-ming (also known as Wang Shou-jen) in the Ming period. As a result it is also known as the Lu-Wang school. Lu Chiu-yuan adopted Ch'eng Ming-tao's ideas, so he shares the intellectual origin of the Chu Hsi school. In consequence, the two schools are not diametrically opposed, although they are frequently contrasted with one another. Both deal with the Principle of Heaven and human desires, discuss human nature, and expound "solitude and inaction, preserving and nourishing, and sitting in quiescence." However, the Wang Yang-ming school

II

It might seem logical to examine how the specific features of the Chu Hsi school analyzed above emerged in the work of the early Tokugawa Chu Hsi scholars, but since these scholars treated Ch'eng I and Chu Hsi with the devotion due to sages, their works are no more than faithful introductions to Chu Hsi's theories. Dr. Inoue Tetsujirō writes:

Although there are many branches in the Chu Hsi school, it is very simple and homogeneous. The Chu Hsi scholars merely described and propagated Chu Hsi's theories. If any of these scholars had been so bold as to criticize or to attempt to present his own ideas, he would not have belonged to the Chu Hsi school. Anyone wishing to belong to the Chu Hsi school had to stick faithfully to Chu Hsi's theories. In other words, he had to be Chu Hsi's spiritual slave. As a result we

---

emphasized more strongly the moralistic element in the Principle. In consequence, it rejected any recourse to an intermediate object such as "Pursuit of the Principle" as a method of training and advocated the cultivation of the "intuitive knowledge" of the subject. Wang Yang-ming therefore emphasized the unity of knowledge and action in contrast to Chu Hsi's theory of "First knowledge, then action." In short, because he completely dissolved the physical element in Chu Hsi's Principle into the moralistic element, he failed to match the comprehensiveness of the Chu Hsi school, and his philosophy was oriented more toward the individual than toward society (this is substantiated by the fact that it is also referred to as *Hsin Hsueh,* the Study of the Heart, or the Idealistic school). But it still depended largely upon the Chu Hsi school for its basic methods of thought. This dependence on the Chu Hsi school was particularly noticeable among the Japanese Wang Yang-ming scholars. Unlike the scholars of Ancient Learning and Chu Hsi, they failed to develop an independent school of thought. As a result, Wang Yang-ming scholars' modes of thought were highly individualistic. With some, Chu Hsi characteristics were very noticeable; with others, they were not. Generally speaking, they reflected the overall intellectual trend, with Chu Hsi influence declining with the passage of time. For instance, if we compare the thought of Nakae Tōju, usually regarded as the founder of the Wang Yang-ming school in Japan, with that of his disciple Kumazawa Banzan, and that of someone like Ōshio Chūsai, who came later in the Tokugawa period, we find that the quiescent, contemplative tendencies become steadily weaker. In Japan, at any rate, it is meaningless to discuss the general characteristics of the Wang Yang-ming school by contrasting them with those of the Chu Hsi school. In light of the fact that our object is not to write a history of Confucian theories but to discuss how a mode of thought or mental outlook widespread during the early Tokugawa period changed, it is convenient to describe the disintegration process of this mode of thought solely in terms of the features of the Chu Hsi school. This process of disintegration also involves certain moments of Wang Yang-ming thought, of course.

can read volumes of the Chu Hsi scholars' works and find that they all say the same thing.[20]

After the middle of the Tokugawa period, that is, after the Chu Hsi system had been subjected to the criticisms of the scholars of Ancient Learning and National Learning, conciliatory elements and compromises, whether conscious or not, began to appear in the works of the Chu Hsi scholars. During the early years of the Tokugawa period, however, their writings were especially orthodox. This was a natural result of the fact that this period was objectively suited to the Chu Hsi mode of thought. To present the views of the Tokugawa Chu Hsi scholars would merely be to repeat the statements of the Chinese Chu Hsi philosophers. I shall therefore simply present some examples, restricting my study to a few points from the founders of the Tokugawa Chu Hsi school, Fujiwara Seika and Hayashi Razan.

Fujiwara Seika linked the concept of "the Way of Heaven," which was widespread as a common moral ideal during the period of strife in the sixteenth century, with the Principle (*li*) of Chu Hsi philosophy. "The Way of Heaven," he explained, "is the same as Principle. When Principle is in Heaven and is unattached to any object, it is called the 'Way of Heaven.' When Principle is attached to the human spirit but has not yet had to take any action, it is called human nature. Human nature then is the same as Principle."[21] This equation of the Way of Heaven with Principle was, of course, made possible by objective circumstances, that is, by the independence of Chu Hsi philosophy and its general dissemination at the beginning of the Tokugawa period. In turn, this equation served as a highly effective device for the propagation of Chu Hsi philosophy. And this conception of the Way of Heaven clearly reflects the continuative character of Principle in Chu Hsi philosophy. Seika writes:

The Way of Heaven is the master of all things between Heaven and Earth. Being shapeless, it is invisible but just as it is responsible for

[20] Inoue Tetsujirō: *Nihon shushigaku-ha no tetsugaku* [The philosophy of the Japanese Chu Hsi school] (Tokyo, 1909), p. 598.

[21] *Nihon rinri ihen*, VII, p. 21 (*Seika bunshū*, Book IX: *Goji no nan*).

the regular sequence of spring, summer, autumn, and winter, it is responsible for the four seasons, the creation of human beings, the blooming of flowers, the bearing of fruits, and the production of grain. In the same way, although man's spirit is shapeless, it governs the body, and its authority extends throughout, from the tips of the hair to the ends of the fingernails. The human spirit, which was formerly an integral part of Heaven, branched off from it and became our soul.[22]

Here Seika has directly linked together heaven and man, natural law and human nature. As a result, "illustrious virtue" (*meitoku*) becomes the Way of Heaven endowed upon man. Illustrious virtue, Seika explained, is absolute goodness, "perfectly clear and free from all evil thought." The sage is "a man who polishes this illustrious virtue so much that it preserves the clarity it had at the time of his birth." But "after birth, human desire arises in man. . . . As human desire gains in strength, illustrious virtue declines. Then, although he may retain the shape of a human being, his soul becomes akin to that of a bird or an animal." However, as illustrious virtue is innate and human desire comes into existence after birth, one can say that "illustrious virtue is like a clear mirror while human desire is like a clouded mirror."[23] As soon as the cloudy film is removed, the intrinsic illustrious virtue will appear in all its brilliance. Clearly this is an optimistic theoretical structure. Seika taught that "we must first clarify the illustrious virtue, instill the human spirit with sincerity, maintain proper conduct, polish the interior of the soul, and faithfully uphold the five cardinal virtues and the five human relationships. Then we too shall become sages and be one with the Way of Heaven."[24] As we might have expected, Seika linked sages and ordinary men together. But as practical ethics, this optimism contained a moral rigorism that abhorred human desire as its "enemy." Hence Seika's statement that "unless this illustrious virtue is polished day in and day out, the stain of human desire will accumulate and the original spirit be lost. Illustrious virtue and human desire are absolute enemies. If one wins, the other has

---

[22] Ibid., p. 31 (*Chiyo motokusa*).
[23] Ibid., p. 32 (all preceding quotations from *Chiyo motokusa*).
[24] Ibid., p. 34.

to lose."[25] Obviously, this mode of thought reflects the distinctive features of the Chu Hsi school described above.

Hayashi Razan was an even more faithful Chu Hsi scholar than Seika, so his writings are no more than conscientious introductions to Chu Hsi's ideas. For example, on the concepts of Principle and Ether he wrote:

> The principle that is ever-present, before the emergence of Heaven and Earth as well as after, is called the Supreme Ultimate. When the Supreme Ultimate moves, *yang* comes into being. When it is quiescent, *yin* comes into being. Originally *yin* and *yang* were of one and the same Ether, but later they separated into two parts. They separated once more and became the five elements, that is, wood, fire, earth, metal, and water.[26]

On human nature:

> The principle which is attached to the human form and resides in the heart is called nature ordained by Heaven. This nature is just another name for Principle and does not contain an iota of evil.
>
> One may wonder why human nature can be evil when it is inherently good. Human nature is like water. If it is poured into a clean container, it remains pure; if it is poured into a dirty container, it becomes dirty. . . . Ether [*ch'i*] is the container of human nature. . . . Thus, depending on the Ether, human nature, although basically good, may be covered by the physical form and be obstructed by desire. Thus the heart [*kokoro*] becomes clouded.[27]

In other words, Razan did no more than present simple explanations of Chu Hsi philosophy.[28] Thus, he pointed out the conflict between the Principle of Heaven and human desires:

[25] Ibid., p. 32.

[26] *Zoku-zoku gunsho ruijū*, X, p. 73 (*Riki no ben*).

[27] Ibid., p. 74.

[28] On Principle (*li*) and Ether (*ch'i*), however, he states: "According to the Sung philosophers, Principle and Ether are two and at the same time one; and are one and at the same time two. But Wang Yang-ming said, 'Principle is the logical principle of the Ether, while Ether is the functioning of Principle.' If we reflect upon this, we find that the Sung philosophers' views have the defect of being fragmentary. Later philosophers, in choosing between the two, must drop the former and adopt the latter. That is, they must adopt the unitary view. This is what is called the human heart" (*Hayashi Razan sensei bunshū*, II, p. 400). In other words, he favored the Wang Yang-

A benevolent man allows propriety and righteousness [*reigi*] and selfish desires [*shiyoku*] *to engage in a conflict within his heart*. When the former subdues the latter and its way is preserved, benevolence prevails. Unless a person is able to free himself from his desires, he cannot become benevolent. Unless a mirror is polished and the stain that clouds it is removed, it will not be clear. Only by removing selfish desires can a person achieve the state in which the principle of Heaven and human nature are present in their full perfection.[29]

But even someone blinded by human desires "is not by nature devoid of illustrious virtue. Just as sunlight and moonlight cannot be seen when the weather is bad and it is cloudy and foggy, but can be seen as soon as a little opening breaks in the sky, illustrious virtue is inherent in all men and is never totally lost."[30] Therefore, "if a person studies well, the bad aspects of the Specific Ether [*kishitsu*] can be corrected and goodness can be made to triumph."[31] This idea is expressed in the Great Learning as "the clarification of the illustrious virtue." After they have clarified the illustrious virtue, people can educate other men. They have become "new men" (*shinmin*).

If, just as a person daily washes and cleanses his body, takes a bath and washes his hands and face, he cleanses his heart each day, his selfish desires will disappear. This is called renovation. *This does not mean that something new which was not originally present has been produced.* It means that a person who was unaware of illustrious virtue until then has been made aware of it just as acutely as he is aware of his own existence.[32]

Thus the body is to be governed by illustrious virtue, and the people are to be governed by the "new men." This is the foundation for "order in the state and peace in the world." Razan

---

ming belief in the unity of Principle and Ether. But in another place, he wrote: "Principle and Ether are two . . ." (*Riki no ben*, op. cit., p. 75). His position in this question is thus unclear (in the last analysis, he was a bibliographer rather than a thinker). However, if we are studying the development of the Chu Hsi viewpoint rather than Chu Hsi philosophy itself, this question is not particularly significant.

[29] *Zoku-zoku gunsho ruijū*, op. cit., X, p. 48 (*Shunkanshō*).

[30] Ibid., p. 76 (*Santokushō*).

[31] Ibid.

[32] Ibid.

asserted that "*if the instruction from above is good, soon the customs of the age will also become good.* Evil will then be transformed and good will prevail. Of this, there is no question."[33] Thus private morality and government are linked together. This is, of course, in accordance with the usual interpretation of the Great Learning. But these expressions also reveal an optimistic mode of thought that is distinctly Razan's own.

This brief examination of the ideas of Seika and Razan has been presented in lieu of a general discussion of the characteristics of Chu Hsi philosophy as manifested in the early Tokugawa period. Before moving on, I should make a few comments about Yamazaki Ansai (1618–82), the founder of the Shikoku school, which, with the Kyoto school of Seika and Razan, was the fountainhead of Tokugawa Chu Hsi philosophy.[34] This was not because of anything unique in the content of Ansai's theories. He was, however, an extremely faithful Chu Hsi scholar, and, because of his distinct personality, his school preserved completely the moral rigorism that was inherent in Chu Hsi philosophy. Ansai had a religious reverence for Chu Hsi philosophy. "If a person errs by studying Chu Hsi," he said, "he errs with Chu Hsi. He has nothing to regret." He edited the works of Chu Hsi that dealt with individual moral training (such editions constitute the bulk of Ansai's writings), insisted on a rigid observation of these maxims, and enforced a rigorous program of moral training among his followers. The ideals of "holding fast to seriousness, and preserving the mind and nourishing nature" were strongly emphasized, and his disciples were strictly forbidden to read anything that did not contribute directly to the attainment of these goals. Discussing the spirit of Ansai's school, Naba Rodō (1736–98), a late Tokugawa Confucian scholar, wrote in his *Gakumon genryū* [The fountainhead of learning]: "Only a limited number of books were to be read. Historical works and the writings of the Hundred Schools were proscribed as useless. A good writing style was not valued, because it was regarded as frivolous and as leading to the loss of lofty

[33] Ibid., p. 83.

[34] Ansai was the disciple of Tani Jichū (1598–1649) and brought to perfection the Shikoku branch of the Chu Hsi school; but in his later years he developed an interest in Shinto and became an advocate of *Suika-Shintō* (a movement to syncretize Shinto with Confucianism), thus ceasing to be a genuine Chu Hsi scholar.

aspirations. Composition of poetry and verse was totally forbidden."[35] Ansai stressed the following passage from Chu Hsi's *Ching chai chen* [Admonitions on reverence and abstention] as the moral code of his school:

> When facing the Emperor, a person must wear a proper robe and headdress, be dignified in his gaze, and in command of his mind. . . . Outside his home, he must behave properly as if he were someone's guest. When he is given an assignment, he must behave as if he were given a sacred task. His attitude must be full of awe and respect. He must not dare to treat things with levity. He must seal his lips like a jug, and control his will like a castle. Reverence and respect must accompany a deep feeling of friendship. He must not dare to treat things lightly. . . . If he relaxes even for a moment, selfish desire in its full strength will burst forth, seemingly without cause, as if heat were present without fire and coldness without ice. A little mistake in the beginning will lead to great errors in the end and upset heaven and earth. If the three principles deteriorate, the nine standards[36] by which to rule the land will collapse. Remember this and be respectful.

This was the strict disciplinarian philosophy that Ansai adopted. The severity of his attitude as a teacher can be grasped from the fact that even his leading disciple, Satō Naokata (1650–1719), confessed: "Each time I arrived at his home and entered his gate, my heart was filled with fear and I felt as if I were entering a dungeon. When the time came to leave, once I got outside the gate, I would heave a sigh of relief just as if I had escaped from the tiger's lair."[37] Hence, when currents of thought emerged in op-

---

[35] Quoted from Iwahashi Junsei: *Dai Nihon rinri shisō hattatsu shi* [A history of the development of Japanese ethical thought] (Tokyo, 1915), I, pp. 397ff. (During the turbulent years of the Warring States [late fifth to third centuries B.C.] in China, a whole host of philosophical schools emerged, each proposing to remedy the moral, social, and political ills of the age. Translator's note.)

[36] The three principles are those that govern the relationships between lord and subject, father and son, and husband and wife. The nine standards listed in the Doctrine of the Mean are "cultivating personal life, honoring the worthy, being affectionate to relatives, being respectful toward the great ministers, identifying oneself with the welfare of the whole body of officers, treating the common people as one's own children, attracting the various artisans, showing tenderness to strangers from far countries, and extending kindly and awesome influence on the feudal lords" (Wang-tsit Chan: *A Source Book of Chinese Philosophy*, op. cit., p. 105). (Translator's note.)

[37] Quoted from Inoue, op. cit., pp. 396–97.

position to the Chu Hsi school, recognizing men's natural characteristics, they always referred to the Ansai school as a concrete example of what they were against.

Hayashi Razan was employed by Ieyasu at the beginning of the seventeenth century, in 1605, two years after the latter was appointed *Seii-tai-shōgun* (Generalissimo in Charge of Subduing the Barbarians). Fujiwara Seika died fourteen years later in 1619. In 1635, thirty years after Razan was retained by the Tokugawa family, the third shogun, Iemitsu, revised the Buke Hatto [Laws Governing the Military Households] and established the *sankin kōtai* system.[38] Razan himself read to the daimyo assembled in Edo the epoch-making new hatto. Yamazaki Ansai was born in 1618, a year before Seika's death, and began to gain recognition as a Confucian scholar around 1645. He is believed to have become a supporter of the Shinto theories of Yoshikawa Koretaru (1616–94)[39] after 1655, so he was active as an orthodox Chu Hsi scholar for over twenty years. Hoshina Masayuki (1611–72)[40] was a zealous Chu Hsi scholar and respected Ansai highly. But around the same period, in the middle of the 1660s, two men of extraordinary ability, Yamaga Sokō (1622–85) and Itō Jinsai (1627–1705), almost simultaneously sought to bring about a general shift from Chu Hsi philosophy toward Ancient Learning. Razan had died a decade earlier, after serving four shoguns: Ieyasu, Hidetada, Iemitsu, and Ietsuna. And Ogyū Sorai, the man who produced the antithesis to the Chu Hsi school, and who is the central figure of my thesis, was born in Edo in 1666. We can thus pinpoint the period from the beginning of the seventeenth century to a date just past the mid-century as the era in which the Chu Hsi school, or, more precisely, the Chu Hsi mode of thought, was universally accepted. This was also the period in which, thanks to the establishment of the Tokugawa government, the confusion and

[38] The system that required the feudal lords to reside in the capital every other year or every other half-year, and leave their immediate families there when they returned to their fiefs. (Translator's note.)

[39] Koretaru sought to introduce Neo-Confucian ideas into Shinto and equated li (Principle) with The Eternal Earth Stander (*Kuninotokotachino-mikoto*), the creator of the earth. (Translator's note.)

[40] The son of the second shogun, Hidetada. He was very influential in the government as an assistant to the fourth shogun, Ietsuna, during the 1650s and 60s. (Translator's note.)

disorder of the Sengoku era came to an end. However, Sorai did not begin to advocate the "study of ancient words and phrases" (*kobunjigaku*) until the Kyōhō era (1716–36), that is, half a century after Sokō and Jinsai had turned to the study of the ancient classics. Compared with the 260 years that Tokugawa feudal society lasted, half a century is not very long. However, profound changes occurred between the Kanbun (1661–73) and Kyōhō eras. The most problematic era of the entire Tokugawa period, the Genroku era (1688–1704), falls within this interval. During this half century, the popularity of Chu Hsi philosophy rapidly declined.

When, in 1666, Yamaga Sokō criticized Chu Hsi philosophy in his *Seikyō yoroku* [Essential teachings of the sages], issuing it, moreover, on the doorstep of the official philosophy, the response was immediate. He was exiled to Akō in the modern Hyōgo Prefecture, leaving behind him this famous statement: "Those who hold me to be a criminal must hold the Way of the Duke of Chou and Confucius to be criminal also. I may be incriminated, but the Way cannot be incriminated. It is the fault of the political currents of our time that the Way of the Sages is incriminated."[41] Before

---

[41] This farewell message is included in his *Haisho zanpitsu* [An autobiography in exile]. He had written it with the intention of having it presented to the government if he were executed, but since he was only exiled, he kept it in his possession. Sokō did not fall into disfavor for intellectual reasons alone. The bakufu was wary of *rōnin* (masterless samurai) in general. (Only ten years earlier, Yui Shōsetsu, 1605–51, had plotted to overthrow the bakufu.) But if the bakufu had really feared the political effects of Sokō's fame among the daimyo, it would hardly have placed him in the custody of the Asano family, a *tozama* house (one without hereditary ties to the Tokugawa family), which had once retained him with a stipend of one thousand *koku*, and still maintained very close relations with him. In fact, Sokō was treated as a guest in his place of exile. Unlike Kumazawa Banzan, who was regarded with disfavor at the same period, Sokō had not criticized or acted against any specific government policy. The official most responsible for his punishment, Hoshina Masayuki, had been influenced by Ansai's fanatical opposition to all unorthodox views. Three years after Masayuki's death, Sokō was pardoned and allowed to return to Edo. Taking all these facts into consideration, it seems obvious that his intellectual position must be regarded as at least in part responsible for his exile. Even if the ban against *Seikyō yoroku* served merely as a pretext for his exile, *the fact that it could serve as such a pretext* shows in itself that Chu Hsi philosophy still had strong support. Jinsai, who had shifted his allegiance to the school of Ancient Learning in the same period, escaped punishment because he was in Kyoto, far from the center of the official school, and because the *publication* of his main works came much later, around the time when Sorai's school was rising into prominence. His *Gomō jigi* [The meaning of the terms in the Confucian Analects and Mencius] appeared in 1705, his commentaries on the Confucian Analects in 1712, those on the Great Learning in 1713, those on Mencius in 1720, and his *Dōjimon* [Boy's questions] also in 1720.

he published *Seikyō yoroku,* Sokō's disciples had told him: "This book should be kept a secret, and admired by us. It should not be shown widely among the people. Moreover, it rejects the Confucians of the Han, T'ang, Sung, and Ming periods. Since it disagrees with the views of the scholars of the land, would not those who see it make slanderous remarks about it?" Sokō had replied: "Ah, you young men do not reflect very deeply. This is the Way of the World. It should not be embraced in secret. It should fill the entire land and be practiced through myriad ages. . . . Once my views are known, people throughout the land will discuss, criticize, and argue about them. If as a result of these discussions, criticisms, and arguments, they correct their errors, it would be an auspicious thing for the Way."[42] He had therefore insisted on publishing it. This episode shows that his disciples were aware of their intellectual isolation.

But what was Sorai's fate in the Kyōhō era? He, too, criticized the Chu Hsi philosophy, on the official philosophers' doorstep. He was forceful in expressing his views, leaving no doubt as to what he meant, and going further than Sokō in this direction. As we shall see later, his methodology contained the germ of rejection of Confucianism itself. But despite, or perhaps because of, this, outstanding men flocked to him to become his disciples. He won such renown that "nobles, sons of nobles, famous men of the various *han* [domains], as well as unemployed samurai and monks from distant regions rushed to see him, hoping to get to him before others did. In extreme cases, a word of criticism or praise from Sorai would send a person into the depths of despair or the heights of elation. . . . In this way, the entire nation submitted to him and followed him like his shadow. As a result, learning underwent revolutionary changes."[43] And until the very last, Sorai retained the deep trust and confidence of the eighth shogun, Yoshimune. No wonder Muro Kyūsō, a loyal Chu Hsi scholar also highly respected by Yoshimune, bitterly complained:

From the ancient period, false theories have frequently harmed the

[42] This question is discussed in the preface to the *Seikyō yoroku.*
[43] Inoue Tetsujirō: *Nihon kogaku-ha no tetsugaku* [The philosophy of the Ancient Learning school in Japan] (Tokyo, 1915), p. 451.

Way, but never have such incoherent falsehoods and crude ideas been expressed as freely as at present. For instance, there is a movement called Ancient Learning. People of this school say that the *Great Learning* is not the work of Confucius. Some claim to be capable of putting an end to the works of the Chu Hsi school [a criticism directed against the followers of Itō Jinsai]. Some hold literature in high regard, and say that the Way does not stem from Heaven or that the Way is not the natural principle of all things [a criticism of the Sorai school]. Countless other erroneous and shallow statements are bandied about. If these ideas had been expressed several decades ago, even ordinary men and youngsters could have seen that they were false and scorned and ridiculed them. But today the situation has changed. Everyone is affected by these views and respects and believes them, even Confucian teachers. If this is true of teachers, what can be expected of students and youngsters? It is only natural that they should all hasten to join the advocates of these views. I am convinced that the Way is daily declining and that the human heart is daily turning more towards falsehood. It is indeed a sad state of affairs.[44]

When Kyūsō says, "If these ideas had been expressed several decades ago, even ordinary men and youngsters could have seen that they were false and scorned and ridiculed them. But today the situation has changed," he reveals the rapid tempo of intellectual change in the preceding half century. By examining the theories of Yamaga Sokō and Itō Jinsai—the two men whose ideas mark the transition between the dominance of the Chu Hsi school and the rise of the Sorai school—and by studying the thoughts of Kaibara Ekken, who, while opposing Ancient Learning, began to have doubts about the Chu Hsi school toward the end of his life, I shall now trace the dissolution of the Chu Hsi method of thought in this half century.[45]

[44] *Kōhen Kyūsō bunshū,* Vol. XVI (Part 2, The collected writings of Kyūsō).

[45] Kumazawa Banzan (1619–91) is another scholar of this period who cannot be overlooked. But he was far more important as an advocate of concrete social and economic policies and as an actual government administrator than as a theorist. For instance, one cannot help but be struck by the incongruity of finding isolated but very penetrating empirical observations surrounded by cliché-ridden moralism in his *Shūgi washo* [A Japanese collection of principles]. "My name is vacuity. How with this name can I make a pretense of learning and serve as a teacher of others?" (ibid., Book IX) he asks. He was a many-sided man and cannot be classified simply as a Confucian

III

In his *Autobiography in Exile*, Yamaga Sokō explained his intellectual motives for advocating the study of the ancient Confucian classics as follows:

In the beginning of the Kanbun era [1661–73], I concluded that the books of the Han, T'ang, Sung, and Ming periods failed to clarify questions that had arisen in my mind. I therefore decided to inquire directly into the works of the Duke of Chou and Confucius and gain a proper understanding of learning by relying upon them. After that, I ceased to use the works of the later ages, and studied the works of the sages day and night. Then for the first time I was able to comprehend the way of the sages. . . . *In accordance with the teachings of the sages, I came to realize that learning was not to be treated as literature. What a person learns today can be put into practice today. It does not include such things as calculation, preserving seriousness, or sitting in meditation.* I clearly understood, therefore, that even if a person's words and actions were correct and he engaged in moral cultivation and recited a thousand words and phrases, he is only involved in trivial learning, not in the pursuit of the teachings of the sages.[46]

---

scholar. Where Confucianism is concerned, his views contained elements unrelated to the Sung school. "I do not rely upon Chu Hsi, nor do I rely on Wang Yang-ming. I only adopt and use the teachings of the ancient sages" (ibid., Book VIII). He also said that "the function of the physical form in perceiving the nature of physical objects is what we call the human heart. It is man's understanding of the temperature of the weather, food and drink, and male and female. It is wrong to regard this as human desire. It is not human desire. If a person arrives at an awareness of things on the basis of just principles and protects himself from the cold weather in accordance with proper principles . . . eats and drinks in accordance with proper principles, and maintains intimate relations with the other sex in accordance with proper decorum and just principles, he is behaving in accordance with the Way. How can the human heart be called human desires?" (ibid., Book XIV). Also, "A friend asks, 'Of what good is it to close one's eyes and sit in meditation?' The answer is, 'It is good if a person wants to recover from fatigue when his spirit is weary. But it is not good if a person engages in it because he dislikes movement and favors quiescence, and hopes to stop thinking by doing so. Movement and quiescence belong to the temporal realm. Things in the realm of human affairs must be taken care of. They must not be disliked' " (ibid., Book XV). But these expressions are only isolated statements and do not harmonize with the rest of his works. Since our aim is not to trace the history of philosophical theories up to the time of Sorai, we need not discuss Banzan centrally in this work.

[46] *Zonsaisōshobon*, ed. Kondō Keizō (133 vols., Tokyo, 1880–87), *Haisho zampitsu*, pp. 16–17.

Thus Sokō was dissatisfied above all with the methods of the Sung schools' practical ethics, the "exhaustive investigation of Principle," and "holding fast to seriousness." About the former, Sokō wrote: "All things in Heaven and Earth derive their forms from *yin* and *yang* and the five elements. They all originate from one and the same source. But once they have been transformed into Heaven and Earth and a myriad of things, they cannot be discussed in terms of one principle alone. The sages spoke of the investigation of things. This cannot be replaced by the 'exhaustive investigation of the Principle.' "[47] Needless to say, Sokō did not abandon the category of Principle. But he rejected its transcendental and metaphysical aspects, emphasizing its closeness to concrete things. "There is the logical principle of things. This is called Principle. Logic permeates all things. When logic is disrupted the order and hierarchy of things are not properly maintained. It is a great mistake to teach that [human] nature and Heaven are the same as Principle."[48] About the latter, i.e., "holding fast to seriousness," he asserted that "the Sung scholars have made 'seriousness' the basis for learning, and the totality of the philosophy of the sages. If a person concentrates on meditation in accordance with this line of thinking, he becomes grave and taciturn, feels oppressed and frustrated, becoming narrow and shallow in his outlook."[49] The Ansai school is the characteristic example of this "oppression and frustration, narrowness and shallowness." The sages do not abhor motion and delight in quiescence, for the human mind "belongs to the realm of fire and is continuously in action, not remaining immobile even for a moment. Motion and action are identical with the human mind."[50] Therefore, "the sages teach man to learn the pattern of things by studying the motion of all things. Both motion and stillness are the nature of things. There is no reason to give primacy to stillness. Motion has a design of its own. Stillness, too, has its own design. All this is in accordance with the investigation of things."[51]

In his practical ethics, Sokō always emphasized this principle of

---

[47] *Nihon rinri ihen*, IV, p. 154 (*Yamaga gorui*, Book XXXIII).
[48] Ibid., p. 21 (*Seikyō yōroku*, Book II).
[49] Ibid., pp. 22–23.
[50] Ibid., p. 26 (*Seikyō yōroku*, Book III).
[51] Ibid., p. 163 (*Yamaga gorui*, Book XXXIII).

"the investigation of things" (*kakubutsu*).[52] He therefore set out to expurgate the quiescent and contemplative characteristics of the Chu Hsi school's conception of "the investigation of things," and to bring out its materiality (*Sachlichkeit*). But as we have seen, the quiescent and contemplative character of the Chu Hsi school derives from the optimistic structure of its theory of human nature. Sokō therefore had to tackle this point too. He claimed that "the nature of things cannot be discussed in terms of good and evil. When Mencius used the term 'good nature' he did so for the sake of convenience. He had in mind the nature of Yao and Shun. But the later generations were unaware of this fact and came to regard human nature as being inherently good, theorizing extensively on the basis of this assumption. This has been the scholars' greatest error."[53] For Sokō, good and evil result from the *motion* of nature. "When things have not yet manifested themselves, there is no basis on which to discuss their brightness or darkness, goodness or badness."[54] The fact that all human hearts prefer good and abhor evil is the effect of the Specific Ether (*kishitsu no sei*), not of any "innateness" (*honzen*) of [human] nature independent of that Specific Ether. Moreover, this preference for good and abhorrence of evil is merely the foundation (*shitaji*) upon which moral training builds: "Unless a person studies and learns, he cannot truly understand good and evil. . . . Just because everyone's foundation is the same, it would be a grave error to compare one's heart to the sages, or even worse, to Heaven and Earth."[55] He warned against the uncritical thinking that Chu Hsi optimism might lead to, and called for an active, practical approach, for "a person must exert himself every day without rest, study without getting disgusted, and teach without becoming weary."[56] Here Sokō was cutting the link between the normative and naturalistic characteristics of the Chu Hsi theory of human nature and attempting to isolate the normative aspect. For Sokō, this trend led to the provision of a theoretical foundation for Bushidō (The Way of the Warrior). The ethical purification of pristine Confucianism

---

[52] *Ko-wu* in Chinese. (Translator's note.)
[53] *Nihon rinri ihen*, IV, p. 25 (*Seikyō yōroku*, Book III).
[54] *Zoku-zoku gunsho ruijū*, X, p. 271 (*Takkyo dōmon*, Book I).
[55] Ibid., p. 273.
[56] Ibid., p. 278.

was left to Itō Jinsai, who will be discussed later. On the other hand, once liberated from the norms of moralistic rationalism, the naturalism too began to develop independently. It is this aspect that is of special significance in the relationship between Sokō's and Sorai's thought. Sokō's social and political interests led him to criticize the moralism of Sung philosophy from a practical point of view, an approach that proved fruitful.

First of all, Sokō did not regard the different human passions and desires as "enemies" to be hated: "The passions and desires of men cannot be avoided. Passions and desires will not arise without the presence of form and character determined by the Specific Ether. Earlier Confucian scholars have spoken in favor of being without desires. This is a grave error."[57] "Those who eliminate all human desires are not human beings; they are no different from tiles and stones. Can we say that tiles and stones can comprehend the Principle of Heaven?"[58] He therefore rejected that rigoristic attitude that "rebukes man for all his errors, even the minute ones, and seeks to turn even slaves and servants into sages, endeavoring to remove every single speck of dust from every nook and cranny, thus bringing misfortune upon itself by its excessive scrutiny."[59] But Sokō did not just negatively tolerate the inevitability of human desire. His standpoint was utterly activist and practical: he assessed human desires positively as the basis for all activity, and hence for all moral conduct. He stated:

Man's intellect is superior to that of other beings. In the same manner, his desires and selfishness are stronger than those of all other beings. Therefore those who desire sex seek the world's most beautiful woman. Those who love music seek the world's most beautiful voice. They are not content unless they have attained perfect beauty. This is the basic nature of man and this has made his intellect superior to that of all other beings. Therefore, he not only likes sex and good music, but also when he serves his parents and lord he does his best. Otherwise he would not be behaving sincerely. Thus, the sages presented the concepts of filial piety and loyalty to guide subjects and children, and established the principles of benevolence and righ-

---

[57] *Nihon rinri ihen,* IV, pp. 167–68 (*Yamaga gorui,* Book XXXIII).
[58] *Zoku-zoku gunsho ruijū,* X, p. 286 (*Takkyo dōmon,* Book II).
[59] Ibid., pp. 265, 225 (*Takkyo dōmon,* Book I).

teousness as the highest paths of proper human relationships. This is so because a beautiful woman is the greatest good in sex, and the eight musical tones are the greatest good in music. Loyalty and filial piety are the greatest good when serving one's prince or father, and benevolence and righteousness are the greatest good of the Way of Man.[60]

Hence what is to be rejected is not human desire, but its misapplication or perversion. By this Sokō meant both excesses and deficiencies. This has important consequences. If human desire is at the bottom of all actions, good or bad, and if there is no Principle of heaven separate from human desire (this followed from his rejection of the separation of innate or Original Nature from Specific Ether), then the measure of the excesses or deficiencies of desire that constitute good or evil can no longer be found within human nature, but must be located outside it. At this point, rites and music become important as objective standards of value. Sokō's claim that "the teachings of the sages consist only in rites and music"[61] is reminiscent of Sorai. However, in comparison with Sorai, Sokō did not think through very thoroughly this concept embodied in his logical processes. He did not yet regard rites as man-made social institutions absolutely unconnected with nature.[62] Nevertheless, for him rites do regulate both the excesses and deficiencies of human sentiments or desire: "Man establishes rites *so that he can control his excesses and deficiencies in accordance with human sentiments* [ninjō]. He can also judge the nature of all things, and investigate the size, value, and quality of all things. By this means the *heart* is brought under control."[63] "The standards of measurement for the proper way and proper decorum in all

[60] Ibid.

[61] *Nihon rinri ihen*, IV, p. 22 (*Seikyō yōroku*, Book II). (*Li* and *yueh*. Rites have two functions: to regulate and refine human desires so that they remain within proper bounds. Music regulates human emotions so that they can be expressed in accordance with right principles. Cf. Fung, op. cit., I, pp. 337–44. Translator's note.)

[62] In another place in his *Seikyō yōroku*, Sokō wrote: "The reason of nature prevails in Heaven and Earth, and among men. This is called rites" (ibid., p. 21). Rites for Sokō still regulated the natural order as well as the social order. On the other hand, his denial of the identification of Principle (reason) and human nature severed the link between the reason of nature, or rites, and the inner nature of man, which had been clear in the school of Chu Hsi.

[63] *Zoku-zoku gunsho ruijū*, X, p. 233 (*Takkyo dōmon*, Book I).

things were established by the sages. *They can thus be regarded as external factors.*"[64] In other words, he considered rites and music to be objective standards outside human nature. Thus Sokō took the decisive first step in the movement toward the externalization of the "Way," or norms, that was completed by Sorai.

As one might expect, this first dissolution of the link between norms and human nature was accompanied by a weakening of the link between personal moral discipline and government. Here, of course, Sokō still basically accepted the Great Learning with its stress on the interconnection of "moral cultivation, regulation of the family, order in the state, and peace in the world," and insofar as he did so, his discovery of "the political" remained crucially limited. He always insisted that "moral cultivation is the beginning of the philosophy of the sages, and maintaining peace in the world is its ultimate goal. . . . Therefore, in order to govern the land, one must first start with moral cultivation."[65] On the other hand, the first signs of an independent development of the political factor can be seen in his statement: "*It is the opinion of the Sung and Ming Confucian schools that peace in the land will immediately follow the completion of moral cultivation.* But it is not sufficient to discuss the affairs of the land only in terms of moral cultivation."[66] Sokō emphasized the word *after* in the phrases from the Great Learning, "*after* moral cultivation" and "*after* order is established in the state." Government does not end with moral cultivation and regulation of the family; rather, "moral cultivation is the root, the basis, the beginning." Hence, "even when there are many people of excellent character, whose speech and behavior are proper and who do not commit any unrighteous or unprincipled acts, should disharmony erupt between family members, not to speak of in the country, the fate of the family would be determined by this situation. In such a case those virtuous people would be unable to cope with or make judgements about the matter. It would be all the more difficult for them to deal with the political problems of the entire world."[67] To prove this, he pointed out

[64] Ibid., p. 220.
[65] Ibid., p. 357 (*Takkyo dōmon*, Book III).
[66] Ibid., p. 358.
[67] Ibid.

that "although the School of the Heart [the Wang Yang-ming school] and Chu Hsi philosophy were popular during the Sung period, they failed to maintain peace in the land. Rites and music did not flourish, disasters wrought by the barbarians occurred daily, and the Southern Sung dynasty finally collapsed."[68]

For Sokō, "virtuous rule" (*tokuji*) is not merely a subjective attitude, but something achieved by means of objective institutions. He wrote: "To say that the people are to be influenced by virtue means that perfection in goodness and beauty is to be achieved after rites and music, law enforcement, and political administration [*li-yueh, hsing-cheng*] have been put in order. . . . When rites and music, law enforcement, and political administration are ill-defined, virtue cannot be practiced."[69] Hence his basic concern was with law and social rules. "Authority was based on these in the age of the sages," he said. "All the more reason for people in later ages to rely upon them."[70] Here Sokō had gone far beyond Jinsai and was close to Sorai.

Why is it that personal morality and government cannot be linked together? Sokō provided an interesting answer: "The manner in which the heart regulates the body is not the same as the manner in which the ruler governs the land. . . . This is because a person's body consists of separate parts which have different names but are all part of the same body. *The land under heaven, however, is a whole which is a combination of dissimilar things.*"[71] Because political unity is achieved not as an organic unity but as the integration of contradictory elements, it follows that it is different from moral cultivation and from the regulation of the family when the members of the latter are "few and very intimate." This partial insight into the dynamics of "the political" inevitably led to the recognition of an irrational moment in politics. This he referred to as the momentum of events (*ikioi*) or the trend of the times (*jisei*). For example, "all the people of the land, young and old, male and female, admire tobacco when it does not serve as food or drink, nor as medicine." "*Sake*, which often leads

---

[68] Ibid., p. 364.
[69] Ibid., p. 365.
[70] Ibid.
[71] Ibid., pp. 343–44 (*Takkyo dōmon*, Book II).

people into a state of frenzy and causes harm, is highly desired."
Nevertheless, "these things cannot be prohibited suddenly. This
is so because one has to follow the 'momentum of events.' "
However, "clever men of shallow learning remain oblivious to
such a momentum and insist that these things are contrary to
the reason of things. They insist that they run counter to the
Way and dogmatically demand that their use be stopped by
prohibiting them immediately. They would thus impose excessively harsh laws. The people may suffer under these laws, but the
attempts to ban the use of tobacco and *sake* will fail. In fact, these
things will tend to become more popular than ever."[72] He applied the same reasoning to attempts to reform the people's
manners and morals: "There are men who believe that, in order
to uphold proper manners and morals, the people must not
indulge in parties and excursions, nor display any taste for elegant
and refined matters; and also there are those who believe that
only when the lower-class people, even young urchins, adhere to
the Way, read books, recite literature, refrain from speaking out
loud or even singing a popular song, will the manners and morals
of society be rectified. These men express the mistaken views of
vulgar scholars, displaying the cleverness of a degenerate age.
They do not understand human feelings. This is the way in which
Sung philosophers seek to interpret the concept of remaking the
people."[73] Clearly, what Sokō consistently criticized was moralistic
Chu Hsi rationalism. These criticisms of Sung philosophy were to
be developed further and in a more forceful manner by the Sorai
school.

IV

As the Chu Hsi system, with its continuity of norms and nature,
began to disintegrate, Sokō sought to transform the negative character of its concept of "human desire" into a positive one by
establishing the independence of nature and attacked Sung rationalism from this position. Itō Jinsai (1627–1705), on the other
hand, sought to purify Confucian ethical philosophy by emphasiz-

---

[72] Ibid., p. 431 (*Takkyo dōmon*, Book III).
[73] Ibid., p. 436.

ing the normative aspects of the system. From this position, he, too, called for a return to pristine Confucianism. Sokō lived mostly in Edo, associated with various daimyo, and maintained a deep interest in government throughout his life. Jinsai, who was born into the family of a Kyoto lumber merchant, refused appointments from the lords of Hizen and Kishū[74] and remained a private scholar throughout his life. Living in considerable poverty, he continued to teach the Way as a true Confucian. While Sokō was successful in his criticisms of the social and political aspects of Sung thought, Jinsai was more successful in analyzing its philosophical aspects. This was due largely to the differences in their attitudes to life.

Jinsai made clear distinctions between categories such as the Way of Heaven, the Way (of Man), the Will of Heaven, Principle, benevolence, righteousness, propriety, wisdom, and the nature of things (sei). His aim was to rescue Confucianism from its decline into a merely contemplative philosophy by reinforcing its practico-ethical character. However, the unforeseen result was to accelerate the dissolution of the Chu Hsi school's continuative mode of thought. Jinsai opened the door to the Sorai school, in a sense his direct antithesis.

First let us consider how he distinguished between the Way of Heaven and the Way (of Man). He wrote: "The 'Shuo Kua' [a chapter in the Book of Changes] clearly explains that the Way of Heaven consists of yin and yang, the Way of the Earth of softness and hardness, and the Way of Man of benevolence and righteousness. *They must not be confused and viewed as being the same.* Just as benevolence and righteousness cannot be identified with the Way of Heaven, yin and yang cannot be identified with the Way of Man."[75] He confined yin and yang, as categories of the natural world, exclusively to the Way of Heaven, and benevolence and righteousness, as moral categories, exclusively to the Way of Man. With Jinsai we can, for the first time, speak of a cosmology that is independent of any theory of human nature.

Compared with the quiescent, rational view of nature held by

[74] Hizen extended into the modern Saga and Nagasaki prefectures, while Kishū was located in Wakayama and Mie prefectures. (Translator's note.)

[75] *Nihon rinri ihen*, V, p. 19 (*Gomō jigi*, Book I).

the Sung scholars, Jinsai's cosmology is strongly vitalistic. "In Heaven and Earth there is only a single monistic Ether, which manifests itself sometimes as *yin*, sometimes as *yang*. The relationship between *yin* and *yang* is a functional one, that is, if one rises the other declines; if one shrinks the other expands; if one goes the other comes; if one induces the other responds. This relationship continues forever. This is the whole of the Way of Heaven. This is the dynamics of nature."[76] A dynamic view of nature of this kind inevitably led to the denial of the supremacy of Principle over Ether assumed in the statement that the former "is the cause and reason of all things." "It is not true," wrote Jinsai, "that Principle exists first and Ether emerges later. On the contrary, the so-called Principle is the logical principle that is in the Ether."[77]

As we have seen, Sokō had already proposed that "Principle is the logical principle of Ether," and the Wang Yang-ming school maintained that "Principle is the logical principle of Ether. Ether is the Principle in actual operation." But as presented by Jinsai, this thesis is far more significant than in Sokō and also differs from that of the Wang Yang-ming school. For Jinsai, Principle no longer provides the link between heaven and man; it is no more than a "physical principle." "In speaking of the Way of Heaven and the Way of Man, the Sages never said that Principle is what governs their course. The *Book of Changes* states that the Principle must be investigated exhaustively, and the nature of things thoroughly studied. In this manner, the Will or Mandate [of Heaven] is to be ascertained. Investigation of the Principle involves material things, the study of the nature of things involves man, and the ascertaining of the Will involves Heaven. *There is a natural order in the way these terms are used. That is, it starts with matter, is followed by man, and then by Heaven. Notice that the word Principle is attached to material things and is not attached to Heaven or man.*"[78] Thus Jinsai opposed the extension of Principle to every domain. Jinsai's

[76] Ibid., p. 11. When he stated, "This is the whole of the principle of the Way of Heaven, this is the force of nature," he ranked nature with the Way of Heaven. This shows that his theory of the Way of Heaven is close to a *natural* philosophy in the true sense of the word.

[77] Ibid., p. 12.

[78] Ibid., p. 21. (Will or mandate: *mei* in Japanese, *ming* in Chinese, it signifies will, command, mandate, destiny. Here I shall use "Will." Translator's note.)

criticisms of the Sung philosophers' theory of Principle and Ether did not, as is often argued, confuse the logical priority they claimed for Principle over Ether with a temporal priority. Rather, he feared that the supremacy accorded Principle by the Chu Hsi school might go beyond a logical supremacy and become a supremacy of *value*.[79] He therefore sought to find a nonrational ultimate origin for a constantly fluctuating but monistic Ether. Hence his concept of the Will of Heaven.

I need not discuss the vicissitudes of the concept of heaven or of the Will of Heaven in Confucian philosophy. However, it should be noted that the Sung schools regarded the "Will of Heaven" simply as a synonym for the Principle of Heaven or the Way of Heaven and thus linked it to human nature. Their pantheistic structures completely buried the personal, individual element implicit in the term "Will of Heaven." Jinsai, on the other hand, distinguished the "Will of Heaven" both from the Way of Heaven and from human nature. He wrote: "The so-called Will refers to Heaven's assignment of good or bad luck, good or bad fortune, to people, after it has observed whether their behavior is good or bad. It says in the *Book of Odes*, 'This is the Will of Heaven. It endures magnificently forever.' "[80] This is a personified view of heaven. "Heaven is like the ruling prince and its Will is like the commands of the prince."[81] The force that takes the place of Sung philosophy's "Principle" as the fundamental causal factor in the constantly fluctuating natural world is this personified heaven. "The

[79] He maintained that "all things are based on the five elements and the five elements are based on *yin* and *yang*. *If we were to inquire further and pursue the reason for yin and yang we would inevitably arrive at the Principle.* Once we arrive at this point, we cannot help but succumb to a sense of nothingness.... *Common sense would inevitably lead us to this conclusion.* This is where ordinary men differ from the sages" (*Dōjimon*, Book II, ibid., p. 131). Although he admitted that pursued to the very end logic leads to the Principle, he denied the "nothingness" that is the practical consequence of this logical analysis. On the other hand, he did of course reject any theory of the origin of heaven and earth: "Who has seen and who has reported on things before and at the time of the creation of Heaven and Earth?" But this is merely to argue that from the standpoint of chronological sequence the theory that Principle came before Ether is untenable, not to confuse the logical relationship between the two. This is clear from his commentaries on Confucius and Mencius (*Gomō jigi*) in the section on "The Way of Heaven." Here, he refuted the Sung Confucians' theory that Principle precedes Ether, and went on to criticize their theory of the genesis of the universe.

[80] Ibid., p. 16 (*Gomō jigi*, Book I).

[81] Ibid., p. 15.

constantly alternating motion of *yin* and *yang*," asserted Jinsai, "can be discussed in terms of fluctuations, and the Will of Heaven which endures magnificently forever can be *discussed in terms of a ruling prince. . . .* In reality, the principle is the same, but *when we are concerned with what makes the Way of Heaven the Way of Heaven, we must speak of it in terms of a sovereign authority.*"[82]

Only a small part of Jinsai's overall philosophical system is concerned with his theory of the Will of Heaven. But its importance in the intellectual structure of his philosophy cannot be ignored. "The Sung Confucians," he remarked, "contend that all things under Heaven can be explained by the single word 'Principle.' They fail to realize that, although nothing stands outside Principle, things under Heaven cannot be judged solely in terms of a single principle."[83] "The beginning and end of all things, past and present, cannot be investigated. The limits of the four directions cannot be known. Things nearby can be known through personal experience, and distant things can be known by means of other things, but the reason for the shape and nature of things cannot be investigated and known."[84] The logical origin of Jinsai's agnostic tendencies can be traced to his theory of the Will of Heaven. The Sorai school adopted and generalized this theory of the Will of Heaven, which was only a small part of Jinsai's philosophy, and used it to sap the foundations of the Chu Hsi school. Jinsai's theory of the Will of Heaven broke down all the defenses of Chu Hsi rationalism.

However, the theory that Jinsai emphasized most heavily and developed in most detail was neither his cosmology nor his theory of the Will of Heaven, but his ethics—the above-mentioned distinction between the Way of Man and the Way of Heaven. "When the sages spoke of the Way," he wrote, "they were all thinking of the way of man. Confucius seldom spoke of the Way of Heaven, and Tzu Kung held that it was not a matter to be inquired into."[85] Jinsai's reason for restricting the Way primarily to the way of man was his fierce ambitions for practical morality. "When morality

[82] Ibid., p. 14.
[83] Ibid., p. 129 (*Dōjimon,* Book II).
[84] Ibid.
[85] Ibid., p. 19 (*Gomō jigi,* Book I). (Tzu Kung: 520–c.450 B.C. A pupil of Confucius. Translator's note.)

flourishes," he asserted, "argument remains in abeyance, but when morality declines, argument gains ascendancy. . . . When morality declines one degree, argument rises one degree; when morality declines two degrees, argument rises two degrees. The more morality declines, the more argument rises, and when argument rises morality is scorned."[86] By insisting that "there is no way without man, and no man without the way,"[87] Jinsai hoped to strengthen the ethical side of the Sung schools' Way, which had been weakened by its extension to cover the natural world. But Jinsai's ambitions for practical morality were not satisfied by simply liberating morality from physical nature. He delved into the theoretical structure of Confucian ethics and sought to purify it into a set of ideals. Having broken the continuity between the Way in general and the Way of Heaven, he now made it transcend human nature also. As we saw earlier, in Chu Hsi philosophy, benevolence, righteousness, propriety, and wisdom are classified with original human nature and also constitute the Way. But according to Jinsai, "The four concepts of benevolence, righteousness, propriety, and wisdom are all moral terms and do not deal with human nature. *Morality is a universal force* and is not the property of one man. On the other hand, *the nature of things has to do with the individual*, and does not have a universal character. That is what distinguishes the nature of things from morality."[88] In Jinsai's opinion, benevolence, righteousness, propriety, and wisdom are not principles endowed upon man at birth, constituting his Original Nature; they are ideal characteristics that men must strive to realize. He was expressing the same idea when he said: "When man exists, his nature exists. When man does not exist, his nature does not exist. *But regardless of whether or not man exists, the Way, by its very nature, has an existence of its own.* It permeates Heaven and Earth, and extends throughout all human relationships. It exists at all times and in all places."[89] This view in no way contradicts the point made earlier, namely that "there is no Way without man, and no man without the Way." The latter

[86] Ibid., p. 81 (*Dōjimon*, Book I).
[87] Ibid., p. 80.
[88] Ibid., p. 27 (*Gomō jigi*, Book I).
[89] Ibid., p. 83 (*Dōjimon*, Book I).

expresses the separation of the Way from the natural world, while the former makes the Way transcend human nature.

Of course, insofar as Jinsai's plan to purify Confucian ethical ideals is concerned, the Way could not be completely external and wholly unrelated to human nature. Because he respected Mencius just as much as Confucius, he could not but support the former's belief in the goodness of human nature. Therefore, while insisting on regarding benevolence, righteousness, propriety, and wisdom as transcendental ideas, he placed the "four beginnings" (ssu tuan), i.e., the senses of commiseration, shame, compliance, and moral judgement, in the realm of human nature. (Since he had already denied the immanence of the Way, by the nature of things he here meant primarily the nature of the Specific Ether, or kishitsu.) The four beginnings are endowed in human nature as predispositions (Anlage) toward the realization of the Way, which has an objective and autonomous existence. Thus, he explained that "unless man's nature were good, he would be unable to attain the virtues of benevolence, righteousness, propriety, and wisdom, even if he desired to do so. But because human nature is good, he is able to realize these four virtues."[90] That is all it means to say that human nature is good. Jinsai did not fail to point out that although Mencius taught that human nature is good, he did not, like the Sung Confucians, "fruitlessly discuss its principles, but emphasized the necessity of augmenting what is lacking, and preserving one's mind and nourishing one's nature."[91] Jinsai repeatedly stressed that Mencius's belief in "the goodness of human nature was expressed mainly for the benefit of *those who were in a state of despair and self-abandonment.*"[92] For him, the core of philosophy was the imperative and transcendental aspects of the Way, while the goodness of human nature was only an expedient notion.[93]

[90] Ibid., p. 28 (Gomō jigi, Book I).
[91] Ibid., p. 82 (Dōjimon, Book I).
[92] Ibid.
[93] The fact that Jinsai included the four beginnings in the realm of human nature while maintaining that benevolence, righteousness, propriety, and wisdom were not aspects of human nature is often pointed out as a contradiction in his work. But whether we should regard absolute good as inherent in human nature or as a goal for human nature to reach, in other words, whether goodness should take the background or the foreground, is a question that has always sharply divided ethical thought. Even

Although Jinsai emphasized the imperative character of Confucian ethics, he was not intolerant of man's natural desires. On the contrary, although he is regarded as the typical moralist, he often revealed the same kind of understanding of "sensual desire" as Sokō. For instance, he said, "if we were to judge things in terms of propriety and righteousness, we would find that passion conforms to the Way and desires to righteousness. There is nothing wrong with them."[94] It may seem strange that Jinsai, who was interested in purifying Confucian morality, should also have this side to his character. But this strangeness disappears once we stop considering Jinsai's thoughts *in isolation* and look at them in their place in the disintegration of the Chu Hsi mode of thought. Rejection of the optimism of the Chu Hsi theory of human nature (by purifying norms of their naturalistic restrictions) inevitably entailed the elimination of the moral rigorism inherent in that theory.

It is thus not so strange as it might seem to find Jinsai, who was content to remain in abject poverty all his life, saying: "Confucians pride themselves on showing little interest in monetary compensations and holding wealth and rank to be worth no more than dust and dirt. Society in general also respects those who hold mundane affairs in disdain and maintain an attitude of transcendence and aloofness. Both show that they are extremely igno-

---

those who regard it as a transcendental idea naturally seek to connect it with the inner feelings of man in some form or another unless they are prepared to accept the position of judging the morality of human conduct solely in terms of its consequences. Jinsai's expressions are often ambiguous because he tried to indicate the transcendental nature of norms by employing terms used by Mencius such as "extension" (*k'uo ch'ung*) and "four beginnings." This causes some difficulties, but if we examine Jinsai's thoughts not in a prosaic, two-dimensional fashion but from the point of view of his concern for the practical, and bearing in mind the disintegration of Chu Hsi thought, they cannot be dismissed as casually as they are by Dr. Inoue Tetsujirō when he writes: "Jinsai seeks to make a rigid distinction between himself and the Sung Confucians by straining the point and insisting that benevolence and righteousness are not aspects of human nature. As a result, he goes completely astray, using words in a crazy way. He says, 'The Sung philosophers' logic is very weak.' But it is not the Sung philosophers' logic that is weak at all. Jinsai's own thinking is so confused that he seems to be groping in the dark" (Inoue Tetsujirō: *Nihon kogaku-ha no tetsugaku,* op. cit., pp. 242–43). I shall not pursue this question any further here. It is enough to remember that in his interpretation of the Way, Jinsai rejected the idea of simply linking it with human nature and tried to objectify it. This point is significant because of its relationship with Sorai's views later on.

[94] Ibid., p. 108 (*Dōjimon,* Book II).

rant of the Way."[95] Compare these words with Motoori Norinaga: "The Confucians of every age extol those who remain unconcerned about their poverty and lowly status, and show no desire nor delight in wealth and prosperity. But these attitudes do not reflect the true feelings of man. Frequently they are deceptions practiced by those who covet honor. Occasionally we find men who truly adhere to these attitudes but they are abnormal. There is nothing praiseworthy about their views."[96] There is obviously a gulf between Itō Jinsai, who regarded himself and was regarded by others as a true Confucian scholar, and Motoori Norinaga, who was a thoroughgoing opponent of the Confucians. Nevertheless, if we look at their views in the context of the dissolution of the Chu Hsi mode of thought, we find that they are not so far apart as they might seem.

We have already seen that the rigoristic conclusions of the Chu Hsi school were inextricably linked to its moral rationalism. The irrationalism in Jinsai's cosmology, arising, as we have seen, from his agnostic viewpoint, recurs here too as a consequence of his opposition to moral rigorism. He believed that "if all things are judged solely on the basis of Principle, cruel and merciless attitudes will triumph, and kindly and humane attitudes will decline."[97] He also wrote:

Upon reading such works as the *Li-tai t'ung-chien tsuan-yao*, I find that in their criticism of people, they regard good as good and bad as bad, showing not one iota of mercy. They are indeed harsh. Their judgement is so severe that in their view there has not been a perfect person in all history. They display nearly the same spirit as Legalists such as Shen Pu-hai and Han Fei-tzu, showing none of the spirit of tolerance that the Sages had. They insist on severe self-discipline and harsh criticism of others. This attitude saturates the heart, permeates the marrow of the bones, and finally makes a person inhumane. Herein lies the error of adhering exclusively to the word Principle. It is indeed a sad state of affairs.[98]

[95] Ibid., p. 88 (*Dōjimon*, Book I).

[96] *Zōho Motoori Norinaga zenshū* [Enlarged edition of the complete works of Motoori Norinaga] (Tokyo, 1926–28), VIII, p. 73 (*Tamakatsuma*, 3). (Motoori Norinaga's views will be further discussed in chapter 4. Translator's note.)

[97] *Nihon rinri ihen*, V, p. 129 (*Dōjimon*, Book II).

[98] Ibid., pp. 129–30. (*Li-tai t'ung-chien tsuan-yao*: a ninety-two-volume historical

Such criticisms of the rationalism of the Sung schools inevitably led to the emergence of the historical consciousness they lacked. Chu Hsi stated that "during and before the time of the Three Dynasties[99] all things were based on the principle of Heaven. Since the Three Dynasties all things have been based on human desire." Commenting on this, Jinsai remarked:

> These are not the words of a benevolent man. A benevolent man does not despise worldly people. He knows that the present is not so different from the ancient period. A person who is not benevolent tends to become enraged at his own age. He knows that the past cannot be revived in the present. The attitudes and tastes of the past and present differ greatly. Just as it is impossible that no virtuous person could exist in later ages, it is impossible that no insignificant men ever existed in antiquity. How can anyone contend that human desires became the basis of all things only after the age of the Three Dynasties?[100]

On the other hand, Jinsai still maintained the historical outlook of Chu Hsi's *Tung-chien kang-mu* [Outline and digest of the general mirror]. "In studying history," he wrote, "it is necessary to read Chu Hsi's *Tung-chien kang-mu*."[101] But he also said, "If the sages were born in the present age, they too would rely on the common ways of today and employ the methods of today."[102] "The sages sought to avoid extremes. For the rest, they sought to govern society by acting in accordance with the times, and in conformity with the common ways. They had no intention of changing this situation. If one were to try senselessly to change the pleasures of today, society would fall into turmoil, for rites and music would not suddenly come into existence. Certainly sages would not act in this manner."[103] This emphasis on the importance of the his-

---

chronicle compiled by a Ming scholar, Li Tung-yang. Shen Pu-hai [d. 337 B.C.] was a Legalist prime minister of the state of Han in the period of the Warring States, and Han Fei Tzu [d. 233 B.C.], who synthesized Legalist thinking, was a prince of Han. Translator's note.)

[99] The three dynasties of Hsia (2183–1752 B.C.?), Shang (1751–1112 B.C.), and Chou (1111–249 B.C.). (Translator's note.)

[100] *Nihon rinri ihen*, V, p. 113.

[101] Ibid., p. 156 (*Dōjimon*, Book III).

[102] Ibid., p. 112 (*Dōjimon*, Book II).

[103] Ibid., p. 113.

torical development of rites and music shows that the quiescent, immobile rationalism of the Chu Hsi school had quite lost its hold on Jinsai's mind. Just as Jinsai the "moralist" was not moralistic, so Jinsai of the school of Ancient Learning did not believe that civilization had steadily declined since the days of the sages and that it was approaching its demise.

Since Jinsai concentrated on the theoretical analysis of Confucian ethics, we cannot expect too much of him in the realm of political theory. And yet there are clear signs in his thought of the disintegration of the continuity of individual morality and government. When Chu Hsi was on his way to the imperial court at the invitation of the Sung emperor Hsiao Tsung (1163–89), someone advised him that "the Emperor does not like to hear about such things as the upright mind and sincere intentions, so it would be wiser not to discuss these matters." To which Chu Hsi replied, "All my learning has been devoted to the upright mind and sincere intentions. How can I bend my way and deceive my lord?" Commenting on this episode in his *Dōjimon* [Boy's questions], Jinsai remarked: "I think that his opinion is fine, of course. But although it may be a proper subject of study for a scholar, it is not a matter that should be expounded to a ruler. A scholar must of course regulate his life in terms of these ideals, but the ruler must have as his basic principle a willingness to share the good and the bad with his subjects. *Of what advantage would it be for the art of government if he aimlessly studied the principle of the upright mind and sincere intentions but was unable to share the good and the bad with his subjects?*"[104] As this shows, Jinsai believed that the ruler's duty was not the advancement of personal morality, but the public task of "sharing the good and the bad with the people."

Jinsai also disagreed with Chu Hsi's opinion that the qualification for a benevolent person was "to be in harmony with Principle and devoid of self-will." He argued that "Kuan Chung was not completely in harmony with Principle and his mind was not free of selfishness, but Chu Hsi holds him to have been a benevolent person because the people benefited from him."[105] In other words,

[104] Ibid., p. 111.
[105] Ibid., p. 100 (*Dōjimon*, Book I). (Kuan Chung: an adviser to Duke Huan of the state of Ch'i in the late Chou period. Translator's note.)

he believed that there was no difference between the benevolence of the sages and that of Kuan Chung. In judging whether someone was benevolent or not, Jinsai believed, social achievements, that is, whether the people benefited from his actions or not, were more important that his personal motives, that is, whether he was selfish or not. Of course, the full development of these aspects had to await the rise of the Sorai school. But when we see the political moment becoming independent of personal ethics in the thought of a moralist like Jinsai, who spoke of virtuous action every time a word passed his lips, and taught the need for constant correction and improvement whenever he spoke, we are forced to realize that the continuative method of thought was disintegrating so rapidly that nothing could forestall its demise.

V

When Kaibara Ekken (1630–1714) published his *Daigiroku* [Grave doubts] and expressed fundamental doubts about the Chu Hsi school, it was 1714, just before the end of his eighty-five years of life. In the preface, however, he indicated that these doubts about the Sung philosophy had arisen in his mind much earlier, in his middle years. He wrote:

> I began to study the philosophy of the sages at the age of fourteen or fifteen. Having read the works of the Sung Confucians early, I respected their theories highly. At the same time, many questions occurred to me. Being a man of limited ability, I was unable to find the answers myself. Nor was I able to consult a wise teacher. Recently, I have been increasingly feeling the effects of old age and have been rapidly losing the intellectual capacity to solve these questions. I have reflected on these matters seriously for the past thirty years and more, but I have failed to find the answer by thinking about the difficulties by myself. It has been a lifelong source of vexation for me. I have therefore decided to record the questions that have been disturbing me for such a long time, in the hope that intelligent men will resolve them for me.[106]

[106] *Ekken zenshū* [The complete works of Ekken] (Tokyo, 1910–11), II, p. 150. (This preface is absent from the version of the *Daigiroku* in the *Nihon rinri ihen*, so I have referred to the *Ekken zenshū*; other citations from the *Daigiroku* have been taken from the *Nihon rinri ihen*.)

But being modest and cautious, Ekken did not wish to advance dissenting opinions imprudently and found his own school of thought. Hence to begin with he kept his misgivings to himself. He criticized both Jinsai and Ansai, saying: "I thoroughly dislike the ways of the Kyoto scholars. They are all partial in their views, presenting their own opinions. They make no effort to consult each other and arrive at a common point of view. It appears that they have done nothing but formulate their own personal views."[107] But once the seed of doubt was planted in his mind, there was no way to remove it. He continued to revere Chu Hsi and disliked the school of Ancient Learning, but he could not but be drawn toward their criticisms of the Sung schools. As a result, the anti-Chu Hsi tendencies that emerged in his *Jigoshū* [Essays for my own amusement] in 1712 and increased in intensity in his *Shin-shiroku* [Record of prudent reflections] in 1714 finally exploded in *Daigiroku*. His remark in the preface that "I have failed to find the answer by thinking about the difficulties by myself. It has been a lifelong source of vexation for me" clearly attests to the conscientious Ekken's intellectual anguish. Relying primarily upon the *Daigiroku,* but with occasional references to the *Shinshiroku* and *Jigoshū,* I shall endeavor to ascertain the aspects of Chu Hsi philosophy that disturbed Ekken.

Ekken first examined Chu Hsi's cosmology and questioned the theory that Principle precedes Ether. "Chu Hsi says that Principle existed before Heaven and Earth came into being. . . . I venture to suggest that it is strange to see a school of thought which was founded upon the wisdom of the ancients and is just and enlightened present such an opinion. This is the same as the Taoists' theory of the creation of Heaven and Earth, and their view that something is created out of nothing."[108] "Principle and Ether are one and the same. They cannot be separated into two substances.

---

[107] *Kinsei shakai keizai gakusetsu taikei* [An outline of the social and economic theories of the Tokugawa period] (Tokyo, 1935–37), XIV, p. 23. As applied to Jinsai, however, this criticism is unjust. Jinsai too stressed the point that learning was a public matter. He bemoaned the fact that the scholars of his day behaved in such a manner that "each person regards his own school as his private possession and vilifies others." He noted that the habit of "welcoming arguments similar to their own and despising dissenting views" was "the common disease of scholars" and emphasized the need for diligent training by contact with different opinions (cf. *Dōjimon,* Book II, sections 47–49).

[108] *Nihon rinri ihen,* VIII, p. 231 (*Daigiroku,* Book II).

Therefore there can be no Principle without Ether, and no Ether without Principle. One cannot be placed before the other."[109] This belief in the inseparability of Principle and Ether brings him close to the opinion of Lo Cheng-an (1465–1547) of Ming China. But he went beyond the belief that the two are inseparable and argued that the Ether alone is fundamental. "I would venture to say that Supreme Ultimate is the term for the Ether when it was still in a state of chaos and confusion, when *yin* and *yang* were not yet differentiated, and all things had not yet been created."[110] He thus identified the Supreme Ultimate not with Principle, but with Ether. He contended that "the Principle is not an independent force. It is merely the principle of the Ether."[111] Ekken, like Jinsai, denied the substantive existence of Principle.

This denial of the substantiality of Principle naturally brought into question the theory of human nature, in particular the concept of "Original Nature." "In the world, throughout history," he asserted, "man has had only one nature. It is not necessary to distinguish between the nature of Heaven and Earth [that is, *honzen no sei*, Original or Innate Nature] and the nature of the Specific Ether [*kishitsu*]. Is not the nature of Heaven and Earth also the nature of the Specific Ether?"[112] By unifying the nature of things in Specific Ether in this way, he transformed the eternal and absolute conflict between good and evil of Sung philosophy into a dynamic, relative relationship. "Goodness is the normal state of human affairs. Evil is the aberration of nature," he wrote.[113] Earlier, Jinsai, too, had argued that "quiescence is movement at rest, and evil is the aberration of good." Here as elsewhere, Ekken did not present his ideas as a positive theoretical system. He was content merely to have "grave doubts." But it is noteworthy that while subjectively he opposed Ancient Learning to the very end, objectively he was heavily dependent on its method of thought.

By denying the concept of Original Nature and arguing that

[109] Ibid., p. 239.
[110] Ibid., p. 229.
[111] Ibid., p. 239.
[112] Ibid., p. 218 (*Daigiroku*, Book I). Similar opinions, though in a less precise form, are expressed in the *Shinshiroku*. For examples, see *Nihon rinri ihen*, VIII, pp. 35, 66–67.
[113] Ibid., p. 213 (*Daigiroku*, Book I).

there was a dynamic relationship between good and evil, Ekken, like Sokō and Jinsai, was led inevitably to criticize the rigoristic practical morality of the Chu Hsi school. He criticized the scholars of his day for their devotion to the concept of "holding fast to seriousness," stating:

> For a scholar to set his life in order and regulate his conduct, he must practice both rites and music, behave in a solemn, serious manner, and enjoy life in a harmonious fashion. Why must one insist only on "solemn seriousness"? Moreover, the tired and stubborn men of to-day do not understand the meaning of "seriousness." They tend to be enslaved by the word and become stubborn, covetous, narrow-minded, and oppressive. Their minds are desolate and withered; they do not know how to be friendly or enjoy themselves. In dealing with people they lack the virtue of being mild and affectionate, and display stern and cold attitudes.[114]

In writing this passage, Ekken probably had in mind the style of Ansai and his school, a group he personally had seen in action in Kyoto. "The teaching of the sages," Ekken continued, "has as its fundamental principle the ideals of loyalty and faithfulness. . . . Those who do not make loyalty and faithfulness their chief ideals but fruitlessly make *ching* [seriousness] their chief ideal, devoting all their attention to its application, will undoubtedly be confined narrowly to the principle of *ching* and end with the maladies of enslavement and stubbornness."[115] Thus he substituted the simple principles of loyalty and faithfulness for "seriousness." Ekken also insisted that monetary matters could not be ignored, commenting, "the scholars of today often say that a gentleman has no desire for profits. But these are the words of men who covet fame and are haughty in their outlook. They do not represent the true senti-

---

[114] Ibid., p. 234 (*Daigiroku,* Book II).

[115] Ibid., p. 48 (*Shinshiroku,* Book II). Similar remarks can be found in the *Daigiroku.* Here, too, Jinsai and Ekken were in complete agreement. In his *Gomō jigi,* Jinsai stated: "A man's face may show that he is a stern Confucian. But if we inquire into his inner thoughts we find that the desire to triumph over others and the tendency to present a false front exist unconsciously within him. This is because he vainly emphasizes the need to hold fast to seriousness and fails to make loyalty and faithfulness his essential principles" (ibid., V, p. 43).

ments of a gentleman. They are pure falsehoods."[116] As his position on this matter is well known, there is no need for me to elaborate on it any further, except to note that the fact that Jinsai held similar views is often overlooked.

Ekken criticized "holding fast to seriousness" and "sitting in quiescence," but he believed in the importance of "the exhaustive pursuit of Principle": "According to Confucian philosophy, it is important to understand the Way. The best method of doing so is to pursue the Principle exhaustively and in this way get at the nature of things."[117] In this respect Ekken seems to differ from the scholars of Ancient Learning. But Ekken's attitude to the investigation of Principle was affected by his wide interest in natural phenomena (as is well known, he was the founder of the science of medicinal botany in Japan) and was experimental and positivistic rather than moralistic in tendency. "If a person takes the measures appropriate to each situation," he wrote, "there is little danger of his being hindered in his activities. Some people today ardently wish to follow this path. But the outlook of society is stagnant and inflexible so this is not possible. *Those born today are bogged down in old etiquettes and are unable to take actions appropriate to the times.* Customs and morals tend to conflict with the necessities of the age. . . . How could this situation be in accord with the way of the Confucians?"[118] This point of view cannot be classified with the moral "rationalism" of Chou Lien-hsi ("Those who wish to govern without restoring ancient music and without changing present-day music are far from their objectives"), or Chu Hsi ("During and before the Three Dynasties all things were based on the Principle of Heaven, but since the Three Dynasties all things have been based on human desire"). On the contrary, Ekken's point of view is closer to the historical consciousness we have seen in Jinsai.

Ekken's views on the investigation of Principle, then, resemble those of the Sorai school and are not inconsistent with the position that stresses the "ancient meaning of words" rather than "the-

[116] *Ekken zenshū*, II, p. 245 (*Jigoshū*, Book IV). A similar view is expressed in *Shinshiroku*, in *Nihon rinri ihen*, VIII, pp. 196–97.
[117] *Ekken zenshū*, II, p. 186 (*Jigoshū*, Book I).
[118] *Nihon rinri ihen*, VIII, p. 196 (*Shinshiroku*, Book VI).

ories."[119] He argued that "in reading the Six Classics, Confucius, and Mencius, it is of course proper to rely first of all on the commentaries of the Sung scholars but the ancient annotations must not be neglected either. . . . Those who read the Classics today do not take into consideration the ancient commentaries. On the contrary, they diligently and avidly study the many theories of the Ming Confucian scholars. This is like abandoning the essential points and concentrating on the trivial ones. By looking at the commentaries of the Han and T'ang Confucians, we can understand the ancient meaning of words and profit greatly in our investigations."[120] Given this transmutation of the "exhaustive investigation of Principle," it is not surprising that Ekken's attitude to the sages in his *Daigiroku* is one of great reverence. "The sages," he wrote, "created the Six Classics. The words of the sages are standards to be followed eternally. We must have faith in them, not question them."[121] "Ah! the word of a sage is a thing to be believed forever. It must not be questioned."[122] This conforms to his opinion of the Sung Confucians, of whom he said in the *Daigiroku*, "even the Sung Confucians and wise philosophers cannot be put in the same category as the sages."[123]

As Ekken repeatedly emphasized, even Chu Hsi may have been mistaken in his theories, since he was not a sage, so he could

[119] The effect on scholarship of the school of Ancient Learning's criticism of the Chu Hsi "exhaustive investigation of Principle" was the adoption of a philological approach, attempting as far as possible to eliminate the subjective element and to give a faithful interpretation of the ancient classics. The Sorai school adhered strictly to this approach. Jinsai also warned against far-fetched interpretations: "Confucian scholarship abhors ambiguity above all. Those who discuss the Way and teach the classics must of necessity be lucid and to the point. . . . They must not make forced analogies or strained interpretations" (*Nihon rinri ihen*, V, p. 162 [*Dōjimon*, Book III]). Closely related is the attitude that makes faith rather than intellect the crucial factor. Jinsai said: "A profound faith in the ancients is the most essential rule for the advancement of learning, and is the greatest virtue under Heaven. Those who have deep faith in the ancients do not retain even a speck of their own views nor add their opinions to those of the ancients" (ibid., p. 173 [*Jinsai nissatsu*]). In these matters Ekken had much in common with the school of Ancient Learning, despite his insistence on the importance of "exhaustive investigation of Principle."

[120] *Nihon rinri ihen*, VIII, pp. 21–22 (*Shinshiroku*, Book I). (The Six Classics: the Books of Odes, History, Changes, and Rites, the Spring and Autumn Annals, and the Rites of Chou. Originally, the Book of Music was one of the six instead of the Rites of Chou, but it no longer exists. Translator's note.)

[121] Ibid., p. 212 (*Daigiroku*, Book I).

[122] Ibid.

[123] Ibid., p. 216.

proceed dispassionately to criticize those theories. This attitude of absolute reverence toward the sages and critical assessment of the wise men (*kenjin*) was also common to all scholars of Ancient Learning. Judged two-dimensionally by modern standards, this dualism may seem a strange contradiction; but viewed historically and three-dimensionally, it is an inevitable stage in the dissolution of the Chu Hsi mode of thought. When continuity of the hierarchy of ordinary men, wise men, and sages broke down, the sages were absolutely exalted, while the wise men in the middle were downgraded.

Ekken died in 1714 and the *Daigiroku* was his last work. In the same year Ogyū Sorai (1666–1728) published his *Ken'en zuihitsu* [Essays from a day-lily garden]. This work is a severe criticism of Jinsai (who had died nine years earlier in 1705) from a Sung school standpoint. Nevertheless, Sorai was already in fact leaning in the direction of Jinsai's Ancient Learning. Before Jinsai's death, Sorai had written him a letter expressing strong admiration for him and seeking guidance. "Upon reading your two books,"[124] he wrote, "I clapped my hands for joy and thought that you, Master, truly stand far above the men of our day."[125]

For some reason Jinsai did not reply to Sorai, who is believed to have vented his anger by writing *Ken'en zuihitsu*.[126] Only three years later, in 1717, he completed the two books that laid the foundation for his school, *Bendō* [On distinguishing the Way] and *Benmei* [On distinguishing terms]. Ekken lived on the eve of the Sorai school's fundamental revolution in Japanese Confucianism, that is, on the eve of the complete collapse of the Chu Hsi mode of thought. Sorai's leading disciple, Dazai Shundai (1680–1747), wrote of Ekken's *Daigiroku*, "In this work we see both Master Sonken's [i.e., Ekken's] ardent belief in Chu Hsi's way and his

[124] *Daigaku teihon* [Standard text on the Great Learning] and *Gomō jigi*. (Translator's note.)

[125] *Sorai-shū*, Book XXVII.

[126] Cf. Inoue Tetsujirō: *Nihon kogakuha no tetsugaku*, op. cit., pp. 498ff., and Iwahashi Junsei: *Sorai kenkyū* [A study of Sorai] (Tokyo, 1934), pp. 73ff., for details about this incident. According to these accounts, it seems that when Jinsai received Sorai's letter he was already on his deathbed with only a few days to live.

misgivings about it."[127] This well expresses Ekken's place in Japanese intellectual history.

I have now traced the disintegration of the Chu Hsi school and arrived on the threshold of the Sorai school. This may seem an excessively roundabout route. My aim has been to show as clearly as possible that although at first glance the Sorai school may seem to have appeared from nowhere, its foundations had been gradually laid down in the intellectual world of the early Tokugawa period—by looking for the logical connections in *the interior of the thought structures* of that period. The appearance of Sorai's school certainly made a striking impact on his age. However, a century of Tokugawa feudal society had imperceptibly deprived the optimistic, continuative mode of thought underlying Chu Hsi philosophy of the universal acceptance it had once enjoyed. After a moment of shock, therefore, the intellectual world was drawn to the Sorai school as iron filings are attracted to a magnet. Of course, the Sorai school was not an arithmetical sum of all the achievements up to this point. The gulf between Sorai and Ekken, not to speak of other members of the school of Ancient Learning, was a decisive one. This gulf can only be understood in relation to the social changes of the Genroku and Kyōhō eras (at the turn of the eighteenth century). Thus far I have concentrated on the connection between the Sorai school and earlier modes of thought. I shall now turn to what distinguishes the Sorai school, that is, to its unique features, and to its social background. These problems will occupy the next chapter.

---

[127] *Nihon rinri ihen,* VIII, p. 206 (*Shundai sensei doku Sonken sensei daigiroku*).

THE UNIQUE CHARACTERISTICS
OF THE SORAI SCHOOL

Two Examples. The Political Nature of the Sorai School. Its Methodology. The Concept of Heaven. The Essence of the Way. The Content of the Way. The Foundations of the Way. The Separation of the Public and the Private in the Sorai School. The Social Conditions from the Genroku to the Kyōhō Eras. Arguments for the Reform of the Political System.

I

Before entering into a thorough study of the Sorai school, I should first mention two incidents in which Sorai became involved while he was a retainer of Yanagizawa Yoshiyasu (1658–1714), the chamberlain of the fifth shogun, Tsunayoshi. Why they serve as an introduction to the main theory will become clear later on. Let us examine the first one.

In 1696 Sorai had just been retained by the Yanagizawa family with a stipend sufficient to maintain fifteen people. At that time, Yoshiyasu was at the zenith of his career as the favorite of Shogun Tsunayoshi. In 1694 he had been made a member of the Council of Elders (*rōjū*) and been given Kawagoe (in the modern Saitama Prefecture) as his fief, thus becoming lord of Kawagoe castle with an income of seventy thousand koku of rice.[1] During this period extreme poverty drove a peasant living in Yoshiyasu's domain to abandon his house and land, divorce his wife, shave his head, and become a monk, taking the name of Dōnyu. Accompanied by his mother, he roamed the land as a vagrant. On their way, his mother fell ill, so Dōnyu abandoned her and proceeded toward Edo alone. His mother was cared for by people living in the vi-

---

[1] One koku equals 4.96 English bushels. (Translator's note.)

cinity of the place where she was abandoned, and she was eventually sent back to Kawagoe. Dōnyu was arrested and charged with the crime of abandoning his parent. Yoshiyasu then asked the Confucian scholars in his service what was the proper punishment for Dōnyu. Sorai later described the affair in his *Seidan* [Political discourses] as follows:

It was soon after I had entered the service of his lordship Mino-no-kami [Yoshiyasu]. All the Confucian scholars pointed out that the laws of the Ming Court did not contain articles dealing with punishments for abandoning one's parents. Nor could anything be found in any book, past or present. Thus, he should be dealt with as an outcaste. Although he was accompanied by his mother when he became a beggar, he merely ceased taking her along with him. He could not be charged with abandoning his parent. He had divorced his wife four or five days before this, but he took his mother with him although he had been reduced to beggary. For an outcaste, this was commendable behavior. If he had remained in his house with his wife and had taken his mother somewhere and abandoned her, he could have been charged with the crime of abandoning his parent; but since he did not intend to abandon his mother he could not be charged with that crime. The Confucian scholars all shared this opinion. But Mino-no-kami was not satisfied. He insisted that abandoning parents could not be tolerated whatever the status of the person committing the crime. He therefore said he would consult the Shogun and seek his advice. In those days, the Shogun was a follower of Chu Hsi philosophy and, in accordance with its rationalistic approach to things, he was concerned primarily with the examination of the heart [*kokoro*]. Mino-no-kami was a Zen Buddhist and did not ordinarily believe in the reasoning of the Confuian scholars. At this point, I expressed my opinion, stating that in times of famine, this sort of incident occurred frequently in other domains too. It could not be called an act of parent abandonment. If it were judged as such and the culprit were punished, it would set a precedent for other domains. I believed that *the responsibility for such incidents lay first with the local magistrates and county commissioners. Next the ministers were responsible. And there were still others above them who were responsible.* Dōnyu's crime was very insignificant. Upon hearing this, Mino-no-kami agreed with what was said for the first time. He sent Dōnyu back to his village with a stipend to maintain one person so that he could support his mother.

From that time on he began to treat me with special consideration as someone who could be put to good use.[2]

This incident was all the more memorable for Sorai in that it was this that unexpectedly set him on his road to fame. He went on to say, "I had lived in the countryside since childhood. At the age of thirteen, I went to live in Kazusa [in the modern Chiba Prefecture], encountered hardships of all kinds, and saw and heard all sorts of things. *Being a country bumpkin, I spoke up to my lord in this fashion and said things that others dared not mention. . . .* When a person lives in the castle-town from the time of his birth, he is naturally influenced by the manners and morals of the town, becomes frivolous and fails to reveal that he has an independent mind. Hence it is understandable that the high officials and hereditary retainers who live in castle-towns have no ideas of their own and, in accordance with customary ways, fail to express themselves."[3] This feeling constitutes an important undercurrent in the theory of political reform that Sorai discussed in the same work, but this will be dealt with later. My immediate concern is Sorai's view of this incident. As he remarked, the Confucian scholars of his day were, in accordance with the Sung schools of thought, concerned only with Dōnyu's subjective motives and argued whether or not his motives were "commendable." But Sorai maintained that "in times of famine, this sort of incident occurred frequently in other domains too"; he looked upon Dōnyu's actions as but one manifestation of an objective pattern, as a recurrent social problem. He therefore concluded that Dōnyu was innocent and that what was at issue was the political responsibility of the ruling officials. Whatever the justice of his opinion, we can already detect the features that characterize Sorai's mode of thought. Let us now turn to the second incident.

On the morning of December 15, 1702, the awakening citizens of Edo were greeted with an astonishing story. During the night forty-six of the former retainers of the lord of Akō had ventured out into the heavy snow and attacked the home of Kira Yoshinaka

---

[2] *Nihon keizai taiten* [Collection of Japanese economic histories], ed. Takimoto Seiichi (Tokyo, 1928–30), IX, pp. 33–34 (*Seidan,* Book I).

[3] Ibid.

(1641–1702), their lord's bitter adversary. After killing Yoshinaka, they had retired to the Sengakuji temple and asked the authorities to pass judgement on their act of vengeance. Their action provoked heated public discussions. The incident implied a direct conflict between the feudal master-servant relationship, on which the bakufu itself was based, and the bakufu's position as the unifying political authority. It also delivered a deadly blow to Confucian ethics, for it placed the moral relationship between lord and subject on the same plane as the *private* relationship between father and son, husband and wife, elder brother and younger brother, friend and friend. Nowadays it is hard to imagine the confusion and embarrassment this incident caused Confucian scholars. The dimensions of the shock are clear from the fact that the debate between Confucians about "the loyal samurai of Akō" continued into the latter part of the Tokugawa period, long after it had ceased to be a real problem and had become a tale of the past.[4] Muro Kyūsō (1658–1734), a very conscientious Chu Hsi scholar, commended the behavior of the samurai without reservation and immediately produced the well-known *Akō gijin roku* [A record of the righteous men of Akō]. This was natural for a member of the Chu Hsi school, which "in accordance with its rationalistic ways, was primarily concerned with the examination of the heart."

But for Hayashi Nobuatsu (1644–1732), the head of the official Confucian college, the situation was not so simple, since he was officially responsible for the education and morals of the country. Hayashi proposed that the lives of the loyal samurai be spared, but his opinion was not accepted by the Council of Elders. At this Hayashi composed a poem expressing his anger and frustration.[5]

---

[4] *Akō gijin sansho* [Collection of works on the righteous men of Akō], ed. Nabeta Miyoshi (20 vols., 1851–52), Vol. I. This work contains most of the important documents dealing with this controversy.

[5] They charged through the gates, scorning Ching K'o (who had failed to assassinate the emperor of ancient Ch'in, Shih Huang).

The cold wind at I Shui (where Ching K'o parted with his friends) is like the spirit of the valiant warriors.

Like Yu Jang (of ancient Chin who drank lye to become a mute, and painted his body with lacquer to become leprous while biding his time to avenge his master's death), they drank lye and allowed their bodies to waste away.

The elegy that mourns T'ien Heng's death (the ruler of Ch'i upon whose death 500 loyal followers committed suicide) draws copious tears.

Sincerity pierces the sun. Why should they hesitate to die?

But if we examine his views on revenge, we find that he was in complete agreement with the bakufu's decision. He states:

> If we consider this matter in accordance with the spirit of the classics, we are forced to conclude that *on the basis of their motives,* it was proper for them to sleep on rush mats, use their swords as pillows, and take revenge upon their sworn enemy, who could not be permitted to remain under the same sky as theirs. It violates the way of the samurai to cling to life and endure shame. *But from the standpoint of the law,* those who behave as opponents of the law must be executed. Although they acted to fulfill the wishes of their dead lord, they broke the law of the land. In this respect, their behavior was wanton and disobedient. Hence it became necessary to arrest and execute them, and to make them an example to the nation and to future generations. In this way we can uphold and clarify the law of the land. *The two* [the motivational approach and the legal approach] *may seem to differ but in fact they can co-exist and do not contradict one another.* At the top of society there must be a benevolent prince and wise officials who clarify the law and issue decrees. Below, there must be loyal subjects and righteous samurai who give free play to their feelings, fulfill their wishes, and willingly accept punishment for the sake of the law. How could they have any regrets as a result?[6]

But the fact that Hayashi made a distinction between discussing the case from the standpoint of the motive (*kokoro*) and discussing it from the standpoint of public law shows that the Chu Hsi mode of thought, which linked personal morality and public norms in "Principle," was already in decline in the very headquarters of the Chu Hsi school. Hayashi could only attempt to shore up the collapsing system with platitudes typical of official scholars, like "above, there are a benevolent prince and wise officials," and "fortunately, we are now living in a time similar to the days of Yao and Shun."

The spirit of justice pierces the mountains. Life is indeed of little value.
All forty-six men will fall to the sword. Heaven shows no signs of saving these loyal and righteous men.

This poem was so sympathetic to the Akō samurai that it immediately became a subject of discussion among the Council of Elders. Cf. *Akō gijin sansho,* I, p. 303.
[6] Ibid., p. 41.

What was Sorai's attitude? None of his important works or collections contains any discussion of the problem of the "righteous samurai." Today only fragmentary comments have survived. But since he was a Confucian scholar retained by Yanagizawa Yoshiyasu, then at the height of his power, he must certainly have had something to do with the case. From existing historical documents his position seems to have been consistently one of demanding that the "righteous samurai" commit suicide. This view is expressed in *Sorai giritsusho* [Sorai's application of the law], a document which Sorai prepared in response to a request from the bakufu and which survives in the Hosokawa family papers.[7] He writes:

> *Gi* [*i*, righteousness] is the way to uphold one's personal integrity. Law is the standard of measurement for the entire society. *Rei* [*li*, rites or etiquette] is used to control the heart, while *gi* is used to control events. The fact that the forty-six samurai avenged the wrong done their lord shows that they possessed the sense of honor of the samurai. They followed the path of integrity. *Their action was righteous. But this aspect of the situation concerns only them and is a private matter.* The fact is that they came to regard Kira as their enemy when Naganori [their lord] was punished for improper behavior in the Palace. And without sanction from the government, they conspired to create this public disturbance. An action of this kind is prohibited by law. If the forty-six samurai are judged guilty and, *in accordance with the principle of rei fitting to a samurai,* are permitted to commit *seppuku,* the petition of the Uesugi family[8] will be upheld, and the loyal conduct of the forty-six samurai will by properly honored. This policy will best serve the public interest. *If private considerations are allowed to undermine public considerations, it will be impossible to uphold the law of the land.*

The forty-six samurai were dealt with in the manner suggested by Sorai. Whether this decision was based on Sorai's proposal, or,

---

[7] Ibid., Supplement, p. 150. Of course it is not clear that this essay was actually written by Sorai. Other documents that contain Sorai's opinions on this case can be found in the *Akō gijin sansho,* Vol. I (*Akō gishiron*), and in the *Yanagizawa hiki* included in Iwasaki Junsei's *Sorai kenkyū* (op. cit.). Although these documents reveal differences in emphasis, they all arrive at the same conclusion as that found in *Giritsusho,* which is quoted here because it best represents Sorai's method of reasoning.

[8] The Uesugi family of Yonezawa han was related to the victim, Kira Yoshinaka. Yoshinaka had married into the Uesugi house. (Translator's note.)

as recorded in the *Tokugawa jikki*,[9] it was ultimately based on the decision of the head priest of Nikko,[10] Prince Kōbenhō, does not concern us here. And, as in the previous incident, we are not concerned with the soundness of Sorai's opinion. What matters is Sorai's attitude (*Geisteshaltung*). Although on the one hand he fully recognized the "righteousness" of the samurai's conduct[11]—and therefore opposed extreme penalties such as decapitation—he saw this as a matter strictly limited to the private realm, and based on personal considerations. He opposed any tendency to allow personal considerations to undermine public ones, that is, he would not permit private morality to influence matters that demanded political decisions.

The unique character of Sorai's mode of thought as revealed in these two problems should now be clear. In the first case, he concluded that Dōnyu was innocent and opposed his punishment. In the second case, he favored punishing the righteous samurai in the face of strong demands that their lives be spared. The principle that made him insist on the innocence of Dōnyu also made him recommend that the righteous samurai be punished. What do the two cases have in common? The answer is the predominance of the political in Sorai's mode of thought. Both these incidents took place in the Genroku era (1688–1704), when Sorai had not yet perfected his own system of thought. But it is this characteristic, the primacy of the political, that runs like a leitmotif through Sorai's later thought. This intellectual leaning first appeared in Sorai's thirties, but it finally bore fruit in his fifties in two famous works, *Bendō* [On distinguishing the Way] and *Benmei* [On distinguishing terms]. In these two works Sorai attempted a fundamental reconstruction of Confucianism, which was on the verge of total collapse, by "politicizing" it. Did Sorai actually succeed in

---

[9] *Zōho kokushi taihei*, XLIII, p. 499.

[10] Ieyasu's shrine, Tōshōgū, is located in Nikko. (Translator's note.)

[11] All the documents of Sorai dealing with the Akō samurai cited show that he was sympathetic to them. Here he is clearly in disagreement with his chief disciple, Dazai Shundai. The *Yanagizawa hiki* states that the bakufu was about to impose the penalty of execution by decapitation, but Sorai, through Yoshiyasu, strongly opposed this measure and had it changed to death by *seppuku* (self-disembowelment). Here, as in many other instances, Dazai's opinion has been ascribed to Sorai, with the result that Sorai's position on this question has been persistently misrepresented. Cf. also Iwasaki: *Sorai kenkyū,* op. cit., p. 468.

rebuilding Confucianism, or did he, on the contrary, in fact hasten its collapse? The answer to this question should become clearer as we analyze both the basic structure of the Sorai school of thought and the pattern that emerged from Sorai's attempt to transform Confucianism into a purely political theory.

II

The starting point of the Sorai school of thought and its methodology is what Sorai called "the study of old phrases and syntax" (*kobunji-gaku*).[12] He contended that a knowledge of the ancient terms was the essential prerequisite for an understanding of the Way of the Sages. Words change historically, so an interpretation of the ancient classics based on the current meanings of their vocabulary could not grasp the true meaning of the ancient texts. Sorai observed that "the world changes, carrying words [or language] with it. Words change, carrying the Way with them. This is the main reason why the Way is not clear."[13] The Sung Confucians, he also stated, "view ancient literature in terms of current literature, and ancient words in terms of current words. As a result, although they have diligently studied the ancient Way, they have not been able to understand it."[14] Jinsai was right, Sorai said, to try to study the original Confucianism directly without relying on the interpretations of the Sung Confucians; but because he was unaware of the changes that had occurred in the meanings of the words themselves, he tended to distort the texts in a subjective way. Jinsai and the Sung Confucians had all tried to construct the Way from scratch. Each scholar had made his own subjective interpretation of the Way, giving many different versions, but none had understood its objective nature. The important thing is the "words" embedded in the Way and the "facts" that these words express. *Sein* (what is) must be understood before it is possible to talk about *Sollen* (what ought to be). Hence Sorai believed

---

[12] In his philological studies Sorai was clearly influenced by Li Yu-lin (also known as Li P'an-lung, 1514–70) and Wang Yuan-mei (also known as Wang Shih-cheng, 1529–93) of Ming China. But as he himself stated, he received little more than hints from them. The philological examination of the Six Classics was his own idea.

[13] *Nihon rinri ihen*, VI, p. 121 (*Sorai sensei gakusoku*).

[14] Ibid., p. 110 (*Benmei*, Book II).

that "the essence of learning is to be found at the lower level of *words* and *facts* and not at the higher level of arguments about the subtleties of life."[15]

What is *Sein*? For Confucians it is clearly *Gewesene* (what has been), the institutions and civilization of the era of Yao and Shun. Hence for Sorai, the Six Classics, which describe this civilization and its institutions, were of fundamental importance. The Four Books had constituted the core of the Chu Hsi philosophy. As we have seen, Chu Hsi placed particular emphasis on the Great Learning and the Doctrine of the Mean. Jinsai had written an essay arguing that Confucius was not responsible for the Great Learning and had rejected the complex but passive method of moral discipline embodied in it. Instead of the Great Learning, Jinsai recommended the Analects and Mencius. But now, the Six Classics came to the fore again for the first time since they had been relegated to the background with the rise of the exegetical schools of the Han and T'ang periods. "The Six Classics," Sorai argued, "deal with *things*. The *Book of Rites* and the *Analects* deal with their meanings. Meaning must be related to things and institutions first. Only then can the Way be fixed."[16] Of fundamental importance are the historical facts described in the Six Classics; the Analects and the Book of Rites do no more than give meaning to these facts. But "the *facts* were discarded and only their meanings discussed,"[17] hence the confusion of the different Confucian schools of later periods. It is therefore important to read the Six Classics carefully and to familiarize oneself with the way in which words and phrases are used in them and also to acquire knowledge of the concrete institutions of the ancient period. Only then will a reading of the Analects reveal the true intentions of Confucius.

Like Jinsai, Sorai ascribed absolute value to the Analects, but he recognized only relative value in Mencius and other Confucian texts (a fact related to his conception of the sages, which is discussed below). Here he raised the extremely interesting question of the polemical nature of ideas. According to Sorai, the Way of

[15] Ibid., p. 138 (*Seihisui shūsai montai*).

[16] Ibid., p. 12 (*Bendō*). (The Six Classics Sorai had in mind are the Books of History, Odes, Music, and Changes, the Spring and Autumn Annals, and the Rites of Chou. Translator's note.)

[17] Ibid.

the Sages still existed absolutely in Confucius's time. But in the days of Mencius and Tzu Ssu a few centuries later, the Hundred Schools came into being, and the intellectual world entered a period of unprecedented disorder. As a result, Confucians such as Mencius and Tzu Ssu had to interpret the Way of the Sages in the light of their struggles with the philosophers of the Hundred Schools. Many of the ideas in the Doctrine of the Mean (believed to be the work of Tzu Ssu) and Mencius are polemical, designed to refute Lao Tzu and Kao Tzu.[18] But later Confucians made the fatal error of "considering these words, which were intended to refute the ideas of other men, as embodiments of the genuine Way of the Sages."[19] In figurative terms, this is like "a doctor who has used a certain medicine to cure a patient insisting that the latter continue to take the medicine when he has fully recovered."[20] Elsewhere Sorai remarked that the opinions of Mencius and Tzu Ssu were *arguments used to meet the problems of their age*. How could they be in perfect accord with *li* [Principle]?"[21] In this way, he insisted that their ideas were inextricably bound to concrete, historical circumstances. The examples Sorai gave will be cited later at relevant points. Thus, by taking historical circumstances into consideration, Sorai ascribed relative values to the various theories and concepts that had hitherto been accepted uncritically as absolutes. Such a mode of thought can be described as a sort of "sociology of ideology." If so, it is an expression, on the methodological level, of Sorai's "politicization" of Confucianism.

Thus there was a shift from the Sung Confucians' stress on the Great Learning and the Doctrine of the Mean, via Jinsai's high evaluation of the Analects to Sorai's concentration on the Six Classics. This shift from later to earlier texts[22] is closely related to two other trends: on the one hand, a tendency to break the continuity between sages and common men, giving the former absolute value; and on the other hand, a gradual elimination of subjec-

[18] Kao Tzu (c.420–c.350 B.C.) appears in the Book of Mencius as Mencius's antagonist, but nothing further is known about him. (Translator's note.)

[19] *Nihon rinri ihen*, VI, p. 11 (*Bendō*).

[20] Ibid., p. 53 (*Benmei,* Book I).

[21] Ibid., p. 19 (*Bendō*).

[22] Of course, the scholars of this period only thought they were studying the classics in reverse chronological order. We know today that some of the Six Classics were written much later than was then believed.

tivity—labeled *shichi* (private intellect) by Sorai—a process that extended from Chu Hsi rationalism, via Jinsai's study of ancient meanings, to Sorai's study of ancient words. What kind of picture do we get of the Way Sorai was attempting to outline through his philological studies?

First, for Sorai, the way meant norms that are valid for man, not laws that govern the natural world. Such terms as "the Way of Heaven" and "the Way of the Earth" are no more than analogies:

> People speak of "the Way of Heaven" and "the Way of the Earth."
> The sun, moon, and stars are fixed in their places in the sky; wind and thunder, clouds and rain, come and go; hot and cold weather, night and day, recur eternally. It is impossible to grasp the secret of these phenomena. The riddle cannot be solved. The causes of the birth and rebirth of all things, good luck and bad, fortune and misfortune, cannot be known, but they exist. *Quiet reflection shows that all these phenomena seem to have certain regularities.* We label this "the Way of Heaven." [The earth] supports high mountains but does not feel their weight. It moves the rivers and seas about but does not spill any water. The immensity of the problem makes it impossible to investigate. Its depth cannot be fathomed. All things continuously reproduce, but they do not themselves diminish in size because of this. All things perish and return to their original source, but the latter does not gain in size because of this. . . . *When we deliberate upon these matters carefully there seems to be an explanation for everything.* We label this "the Way of the Earth." *But although we call these "the Way," they are merely modeled on the concept of "the Way of the Sages."*[23]

As we have seen, Jinsai had severed the link between the Way of Heaven and the Way of Man and made the theory of the universe independent of ethical philosophy. Jinsai placed special emphasis on his theory of "the Way of Man" but he also discussed the theory of the universe. But Sorai transformed the Way of Heaven into a mere analogy for the Way of Man, eliminating the traditional conception of the Way of Heaven from his schema. Instead, he emphasized the incomprehensible and mysterious nature of heaven. "Heaven," Sorai concluded, "is not a thing to be known.

---

[23] *Nihon rinri ihen*, VI, p. 32 (*Benmei*, Book I).

Moreover, the Sages feared Heaven. As a result, they said that the only thing they knew was the necessity to obey its commands. They also believed that Heaven understood them, but they never once spoke of their understanding Heaven. In this they showed an attitude of complete respect towards Heaven."[24] Thus he did not look on heaven as an object of knowledge but as an object of respect. The personified concept of heaven, which formed only one part of Jinsai's theoretical system—the Will of Heaven—broke its bounds and permeated Sorai's entire system:

> Scholars of later ages delight in exercising their private intellects without any restraint. They are arrogant and have high opinions of themselves. They do not follow the teachings of the ancient kings and Confucius. They express opinions based on their subjective views, and confidently expound the theory that Heaven is the same as Principle. . . . They base their concept of Heaven upon their own subjective notions and claim to "understand Heaven." Is this not the extremity of irreverence? Ch'eng Hao says, "Heaven and Earth do not have a mind of their own but cause things to change." How can this be so? The *Book of Changes* states: "Are divinations used to perceive the heart of Heaven and Earth?" *Is it not clear beyond doubt that Heaven has a heart?*[25]

In Sorai's opinion, the existence or nonexistence of heaven's heart could not be a proper subject of discussion given the conditions of human reason. That is to say, man is separated from heaven by a wide gulf. He explained this with the following analogy: "Heaven is not the same as man, just as man is not the same as birds and beasts. Man cannot comprehend the hearts of birds and beasts. But from this we cannot conclude that birds and beasts do not have hearts of their own."[26] The same can be said of heaven. Sorai elevated this conception of a personified heaven to the level of a religious faith. In his opinion, both the Sung theory of the primacy of Principle over Ether and Sokō's and Jinsai's theory of a unitary Ether were meaningless. They were the result of the abuse of the "private intellect" by theorists who were so ar-

[24] Ibid., p. 81.
[25] Ibid., p. 79.
[26] Ibid., p. 80.

rogant as to draw conclusions about the Principle of Heaven from human norms. Thus, *without leaving the framework of Confucian philosophy*, Sorai transformed Sung rationalism into its very opposite, irrationalism.

For Sorai, the Way is simply the Way of the Sages. What, then, is the Way of the Sages? To answer this question, I must first differentiate between the essence of the Way of the Sages and its content. "The founders of our Way," he explained, "were Yao and Shun. Yao and Shun were rulers of the people. This means that the Way of the Sages is primarily the way to govern the world."[27] Yao and Shun were the so-called Early Kings, and the Way of the Sages is also called the Way of the Early Kings. "The Way of the Early Kings," Sorai explained, "is the way which brings peace to the world. *The Way is complicated but the ultimate purpose is to bring peace to the world.* It is founded upon respect for the Will of Heaven."[28] Thus, the essence of the Way of the Sages, or of the Early Kings, is primarily political, that is, it is the establishment of order in the state and peace in the world. Locating maintenance of order in the state and peace in the world as the core of the way implied a firm rejection of the mode of thought that implied a continuity of personal morality and government, but this comes as no surprise after one has followed the disintegration of Chu Hsi philosophy from Sokō to Jinsai. "The Confucian scholars," Sorai argued, "downgraded the notion that the Way of the Sages is the way to govern the state and the world in favor of high-flown theories about the principles of Heaven, human desires, *yin* and *yang*, and the five elements. They believe in theories suitable for Buddhist monks, such as holding fast to seriousness, maintaining quiescence, investigation of things, extension of knowledge, sincerity of intention, sincerity of the heart, etc."[29] "Whose fault is it that the only heated arguments are about who is right or wrong, and that *people have finally been led to believe that the Way of the Sages and the way to govern the land are two different things?*"[30] "The theory that the Way of the Sages will prevail if a person keeps his

[27] Ibid., pp. 87–88 (*Tōmonsho*, Book III).
[28] Ibid., p. 15 (*Bendō*).
[29] *Nihon keizai taiten*, IX, p. 199 (*Taiheisaku*).
[30] Ibid., p. 197.

body and heart in proper order, and that as long as his body and
heart are in proper order, the world and the state will automatically be well governed, is a simple-minded argument presented by
Buddhists and Taoists. . . . However well a person governs his
heart, orders his body, and disciplines himself to be as perfect as a
jewel, all his efforts will be of no avail if he does not make the
affairs of those below him his concern, and remains ignorant of
the way to govern the state."[31]

Sorai gave a clear illustration of the discontinuity between
personal morality and government: "*The government prohibits violence but uses military law to execute people. Can this be called benevolence?*
But it all stems from the need to maintain peace in the land."[32]
On the other hand, "Confucians of later ages speak of benevolence
and explain the principles of sincerity and commiseration. But
even if they possess the spirit of sincerity and commiseration, if
they fail to bring peace to the people, they are not benevolent;
however much compassion they have, it will all turn out to be
wasted benevolence, the benevolence of a woman."[33] Sorai did
not stop here. He pursued his logic further, attempting to make
personal morality an instrument of government. The ruler worries
about his own individual moral discipline only because "unless he
who is above others behaves properly, those below him will not
respect and trust him. Then his commands will not be obeyed, and
he will fail to bring peace to the people. He must therefore behave
properly. It is not because the effects of his moral discipline will
overflow and enable him to govern the people."[34] This is only one
step away from the conclusion that "therefore, the ruler of the
people must carry out all measures, *even if they conflict with just principles and become the object of ridicule, so long as this brings peace to the
people.* A ruler who maintains such an attitude is truly the father
of his people."[35] The ruler may act against just principles so long
as he pursues the political goal of maintaining peace among the
people.

[31] *Nihon rinri ihen,* VI, pp. 151–52 (*Tōmonsho,* Book I).
[32] Ibid., p. 17 (*Bendō*).
[33] *Nihon keizai taiten,* IX, p. 213 (*Taiheisaku*).
[34] Ibid., p. 214.
[35] Ibid.

This is clearly a transvaluation of Confucian morality reminiscent of Machiavelli's *The Prince*. For example, Machiavelli wrote:

Everyone will agree, I know, that it would be a most praiseworthy thing if all the qualities accounted as good in the above enumeration were found in a Prince. But since they cannot be so possessed nor observed because of human conditions which do not allow of it, what is necessary for the prince is to be prudent enough to escape the infamy of such vices as would result in the loss of his state; as for the others which would not have that effect, he must guard himself from them as far as possible, but if he cannot, he may overlook them as being of less importance. Further, he should have no concern about incurring the infamy of such vices without which the preservation of his state would be difficult.[36]

The Florentine citizen continued:

So a Prince need not have all the aforementioned good qualities, but it is most essential that he appear to have them. Indeed, I should go so far as to say that having them and always practicing them is harmful, while seeming to have them is useful.[37]

Of course, even this brief glimpse shows that in its total liberation of government from the constraints of personal morality, Machiavelli's *The Prince* was far more thoroughgoing than Sorai's *Taiheisaku* [A policy for great peace]. This can be explained by the two men's different historical and social stations. But given the fact that Sorai did remove moralistic restrictions on political thought, even to the extent described above, just as the honor of having established political science as a science in modern Europe is conferred upon the author of *The Prince*, so it would not be inappropriate to call Sorai the "discoverer of politics" in the Tokugawa feudal system.[38]

Since the essence of the Way is the maintenance of order in the

[36] Cf. *The Prince*, ed. T. G. Bergin (New York, 1947), p. 45.

[37] Ibid., p. 51.

[38] To avoid any misunderstanding, let me stress that I do not say that politics and ethics are unconnected. But I do believe that the inherent characteristics of politics must be identified if this relationship is to be understood. As long as politics is uncritically linked to ethics, there is no room for political science in the true sense.

state and peace throughout the land, its content obviously cannot be any quality inherent in man such as human principles or human nature. Nor can it be merely a transcendental idea. Sorai defined the Way as follows: "The Way is a comprehensive term. It includes all the ideas set down by the Early Kings about such matters as rites and music, law enforcement and political administration. Apart from rites and music, law enforcement and political administration, the Way does not exist."[39] This definition implies two things. First, that the Way is universal and inclusive. Sorai noted again and again that the Way cannot be expressed in abstract concepts. "The Way," he observed, "is difficult to understand and difficult to explain because of its magnitude. Confucians of later ages all expressed their understanding of the Way, but they had comprehended only a part of its meaning."[40] "In discussing the days of the Early Kings and Confucius, how can we try to explain everything about the Way in one word? Those who do so are seeking to separate the Way of the Sages from other ways."[41] Special note should be made of this last remark.

As we have seen, Sorai believed that the theories of Mencius and Tzu Ssu had only relative value because of their polemical nature. For Sorai, the Way of the Sages is absolute, and therefore, far from being opposed to other modes of thought, it includes them all within it. Thus, he said, "the opinions of all scholars, from the Hundred Schools and the Nine Groups to Buddhists and Taoists, *are all derived from the Way*. They are also all founded upon human sentiments. Thus it is proper to say that the Way of the Sages is the perfection of human sentiments. Otherwise how could there be order and peace? If we carefully select the strong points, master and possess them, there is nothing but the Way of the Sages."[42] Sorai's comprehensive interest in learning sprang from this attitude.

Although he carefully distinguished his theories from those of other men, his attitude to other schools of thought was one of considerable tolerance. For example, he had many friends among

---

[39] *Nihon rinri ihen*, VI, p. 13 (*Bendō*).

[40] Ibid., p. 11.

[41] Ibid., p. 17.

[42] Ibid., p. 124 (*Gakusoku*). (The Nine Groups: Confucian, Taoist, Yin-yang, Legalist, Names, Mohist, Diplomatist, Eclectic, and Agrarian. Translator's note.)

Buddhist priests, whom Confucian scholars generally intensely disliked, and there were a fair number of priests among Sorai's students. He laughed at the anti-Buddhist positions of the Chu Hsi philosophers: "The teachings of the Sung Confucians stemmed originally from Buddhism. So it would seem reasonable to dislike kindred things and contend with them."[43] Compare this with the Ansai school's fanatical rejection of "heresies" for example. Can we simply say that the Chu Hsi school, which insisted on "the exhaustive study of the Principle," was closer in spirit to the modern age than the Sorai school, which demanded an absolute belief in the Way of the Sages?

The Way is not just universal and all-embracing. The second implication of the definition given above is that it is also objective and concrete. This is clear from the thesis that "apart from rites and music, law enforcement and political administration, the Way does not exist." Rites and music, law enforcement and political administration, are general terms for the *civilization and institutions* of the era of Yao and Shun, which, in his methodology (philology), Sorai referred to as "facts" and "words." These institutions were specific products of history, but for Sorai, as we shall see, they acquired suprahistorical significance. Of course, as an objective reality, the Way cannot be inherent in human nature. Sorai observed:

> The heart is a formless thing. It cannot therefore be grasped and brought under control. The Way of the Early Kings therefore controls the heart by means of rites. Those who speak of governing the heart by means other than rites profess false notions based on private intellect. For they propose to use the heart as an instrument of control. But the thing that is to be brought under control is the heart itself. In other words, one is to control one's heart by means of one's heart. It is like a madman trying to bring his madness under control by himself. How could he succeed in so doing?[44]

From this standpoint, Sorai frequently cited Mencius to the effect that "if a person wears the apparels of Yao, speaks the words of Yao, and follows the behavior of Yao, he is Yao." It is unnecessary

---

[43] Ibid., p. 160 (*Tōmonsho*, Book I).
[44] Ibid., p. 22 (*Bendō*).

to "inquire into the relationship between the heart and virtue."[45]
In other words, the objectification of the Way aimed at by Sokō
and Jinsai was achieved by Sorai. But because for him the Way
has a concrete as well as an objective existence, it can no longer
be merely something that "ought to be" or a transcendental idea,
as it was with Jinsai. Sorai remarked on the hollowness of Jinsai's
"morality." He wrote:

> Master Jinsai was confident that he understood virtue. But he merely
> argued about the terminology of nature and virtue. Moreover, he
> misread Mencius and extended the meaning of the four beginnings,
> turning them into moral principles. How then does he differ from
> Chu Hsi? . . . He only disagrees with Chu Hsi as to whether [the Four
> Beginnings] are perfected by nurture or whether they are perfect by
> nature from the beginning. *When he speaks of virtue, therefore, he is
> merely discussing something that has not yet been formed. He offers words
> without substance.* In this he does not differ from the Sung Confucians.[46]

Sorai was not concerned with *Moralität*, that is, with abstract concepts, with a way that "is not yet formed," but with *Sittlichkeit*,
which exists concretely as (real) rites, music, law enforcement,
and political administration.

Since the Way is no longer merely "what ought to be," the
theory that man is good by nature, which had retained a vestigial
existence for Jinsai as a means to turn the despairing towards the
Way, was, as might be expected, decisively rejected by Sorai.
However, he did not adopt Hsun Tzu's[47] belief that human nature
is evil. The Way is absolute and all-embracing. Hence it is impossible for it to conflict with human nature. According to Sorai,
Mencius expounded the theory that man is good by nature in

---

[45] For example, ibid., p. 134 (*Kukkeizan tōsho*).

[46] Ibid., p. 35 (*Benmei*, Book I).

[47] It is often said that Sorai took his ideas from Hsun Tzu. Dr. Tsuda Sōkichi (1873–
1961) for one holds this opinion. Clearly the two have some things in common. But
my fundamental position is that Sorai's intellectual system can only be properly understood if it is viewed as the end product of the disintegration of the Chu Hsi school.
From this position, it is clear that there are decisive differences between Sorai and Hsun
Tzu. If a comparison is to be made, it would be more appropriate to compare Hsun
Tzu with Dazai Shundai. See note 107 of section 4 below. (Hsun Tzu was active during
the first six decades of the third century B.C. He was a Confucian but, unlike Mencius,
he did not believe that man was good by nature. He also emphasized the importance
of law and was a Confucian who leaned toward the Legalist school. Translator's note.)

order to contest Lao Tzu's argument that the Way of the Sages is false. Hsun Tzu insisted that man is evil by nature, fearing that the opposite theory would lead to the abandonment of moral discipline. Both notions belong to the category of polemical concepts discussed earlier. The result of making such theories as absolute as the Way of the Sages is to downgrade and relativize the Way of the Sages, placing it on a par with other, conflicting theories. The issue is not whether man is by nature good or bad, but whether one believes in the Way of the Early Kings or not. "When a person who believes in the Way of the Early Kings hears that man is good by nature, he strives more strenuously, and when he hears that man is bad by nature, he makes a greater effort. When a person does not believe in the Way of the Early Kings, he indulges himself when he hears that man is good by nature, and falls into despair when he hears that man is bad by nature. The arguments of Hsun Tzu and Mencius are thus both useless. That is why the Sages did not discuss such matters."[48] Thus Sorai dismissed as useless all theories as to whether human nature is good or bad, although this problem seemed to have been the chief concern of Confucianism hitherto. But Sorai's transformation of the theory of human nature was not just passive and negative. He went on to propose positively that human nature is inalterable.

Sung philosophy held that the Original Nature of man (honzen no sei) is an a priori, solitary, and immobile reality and attempted to transform the Specific Ether (kishitsu) so that it conformed to this Original Nature. Sokō, Jinsai, and Ekken denied that man has an Original Nature and concentrated on changing the Specific Ether. Sorai, however, reversed this, contending that the Specific Ether has an a priori existence and is inalterable. The optimism of Sung philosophy has come full circle to its direct opposite, pessimism. The Sung philosophers' thesis that "all men are capable of becoming sages" has been replaced by its opposite, the thesis that "the sages can be studied but one cannot achieve the status of a sage."[49] This pessimism is, however, completely different from Hsun Tzu's theory that man is bad by nature. The theory that human nature is bad arrives in practice at the same rigorist posi-

[48] *Nihon rinri ihen,* VI, p. 91 (*Benmei,* Book II).
[49] Ibid., p. 15 (*Bendō*).

tion as its *theoretical* opponent, Sung philosophy, because it seeks to change or suppress human emotions and desires by means of objective standards, that is, rites and music. That is why Hsun Tzu argued that "learning consists of learning how to become a Sage."

Sorai's pessimism, on the other hand, leads to the humble recognition, first, of man's impotence in the face of the authority of the Will of Heaven, and, second, of the fragmentary and particularistic nature of human existence in contrast to the all-inclusive and universal nature of the Way. "Specific Ether," he wrote, "is the nature of Heaven. Even if we try to oppose and overcome Heaven by human strength, we are unsuccessful. If we try to coerce someone else to do what is impossible, we make him feel bitter towards Heaven and reproachful towards his parents. The Way of the Sages does not follow this path."[50] The result is an attitude of tolerance towards the natural inclinations of human beings. This point will be discussed further later. Here I shall concentrate on the second point.

What significance is there in the fact that the nature of man is fragmentary and particularistic in contrast to the all-inclusive, universal nature of the Way? First of all, both the Sung philosophers and Jinsai believed that the variability of the Specific Ether is the necessary premise for the individual to realize the Way. But for Sorai, the Way is fundamentally social; it is not a goal to be realized by the individual. That is why he said, "the way of man cannot be discussed in terms of one man only. It must be discussed in terms of millions and billions of people."[51] Moreover, the Way has already acquired a concrete existence as rites, music, law enforcement, and political administration and is not something the individual needs to realize in the future. Hence the goal implied by the theory of the variability of Specific Ether has no place in Sorai's system. If at first he had regarded the variability of the Specific Ether as impossible, he now judged it to be unnecessary, or even harmful:

The idea of transforming the Specific Ether is an absurd notion

[50] Ibid., p. 20.
[51] Ibid., p. 15.

presented by the Sung Confucians. They are asking people for the impossible; it is the height of irrationality. The Specific Ether simply cannot be changed. Rice always remains rice, and beans remain beans. The object of learning should be the cultivation of the Specific Ether and the development of what one is born with, just as we provide rice and beans with fertilizer so that they will yield good crops in accordance with their natural characteristics. . . . *For the world, rice is useful as rice and beans are useful as beans*. . . . If, as the Sung Confucians insist, Specific Ether is blended and harmonized, *we will have something which is neither rice nor beans*. Is this what they want? The product would be of no use at all.[52]

Here too Sorai considered the question holistically, that is, he brought the whole world into his discussion. The Sung Confucians' and Jinsai's concern with the relationship between *reality* and *goal* changes with Sorai into one for the relationship between the part and the whole. A part is a part of the whole (*pars totalis*) only if it retains its *uniqueness*. Each person should retain his unique, innate Specific Ether and strive to develop his individuality. To express the idea of developing one's uniqueness, Sorai used the word "move" (*utsuru*): "Human nature differs in a myriad ways. A person may be strong or weak, frivolous or serious, ponderous or agile, dynamic or static. These characteristics cannot be changed. But it is also characteristic of human nature to *move* readily. It becomes good when it imitates goodness, and bad when it imitates evil."[53] In other words, human nature is not something to be changed, but something to be moved. Use of the words "change" (*henzu*) and "move" (*utsuru*) tends to make Sorai's explanations vague, but when he used the word "change," he meant a qualitative change in the Specific Ether (in the example given above, changing rice into beans), and by "move" he meant a quantitative change in the Specific Ether (increasing the yield of rice). Believing the former to be impossible, and even harmful, Sorai focused on the latter. His explanation of the sentence "It becomes good when it imitates goodness, and bad when it imitates evil" helps to clarify this: "By 'it becomes good when it imitates goodness,' *I mean that the cultivation of human nature makes it a useful material.*

[52] Ibid., pp. 175–76 (*Tōmonsho*, Book II).
[53] Ibid., p. 89 (*Benmei*, Book II).

It is like a rich harvest of grain which can be eaten as food. By 'it becomes bad when it imitates evil,' I mean that *failure in proper cultivation results in a failure to bear fruit.* It is like blighted grain which cannot be consumed. In other words, there is no need to attempt to change the Specific Ether in order to attain the status of a Sage."[54]

Sorai called the *achievement* of each individual who "moves" his innate Specific Ether "virtue." Jinsai had seen "virtue" as identical with the Way, whereas Sorai, like the Sung Confucians, but on entirely different grounds, separated the two. In Sorai's opinion, virtue serves as the intermediary factor that enables the fragmented and particularistic individual to participate in the universal and complete Way:

> Virtue [*toku*] means acquisition [*toku*]. It means that each person acquires a share in the Way. . . . *Human nature is different in each individual. Thus virtue too is different for each person.* The Way is broad. As long as one is not a Sage, how can one be in complete unity with the Way? . . . Differences in human nature can be compared to trees and grass, which are separate and distinct. Even the moral teachings of the Sages cannot be forced upon the people. *Each individual must follow what is suitable to his nature, and develop his virtues by cultivating his natural tendencies.*[55]

Thus in contrast to the universal, all-inclusive Way, virtue is necessarily unique and discrete.

Sorai separated benevolence, righteousness, propriety, and wisdom, which had been grouped together since the time of Mencius, and assigned propriety and righteousness to the Way and benevolence and wisdom to virtue. But virtue is not restricted to benevolence and wisdom alone. And these two, like all other virtues, are distinct in nature. The essence of benevolence is to bring peace and security to the people, while the essence of wisdom is to know people, that is, to recognize men of wisdom and talent and to utilize them. But they are both virtues peculiar to political rulers; they are not to be acquired by all men: "If benevolence is

---

[54] Ibid., p. 90.
[55] Ibid., p. 34 (*Benmei,* Book I).

made the totality of virtue, what would become of what is called the virtue of the masses?"[56] "When people study the Way of the Sages, the virtue they acquire varies in accordance with their nature. They would not all acquire the virtue of benevolence."[57] Thus he was strongly opposed to the idea that benevolence is the whole of virtue. When Sorai spoke of virtue, he did not mean virtue in the narrow sense; as his use of the term "material" (*zai*) indicates, he included special talents and skills under the same head. The cultivation and development of the skills and talents most appropriate to his nature is the method by which each individual can participate in the universal Way.

However, as we have seen, Sorai's Way is the Way of the Early Kings, and the latter is essentially political in nature, that is, its goal is the maintenance of order in the state and peace in the world. If this is so, what does it mean to say that all men can participate in the Way through virtue? We can expect benevolence and wisdom, both virtues of a political nature, to mediate between the individual and the Way, but what connection is there between politics and the cultivation of the individual's particular talents? "After the king has caused his people to study and develop their virtues," Sorai wrote, "how should he utilize their virtues? *His object should be to employ them in the government according to their talents and make them work for the peace and security of the people.*"[58] In other words, the king is to select those who have developed their special talents and to promote them into the ranks of the bureaucracy. In this way they are to assist the king in the exercise of political power and to participate in the task of maintaining order in the state and peace in the land. But other questions remain. Is it unnecessary for those who do not wish to or are unable to enter government service to cultivate their virtues? Are they to have no connection with the Way of the Sages? Perhaps we should have asked these questions earlier. Sorai's system sees the Way of the Sages in terms of its political significance and subordinates individual morality to politics. To answer these questions, we must therefore inquire into the basic problem of the relationship between the limitations of

[56] Ibid., p. 38.
[57] Ibid., p. 37.
[58] Ibid.

the political ruler and the universal validity of the Way of the Sages. Sorai's *Tōmonsho* [Questions and answers] contains the following significant remark:

> The farmers till the soil and support the people of the world; the artisans make household goods and enable the people of the world to use them; the merchants move goods from one place to another and thus serve the people of the world; and the samurai govern the world and maintain order. Although they all perform their own tasks, they also help each other. If even one part were missing, the country would collapse. People are social beings; they cannot exist in isolation, separated from one another. *All the people of the world are officials who assist the ruling prince, who is the parent of the people.*[59]

The entire population is made up of officials! This is the only way to solve the question asked above without any contradictions. The politicization of Confucianism is complete.

III

So far we have discovered that the essence of the Way in Sorai's system is political in nature, its object being the maintenance of order in the state and peace in the world. As a result, we have found that it has for content the objective, concrete principle of "rites, music, law enforcement, and political administration." Our next problem concerns the basis for making a way with such an essence and content the Way. In Sorai's system, the Way is a general term for the institutions and civilization of the era of Yao and Shun. How can such a historically and geographically restricted way transcend both time and space and acquire an absolute, universal validity? In Sung philosophy, needless to say, the ultimate basis for the Way lies in the Supreme Ultimate or Principle. The Way of the Sages is identical with the principles of the universe and nature, and therefore absolute. But this metaphysical-type principle was Sorai's bête noire. Of course, he did not deny that Principle existed, but he placed it beyond the bounds of human understanding. In other words, from the human point of

---

[59] Ibid., p. 151 (*Tōmonsho*, Book I).

view, "Principle does not have fixed standards."[60] If Principle
were made the basis for the Way, each individual could interpret
Principle according to his own judgement and hold this to be the
Way. The inevitable result would be to destroy the unity and
coherence of the Way. Such an interpretation had produced the
disputations of the Hundred Schools. Sorai could not accept it, for
he wanted to see the Way transcend the oppositions between the
schools.

Can the Way be a self-sufficient value system that needs no
basis outside itself? Jinsai evidently thought so. As we have seen,
he denied any connection between "investigation of Principle"
and moral conduct, emphasizing the normative significance of the
Way. In any idealistic philosophy, there is no reality that transcends the idea, the ultimate standard. The idea embodies within
itself the proof of its own truth. Jinsai ascribed a priori and absolute value to benevolence, righteousness, propriety, and wisdom.
"If there is a universe besides this one," he wrote, "and people
inhabit it, there will undoubtedly be moral principles based on the
Way of benevolence, righteousness, propriety, and wisdom governing the relationships between lord and subject, father and son,
husband and wife."[61] Thus insofar as he rejected Sung philosophy's continuity of the Way and natural law (the Way of Heaven)
and emphasized human relationships, Jinsai's Way is not naturalistic; but it is naturalistic insofar as he believed the Way to have
an a priori existence, sufficient unto itself, transcending actual
human behavior. For instance, he remarked that "the Way is the
path that we must follow each day in our relationships with other
men. It existed before moral teachings came into being. It was not
perfected by man-made improvements. *It is as it is by nature.*"[62]

As we have seen, Sorai rejected Jinsai's idealism as "words with-

---

[60] *Nihon rinri ihen*, VI, p. 97 (*Benmei*, Book II). It is clear that he did not deny the validity of Principle itself from his remark on the same point that "only the Sages are capable of investigating the Principle and grasping its ultimate meaning, which consists
of propriety and righteousness. Thus when a chapter of the Book of Changes, 'Shuo
Kua,' refers to the extensive study of the Principle it has in mind the Sages. It is not
possible for an ordinary man to study it. So the Way of the Early Kings and Confucius
does not deal with Principle but with righteousness. But it does not, of course, intend
to abandon Principle." In other words, Sorai believed that only the sages had the
ability to make an extensive study of the Principle.

[61] *Nihon rinri ihen*, V, pp. 80–81 (*Dōjimon*, Book I).

[62] Ibid., p. 19 (*Gomō jigi*, Book I).

out substance." He was not satisfied with the insubstantiality of abstract concepts, and, seeking more tangible and concrete evidence for the Way, turned to the institutions and civilization of the era of Yao and Shun. But if he had ascribed an a priori, self-sufficient value to the institutions and civilization themselves, he would in effect have reverted to Jinsai's position. Hence he had to reject this second solution also. In erecting a system that places substance over name and objective human relationships over subjective morality, the only way to avoid erecting a Tower of Babel was to establish an absolute personality standing behind the Way as its creator. All the values of the Way had to be rooted in the personified entity. In Sorai's system, the Early Kings and the sages emerged as such ultimate entities.

The Way was created by the sages. Conversely, the term "sage" is nothing but the name for those who created the Way.[63] The most ancient political rulers, Fu Hsi, Shen Nung, and Huang Ti (the Yellow Emperor), are all sages in this sense. For instance, Fu Hsi invented the ethical principles that govern the relationship between husband and wife, Shen Nung introduced agriculture, and Huang Ti taught architecture and sewing.[64] But the men who systematized the Way in rites, music, law enforcement, and political administration were the rulers of the Three Dynasties, Yao, Shun, Yu, T'ang, Wen, Wu, and Chou. These men are sages among the sages. Thus the sages are the ancient political rulers who established the Way, and therefore for Sorai the sages are identical with the Early Kings.[65] Moreover, these sages are sages because they established rites and music, *not because they were en-*

---

[63] Cf. *Benmei,* Book I, ibid., VI, p. 43.

[64] Cf. *Tōmonsho,* Book III, ibid., pp. 196–97.

[65] If the view that the sage is to be defined as the inventor of the Way is carried to its ultimate conclusion, it implies that not only the wise men, from Mencius on, but even Confucius himself cannot be classified as sages. Obviously, even Sorai wanted to avoid this conclusion, so he explained that, although Confucius is not one of the creators of the Way, if he had not edited the Six Classics, the Way of the Early Kings would have fallen into decay and not been transmitted to later ages. As a result, the origin of the Way is now ascribed to Confucius. But not being a sage himself, Sorai held that it would be presumptuous for him to decide who should be classified as a sage. Hence he could not give a final word as to whether Confucius is a sage or not: "I shall therefore compare him with the ancient inventors of the Way for the time being and call him a Sage." The idea of the absolute character of the sages discussed below is introduced as a cunning evasion of the issue.

dowed with impeccable virtue. "The sages, too, are no more than human beings. Men's virtues differ with their natures. Even sages are not identical in their virtues. But we call these men sages because of what they invented."[66] The Sung philosophers' insistence that the sages are "identical with the principles of Heaven and do not have a speck of selfish human desire" is no more than "their own personal opinion."[67] The fact that Sorai defined the sages without reference to their virtue does not lower their value for him. On the contrary, as the sages are cut off from ordinary men, they acquire absolute value. In his conception of the sages, too, we can detect the predominance of the political factor.

Thus the Way is ultimately based on the invention of the sages or Early Kings. To hold, like the Sung Confucians, that the Way exists in the universe and nature, or that it is based on a principle of correct behavior in all things, results, Sorai concluded,

from the fact that they believe strongly in themselves and have little faith in the ancient Sages. They train themselves in the art of extending knowledge through the investigation of things and make inquiries and conclusions on the basis of their own judgements. Thus they say that this thing should be so and that fact should be thus, *insisting that these views are identical with the Way of the Sages. But what they say is no more than conjecture.* . . . The Way of the Sages is extremely profound and very extensive. It cannot easily be perceived by scholars as a "principle that ought to be." To pretend to understand everything in spite of this and to conclude that "naturally it ought to be so" is indicative of *an attitude that presumes to give the seal of approval to the Sages. Certainly it is the height of audacity.*[68]

So far as Sorai is concerned, any attempt "to make inquiries and conclusions on the basis of one's own judgement" about the foundation of the Way is "conjecture" and a sign of "audacity" towards the sages. The establishment of standards must move from the sages to man, not from man to the sages. Thus he insists that "those who follow the Way of the Early Kings are just; those who do not follow the Way of the Early Kings are evil. . . . The Way of

[66] *Nihon rinri ihen,* VI, p. 45 (*Benmei,* Book I).
[67] Ibid., pp. 18–19 (*Bendō*).
[68] Ibid., p. 195 (*Tōmonsho,* Book III).

the Early Kings is the yardstick and plumb line. Only by following the Way of the Early Kings can we attain justice."[69] "My humble desire is to preserve a deep faith in the Sages and even if something may seem improper to me, I shall carry it out in the conviction that so long as it is the Way of the Sages, it could not be improper."[70]

At this point, it would appear as if the sages had been elevated into absolute religious figures. Indeed, when Sorai said, "This ignorant old man does not believe in Shākyamuni Buddha, he believes in the Sages,"[71] this was no metaphor. As we have seen, for Sorai heaven is an otherworldly (*jenseitig*) object of faith. He now identified the Five Emperors who have the oldest places in the line of sages with heaven itself: "Emperors are the same as Heaven. . . . The arts of hunting and fishing, farming and sericulture, weaving, architecture, transportation, sailing, and writing were created by Fu Hsi, Shen Nung, Huang-ti, Shao Hao, and Chuan Hsu. They have not declined in importance through the ages and are still used daily by the people who consider these things normal aspects of man's way of life and remain ignorant about their origins. Because of their invention, Sages of later ages deified them, equated them with Heaven, and called them Emperors."[72] The sages have already been cut off from ordinary men; here they are clearly linked with a personified heaven. This otherworldliness (*Jenseitigkeit*) of the sages is Sorai's ultimate guarantee for the universal validity of the Way.

Thus Sorai's system based the Way on the institutions of the era of Yao and Shun, institutions limited both in time and place. Why

---

[69] Ibid., p. 70 (*Benmei*, Book I). On the other hand, he stated, "Goodness is the opposite of evil. This is a universal concept. Mencius in explaining this says: 'What is desired is goodness.' Even though it is not included in the Way of the Sages, anything that benefits and helps the people is good" (ibid., p. 74). Here he seems to have made good and evil prior to the Way of the Early Kings. But for Sorai, as we have just seen, good and evil are expressions of desires rather than standards of value, and hence there is no absolute conflict between the two. In the same way, as we saw earlier, in discussing the Specific Ether, he held that evil arises when someone's nature is not successfully cultivated and developed. Evil is "the potential form" of good. There is only a relative difference between the two. When one is compelled to choose between "this and that" the value judgement must be based upon the Way of the Early Kings.

[70] Ibid., p. 196 (*Tōmonsho*, Book III).

[71] Ibid., p. 172 (*Tōmonsho*, Book II).

[72] Ibid., p. 83 (*Benmei*, Book II).

was it that instead of turning into an ahistorical dogmatism, it produced a level of historical consciousness unparalleled in Confucian thought? This question remains obscure until we consider the otherworldly character of the sages on whom the Way is founded. The institutions of the era of Yao and Shun are absolute simply because they were invented by sages with these otherworldly characteristics.[73] This basic proposition calls out for historical consciousness, both in the positive and in the negative sense.

First of all, negatively, once this otherworldly period has passed, all institutions, rites, and music are clearly relative, limited in time and space. In a letter to Yanagawa Naisan, Sorai wrote, "After the Three Dynasties, even the Middle Kingdom was disturbed by the barbarians. It was no longer the Middle Kingdom of old. Thus those who are vainly enraptured with the term Middle Kingdom are mistaken. Please bear this in mind." As one might expect, given this basic position, Sorai was deeply interested in the study of law. His investigations in this area were crystallized in his famous work *Min-ritsu kokuji-kai* [An analysis of Ming law in Japanese]. When he lectured on Ming law at the Ken'en school, he made his students sign an agreement,[74] one of whose articles stated, "*These laws are the institutions of a different era and a different country*. One must not simply employ them in the present era and destroy the existing laws." Second, because the Way is absolute in its otherworldliness, it displays its binding power concretely and empirically only in historically unique circumstances. This is the positive aspect of the Sorai system's historical consciousness.

At this point we should recall the philological studies that provided Sorai with his methodology. Here, "things" rather than "meaning," and "facts and words" rather than "arguments," that is, *Sein* rather than *Sollen*, are held to be of fundamental importance. The institutions and civilization of the Three Dynasties,

[73] Sorai had this otherworldly, absolute nature of the Way in mind when he said: "There is no past or present in the teachings of the Way. The nations and world of today can be governed in accordance with the Way of the Sages. . . . If a principle is not applicable regardless of time, it is neither the Way of the Sages nor their teaching" (ibid., p. 190 [*Tōmonsho*, Book III]). Not only does this view not contradict Sorai's historical consciousness, it is what made it possible.

[74] This is in his *Ken'en zatsuwa, zoku jurin sōsho,* Vol. I. The Sorai quotation is from *Sorai-shū,* Book XXV.

regarded simply as Sein, were based upon the otherworldliness of
the sages and are not made absolute in their normative significance. When, therefore, the Way functions as Sollen in a given
time and place, there is nothing to prevent it from adopting the
form appropriate to the given, specific circumstances. Sorai distinguished between those who establish rites, those who propagate them, and those who practice them on this basis.[75] Needless
to say, those who establish rites are the sages of the Three Dynasties, and those who propagate them are Confucius and his disciples. The problem here is the third group, those who practice the
rites.

Sorai vigorously rejected any subjective component, any private
intellect, in his conception of the rites of the Early Kings, but in
practice he held that when these rites are performed in later ages
by people who have not lived under the rule of the Early Kings, it
is not only inevitable but in fact in accordance with the Way of the
Early Kings to make adjustments in their rites according to personal judgements. "What do I mean by adjustments [shinshaku]?"
he asked. "I mean the attempt to conform with human feelings,"
because "in establishing the Way, the Sages were guided by human feelings. Thus, in performing the rites, it is not contrary to
the Way to attempt to make them conform to human feelings."
Hence Sorai could say, "From the standpoint of the establishment
of the rites, it was wrong for Ch'eng I and Chu Hsi to imitate the
Sages. From the standpoint of propagating the rites, it was wrong
for Ch'eng I and Chu Hsi to disrupt the ancient institutions."
However, "*from the standpoint of the application of the rites,* it is proper
to perform the rites of Ch'eng I and Chu Hsi as well as the popular
forms of the rites. It is also permissible to make adjustments in the
rites of the Early Kings on the basis of one's own judgement."

Although Sorai denied the independent existence of Shinto—
naturally enough, given his belief in the universal validity of the
Way of the Sages—he maintained, on the same theoretical
grounds, that "Shintoists of our country worship their ancestors
and place them in Heaven. They identify Heaven and their an-

---

[75] Cf. *Sorai-shū* (30 vols., c. 1736), *Fukuantanpaku* [Letters replying to Azaka Tan-
paku], Vol. XXVIII, chapter 6. The quotations that follow in connection with this
discussion are all taken from this work.

cestors, and perform everything in accordance with the commands of the spirits and demons. . . . This is the same as the ancient Way of the Three Dynasties." "There is no such thing as Shinto, but these spirits and demons must be worshiped. The Way of the Sages expects those of us born in this country to revere the gods of the country. We must endeavor not to neglect them."[76] Thus nothing is more remote from Sorai than a dogmatism blind to historical reality.[77]

It should be clear that this increasing historical consciousness is closely related to the decline of Chu Hsi rationalism that we have glimpsed in Jinsai and Ekken (see pp. 58–60 and 65–67). However, so long as the Way is seen as the way of the universe and nature, in other words, so long as it is based ultimately on an impersonal idea, history is inevitably examined only to see whether or not it corresponds to this idea, a moralistic idea at that. Such a historical consciousness is crucially limited (note that Jinsai and Ekken still regarded the *T'ung-chien kang-mu* as the historical classic). Only by denying the idea that the Way itself is the ultimate source of authority, by founding it upon a number of personalities who have made a unique appearance in ancient China, and by raising these personalities to an otherworldly level is it possible to free "this-worldly" (*diesseitig*) history for the first time from the fetters of fixed standards; only then is it possible for history to develop freely.[78]

In the fourth article of his school's regulations, Sorai stated,

---

[76] *Nihon keizai taiten*, IX, p. 201 (*Taiheisaku*).

[77] Hence the criticism that Sorai believed in the supremacy of the Middle Kingdom is completely wrong, insofar as it implies that he held a specific country, China, to be the greatest of all nations. But here too Dazai Shundai is rather unhistorical in his outlook and tends to apply the Way of the Sages in a mechanical fashion. This is related to the fact that he emerged after the split between the public and private aspects of Sorai's system (a matter discussed below) and inherited only the former. On the common misconception of this aspect of Sorai's thought, see Iwahashi Junsei: *Sorai kenkyū*, pp. 242ff., 464ff.

[78] He did not see the Way of the Three Dynasties as stationary and inflexible, however. It changed from the Way of Hsia via the Way of Shang to the Way of Chou. But should this not be understood to mean that his awareness of "*this*-worldly" historical changes was projected back into the period of the Three Dynasties? Hence, whereas in general history he stressed the need to understand the historical uniqueness of each era, in the Three Dynasties, Sorai held that "because we do not possess the wisdom of the Sages, we cannot comprehend the reason why the Way had to be revised." *Nihon rinri ihen*, VI, 32 (*Benmei*, Book I).

"No Sages have appeared since the Ch'in and Han eras. But each age has established its own institutions. . . . The uniqueness of things must be understood by referring to the records. Only after a person has considered the uniqueness of different things should he express his opinion about the age. *On the other hand, it is very simple to criticize all ages by judging them in terms of fixed scales of measurement.* Anyone who does so considers himself to be right and does not weigh the circumstances of any era. *Of what value then is history?*"[79] Thus Sorai absolutely rejected the theory that in history the good are rewarded and the evil punished, the concept that governs Chu Hsi's *T'ung-chien kang-mu:* "The arguments in the *Kang-mu* are like the application of a rubber stamp. The form is fixed, the reasoning follows a single pattern, and the manner of presentation is the same. But Heaven and Earth are active forces. So are human beings. Learning which looks upon these things as if they were fettered by a rope is of no value. It does nothing more than make people clever. *Tzu-ch'ih t'ung-chien* [A general mirror for the aid of government], *which concerns itself only with facts, is far superior.*"[80] What Sorai looked for above all in history was "facts." Thus he firmly rejected the antipositivism revealed, for example, in "the arguments of the Chu Hsi school," which "leap over factual evidence" and, "disregarding facts, are designed only to sound reasonable."[81]

We have seen that, as a counterpart to his transformation of the sages and of the Way of the Sages into religious absolutes, Sorai rejected any subjective admixture in the study of the Six Confucian Classics. But he extended this positivist approach beyond the Confucian Classics, applying it to all historical phenomena. As he said: "It is necessary above all to look at history. It is of the utmost importance to understand each age. Unless the studies of literature, government, and classical texts are all undertaken by first understanding *the changes that occurred in each age,* there will be difficulties. *Changes in a particular age produce changes in language and institutions.* In order to study history without difficulties, it is necessary to bear

[79] Ibid., p. 123.

[80] Ibid., p. 153 (*Tōmonsho,* Book I). (*Tzu-chich t'ung-chien* was written by Ssu-ma Kuang [A.D. 1018–86], an orthodox Confucian scholar of the Sung period. Translator's note.)

[81] Ibid., pp. 153, 155.

this in mind."[82] This is simply a general application of the philological interpretation of the words (language) and facts (institutions) in the Six Classics. Sorai's theory of learning, too, broke out of its original circumscribed bounds. He had once said, "Learning consists in studying the Way of the Early Kings. The Way of the Early Kings is contained in the Books of *Odes*, *History*, *Rites*, and *Music*. Learning consists only of the study of these texts,"[83] but now that his approach had become independent of "fixed scales of measurement" or "reasoning" he argued that "learning consists of the extensive knowledge of facts. Thus learning means a thoroughgoing study of history."[84] "Learning means the broadening of one's knowledge by the incorporation of everything."[85] His scholarly interests were thus spurred on into a boundless open plain.

A scholar of Okayama *han* and an epigone of Sorai, Yuasa Jōzan (1708–81), stated in his *Bunkai zakki* [Miscellaneous essays]: "It is said that Sorai listened intently to what people had to say about different places and all sorts of things. After his death they say that a box was found containing old letters and scraps of paper on which he had written down the various things that he had heard."[86] As this shows, Sorai put his theory of learning into practice. The catalogue of his works covers the entire range of culture in encyclopaedic fashion, including not only discourses on the traditional Confucian Classics, but also essays on military science, law, history, literature, and music. Of course, Sorai would have said that the Way of the Sages is absolutely and concretely universal. All learning is "only a fragment of the Way." But what do the extraordinarily detailed investigations in his *Narubeshi* [How it is], which covers four hundred Chinese and Japanese matters, past and present, have to do with the art of "maintaining order in the state and peace in the world"?

The elevation of the sages to an otherworldly level had aroused an interest in the nature of individual things, which surged forth like a tidal wave threatening to sweep away Sorai's original object. His elevation of the Way above all dispute led to an unexpected

[82] *Nihon bunko*, III, pp. 9–10 (*Shibunkokujitoku*).
[83] *Nihon rinri ihen*, VI, p. 106 (*Benmei*, Book II).
[84] Ibid., p. 153 (*Tōmonsho*, Book I).
[85] Ibid., p. 156.
[86] *Nihon zuihitsu zenshū* [Collection of Japanese essays] (Tokyo, 1927–30), II, p. 578.

split in the goal he attributed to learning: on the one hand, the study of the Classics, with the direct aim of preserving order in the state and peace in the world; on the other, the acquisition of "an extensive knowledge of facts" and "total inclusiveness." I shall call the former the public and the latter the private aspect of Sorai's system. As we investigate his opinions we shall find that this division is a fundamental characteristic running through the entire structure of his system.

IV

My use of the terms "public" and "private" is not based on any arbitrary interpretation of my own. Let us consider how the two terms were used by Sorai. The example that first comes to mind is Sorai's *Giritsusho* [Application of the law] and the above-mentioned incident of the "just samurai of Akō." In that work he argued that the "honorable" convictions of the samurai that led them to avenge their dead lord were a "private" matter, while the state's need to punish them was a "public" matter. To give another example from the first section of the fourth book of his *Seidan*, in 1651, two masterless samurai (rōnin), Yui Shōsetsu and Maru-bashi Chūya, conspired to overthrow the bakufu. Marubashi was arrested before their plans could be carried out because an informer exposed the plot to the authorities. However, the informer was not rewarded with a government position as he had anticipated. Sorai was critical of this. He admitted that those who informed on or brought charges against others were usually regarded as cowards without the courage to avenge their wrongs themselves, so they turned to the government to settle their personal grudges. But, Sorai argued, accusations brought out of a sense of loyalty to the government should be distinguished from those stemming from personal grievances. Usually, however, the two categories were completely confused and both samurai and townsmen refused to inform on or bring charges against anyone. "*Generally speaking,*" wrote Sorai, "*the opinion that those who complain to the government about another person are cowards is based on the principle of private obligations.* However, the person concerned (the man who informed on Maru-bashi) was an extremely loyal man. . . . Generally there is a conflict between private obligations on the one hand and public obligations and loyalty on the other. *Private obligations can be upheld if they conform to public interests, but if they conflict seriously with the public good and are inimical to it, private obligations must not be sustained.*"[87] Sorai believed that to regard informing as dishonorable is to adhere to a "private" code of duty, while a willingness to inform in the interest of the state is an example of "public" loyalty. In both cases he was clearly using the terms "public" and "private" with the same meanings. That is, "public" refers to political, social, or external matters, while "private" refers to individual, internal matters. As these definitions are more or less identical with the meanings these words have today, it hardly seems necessary to discuss them. But things are not so cut and dried.

From an ideal-typical point of view, the distinction between the public and the private is rarely found in nonmodern, or more accurately, premodern modes of thought. This reflects the fact that, as an ideal type, premodern social structure itself is not divided into public and private spheres in this sense. In other words, relationships of political power and private economic relationships are interwoven in premodern society. The ruler's public financial outlay is not distinct from his personal consumption. The execution of administrative business is also the performance of the duties the servant owes his master. Public law is at the same time private law, and private law, public law. The independence of the public domain in every sphere of human activity, which implies the liberation of the private domain, is surely the crucial hallmark of "the modern."

Of course, a somewhat different opposition between public and private matters is not entirely unknown to premodern modes of thought. For example, there have been various attempts to distinguish between the "public" and the "private" in terms of *ethical standards* rather than as different *spheres*, so that "public" means good and "private," bad. But the two words have no such meanings for Sorai. He did place "public" before "private" affairs, but we have attributed this to his tendency to give primacy to political questions. It is not an attempt to reject "private" matters in themselves. In his *Giritsusho* he said that the forty-six Akō warriors "fol-

[87] *Nihon keizai taiten,* IX, p. 167.

lowed the path of integrity. Their action was righteous." Thus he insisted that they be given "the courtesy due to a samurai" and be allowed to commit seppuku rather than be beheaded. He merely condemned private righteousness *when it goes beyond its true sphere* and violates public law. He adopted a similar position on the other incident involving Marubashi Chūya. Although he recognized the legitimacy of private obligations, he argued that "if they conflict seriously with the public good and are inimical to it," that is, if a conflict of duty (*Plichtenkonflikt*) arises between public and private matters, then public interest should prevail.

In both these cases, the main issue is the boundary line between the public and private domains, not the rejection of either of these categories. Sorai made this point quite clear in his definition of the two terms in *Benmei* [On distinguishing terms]. Here he wrote: " 'Public' is the opposite of 'private.' What the people share in common is called 'public.' What concerns the individual alone is called 'private.' Part of the way of the prince is concerned with matters that he shares with the people, and part of it concerns only himself. . . . *Both public and private matters have their proper places. The prince, too, is not free of private affairs. To govern the state and the world and to have respect for public matters is the Way of those who rule over others.*"[88] As examples of public affairs Sorai cited the Way of the King discussed in the Book of History and the concept of preserving peace in the world found in the Great Learning. As examples of private matters he cited Confucius in the Analects where he says, "The father conceals the son, and the son conceals the father," and Mencius's statement that "I have heard that a gentleman [*chun tzu*] does not economize where his parents are concerned by using the good of the world as an excuse." (This has been variously interpreted, but it seems to mean that a gentleman does not economize on the furnishings for his parents' funerals in order to save public resources.) It is clear that Sorai's use of the terms is exactly the same here as in the incidents discussed earlier.

By contrast, let us look at the Chu Hsi school. Here "public" is synonymous with the principles of heaven, and "private" with human desires. We have already noted that there is a sharp ethical

---

[88] *Nihon rinri ihen,* VI, p. 69 (*Benmei,* Book I).

conflict in the relationship between the principles of heaven and human desires. Hence a "private" matter is an *evil* that must be rejected. The Chu Hsi scholars of the early Tokugawa period faithfully followed this interpretation. Hayashi Razan, for example, argued that "a benevolent man is a person who has eliminated selfish desires and has adhered to the public good based on the *principles of Heaven*. Public good based on the principles of Heaven means righteousness. . . . This is the path that is natural *and does not involve private considerations. Private matters based on human desires* are the desires and wanton thoughts aroused when a person sees a woman, hears her voice, smells a certain scent, or tastes a certain flavor."[89] Given the general acceptance of this Chu Hsi school interpretation throughout the intellectual world of the period, there is no denying the revolutionary nature of Sorai's conception of public and private.

It must be clear by now that I have stressed this separation of public and private in Sorai's system because it is deeply rooted in his very mode of thought, and that this is not just an analysis of his system of thought from an arbitrary standpoint. It should not be necessary to discuss in detail the fact that he treated the Way of the Sages primarily in its public aspect. The Way is, of course, absolute, so the division between public and private is always a division within the Way itself; nevertheless, it is clear that since the essence of the Way is to maintain "order in the state and peace in the world," it belongs more directly to the public domain, the domain where "the people hold things in common." Conversely, the same thing is revealed by the concept of "self-discipline," which Sorai included in the private domain: "Self-discipline means the effort to develop one's own virtues. *The Way of the Early Kings usually functions as an external force.* Propriety and righteousness come into being *in relation to other people.* As a result, scholars tend to regard the Way as an art, and many do not attempt to develop their own virtues. It therefore became necessary to speak of self-discipline."[90] In other words, the Way of the Early Kings is above all external and socially oriented.

What then makes up the major part of the private domain, the

[89] *Zoku-zoku gunsho ruijū*, X, p. 48 (*Shunkanshō*).
[90] *Nihon rinri ihen*, VI, p. 65 (*Benmei*, Book I).

domain from which, Sorai claimed, even a prince is not free? Obviously the "self-discipline" and "private obligations" discussed earlier. But Sorai was hardly concerned with individual morality. By maintaining that "those who speak of governing the heart by means other than rites profess false notions based on private intellect" (see p. 85, above), he made rites and music the only things the individual can use to exercise inner control. But these rites and music are completely political in nature and are sharply distinguished from the troublesome rites that have hitherto served as a means to govern everyday life. "When the Sung scholars," said Sorai, "talk about *rei* [*li,* rites], they talk as if this were something trivial and petty used by old women to discipline young girls in daily conduct. But it is stated in the *Tso chuan* that *rei* are the pillar of the nation. *The most important matter for the state is rei.*"[91] If this is so, all that can fill the vacuum created in the individual's inner life by this externalization of the Way is the natural human sentiments suppressed by the moralistic rationalism of Chu Hsi philosophy. It should now be clear why Sorai's separation of the public and the private is so significant for the history of Japanese Confucianism. *The disintegration of the continuity between moral standards and nature that we have been following culminated in the Sorai school in the liberation of the private or inner life from all rigorism as a result of the sublimation of standards (the Way) in the political.*

Sorai concluded his academy's regulations with the statement that "even if scholars have to become acrobats of the Hundred Schools, they should not become moralistic teachers of the Way." The extent of his dislike for the moralistic philosophers is revealed in his remark that "the Confucians of today are drunk with the concept of Principle and ceaselessly speak of morality, benevolence, righteousness, heavenly principles, and human desires. Whenever I hear these words I immediately feel so upset I have to go and play some music."[92] He therefore rejected the *T'ung-chien kang-mu* once again, this time not for theoretical reasons, that is, for its disregard for historical facts, but because of the practical effects

---

[91] *Keijishi yōran,* Book I. *Tso chuan* is Tso's Commentaries on the Spring and Autumn Annals. This commentary has traditionally been attributed to Tso Ch'iu-ming, a contemporary of Confucius, but some hold that it was not written until the fourth century B.C. (Translator's note.)

[92] *Nihon rinri ihen,* VI, p. 136 (*Benmei,* Book I).

of its moral rigorism. "The fact that even many men of good character become bad after the pursuit of learning is entirely due to the harmful effects of Chu Hsi rationalism. According to the *T'ung-chien kang-mu,* there has never been a satisfactory person, past or present. Anyone who views the people of today with this kind of attitude naturally becomes a man of bad character."[93] Sorai's best examples of those who had succumbed to the evil influence of Sung philosophy were the members of Ansai's school. "Those who subscribe to the Sung scholars' version of Confucianism," he wrote, "insist on making a rigid distinction between right and wrong, good and evil. They like to have every aspect of all things thoroughly clarified, and in the end they become very proud and lose their tempers easily. Many tend to dislike relaxing activities that involve refined tastes and literary talent, and develop bad personal characteristics. The personality of Asami Keisai is well known. It was not entirely his own fault. The narrow outlook of the school to which he belonged was responsible."[94]

Sorai's theory that human nature cannot be changed but must be "moved," and his belief that individuality (virtue) must be developed, were put into practice as outstanding men from many fields gathered in his school, the *Ken'en,* like a hundred brilliant flowers. Thus the natural human sentiments that Sorai released from the fetters of moral rigorism moved, as one might expect, in the direction of "refined tastes and literary talent." The Ken'en's reputation for putting literature above everything else was not completely unmerited. Just as Sorai rejected moralistic restrictions in politics and history, he insisted that literature should be independent of ethics. Here, too, his protest was directed at the Chu Hsi school: "I shall discuss the more significant errors of the Sung scholars in their interpretation of the Book of Odes. They insist that the Book of Odes was written in order to reward good and punish evil. This is a great mistake. If that had been its purpose, it would have been presented in a better form. . . . There are many lascivious poems in the Book of Odes. In his commentaries, Chu Hsi states that the poems were intended to punish evil but I believe

---

[93] Ibid., p. 153 (*Tōmonsho,* Book I).

[94] Ibid., p. 201 (*Tōmonsho,* Book III). (Asami Keisai [1652–1711] was one of Ansai's three principal students. Translator's note.)

that they are more likely to lead to lasciviousness. . . . There is no difference between the poems in the Book of Odes and poems of later ages. *It would be best to regard the poems in the Book of Odes simply as poems.*"[95] He also observed that "[Chinese] poems are usually regarded as rigid and serious. But they should be considered in the same light as Japanese songs [*uta,* poems]." The same attitude is manifested in his theory of poetic composition. "As I reflect upon the poems that are being composed today, I find that they are generally feeble and lack vigor; they are withered and lack richness. After all, it is important for poems to present images such as flowers and trees in beautiful profusion enveloped in a soft spring breeze. That is, they should describe nature and the richness of things. It is entirely pointless to compose in the feeble and withered style mentioned above."[96]

Of course, it is impossible to escape one ultimate restriction, the Way of the Sages. Hence although Sorai held that poems are written to express human sentiments rather than to reward good and punish evil, he also argued that because the Way of the Early Kings harmonizes with human sentiments, the investigation of human nature through poetry is essential to an understanding of the Way of the Early Kings, and therefore poetry is after all related to the Way of the Early Kings. Although he held that Chinese poems (*shi*) and Japanese poems (*waka*) were the same,[97] he could not avoid the conclusion that "Japanese poems have a feminine air to them. This is because they are poems from a country without Sages."[98] This last remaining restriction was not lifted until the advent of the school of National Learning. Only then could the concept of "art for art's sake" come into being. Nevertheless, Sorai did maintain this:

The ancients learned poetry for the same reason that people learn *Nō* songs today. . . . It is the nature of the mind to think. Even when a person has leisure and no worries, he thinks about various things. So when he is moved by something and sentiments of joy, anger,

---

[95] Ibid., p. 202.

[96] *Nihon bunko,* III, p. 29 (*Shibunkokujitoku*). The previous quotation is from *Kunyaku jimō,* Book I.

[97] Cf. *Benmei,* "Gihachisoku."

[98] *Nihon rinri ihen,* VI, p. 180 (*Tōmonsho,* Book II).

sorrow, elation, love, or hatred are stirred within him, he automatically gives expression and voice to these feelings. [Chinese] poems [*shi*] are the same as Japanese poems [*waka*]. They are not meant to expound the Way, to discipline oneself, and to govern others. Nor are they meant to show how to maintain order in the state and peace in the world.[99]

Thus Sorai's position was barely within the bounds of the Confucian philosophy of art. By insisting that poetry is not intended to "show how to maintain order in the state and peace in the world," he clearly indicated his belief that literature belongs to the private domain.

The division between the traditional study of the Chinese classics and "learning which consists of the extensive knowledge of facts" is no more than a manifestation of the theory of the duality of private and public in learning, which runs through Sorai's system. The *public realm* of learning is monopolized by the Way of the Sages in the narrow sense as embodied in the Six Classics. As a result, Sorai firmly opposed any encroachment on the public domain by all schools of thought that, in his opinion, did not have as their goal the preservation of order in the state and peace in the world. These included the Chu Hsi school, the Wang Yang-ming school, the Jinsai school, Taoism, and Buddhism. But although they were to be kept out of the public domain, these heterodox schools of thought were all permitted to survive in the private domain. For instance, Sorai said: "Shākyamuni Buddha forsook the world, left his home, and joined the world of beggars. In this condition he formulated his Way. Consequently he dealt only with matters that concern man's mind and body; he did not explain the way to govern the state and the world. . . . It is the primary object of the Way of the Sages to establish the way to govern the state and the world." Thus Sorai conceded Buddhism a place in the individual sphere precisely because he sharply distinguished it from the public Way of the Sages: "Because Buddhism teaches the individual how to govern his mind and body, it has never come into conflict with the Way of the Sages."[100] He argued that *even if*

---

[99] *Keijishi yōran*, Book I.
[100] Ibid., p. 151 (*Tōmonsho*, Book I), and p. 159.

a person "secretly favors Buddhism in order to gain comfort for his mind and body, it does not matter so long as he believes in the Way of the Sages and concerns himself with the state and the world."[101] This is possible because the two belong to separate domains.

On Distinguishing the Way (Bendō), the work in which Sorai clearly stated his total opposition to the "heterodox" schools, particularly Sung philosophy, for the first time, and a work that he himself regarded very highly, remarking, "Ah, it has been over a thousand years since Confucius died, and now for the first time the Way has been clarified,"[102] ends with these extremely tolerant words: "I have no desire to see scholars abandon the theories of the Sung Confucians and other philosophers because of what I say. . . . The world of learning respects thought. When a person is engaged in thinking, even the words of the Taoists and Buddhists are helpful. This is truer still of the theories of the Sung Confucians and other Confucian philosophers."[103] This, too, is an example of Sorai's desire to "broaden one's knowledge by adopting everything."

This distinction between public and private is not confined to the object of learning but involves its very nature. Insofar as the teachings of the sages are concerned with the maintenance of order in the state and peace in the world, they are indispensable for political rulers. Hence Sorai deeply regretted the absence of learning among the samurai class:

Although they are called warriors [*bushi*], so long as they are concerned with the task of governing the state and the world, the samurai are rulers of the people. When a person becomes a commissioner or occupies other official positions, he is equivalent to a chief minister or a high official. The samurai occupy the positions of king, duke, chief minister, or high official, but they fail to realize that they are gentlemen [*chun tzu*]. . . . *They fail to realize that talent and intellect are to be developed and broadened by learning and that the state is to be governed by letters.* It is stupid in the extreme to think that the land can be governed by thrusting out one's elbows and glaring at the people, and

---

[101] *Nihon keizai taiten,* IX, p. 200 (*Taiheisaku*).
[102] Cit., Iwahashi: *Sorai kenkyū,* op. cit., p. 182.
[103] *Nihon rinri ihen,* VI, p. 27.

by repressing the entire population by terrifying it with the threat of punishment.[104]

He therefore proposed in his *Political Discourses* (*Seidan*) that Confucian scholars be placed throughout the city of Edo to lecture to the shogun's immediate retainers (*hatamoto*) and that *hatamoto* recommended by these scholars be appointed as officials.[105] Here learning is clearly given a public character, but only insofar as it is a way to maintain order in the state and peace in the world. The pursuit of learning for its own sake is evidently regarded as a private matter, as can be seen from Sorai's statement that "learning is different from public duties; *after all, it is a private matter.*" In the light of this, although those Confucian scholars who regard learning itself as the ultimate goal do participate in the maintenance of order in the state and peace in the world *through* their learning, in the broad sense in which everyone is a government official, their basic function is to serve in the private, nonpractical realm. Hence the humble confession that "*the task of Confucian scholars is to preserve phrases and sentences and pass them on to future generations. They have only to exert themselves and follow the established tradition. This is their only duty. As for such things as the Way, it should be left for future Sages to deal with. This would be the proper attitude to take.*"[106]

The Chu Hsi school and Sorai here had diametrically opposed views on the relationship between Confucian teachings and Confucian scholars. For the Chu Hsi school, which directly linked "the extensive pursuit of the Principle" with virtuous conduct, and virtuous conduct (cultivation of the personal life and regulation of the family) with the preservation of order in the state and peace in the world, the Confucian scholar has a political task precisely because the school was nonpolitical in its theory. But for Sorai, who had broken the continuity between private morality and politics, the Confucian scholar's tasks are nonpolitical because he saw the essence of Confucianism as the maintenance of order in the state and peace in the world. For Sorai the scholar's work is at most to

[104] *Nihon keizai taiten*, IX, p. 202 (*Taiheisaku*).
[105] Ibid., pp. 188–89.
[106] *Nihon rinri ihen*, VI, p. 127 (*An Tampaku tōsho*).

gain an understanding of the Way and to explain it. Inventing the
Way or putting it into practice is a task left to political rulers.
Sorai's methodology (the study of ancient words and terms), with
its emphasis on *Sein* rather than *Sollen,* is no more than a concretization of this point of view. Remember that the criteria for his
conception of the sages are primarily political. As we have explained, his opposition to the intrusion of "private intellect" and
his insistence on fidelity to the words of the classics are the counterpart to his deification of the sages. Ironically, by making the
sages absolute *in their political merit* while seeking the essence of
learning in "the lowly realms of words and facts," Sorai had de-
politicized his own position.

My study began with an examination of Sorai's philological
methodology, so I now find I have come full circle. I have at least
completed my survey of the basic structure of Sorai's system. To
sum up, I have found that Sorai's thought is everywhere antitheti-
cal to Chu Hsi philosophy. He replaced the rational Way of
Heaven with a nonrational Will of Heaven. He ended the functions of "the extensive pursuit of the Principle." He made the sages
into beings essentially different from ordinary men. He made a
break in the continuity of moral norms and nature and abandoned
moral rigorism. He made the maintenance of order in the state and
peace in the world independent of the cultivation of personal life
and the regulation of the family. Thus the continuative mode of
thought of the Chu Hsi school completely disintegrated and its
various component parts became independent. This was the ultimate result of the development that I traced step by step in the
ideas of Sokō, Jinsai, and Ekken.[107] As I have pointed out, the

[107] In order to substantiate the theory that the establishment of Sorai's system would
have been impossible had it not been for the disintegration of the Chu Hsi mode of
thought in the background, let me quickly point out that the specific features of Sorai's
system described above cannot be found in the thought of Hsun Tzu, with whom Sorai
is often compared.

First of all, for Hsun Tzu, cultivation of one's personal life and government are completely continuous. He wrote: "I am asked about the way to govern the nation. I reply:
I have heard of the way to discipline one's own life but I have not yet heard of the way
to govern the nation. The prince embodies in himself the standard of righteousness.
When the standard of righteousness is correct, the external forms are also correct. The
prince is like a water basin. If the basin is round, the water is round. . . . Emperor
Chuang of Ch'u liked willowy people. At his court, therefore, some people starved
themselves. So I say, I have heard of the way to discipline one's life but I have not yet

universality of the Chu Hsi mode of thought in the early years of the Tokugawa period was based on the stability of Tokugawa feudal society. In that case, what kind of historical development was taking place in Tokugawa society as a background to this disintegration of Chu Hsi optimism? In particular, what was the social basis for the sudden acceleration in this disintegration with Sorai? What factors led him to such a drastic "politicization" of Confucianism? To answer these questions, I must leave the world of ideas for a time and descend into the practical world in which Sorai lived and observed in the years immediately preceding and following the end of the seventeenth century. The next section presents a very broad outline of this period.

V

"Spring in Edo, not a day goes by without a temple bell being sold."[108]

Eighty years had passed since the founding of the Tokugawa

---

heard of the way to govern the nation" (*Chun tao* [The way of the prince], Chapter XII). For Hsun Tzu, propriety (*li*) is exclusively ethical, as can be seen from the fact that he related it closely to his theory that man is bad by nature. It is not transformed into something purely political as it is in Sorai. The same goes for Hsun Tzu's conception of the sages. He defined them ethically, establishing a hierarchy of men who rely on force, gentlemen, wise men, and sages. Hence, unlike Sorai, who believed that "one cannot attain the status of a Sage by learning," Hsun Tzu held that "of course, one studies in order to become a Sage."

In view of the fact that Hsun Tzu's definitions of the sages and propriety differ from those of Sorai, his thesis that "rules of proper conduct and standards of justice and law are created by the Sages" (*Hsun tzu*, Chapter XXIII) also has an entirely different objective meaning, although it may have given Sorai a hint. Ethics and politics are continuous in Hsun Tzu's thought because he lacked Sorai's division between public and private. Hsun Tzu's use of public and private is identical with that of the Chu Hsi scholars. He said, "The Book of *History* states: 'Do not behave according to your likes and dislikes but solely follow the kingly way.' This indicates how a gentleman is to *control his selfish (private) desires by means of public justice*" (*Hsiu shen* [Moral cultivation], Chapter II). As a result, the peculiar factors that produced Sorai's private domain— his historical consciousness, his opposition to moral rigorism, his tolerance toward other schools of thought, his respect for literature, and so on—are completely lacking in Hsun Tzu. It is Dazai Shundai rather than Sorai who closely resembles Hsun Tzu, because the former inherited only the public aspect of his master's philosophy (of course, he could only do so once a division had been made between public and private, so a careful analysis would show that Shundai's thought too differs from Hsun Tzu's). At any rate, these differences show that the modern consciousness germinating in Sorai's system was completely absent from Hsun Tzu.

[108] *Kane hitotsu | urenu hi wa nashi | Edo no haru.*

Bakufu. The spirit of political and social activity created by internal disorder and international contacts in the Sengoku era had temporarily subsided because of internal stabilization and seclusion from the outside world. But the people's energies, denied an outlet abroad, turned inward and produced the dazzling and enchanting picture scroll of Genroku culture. The fifth shogun, Tsunayoshi, revised the first article of the Rules Governing the Military Households to read: "Learning and military skill, loyalty and filial piety, must be promoted, and the rules of decorum must be properly enforced," thus emphasizing the importance of learning for government. In 1690 he built a Confucian shrine at Yushima (in Edo) and wrote the words "The Palace of Perfection" (*Taiseiden*) to be displayed in the shrine. The following year he promoted Hayashi Nobuatsu to junior grade fifth rank[109] and made him minister for higher learning (*daigaku no kami*). He also assembled the daimyo, hatamoto, and Confucian scholars and lectured to them personally on the Confucian Classics. In addition he sponsored debates between Confucian scholars. Thus he strove to promote literature and learning. The scholarly prestige of the Hayashi family declined in inverse ratio to the official favors it received,[110] and Sorai later severely criticized Tsunayoshi's half-dilettante interest in these lectures: "During Shogun Tsunayoshi's regime, the Shogun amused himself by listening to lectures, so that the Confucian scholars neglected all other learning and literature and behaved as if it was their sole duty to lecture on Confucianism.

[109] There were nine court ranks, each rank being divided into two categories, senior and junior. (Translator's note.)

[110] *Sentetsu sōdan* states that the minister for higher education, Hayashi Nobuatsu, was a man of "wide knowledge and broad learning" (*Dai Nihon bunko*, p. 14), but Arai Hakuseki dismissed him as an "intellectual sycophant," and lamented: "Is it not sad that learning in our country has declined to such a level as this?" (*Oritaku shiba no ki* [Recorded while burning brushwood], ed. Iwanami Bunko, pp. 187 and 193). Of course, we cannot accept Hakuseki's opinion without question because he and Nobuatsu were political enemies, but the fact that, although they disagreed about everything, Hakuseki's views always prevailed does not reflect much credit upon the official school of Confucianism. In his *Ken'en zatsuwa* [Miscellaneous remarks from the Ken'en], Sorai wrote that when he was asked by Shogun Yoshimune to punctuate the *Luyu-yeni* (Commentaries on the six moral precepts set down by the Emperor K'ang Hsi of the Ch'ing dynasty) so as to make it easier to read the Chinese, "The lords Kanō Tōtomi-no-kami and Arima Hyōgo-no-kami had *asked the Hayashi family* to work on the *Luyu-yeni*, *but their work proved to be unsatisfactory*. As a result I was asked to punctuate it." The scholarly prestige of the Hayashi family was undoubtedly on the decline by Nobuatsu's day.

As a result, they have all now become ignorant and useless."[111] Nevertheless, the initiative from above for the promotion of learning and education undoubtedly contributed to the ascendancy of learning in the Genroku era, of which it was said that "literature and learning flourished widely. Every house read and every family recited [the classics]. Such a thing has not happened since."[112] Tsunayoshi was interested not only in Confucianism but also in Japanese poetry. He invited the poet Kitamura Gigen (1624–1705) and his son from Kyoto and gave them employment. He also held poetry readings at the house of Yanagisawa Yoshiyasu.

But what is unique about the learning and art of the Genroku era is their independence. In all areas, free and independent schools sprang up in opposition to traditional forces. The rise of Jinsai's Horikawa school and Sorai's Ken'en school is merely a reflection of the general trend within the Confucian circle. Thus we find that in Japanese poetry, the efforts of the court aristocracy were demolished by the criticism of Toda Mosui (1629–1706) and Keichū (1640–1701). In belles lettres Matsuo Bashō (1644–94) emerged in opposition to the Danrin school of haiku (which emphasized humor) and started his own Shōfū school. Ihara Saikaku (1642–93), who began as a haiku poet in the same Danrin school, founded the *ukiyozōshi*, the realistic literature of the "floating world," and depicted in realistic fashion the passionate pursuit of material and sexual pleasures by the *chōnin* (townspeople), who were supposed to count for nothing politically. Significant advances were made in the field of drama, which was the chōnin's main outlet besides the gay quarters. Here Chikamatsu Monzaemon (1653–1725) emerged as the outstanding *jōruri* (puppet play) dramatist. Among kabuki actors, there were Sakata Tōjūrō (1645–1709) in the west, and Ichikawa Danjūrō (1660–1704) in the east. In the field of painting, we find rebels such as Hanabusa Itchō (1652–1724) emerging from the Kanō school, the academy in the world of painting comparable to the Hayashi family in Confucianism. Itchō freed himself from the restrictions of his master's style and produced satirical genre paintings. Hishikawa Moronobu (1618–94), who established this type of genre painting as the art

---

[111] *Nihon keizai taiten*, IX, p. 192 (*Seidan*, Book IV).
[112] *Sentetsu sōdan*, p. 14.

of the chōnin and initiated ukiyo-e wood-block printing, and Ogata Kōrin (1658–1716), who rivaled government-backed gold-lacquer workers such as Koami (1599–1651) and Koma (d. 1663) and made Jōken'in (the Buddhist name of Shogun Tsunayoshi) period gold lacquer famous, both belong to this era. Thus the entire cultural sphere was seething with creative activity. The brilliant yet delicate color of Genroku designs reveals the fundamental spirit of Genroku culture.

This increase in creativity in the cultural sphere was based, of course, on a desire for improved living standards, but at the same time it fostered this desire. Needless to say, the fact that these creative activities were concentrated in large cities like Edo, Kyoto, and Osaka is closely related to the growth in the economic power of the chōnin. Thus the Genroku spirit first took the form of increasing chōnin extravagance. In 1692 Ihara Saikaku wrote:

> Nowadays all housewives have grown extravagant. Although they are not lacking in apparel, they must have another wadded-silk garment of the latest fashion for the New Year. It must be made of glossy silk costing forty-five *momme*[113] for half a roll. They have it dyed in a thousand delicate tints and colors, which cost even more: one *ryō* of gold. Thus gold and silver are squandered for something that others would hardly notice. The *obi* they wear around their waists is of genuine satin, twelve feet long and two feet wide, imported long ago from China. It costs two pieces of silver. On their heads they wear ornamental combs that cost two *ryō* in gold coins, the equivalent of three *koku* of rice. Their undergarments are made of a double layer of pure crimson silk, and they wear white silk *tabi* on their feet. Formerly, even a daimyo's lady would not have dressed in this manner. As wives of townspeople they are dressing far beyond the manner befitting them. The divine retribution that will strike them is frightful to contemplate.[114]

The samurai, too, were influenced by this atmosphere. Sorai observed:

[113] Sixty *momme* equaled one *ryō*, which was a gold piece weighing 17.86 gm. (Translator's note.)

[114] *Saikaku meisaku-shū* [A collection of Saikaku's masterpieces], published by the Nihon Meicho Zenshū Kankō Kai, II, p. 571 (*Seken munazanyō*, chapter 1). See Saikaku Ihara: *This Scheming World*, trans. Masanori Takatsuka and David C. Stubbs (Tokyo, 1965), p. 20.

Thirty or forty years ago, none of the lower police officials had *tatami* in their houses, and none wore formal ceremonial suits [*kami-shimo*]. Now they have *tatami* on the floor and sliding doors covered with Chinese paper. The houses and private circumstances of these well-to-do samurai are as good as those of their superiors. Formerly those who wore formal suits when they went out were the recipients of sizable stipends. When the founder of the Tokugawa Bakufu first established his domain in Kanto, the younger samurai never wore *hakama* [formal skirts]. No one wore silk or anything better. . . . But all this changed because it was said that the *hatamoto*, being the immediate retainers of the Shogun, should be of equal standing with the daimyo. Then the retainers of the *hatamoto* came to be regarded as the equals of the vassals of the daimyo. Finally even *wakatō* [lower-class samurai] began to live in a grand style.[115]

If the living conditions even of the hatamoto and their retainers had improved, the feudal lords were even better off. "In the way in which they behave throughout the day, in their garments, food and drink, household furnishings, dwellings, and utilization of servants, in the conduct of their wives, the manners of the messengers they send with letters and gifts, the retinues that accompany them in processions through the city, the style in which they travel, and in their ceremonies of coming-of-age, marriage, and burial . . . in all these they naturally tended to be more extravagant in accordance with the trend of the times."[116] Soon the hair of the samurai began to smell of aloeswood oil and their sword guards to be decorated with fine gold and silver inlay. Nor were the gay quarters, of which it was said that "indecent places so flourished during the Genroku [1688–1704] and Hōei [1704–11] eras that they seemed like paradise during the day and the Sea God's palace at night,"[117] completely unfamiliar to the samurai class.[118]

From all levels of society came the sounds of gaiety, echoing

---

[115] *Nihon keizai taiten,* IX, pp. 77–78 (*Seidan,* Book II).

[116] Ibid., p. 68.

[117] *Enseki jisshu* [Ten imitation jewels] (Iwamoto Darumaya, 1863), I, p. 141 (*Waga koromo*).

[118] This can be surmised from the fact that daimyo and hatamoto frequenting the gay quarters were admonished during the Kyōhō era, a period of moral retrenchment. Cf. Takayanagi Shinzō and Ishii Ryōsuke, eds.: *Ofuregaki kampō shūsei* (Tokyo, 1934), pp. 580–81.

through the *yashiki* (the Edo residences of the daimyo) and flooding the city streets. The warlike atmosphere of the Sengoku period
had vanished completely. Moreover, the stringent and cunning
methods introduced by the bakufu at the beginning of the Tokugawa period to control the daimyo had completely fulfilled
their purpose by now, and even daimyo from the outlying regions
abandoned their old political ambitions and plunged into the
hedonistic life of Edo. Ronin with secret hopes of an uprising had
nearly all been disposed of, and the Keian incident (Yui Shōsetsu's
plot to overthrow the Tokugawa government in 1651) had become a tale of bygone days told by old men. Both the samurai and
the townspeople congratulated themselves on their "Era of Tranquillity." Culturally and politically, as historians tell us, the Genroku era was the high point reached by the Tokugawa Bakufu.

But once we turn our eyes away from the dazzling forestage of
the Genroku era and look behind the scenes, we cannot miss the
slow growth of a situation that was soon to pose grave difficulties
for the feudal authorities. Its roots lay deep in the formative period
of Tokugawa feudal society itself. Tokugawa society made clear-
cut status distinctions between the samurai (*shi*) on the one hand,
and the peasants, artisans, and merchants (*nō, kō,* and *shō*) on the
other, and firmly fixed the hierarchical relationships between ruler
and subject, superior and inferior persons, thus constituting the
perfect form of Japanese feudalism. But it lacked an essential
characteristic of feudalism in that political control was distinct
from the real usufruct of land. This had been brought about by
the division of the country into separate feudalities from the late
Muromachi period (1336–1573) on, and the concentration of the
samurai in castle-towns.[119] The samurai with a fief of his own
managed to maintain some contact with the land through his fief
and the need to tax it, but the vast majority of lower-class samurai
were left with only a symbolic tie to the land through the grant of
a rice stipend.

On the other hand, the money economy, which was already so

[119] Gierke's view that the hallmark of feudalism is "the fusion of authority and real
estate" (*Verschmelzung von Herrschaft und Dinglichkeit*) is more or less applicable to the
Japanese feudal system of the middle ages. A feudal system separated from the land
is like a kinship system without blood ties.

extensive when the Tokugawa Bakufu came to power that the latter needed a minting monopoly, grew even more because of the many feudal retainers concentrated in the castle-towns. The introduction of the *sankin kōtai* system made this trend nationwide. As a result, not only the castle-towns and the agricultural villages but Edo and all the feudal domains were bound closely together by the commercial economy. The samurai's way of life changed from one founded on real wealth to one based on credit. His life began, in Sorai's words, to be like that of "a traveler at an inn." If it is generally true that "life under law is static in character as long as it is based predominantly on title to property, but dynamic in character when the chose in action [i.e., incorporeal rights] becomes its principal foundation,"[120] then we can say that the samurai class was now compelled to deal with expenditures that were dynamic with incomes that were static. The spread of Genroku culture to the samurai class quickly aggravated this contradiction.

The resulting crisis first emerged in the bakufu's financial management. Sorai recalled: "When the Lord of Harima was in charge of the treasury he confided to a close friend that the government's expenditures exceeded its revenues. A sum of ten to twenty thousand *ryō* had to be taken out of the reserve. In the future, officials of the government will be faced with grave difficulties. This was told me by my father."[121] As he anticipated, the financial difficulties whose symptoms were visible at the end of the reign of the fourth shogun, Ietsuna, became a full-scale crisis because of the extravagance and personal largesse of the fifth shogun, Tsunayoshi. As a result, in 1695, Finance Commissioner Hagiwara Shigehide proposed a policy of recoining gold and silver bullion. The object was to debase the currency in order to increase government funds. This was the first but not the last time this measure was employed, for it served time after time as a financial stopgap until the end of the Tokugawa Bakufu. In this respect, the 1695 debasement was a measure of historical significance vis-à-vis the decline of Tokugawa feudalism. The amount of money the bakufu raised by this policy during the Genroku era is estimated to have

---

[120] G. Radbruch: *Rechtsphilosophie*, 3rd ed. (1932), p. 141; translated by Kurt Wilk in *The Legal Philosophies of Lark, Radbruch and Dabin* (Cambridge, Mass., 1950), p. 168.
[121] *Nihon keizai taiten*, IX, p. 78 (*Seidan*, Book II).

been between 4.7 and 5 million ryō.[122] But all this added revenue was quickly consumed through continuing financial recklessness and a succession of natural calamities like the great fire in Edo in 1698, the earthquake and fires that ravaged the Kanto region in 1703, and the eruption of Mount Fuji in 1707. Lacking any other solution, the bakufu continued its policy of debasing the silver coinage from 1706 on, flooding the market with inferior coins, which were said to be "black in color and tarnished. None of the characteristics of silver remained and they were exactly like lead or tin coins."[123]

Repeated debasements of course forced prices up, creating a situation the bakufu had not anticipated. The samurai class as a whole was badly hit, while the officially retained merchants of the gold and silver guilds were enriched, together with treasury officials like Shigehide who worked in collusion with them.[124] The decline in the value of gold and silver pieces meant a rise in the value of copper coins. This affected the samurai adversely, because they exchanged their rice stipends for gold pieces and then turned these in for copper coins to purchase their everyday necessities. But the price of everyday necessities purchased with copper coins did not drop to compensate for the rise in the value of copper coins, because the demand for these goods remained relatively stable.[125] In 1708 (the fifth year of the Hōei era), the bakufu issued a large copper coin (known as Hōei currency) worth ten times any existing denomination in copper. But, as Dazai Shundai observed, this did no more than expose the weaknesses of the bakufu. Shundai wrote:

[122] Cf. Arai Hakuseki: *Oritaku shiba no ki,* op. cit., p. 100, and Takekoshi Yosaburō: *Nihon keizai shi* [Japanese economic history], 8 vols. (Tokyo, 1920), IV, p. 87.

[123] Dazai Shundai: *Keizairoku,* Book V, in *Nihon keizai taiten,* IX, p. 525.

[124] This question is discussed in detail in Arai Hakuseki: *Oritaku shiba no ki,* op. cit., pp. 163–65.

[125] Dazai Shundai observed: "The samurai benefit when the value of copper coins is low, and the common people benefit when it is high. When the value of copper coins is high, the value of gold pieces is low. When the value of copper coins is low, the value of gold pieces is high. . . . The samurai sell their rice, receive gold pieces, purchase copper coins with them, and then buy all their necessities. So, if the value of gold coins is low and that of copper coins is high, they cannot pay for their daily needs. The situation is different for those in commerce, for even when the value of copper coins is low, they do not suffer any losses. The best policy today, then, would be to increase the supply of copper coins and lower their value." *Nihon keizai taiten,* IX, p. 528 (*Keizairoku,* Book V).

When these coins were issued, the people were greatly inconvenienced and came to dislike them intensely. The government issued stern edicts to make the people use them, but they stubbornly resisted. The government then issued stricter edicts threatening anyone who refused to use these coins with severe punishment. Although it issued new edicts daily, the people continued to ignore them. Thus, even the government with all its authority was unable to force the people to comply with its wishes. Indeed, any measure which runs counter to the sentiments of the people cannot be enforced even if it is backed by harsh penalties.[126]

By the time Shogun Tsunayoshi died, there was unprecedented confusion in economic life because of the simultaneous issue of different types of currency and fluctuations in the comparative values of gold, silver, and copper. On taking office, the sixth shogun, Ienobu (1663–1713), removed Hagiwara Shigehide, the originator of the reckless financial policy, from office and sought to restore the values of the currencies with Arai Hakuseki (1663–1713) as his chief adviser. Hakuseki attempted to restore order in the financial world by reviving the office of comptroller (*kanjōgimmi*), restricting the volume of foreign trade at Nagasaki, and so on, but his aristocratic stress on ceremonials made it impossible to cut down extensively on bakufu expenses. When Ienobu and Ietsugu (the seventh shogun) died in rapid succession, the problem was passed, still unresolved, to the eighth shogun, Yoshimune (1684–1751).

Yoshimune introduced the Kyōhō (1716–36) Reforms, the first large-scale attempt in the Tokugawa period to reinforce the feudal structure. In the financial realm this meant a policy of drastic retrenchment. Gold and silver pieces were recoined to restore their value to that of the coins of the Keichō era (1596–1615), bakufu expenses were drastically reduced, and edicts were issued urging frugality on the general public. But these measures could not fundamentally reconstruct the finances of the bakufu, which were in deep crisis. Finally the bakufu began to find it difficult even to pay the stipends of its own retainers. In 1722 it was forced to impose a levy on daimyo with incomes of over ten thousand koku. This "presentation rice" (*agemai*) amounted to one percent of their in-

---

[126] *Nihon keizai taiten,* IX, p. 527.

comes. In return, their period of residence in Edo (as laid down in the sankin kōtai system) was reduced by half. This reveals the gravity of the situation, for the government that had aspired to revive the era of the founding father, Gongen, the deified Ieyasu, was forced to relax the fundamental policy of the bakufu, the sankin kōtai system, because of financial necessity. The official proclamation itself admitted this: "*This request is being made regardless of shame.*"[127] As might have been expected, this policy could not last, and in 1730 the original measures of the sankin kōtai system were restored. However, the new system was discontinued "*not because the government coffers had been sufficiently filled,* but because it had been in effect for a number of years."[128]

The government coffers were further depleted by a decline in the price of rice starting in the early years of the Kyōhō era. After 1728 a series of abundant harvests depressed rice prices even further. In contrast, the price of other commodities not only did not decline with the price of rice but instead tended to rise. In consequence, the difficulties of the bakufu and the samurai class grew worse. The bakufu sought to remedy this situation by limiting the volume of rice that could be shipped to Edo from Osaka, by setting price ceilings, and so on, but all these measures proved ineffective. As a result, in 1736, it reverted to the Genroku policy of currency debasement. The policies intended to create sound finances had failed. The Kyōhō Reforms, which failed first in this area of currency policy, collapsed like a castle built on sand when Yoshimune retired. In the Tanuma era, the period of Ieshige (the ninth shogun) and Ieharu (the tenth shogun), the country experienced a period of financial irresponsibility worse than that of the Genroku era. Then came the Kansei (1788–1801) Reforms of Matsudaira Sadanobu (1758–1829), followed in turn by the luxurious eras of Bunka (1804–18) and Bunsei (1818–30). Next came the Tenpō (1830–44) Reforms of Mizuno Tadakuni (1793–1851). Thus the Tokugawa Bakufu seesawed between extravagance and retrenchment before plunging into its final ruin in the so-called Bakumatsu period (the period of the downfall of the bakufu). In this sense, the Genroku and Kyōhō eras can be viewed as a proto-

---

[127] *Ofuregaki kampō shūsei*, op. cit., p. 162.
[128] Ibid., pp. 563–64 and 876–77.

type of the alternation of historical eras that characterized the latter period of Tokugawa feudal society.

Needless to say, the financial difficulties of the bakufu and hence of the hatamoto and *go-kenin* (the immediate retainers of the bakufu) also to a greater or lesser degree confronted the daimyo and their retainers, who had an economic basis similar to the bakufu's. Once initiated into Genroku culture, the samurai could no longer live in the same sober style as in the days when they ran about the battlefield with nothing but a lance. As a result, their dependence on the warehouse managers, financial agents, and exchange brokers who managed their finances grew greater and greater. These usurious capitalists steadily increased their wealth by cleverly taking advantage of the fluctuations in the relative values of gold and silver, and the general inflation. In addition, the construction projects initiated by Shogun Tsunayoshi and those that followed natural calamities were very profitable for the lumber dealers and other officially employed merchants.[129] Of course, the unstable currency was bad for the chōnin too, but generally speaking Hakuseki's observation that "it is not true that people at all levels of the society are experiencing financial difficulties. It is true, however, that the samurai are in dire financial straits"[130] and Sorai's comment that "since the beginning of history, there has never been a time, either in foreign lands or in Japan, when merchants have been able to double their profits as readily as in the past hundred years"[131] are both accurate enough. As a result, from around the Kyōhō era, the relative social statuses of the samurai and the merchant began to show signs of reversing. According to Shundai,

> Both large and small daimyo at present must bow their heads and ask the *chōnin* for favors. They depend on the support of the rich merchants of Edo, Kyoto, Osaka, and other cities, and are able to survive only by their continued assistance. . . . They are constantly plagued by creditors who come to collect their loans. The daimyo lack peace of mind through worrying about how to make excuses.

[129] Cf. Arai Hakuseki: *Oritaku shiba no ki,* op. cit., p. 162.

[130] *Arai Hakuseki zenshū* [The complete works of Arai Hakuseki] (Tokyo, 1905–7), VI, p. 159 (*Shoseikengi*).

[131] *Nihon keizai taiten,* IX, p. 52 (*Seidan*).

They fear the sight of money-lenders as if they were devils. Forgetting the fact that they are warriors, they kow-tow to the *chōnin*.[132]

If the daimyo had to behave like this, the ordinary samurai were
much worse off. One observer remarked:

Nowadays when [a samurai] writes a letter to a merchant who
possesses some wealth, he addresses the latter in the same manner
as he would address an exalted personage. When they meet each
other on the street and exchange greetings, they both address each
other as *dono* ["sire"] so that it is difficult to distinguish between the
samurai and the merchant. They behave as if they were equals.[133]

Thus the samurai found it difficult to maintain their dignity. Inversely, of course, the chōnin's self-confidence rose, as the playwright Chikamatsu shows when a chōnin in one of his plays (*The
Love Suicides at Amijima*) says:

Well, a customer is a customer, whether he is a samurai or a townsman. The only difference is one wears swords and the other doesn't.
But even if he wanted to he couldn't wear five or six swords. At
most he'll wear two, the broadsword and the dirk. I'll take Koharu
[the *geisha*] and if necessary the samurai too.

He also says: "Being a townsman I have never worn swords but
the luster of the mass of silver I have at home should bend and
twist any sword."[134]

But we should not overestimate the historical significance of this
ascendancy of the chōnin. Whether they were warehouse managers, financial agents, merchants of the gold and silver guilds, or
lumber dealers, the wealthy merchants to whom the samurai
"bowed their heads" were all parasitic upon the feudal authorities. They were commercial, money-lending capitalists who lacked
the ability to invent new methods of production. They cannot be
considered to have gained their profits in the normal way, but

---

[132] Ibid., p. 512 (*Keizairoku*, Book V).
[133] Ibid., XI, p. 281 (Memorial of Yamashita Kōnai).
[134] Chikamatsu Monzaemon: *Shinju ten no amijima* (Iwanami Bunko), pp. 69–70. This
play was written in 1720. Cf. the English translation by Donald Keene: *Major Plays
of Chikamatsu* (New York, 1961), pp. 387–425.

rather in a manner highly reminiscent of *wucherischer Kapitalismus* (usurious capitalism).[135] They lived off the feudal authorities and could only survive by directly or indirectly siphoning off part of the income the feudal authorities exacted from the peasants. Hence their status was so insecure that if they ever incurred the wrath of the authorities, they collapsed instantly. The fate of Yodoya Tatsugorō[136] provides us with concrete evidence of the fragility of the foundations on which commercial capitalism rested. The merchants therefore quickly dissipated the fortunes that they had accumulated in extravagant pleasures. The many absurd stories about Kinokuniya Bunzaemon and Naraya Monzaemon[137] may have been exaggerated, but they reflect one aspect of the chōnin's attitude to life.

Although the chōnin of Osaka were scorned by their counterparts in Edo for their parsimony, the picture of them drawn by the novelist Ihara Saikaku clearly shows that they were not so far apart in this matter. Take one of the tales from his *Nippon eitaigura* [The Japanese family storehouse], "A Medicine Concocted in an Unusual Manner." A poor man asked a man of fortune for a way to cure a "disease called poverty" and was taught how to concoct "the Millionaire Pill." The prescription was: five ryō of early rising, twenty ryō of the family trade, eight ryō of overtime, ten ryō of economy, and seven ryō of good health, the total of fifty ryō to be chopped into small pieces and taken morning and night. At the same time, certain noxious things had to be avoided: "fancy foods, dissipation with women, use of silk garments as day-to-day wear, palanquins for wives, music, and poem-cards for eligible daughters . . . ambling around at night, gambling, the game of *go*, backgammon . . . *sake* with supper, tobacco, unnecessary trips to Kyoto . . . familiarity with actors and brothel quarters, and borrowing money at a monthly rate of eight-tenths of one percent." In other words, practically all forms of enjoyment were to be avoided. The poor man followed the prescription faithfully,

---

[135] For a definition of usurious capital see Max Weber: *Wirtschaftsgeschichte* (1924), p. 286; trans. F. H. Knight as *General Economic History* (New York, 1961), pp. 246–47.

[136] A wealthy merchant whose entire property was confiscated by the bakufu in 1705 on the grounds that he was leading too extravagant a life. (Translator's note.)

[137] Wealthy lumber merchants of this era who were known for their extravagant behavior in the gay quarters of Edo. (Translator's note.)

worked industriously for forty years, and became a great lumber merchant with savings of a hundred thousand ryō. The man then decided that "all this resulted from taking the millionaire pill when I was young. Now that I am over seventy years of age a little intemperance should do no harm," and changing his way of life completely, spent the rest of his life in luxury. Saikaku adds: "It is important to save in youth and spend in old age."[138] In other words, pursue a life of strict abstinence in order to enjoy a life of hedonistic consumption later on. Just as the chōnin did not yet constitute a middle class, the "chōnin disposition" was still far removed from Max Weber's spirit of capitalism, the psychological motor of the development of industrial capitalism.[139]

Now that we have viewed the Genroku and Kyōhō eras from the front of the stage and also from behind the scenes, we must descend into the pit to obtain a complete understanding of the period. There we find the peasants, the ultimate mainstay of the feudal society, living on in uncomplaining silence. From the beginning of the Tokugawa period, the bakufu and the other feudal lords devised various measures to ensure the inflow of the taxes, their economic base. Especially significant was the extensive intervention in the daily life of the peasants. The kind of food the peasants could eat was restricted: "As for the peasants' food, they

[138] *Saikaku meisaku-shū*, II, pp. 121–23. Cf. *The Japanese Family Storehouse*, trans. G. W. Sargent (Cambridge, 1959).

[139] Cf. Max Weber: *Die protestantische Ethik und der Geist des Kapitalismus* (1934); trans. Talcott Parsons as *The Protestant Ethic and the Spirit of Capitalism* (London, 1930). The following passage is suggestive for the nature of commercial capitalism in the Tokugawa period: "This is not wholly because the instinct of acquisition was in those times (ancient times and the middle ages) unknown or undeveloped, as has often been said. . . . The difference between the capitalistic and pre-capitalistic spirits is not to be found at this point. . . . The universal reign of absolute unscrupulousness in the pursuit of selfish interests by the making of money has been a specific characteristic of precisely those countries (Southern European and Asiatic) whose bourgeois-capitalist development, measured according to Occidental standards, has remained backward. . . . *Absolute and conscious ruthlessness in acquisition has often stood in the closest connection with the strictest conformity to tradition. Moreover, with the breakdown of tradition and the more or less complete extension of free economic enterprise, even to within the social group, the new thing has not generally been ethically justified and encouraged, but only tolerated as a fact. And this fact has been treated either as ethically indifferent or as reprehensible, but unfortunately unavoidable*" (Parsons translation, pp. 56–58). The last three sentences apply directly to the situation in Tokugawa Japan. Paradoxically, the feudal outlook manifested most typically in the Chu Hsi mode of thought that regarded "human desires" as *eo ipso* evil expelled such desires from the field of ethics and thus prevented the moralization of the two most significant realms of human desire, love and the acquisition of wealth.

must be instructed to consume the minor cereals and not eat much rice."[140] Also, "they are not to buy and drink *sake* and tea. The same applies to their wives and children."[141] Edicts on clothing stated: "Wives and children of village heads may wear garments made of pongee and cotton. Ordinary peasants may only wear garments made of cotton. Even for neckbands and sashes only cotton may be used."[142] An edict regulating land use stated: "Because it interferes with the production of the five grains, tobacco is not to be grown on regular farm land, regardless of whether it is wet or dry. Nor can it be grown on newly reclaimed farm lands."[143] In addition, there were such "solicitous" instructions as the following: "A wife who neglects her husband's affairs, drinks a great deal of tea, and likes to go on trips and picnics should be divorced. . . . Even if a wife is unattractive physically, if she manages her husband's household carefully, she must be treated in a kindly fashion."[144] The ultimate purpose of these regulations was expressed most succinctly in a Keian era (1648–52) proclamation which stated: "As long as he pays his taxes, no one's life is as care-free as that of the peasant." For this reason, although change of residence by peasants was strictly controlled, it stated: "If the lords of the fiefs or the bakufu's deputies behave improperly and the peasants find it unbearable, *they may move to neighboring villages after they have paid all their taxes.* As long as they do not have any unpaid taxes, neither the lords of the fief nor the deputies may interfere with their departure."[145]

But the rise of the commercial economy also affected the peasantry in many ways. As we have seen, it impoverished the samurai class, and they were forced to become quantitatively and qualitatively more exacting in their collection of taxes. The market economy also directly infiltrated the rural village, gradually dissolving the natural economy of the peasantry. This trend gradually accelerated after the Genroku era. As Sorai observed: "In a cer-

---

[140] *Ofuregaki kampō shūsei,* op. cit., p. 685.
[141] *Tokugawa kinrei-kō* [The Tokugawa prohibitions], pub. the Department of Justice (1932), V, p. 243.
[142] *Ofuregaki kampō shūsei,* op. cit., p. 686.
[143] Ibid.
[144] Ibid., p. 244.
[145] Ibid., p. 687.

tain village money was once very scarce and rice and wheat rather than money were used to purchase everything. But recently, starting with the Genroku era, I hear that money has begun to circulate in the rural areas too, and things are now purchased with money."[146] The fact that the rural villages were drawn into the market economy meant, of course, some diffusion of Genroku culture into these villages. In spite of the restrictions mentioned above, the peasants' aspirations to improve their living conditions grew stronger and stronger. The edict issued to the peasants in the bakufu's domains in 1713 touches upon this trend. "Recently the laws have not been observed faithfully in many areas, and the manners and customs of many places have become corrupt. People neglect their duty and fail to work the land. Instead they indulge themselves with things unrelated to their vocation, that is, with affairs of the entertainment world. In all things—housing, clothing, and food—they are living in a style improper to their status."[147]

There was inevitably friction between the increasingly stringent tax exactions and the growing aspirations for an improved standard of living. The relation between feudal lord and peasants had so deteriorated by the second decade of the eighteenth century that Sorai observed: "The lord of the fief is convinced that his sole function is to collect taxes while the peasants see him as doing nothing else. The former seeks to collect as much tax as possible while the latter seek to pay as little as possible. Both sides are concerned with nothing else but this struggle over taxes. *As a result, the lord of the fief and the peasants look upon each other as sworn enemies.*" On the other hand, the penetration of the village by commercial capital meant that land began to be drawn into the money economy. The law prohibiting the sale of agricultural land was circumvented in various ways, producing a simultaneous concentration and fragmentation of landholding. When all else failed, the peasants whose income was thus reduced to subsistence level resorted to the desperate rebellions called *ikki*. According to the figures given by Professor Kokushō, from the Hōei era to the

[146] *Nihon keizai taiten,* IX, p. 76 (*Seidan,* Book II).
[147] *Ofuregaki kampō shūsei,* op. cit., p. 707.

Kyōhō era (1704–36) there were forty peasant ikki, a sudden jump to twice the previous average of less than one per annum.[148]

But not until the Hōreki era (1751–64) had the agrarian situation so deteriorated that the very existence of the feudal society was threatened. In this respect, too, the Genroku and Kyōhō eras are a watershed. The increase in the number of peasant ikki during the Kyōhō era is insignificant in comparison with the sudden leap in the Meiwa era (1764–72), the An'ei era (1772–81), and the Tenmei era (1781–89). And infanticide only became widespread among the peasantry after the Kyōhō era. The population increased at a fairly normal rate during the Tokugawa period until the Kyōhō era, when it became stationary or even occasionally decreased.[149] This can be understood only if we take into consideration the changes in the living conditions of the peasantry, who constituted over 80 percent of the total population.

This concludes my outline of social conditions from the Genroku to the Kyōhō eras. What can we say about what we have found? These are typical phenomena of a transitional period. The colorful Genroku culture concealed all the moments, both urban and rural, that were to undermine the feudal political structure, either by quiet corrosion, or by active resistance. But these moments had not yet developed in sufficient strength to deal a mortal blow to the feudal society. Although the Tokugawa feudal system was experiencing its first significant difficulties, it had not yet lost its overall strength. It was these circumstances precisely that led Sorai to "politicize" radically the Confucian system.

There are two limiting factors that will prevent a political mode of thought from gaining supremacy in ruling circles. On the one hand, so long as there is stability in the society, the prevalent attitude is one of optimism about the social order. Only when the life basis of the ruling class of the society is disturbed by some kind of social change does the awareness of a crisis germinate in the minds of sensitive thinkers, bringing "the political" to the fore in

[148] Kokushō Iwao: *Hyakushō ikki no kenkyū* [A study of peasant uprisings] (Tokyo, 1928), pp. 271ff. and the chart on p. 263. The Sorai quotation is from *Kinroku,* Book I.

[149] Cf. Honjō Eijirō: "Tokugawa jidai no jinkō oyobi jinkō seisaku" [The population and demographic policy in the Tokugawa period], *Keizaishi kenkyū,* ed. Iwanami Shoten.

their thought. On the other hand, and this is the second limiting factor, the society may fall into such a hopeless state of confusion and decay that the political mode of thought fades away again. Instead, escapism, decadence, and dissimulation spread through the society. Thus serious political thought capable of confronting reality is possible only in a situation between these two extremes (*Grenzsituation*).[150] As he was in such a situation, Sorai was able to reject the optimism of the Chu Hsi philosophy—"Whose fault is it ... that people have finally been led to believe that the Way of the Sages and the way to govern the land are two different things?"— and to try, by politicizing Confucianism, to make it the philosophical basis for "the Way to govern the land." On the other hand, however, the cultural factors (that is, Genroku culture) that had agitated the feudal society were bound to leave an imprint on Sorai's philosophy, particularly in its private aspects. Problems serious for the future of Confucianism were inherited unsolved by the intellectuals of the following eras. This development is the theme of the next chapter.

VI

Given this social background, we are now ready to consider Sorai's theories of political and social reform, the specific applications of his philosophy of the maintenance of order in the state and peace in the world. This aspect of Sorai's thought is, however, relatively familiar and there are a number of excellent introductory works[151] so I shall merely summarize his political theories, for my chief objective is to examine the mode of thought concealed beneath these theories.

Sorai successfully applied his methodology, with its emphasis on *Sein,* to the existing society and made an incomparable, percep-

---

[150] Cf. Kurt Schilling: *Geschichte der Staats- und Rechtsphilosophie* (1937), p. 22. However, Schilling's use of *Grenzsituation* is not exactly the same as mine.

[151] Nomura Kanetarō: *Ogyū Sorai* (Tokyo, 1934) is an excellent introduction to Sorai's social and economic thought. There are many works which deal with certain aspects of Sorai's ideas. For example, Honjō Eijirō: *Kinsei no keizai shisō* [Economic thinking of the Tokugawa period] (Tokyo, 1937), and Nakamura Kōya: *Genroku oyobi Kyōhō jidai ni okeru keizai shisō no kenkyū* [Study of economic thought in the Genroku and Kyōhō eras] (Tokyo, 1927). In English, see J. R. McEwan: *The Political Writings of Ogyū Sorai* (Cambridge, 1962).

tive, theoretical analysis of the crisis confronting feudal society. This analysis led him to the basic sources and immediate causes of the difficulties of the samurai class. The basic sources were two-fold: (1) The entire samurai class, from top to bottom, lived like guests at an inn, that is, "even a single chopstick had to be paid for."[152] (2) There was no order in things, that is, while the supply of everything was limited, the demand was unlimited. As for the immediate causes, he noted: (1) "The price of things has become excessively high"; (2) "The number of gold and silver pieces has decreased"; and (3) "Because of heavy debts, the circulation of gold and silver coins has diminished."[153] In other words, the first of these immediate causes had to do with commerce, and the other two with currency.

As an interim solution, he proposed that the direct causes be eliminated first. After that, basic reforms should be gradually introduced. "The fundamental policy in governing the state and the world should first of all be to increase the wealth," he believed.[154] "Unless the immediate difficulties are corrected, it will be extremely difficult to end the situation in which the samurai live like guests at an inn or to establish any sort of systematic order in things."[155] His immediate solution, increasing the currency by minting more copper coins, was to offset the increase in value of copper coins, which was one of the samurai class's difficulties. But he recognized that the basic sources would have to be removed before the problem could be solved: "If we merely increase the supply of copper coins and fail either to correct the situation that forces the samurai to live like guests in an inn or to establish a new system of institutions, the world may prosper for a short while . . . but extravagant ways will revive and the same difficulties will recur."[156] On the one hand, therefore, in order to give permanence to the existence of the samurai, he proposed that they should each be given a fief and be made to live on the land, and that a system of registration should be established to control people's movements. On the other hand, in order to balance supply and demand,

---

[152] *Nihon keizai taiten,* IX, p. 51 (*Seidan,* Book II).
[153] Ibid., p. 72.
[154] Ibid., p. 48.
[155] Ibid., p. 79.
[156] Ibid., pp. 80–81.

he suggested the establishment of a new system of regulations in which people's desires would be fixed in accordance with status.

The first of these proposals was, of course, designed to free the samurai from their dependence on commercial capitalism by restoring the natural economy. But Sorai also listed several secondary advantages which would accrue if the samurai lived in the villages. For example, they would abandon the frivolous spirit of the chōnin and lead a more vigorous and robust way of life, and the conflict between the samurai and the peasantry would be resolved. The second proposal, the establishment of a system of regulations, is a concretization of Sorai's basic philosophy, the Way understood as rites and music. Hence Sorai's whole mode of thought as we have described it comes into play here. His position is not, therefore, as is frequently and erroneously claimed, the same as that of the so-called Legalist school. Sorai's institutions are always founded upon "human feelings." For example, he contended that any attempt to curb rising prices "simply by issuing commands and laws is an unrealistic solution because it is an attempt to force people to do things that are not in accord with manners and customs."[157] He therefore opposed price controls. Just as the Way is not an autonomous, self-sufficient entity, but the product of human beings, the sages, so institutional changes depend ultimately on human decisions, too. "Man is more important than laws. Even if laws are bad, considerable benefits accrue from them if the men who enforce them are good. It is useless to examine the laws if evil men prevail."[158] The plan to utilize men of talent and merit discussed in his *Seidan* [Political discourses] and *Taiheisaku* [A policy for great peace] is the most brilliant aspect of his political theory. The theory that human nature is inalterable is rigorously applied here, and great stress is laid on the need for a full development of the uniqueness of each individual. No hint remains of the typical feudal view of man.

Sorai's theories of social and political reform are undoubtedly restorative in tendency. But we should not overlook the fact that just as he sought to sustain pristine Confucianism by means of a method of thought that is not strictly Confucian, his political

---

[157] Ibid., p. 210 (*Taiheisaku*).
[158] *Nihon rinri ihen*, VI, p. 161 (*Tōmonsho*, Book II).

thought, in which he called for a restoration of feudalism in its original form, conceals a countervailing tendency favoring political centralization. His proposal to utilize men of talent is one example. Here we should note the *germ* of a notion of absolutism, an absolutism centered around the Tokugawa family, of course. The shogun himself, explained Sorai, "is like a guest at an inn. He too buys all the things he needs. . . . *But the entire nation is his fief; he owns the entire country of Japan.* He can make immediate use of all things in the land. So it should not be necessary for him to purchase them."[159] This view is in clear contradiction with the real political position of the Tokugawa Bakufu, which was no more than the government of the preeminent feudal house, although it did exert great authority over the other clans. Sorai's concept of the shogunate led him to conclude that "it is a great error to think that the daimyo do not have to contribute taxes."[160] He therefore criticized the statement that Shogun Yoshimune's rice levy (age-mai) was ordered "regardless of shame" (see p. 122, above). He complained: "What do they mean by calling it a 'loan'? All the feudalities of the land are under the authority of the state. Anything the government needs can be commandeered. What do they mean by calling it a loan?"[161] Sorai also wanted to limit the size of the daimyo's fiefs to three hundred thousand koku, contending that "daimyo with fiefs of 400,000 and 500,000 koku are too large for a small country like Japan."[162] His aim here is an "equalization" of subjects beneath a Tokugawa absolutism: "Unless the affairs of the entire land can be dealt with as the Shogun wishes, the course of government will from time to time be obstructed."[163] Hence although at first sight Yoshimune's restorative reforms seem to be in accordance with Sorai's ideas, Sorai criticized them: "Alas, the spirit needed to effect a restoration was absent!"[164]

Sorai believed that the kind of major institutional reforms he envisioned could best have been introduced during the Genroku

---

[159] *Nihon keizai taiten,* IX, p. 52 (*Seidan,* Book II).

[160] Ibid., p. 64.

[161] *Nihon zuihitsu zenshū,* II, p. 572 (*Bunkaizakki,* Book II).

[162] *Nihon keizai taiten,* IX, p. 159 (*Seidan,* Book IV).

[163] Ibid.

[164] *Nihon zuihitsu zenshū,* II, pp. 585–86 (*Bunkaizakki,* Book II). This statement, however, is not directly related to his theory of absolutism.

era. The Kyōhō era was already too late.[165] Hence by his own
times the situation seemed rather hopeless. The feudal society he
could see was neither the era of Yao and Shun nor an age blessed
with "a benevolent prince and wise subjects" that Hayashi Nobuatsu eulogized. On the contrary, it was an age in which "the
proper order of things in the land has deteriorated and an age of
military conflict is about to emerge."[166] "Because those at the top
lack learning and are ignorant of the Way of the Sages, the world
has rapidly decayed. In the future, power will pass to those at the
lower levels of society. . . . When the authority and prestige of
those at the top decline, disturbances are easily fostered. Indica-
tions of this are present already."[167] While shallow observers were
singing the praises of the "Kyōhō Restoration," Sorai's unclouded
vision already detected the twilight shadows. Indeed, Ogyū Sorai
was the first great crisis thinker produced by Tokugawa feudal
society.

---

[165] *Nihon keizai taiten*, IX, p. 212 (*Taiheisaku*).
[166] *Nihon zuihitsu zenshū*, II, p. 573 (*Bunkaizakki*, Book II).
[167] *Nihon keizai taiten*, IX, p. 202 (*Taiheisaku*).

THE SORAI SCHOOL'S RELATIONSHIP TO NATIONAL LEARNING, ESPECIALLY TO THE NORINAGA SCHOOL

The Diffusion of Sorai's Mode of Thought and Counter-
currents to It. The Schism in the Ken'en School. The
Decline of Confucianism after Sorai. The Negative Relationship between National Learning and the Sorai
School. Common Aspects of Their Methods of Thought.
Various Features of Their Positive Relationship. A Summary of This Relationship—National Learning's Place
in the History of Thought.

I

The emergence of the Sorai school was widely acclaimed in the
intellectual community, and this is natural, given the contempo-
raneity of its theoretical content—or, to look at it from the opposite point of view, given the anachronistic character of the Chu
Hsi mode of thought. But the magnitude of the sympathetic response it elicited is hard to imagine today. It surprised Sorai more
than anyone else. In a letter to Hori Keizan (1688–1757), he
wrote: "I am an ignorant and indolent weakling. . . . I have never
sought to guide or instruct other men. Needless to say, I have
never engaged in controversy with others. *It is difficult for me to believe that the entire country is, as you say, falling under my sway.* This
phenomenon is produced either because shallow men blindly echo
the sounds emanating from men who do not understand my philosophy, or because that philosophy accords with the temper of the
times. At any rate, I fail to understand it."[1]

This statement should not be dismissed as a rationalization invented on the spur of the moment. Sorai's open-mindedness made
him abhor and oppose the formation of a guildlike school of

---

[1] *Sorai-shū*, Book XXVII.

followers. Nevertheless, his personal inclinations notwithstanding, the magnetic force of his philosophy brought into being the Ken'en school, numbering several hundred adherents. Among those under the sway of "Sorai-ism" were Dazai Shundai (1680–1747), Yamagata Shūnan (1688–1732), Andō Tōya (1683–1719), and Usami Shinsui (1710–66). The fact that they were the outstanding minds of the period ensured the survival of the Ken'en school even after Sorai's death. Indeed, where its social influence is concerned, the golden age of the Sorai school began after Sorai died. Commenting on this situation, Naba Rodō (1727–89) wrote:

> From about the middle of the Kyōhō era, we can truthfully say that Sorai's theories dominated the whole society. His ideas reached the peak of their popularity in Kyoto after his death, during the twelve or thirteen years from the beginning of the Genbun era [1736–41] to the eras of Enkyō [1744–48] and Kan'en [1748–51]. In these years, people were so enthusiastic to learn his theories that they behaved as if they had lost their minds. . . . Everyone stopped attending lectures given by scholars who relied on the commentaries of the Ch'eng brothers and Chu Hsi. . . . If any critical work written since the middle ages, any classical text, commentary, or literary work were criticized even slightly by Sorai, people refused to read it, considering it to be worth no more than the paper it was written on.

This is not to say, of course, that the Sorai school did not have any opponents. No rebellion occurs without friction. As opposed to all the existing schools of Confucianism, the Sorai school had made a revolutionary contribution. It was thus inevitable that it would encounter the resistance of Confucian scholars intent on preserving the traditional grounds upon which they stood. However, while Sorai was alive, this friction remained relatively invisible. Active opposition was curbed by Sorai's incomparable scholarly stature, and by the fact that he avoided personal attacks and sought friendly associations with a broad range of other schools of thought. But this latent and confined anti-Sorai current gained in strength soon after his death. Thus the more the Ken'en school's attraction was such that "people . . . behaved as if they had lost their minds," the more vociferous became its critics. Between about 1750 and 1790 more than thirty books appeared attacking the Sorai school.[2] It was undoubtedly unprecedented in the history of Japanese thought for so much criticism to be directed against a single school of thought in this way. But the many works written to refute Sorai's theories contain very little of theoretical value. Either they consisted of commonplace criticisms from hackneyed old viewpoints, or else the critic himself, while attacking the Sorai school, was using some aspect of Sorai's own method of thought.

Hirata Atsutane (1776–1843),[3] an uncompromising opponent of all Confucianism, including Sorai's, made a just assessment of this situation: "Since antiquity, there have been innumerable Confucian scholars in this imperial country, but not one of them possessed so much vision and talent as Ogyū Sorai. . . . Why then do so many slanderers, forgetting his great influence, disgrace themselves by making minute searches for his mistakes? In extreme cases we find men slandering him by saying that he was not well versed in the methods of research, or that he was ignorant of ancient words and letters. *But these critics have obtained their ability to detect the errors in Sorai's mode of thought because they themselves have been influenced by his methods. . . . It would not be wrong to call Sorai the father of most of the Confucian scholars alive today.*"[4] In other words, Sorai's enormous intellectual influence was more often demonstrated in the thought of his opponents than in that of his followers.

Within the Ken'en school itself, however, no theoretical advances were made beyond Sorai's own formulations. Instead, even as it gloried in its golden age, a schism was beginning to develop behind the prosperous facade of the Ken'en school. In the last chapter we saw how while he politicized Confucianism, and indeed because he politicized Confucianism, Sorai introduced a nonpolitical option into his system with the division between public and private. The objectives of Sorai's philosophy were twofold:

---

[2] Among them Karazaki Genmyō's *Butsugaku benshō* [Analysis of the Sorai school], Ishikawa Rinshū's *Bendō kaihei* [An analysis of Sorai's Bendō], Kani Yōsai's *Hi-Sorai-gaku* [Against the Sorai school], and Goi Ranshū's *Hi-butsu hen* [Against Sorai]. The Naba Rodō quotation is from his *Gakumon genryū*.

[3] A member of the school of National Learning who placed great emphasis on the sacred nature of Japan. (Translator's note.)

[4] Quoted from Iwabashi Junsei: *Sorai kenkyū*, op. cit., pp. 474–75.

on the one hand, the maintenance of order in the state and peace in the world, and, on the other, "broadening one's vision and dealing with facts." Poetry, literature, and history all belonged to the latter, the private domain. The study of ancient words and terms was originally meant to provide a methodology for the study of the Way of the Early Kings, but under the impact of the historical consciousness of the Sorai school, the critical study of words and terms themselves became the primary object. Structural unity of a sort was given to the public and private realms by absolutizing the sages and the Way of the Sages, and by treating the division as "merely a branching in the Way." But this structural unity, achieved and maintained by a single person, was possible only because of Sorai's nearly superhuman breadth of knowledge and learning. Although there were many men of ability in the Ken'en school, there was no other scholar whose knowledge extended from the science of the maintenance of order in the state and peace in the world to the investigation of historical events and their causes. As a result, the division in the Sorai system first took the form of a division between individuals among his followers. The public and private aspects of Sorai's philosophy came to have different supporters (*Träger*) in the Ken'en school. Dazai Shundai and Yamagata Shūnan represented the public aspect, while Hattori Nankaku, Andō Tōya, and Hirano Kinka became the custodians of the private domain. Tsunoda Kyūka (1784–1855) had this situation in mind when he remarked: "After Sorai's death, his followers split into two groups. Hattori Nankaku had a reputation for poetry and literature, while people praised Shundai for his erudition in the Chinese classics."[5]

Because the science of the maintenance of order in the state and peace in the world on the one hand and poetry and literature, history, and the methods of research on the other were studied by different men, the theoretical unity of the Sorai school, too, inevitably disintegrated. This happened because each of Sorai's followers, as a true epigone, consciously or unconsciously absolutized

[5] *Kinsei sōgo,* Book II. Of course, this is not to say that those who adopted the public aspect ignored the private aspect completely and vice versa. For example, Shundai wrote an excellent essay on poetry and music entitled *Hitorigoto* [A monologue], and this reflects the common style of the Ken'en school. The problem is whether the private or the public aspect constituted the essence of the Sorai school.

the aspect he had inherited as the sum total of Sorai's philosophy. They began to argue about all aspects of his philosophy, ignoring the proper bounds of their special domains. This confusion is clearly visible in Shundai and Nankaku. On the one hand, Shundai scorned playing about with ancient words and terms as "filthy trash" and argued: "The Way of the Sages is meant only to serve as a means to maintain order in the state and peace in the world. . . . Those who forsake it and neglect its study in order to spend their lives writing about poetry and literature are not true scholars. They are just like entertainers who occupy themselves with playing the *koto, go,* calligraphy, painting, and the like."[6] On the other hand, Nankaku was "a learned man, but he did not pose as an authoritative teacher, remaining a recluse. *He always occupied himself with literary matters.* If anyone questioned him about current events, he would laugh and say: 'Literary men are foolish and unfamiliar with such things. But they aimlessly discuss these matters for their amusement. That is just like a lame man trying to measure the length of a road. *That is why I do not engage in such discussions.'*"[7] In other words, he ignored political realities and enjoyed himself by composing poems and pursuing philological studies.

Only a relatively small number of Sorai's followers inherited and developed his studies of Confucian classics as Shundai and Shūnan did. In the main, the Ken'en scholars took Nankaku's path. In spite of Shundai's warning, the overwhelming majority soon became mere "entertainers" and "spent their lives writing about poetry and literature." The sincere awareness of crisis evident in Sorai's thought was soon forgotten, and mere frivolous literary taste began to inundate the school. However, Nankaku's philological and literary studies were not lacking in a lively originality. It was said that "when men of later ages spoke of philology, they always mentioned Nankaku first of all."[8] But the later epigones did no more than blindly imitate the philological writings

[6] *Nihon keizai taiten,* IX, pp. 394–95 (*Keizairoku,* Book I). *Koto* is a harp-like musical instrument, and *go* is a complex game of "checkers."

[7] *Kinsei sōgo* [Writings from recent times], ed. Tsunoda Kan (c. 1822), Book III.

[8] Ibid.

of Li Yu-lin and Wang Yuan-mei, which had constituted only one stage in the development of Sorai's philosophy.

These low standards persisted, both in art and in scholarship. During the Bunsei era (1818–30), Ōta Kinjō (1765–1825) said of them: "These men occupy themselves with tea and *sake* and live a life of dissipation. They amuse themselves with calligraphy, painting, and other playthings. They seduce the sons of the nobility and the rich and lead them into elegance and immorality. As a result, not a few ruin themselves and their families. Upright and prudent men therefore dislike the Confucian scholars of today as they dislike gamblers and pederasts."[9] Severe and slightly unfair though it is, this criticism was not far from the truth. These tendencies probably derive from Sorai's own views on private life, in which he, too, professed his attachment to "refined tastes and literary talent." But these later tendencies differ in their basic tone from the early Ken'en school's interest in literature and art. The latter reflected Genroku culture, which, although garish, revealed throughout an exhilarating desire for life. The former, on the contrary, had something in common with the spirit of decadence and decay of the Bunka (1804–18) and Bunsei (1818–30) eras. This degeneration of the Ken'en school began in the Meiwa (1764–72) and An'ei (1772–81) eras, soon after the deaths of most of Sorai's immediate disciples. As a result, from about the Tenmei era (1781–89), the Ken'en school, which had enjoyed great prestige and popularity, rapidly began to lose its intellectual hegemony. This decline was not induced by the numerous anti-Sorai writings or by Matsudaira Sadanobu's Kansei Edict prohibiting the pursuit of unorthodox studies; it was brought about by the Ken'en school itself.

While Sorai's successors were allowing his school of thought to fall into decay and fragmentation, and the Sung school was still convalescing from the wounds inflicted on it by the school of Ancient Learning, a new school of thought emerged among the Confucians, the so-called Eclectic school, represented by such men as Inoue Kinga (1732–84), Yamamoto Hokuzan (1752–1812), Kameda Bōsai (1752–1826), Hosoi Heishū (1728–1801), Kata-

---

[9] *Nihon zuihitsu zenshū*, XVII, pp. 66–77 (*Gosō Manpitsu*, Book II).

yama Kenzan (1730–82), Yoshida Kōton (1745–98), Minagawa
Kien (1734–1807), and Ōta Kinjō (1765–1825). Their views are
really too diverse to call them a school, but they were on common
ground in rejecting factional extremes and searching for the right
way by "adopting the strong and supplementing the weak" in all
schools of thought. They endeavored to support this position by
extensive investigatory philological readings. Because this school
came into existence as a reaction against the dominance of the
Ken'en school and the factional disputes it caused, it was only
natural that, while they rejected the Sung schools, these scholars
were also strongly opposed to Sorai. On the other hand, they were
all more or less influenced by the Sorai school even though not all
of them had, like Inoue Kinga and Katayama Kenzan, at one time
belonged to that school. To sum up, although these men did display some initiative in criticizing the dogmatic factionalism of the
different schools and insisting on the virtues of free inquiry, eclecticism is eclecticism and implies little creativity, so they contributed very little that was theoretically new.

This kind of eclecticism was not confined to the so-called Eclectic school. After the decline of the Sorai school, it became a general
trend throughout Confucianism, the only differences being differences of degree. The Chu Hsi school could no longer retain the
purity of Chu Hsi philosophy, as it had in the early years of the
Tokugawa period, because the method of thought on which Sung
learning was based had lost its compatibility with existing social
conditions. This will be clear if we compare the style of the Kaitokudō school,[10] which alone among the Chu Hsi factions had
retained its vigor, and the Chu Hsi school that had earlier been
the target of the criticisms of the school of Ancient Learning. The
first head of the Kaitokudō school, Miyake Sekian (1665–1730),
was described as "chimeric" because of the eclecticism of his theories. Itō Tōgai (1670–1736), the son of that formidable foe of Sung
learning, Jinsai, was also invited to lecture at the Kaitokudō
school. The fourth head of the school, Nakai Chikuzan (1730–
1804), was the author of one of the more important anti-Sorai
works, but he also constantly criticized the narrow and dogmatic

---

[10] A Chu Hsi school founded in 1724 in Osaka with the aid of the rich merchants of
that city and the approval of Shogun Yoshimune. (Translator's note.)

outlook of Yamazaki Ansai. In general, the Kaitokudō school did not unilaterally emphasize the Confucian Classics. It also had a high regard for poetry and literature.

This eclectic tendency culminated in *shingaku* (teachings of the heart), which began to gain popularity among the common people around the later years of the Kyōhō era (1716–36). The pivotal ideas of shingaku came from Sung philosophy, but with none of the latter's exclusiveness (*Geschlossenheit*). Shingaku did not just compromise with Shinto, it also embraced Buddhism, for "how could the heart [*kokoro*] that derives from Buddhism and the heart that derives from Confucianism be two different entities? *Regardless of the particular Way from which one's heart derives, as long as one rules benevolently and governs the world and the state on the basis of the heart, all will be well.*"[11] Furthermore, "the teachings of *Buddha, Lao Tzu,* and *Chuang Tzu* are all lessons on how to polish our hearts. They should not be discarded." "The main thing is to avoid resisting [the Ways of] Heaven and Earth by abandoning any philosophy or getting bogged down in any one philosophy."[12] In other words, the shingaku philosophers insisted on adopting all teachings capable of furthering the individual's moral cultivation. This attitude cannot be seen as the same as the tolerance found in Sorai's thought. Sorai rigidly preserved the purity of the Way of the Sages while admitting heterodox ideas in other areas, but shingaku allowed a variety of theoretical systems to enter and penetrate the whole school. A mere broadmindedness without any consistency of principle does not deserve the name of scholarly tolerance. Shingaku may have prided itself on its broad dissemination as a popular moral philosophy, but in theoretical value it did not even rise to the level of the Eclectic school.

This eclecticism, which permeated the entire Confucian world, meant that original development had ceased in Tokugawa Confucianism. The Sorai school, as the last Japanese revival of Confucianism, was also theoretically its high point. The intellectual development of Tokugawa Confucianism, which began with Fujiwara Seika, ended for the time being with Sorai. Near the end

---

[11] *Shingaku dōwashū* [Collection of talks on shingaku] (Tokyo, 1914), p. 524 (*Tohimondō*, Book III).

[12] Ibid., pp. 527–28.

of the Tokugawa period, in the Tenpō era (1830–44), a Confucian scholar[13] reviewed the history of Tokugawa Confucianism and commented: "In the light of this, we can say that the two masters, Seika and Sorai, are the patriarchs of the learning of the Tokugawa period."[14] This was no arbitrary opinion. The decline of the Ken'en school meant that Confucianism itself was relinquishing its leadership in the intellectual world. The school of thought which now opened fire on Confucianism in order to replace it as the hegemonic movement in the intellectual world was the school of National Learning.

II

How should the term National Learning (*kokugaku*) be interpreted? Should it be defined categorically or historically? And if it is defined historically, who was its founder? Was it Toda Mosui (1629–1706), the monk Keichū (1640–1701), Kada-no-Azumamaro (1668–1736), or Kamo Mabuchi (1697–1769)? These questions are too complex to be treated in this study, for each constitutes a theme of its own. For my purposes, I shall define National Learning as the set of intellectual systems developed by these men, in particular the system developed by Kamo Mabuchi and perfected by Motoori Norinaga (1730–1801).[15] Many complex factors went into the makeup of National Learning, and its origins as a school cannot easily be identified, but it cannot be denied that Sorai's theory was an important moment in that makeup,[16] so my object will be to analyze the intellectual relationship

[13] Kayabara Sadame in his *Bōsō manroku* [Random records from a hastily built hut], written in 1829.

[14] *Nihon zuihitsu zenshū*, VII, p. 420.

[15] I believe that National Learning's role in the history of ideas was complete with the emergence of Norinaga's system. In a sense, Atsutane's philosophy pointed National Learning in an entirely different direction. Lacking the space to explain my grounds for this interpretation, I can only bluntly present my conclusion. The discussion that follows, however, should clarify these grounds, though not in a completely satisfactory fashion.

[16] Earlier scholars have noted the Sorai school's influence on National Learning. Muraoka Tsunetsugu's *Motoori Norinaga* (Tokyo, 1911), a classic among interpretative works on Norinaga, was probably the first to deal with the relationship between the two schools in a systematic way. While Professor Muraoka holds that although the Confucian school of Ancient Learning constituted one, but only one, important structural element in the intellectual genealogy of National Learning, Dr. Tsuda Sōkichi

between the two schools. Sorai's influence upon individuals in the school of National Learning can be traced as far back as Kada-no-Azumamaro. But my object is not to trace Sorai's *influence on individual scholars but to ascertain how the process of disintegration of the Chu Hsi mode of thought made way inwardly for the formation of a uniform mode of thought known as National Learning, and as a result to examine the kind of structural relationship that developed between the two*. I shall therefore concentrate on the man who perfected National Learning, Norinaga, mentioning Mabuchi from time to time. Limitation of space, of course, precludes a detailed analysis. I must confine myself to presenting an outline of the fundamental location of the problem.

First it should be noted that this influence or relationship cannot be restricted solely to conscious influence or relationship. Once National Learning had been established on a firm footing in the intellectual world by Norinaga, there were some scholars of this school who consciously acknowledged such a relationship,[17] but at a time when the rapidly ascending school of National Learning was trying to make a thoroughgoing opposition to Confucianism in general its distinctive feature, it is only natural for its members to have adopted the attitude of absolutely denying any influence by any of the Confucian schools in the genealogy of National Learning. Because the scholars of National Learning also referred to their school as the "school of Ancient Learning," the Confucian scholars of the day believed that it originated in the Confucian school of Ancient Learning, and therefore the scholars of National Learning had to make a special issue of the absence of any relation to that school. For instance, in an essay entitled *Aru hito no ieru koto*

---

believes that the school of Ancient Learning, and the Sorai school in particular, played a decisive part in the formation of National Learning. Cf. Tsuda Sōkichi: *Bungaku ni arawaretaru kokumin shisō no kenkyū: heimin bungaku no jidai* [A study of the nation's thought as seen in literature: The literature of the common people], Vol. II. He presents a similar position in his article "Nihon ni okeru gairai shisō ishokushi" [The history of the transplantation of foreign thought into Japan] in *Iwanami kōza: tetsugaku* (Tokyo, 1931–33). Differences as to the extent of this influence notwithstanding, it is a commonly accepted theory among students of the school of National Learning that it was influenced by the Sorai school.

[17] In the genealogy (entitled Onrai) of the Norinaga school prepared by Norinaga's adopted son, Tahei, the names Sorai, Dazai, and Tōgai (the son of Itō Jinsai) are all included. See the appendix in Muraoka Tsunetsugu: *Motoori Norinaga*, 1928 ed.

[According to some people], Norinaga wrote: "Some people say that the writings of the Confucian scholars who study ancient words and terms are responsible for the birth of Ancient Learning, but that is incorrect. Our school of Ancient Learning was founded by Keichū. As for the origin of the Confucian school of Ancient Learning, Itō was active about the same time as Keichū, but the latter preceded the former somewhat. Ogyū was active still later. How then could National Learning have been modeled on them?"[18]

The scholars of National Learning did not just passively insist on the lack of any relationship between the two schools; in attacking Confucianism, they often deliberately directed their fire at the Ken'en school. Dazai Shundai was the object of particularly severe criticism. Attacks on Shundai naturally led to criticism of his master. Mabuchi's magnum opus *Kokuikō* [Consideration of the national will], written to explain the ancient way, is mainly a refutation of Shundai's *Bendōsho* [Discourse on distinguishing the Way]. Hirata Atsutane (1776–1843) made his intellectual debut with a work that was also a rebuttal of the *Bendōsho, Kamōsho* [Critique of a misguided work]. Norinaga did not produce any essay directed solely against Shundai or Sorai, but it is clear that in his acid criticisms of the thinkers who worshiped China, he had the Sorai school primarily in mind. And the target of polemic in his *Kuzubana* [Arrowroot], Ichikawa Kakumei (1739–85), was a Confucian of the Ken'en school. Of course, neither these subjective denials by the scholars of National Learning of their school's relationship with the Sorai school, nor their active criticisms of the latter alter the fact that there was an objective relationship between the two. In my opinion, these denials and criticisms are themselves the best proof of the close similarity between National Learning and the Sorai school. For National Learning, the scholars of the Sorai school resemble the Jews in that "it is precisely because they stand directly before the door of sal-

---

[18] *Zōho Motoori Norinaga zenshū,* VIII, p. 239 (*Tamakatsuma,* 8). This is the only complete collection of Norinaga's works available, and for the sake of convenience I shall use it as a reference for all the Norinaga quotations that follow. However, the quotations are not necessarily all based on the texts of this edition.

146 INTELLECTUAL HISTORY OF TOKUGAWA JAPAN

vation that they are and have been the most reprobate and abandoned."[19]

I shall first consider the relationship between the Sorai school and National Learning in personal terms. Kamo Mabuchi studied Chinese learning under Watanabe Keian, a student of Dazai Shundai. More significant is the close friendship between Mabuchi and Hattori Nankaku. Shimizu Hamaomi (1776–1824), a scholar of National Learning and a student of Murata Harumi (1746–1811), wrote of this relationship: "After the Old Master [Mabuchi] went to the Eastern capital (Edo), a close friendship developed between him and Master Nankaku. The Old Master learned poetry from Master Nankaku and in turn taught him National Learning. They were good competitors in learning. Because Nankaku is buried in this temple, it is said that the Old Master has also selected this site as his burial ground."[20] Remember that Nankaku was one of the heirs to the private aspect of Sorai's philosophy; the importance of this will emerge later. Although Norinaga did not have any immediate personal contacts with any member of the Ken'en school, the man he went to Kyoto to study under and from whom he acquired the major part of his Confucian education was Hori Keizan, who, under the name of Kutsu Keizan, appears as one of Sorai's correspondents in the latter's *Sorai-shū* [Collected works]. Keizan was originally a Confucian of the Chu Hsi school. Perhaps under the influence of his correspondence with Sorai, perhaps because he began to associate with Sorai after he had moved away from the Chu Hsi mode of thought, and probably for a combination of both reasons, his thought came to resemble Sorai's very closely.

For example, Keizan argued that *li* (Principle) cannot be an absolute standard: "Ultimately, although *li* seems to be the Ultimate Principle, it is not so. Since it is an abstract principle, it can be used in any way whatsoever. It is like being able to call a white thing black or any other color. It is all a matter of one's intentions. People speak of comprehending the true *li* but this is possible only for Sages. For a person with ordinary brains it

---

[19] G. W. F. Hegel: *Phänomenologie des Geistes, Sämtliche Werke,* ed. H. Glockner, II, p. 265 (trans. J. Baillie [Oxford, 1931], p. 366).
[20] *Nihon zuihitsu taisei* (Tokyo, 1927–31), IV, p. 752 (*Hakubaku-hitsuwa*).

could be interpreted in any way he pleases."[21] He also emphasized the importance of studying the meaning of words. "Regardless of what is said, unless a man thoroughly understands the meanings of words, he cannot understand the true intentions of the Sages. It may be very interesting to listen to those who lecture on the Confucian classics present various interpretations and wag their tongues as if they were omniscient, but if the meanings of words are misunderstood, however embellished their speech . . . . what they say is frequently not in accord with the intentions of the Sages."[22] Moreover, he stressed the political character of the sages and rites and music, observing: "In ancient times the term 'Sages' was generally used to refer to emperors who governed the world virtuously. The only common man to be called a Sage was Confucius. . . . Even the *Book of Rites* states that 'the founder [*sakusha*] is called a Sage.' The term 'founder' signifies the emperor of an epoch. It applies to a man who has founded the rites and music of a country, edified the people, and rectified their manners and morals. Only an emperor can found rites and music."[23] These statements accord all but completely with the positions of the Sorai school.

Particularly interesting is Keizan's rejection of moral rigorism: "In examining man's five basic relationships, I find that no other relationship exceeds that of husband and wife in the depth of human sentiments." "It is a grave mistake to regard all desires as evil. Human desire is a part of human feelings. Anyone who has no desires is inhuman. . . . He is just like a piece of wood or stone."[24] He then openly criticized the Chu Hsi philosophy of art. "In studying the Confucian classics, I follow more or less the Chu Hsi school, but where the interpretation of poetry is concerned, I find that Chu Hsi's commentaries fail to grasp the essence. In his commentary on the phrase 'thought without evil' in the Confucian *Analects,* Chu Hsi states that this means the rewarding of good and the punishment of evil. But this concept—rewarding good and punishing evil—is a precept found in the *Spring and Autumn Annals*

[21] *Nihon keizai taiten,* XVII, p. 324 (*Fujingen*).
[22] Ibid., p. 319.
[23] Ibid., p. 344.
[24] Ibid., pp. 370–71.

and not in the *Book of Odes*."[25] His position was to seek to liberate art from the control of ethics. "Of course we consider poems that do not stem from evil intentions to be good, but among the three hundred verses in the *Book of Odes*, there are many poems which were the products of evil intentions. . . . Regardless of good or bad intentions, *these poems are spontaneous expressions of the true sentiments of the composer*."[26] "Japanese poems [*waka*] are basically the same as Chinese-style poems [*shi*]. . . . Both their seeds come to life deep in the human heart. Upon coming into contact with all sorts of visible and audible things, these seeds then blossom forth in words which are spontaneous and unplanned."[27] Thus Keizan reveals Sorai's influence in his method of argument as well as in his manner of expression. Nor should we overlook the fact that Norinaga spent the impressionable years of his youth under this teacher.[28] We shall see later how much Sorai's philosophy of art, transmitted through Keizan, affected Norinaga's views on *mono no aware* (the "sadness of things"). However, although these direct and indirect personal contacts between the Sorai school and the school of National Learning reinforced the essential relationship between them which I discuss below, the relationship was not based on these contacts.

Let us now refocus our attention on the vicissitudes of the Confucian "Way" from the Chu Hsi school to the Sorai school, i.e., on the process outlined in the previous chapters. The Way of the Chu Hsi school was founded upon the Principle of Heaven, earth, and nature. This Principle permeates heaven and man, it encompasses society and nature. It is a normative standard as well as a (natural) law. It defines "what ought to be" but it is also "what exists," i.e., Original Nature (*honzen no sei*). But as a result of the disintegration of the continuative mode of thought, which I have traced through Sokō, Jinsai, and Ekken, the different elements of this absolute, all-embracing Chu Hsi Way gradually became independent. The Way of Man split away from the Way of Heaven, normative standards from human nature, and "what ought to be"

[25] Ibid., p. 364.
[26] Ibid., p. 363.
[27] Ibid., p. 362.
[28] On Keizan's relations with Norinaga, see Kōno Shōzō: "Motoori Norinaga to Hori Keizan," in his *Kokugaku no kenkyū* [A study of National Learning] (Tokyo, 1943).

from "what (naturally) exists." But even for Jinsai, who gave the most detailed theoretical justification for these divisions, the Way remained transcendental, being an idea "which does not depend upon the existence or nonexistence of man."

Sorai was the first person to deny that the Way is an ultimate principle, by making it dependent on certain human beings, the sages. But because these human beings were raised to an other-worldly level, the Way retained its absolute and universal validity. At this point a warning sounded for the development of the Confucian Way. Its validity no longer lay in the fact that it conforms to the true principles of nature, nor in the fact that it is in itself an ultimate idea, but only in the fact that it was established by the sages. What makes the Way the Way is not Principle, but authority: "*Autoritas, non veritas, facit legem!*" (Hobbes). But authority is only authoritative for someone who believes in that authority. For the Sorai school, anyone who does not believe in the authority of the sages cannot possibly be persuaded to accept the truth of the Way. In the last analysis, Sorai's elaborate system turns out to depend absolutely on one point, namely: "This ignorant old man does not believe in Shākyamuni Buddha, he believes in the Sages" (see p. 96). How precarious! Remove this keystone, and the Way of the Sages, and with it the entire system, instantly crumbles. The sages are the political rulers of ancient China. Why should a Way created by historically and geographically restricted personalities be thus revered and respected? The Sorai school inevitably led those with the capacity to reason things out by stepping outside the shell of the Confucian mode of thought to this question. As a result, this was the point the scholars of National Learning first attacked.

As Mabuchi put it, "The Way of the scholars of the land of T'ang is a very puny thing *founded by men, distorting the spirit of heaven and earth.*"[29] "Man makes transitory institutions, but these must differ according to each country and each place, just as the trees and the grass, the birds and the animals, differ from one another."[30] Therefore, "it is foolish to think that when institutions

[29] *Zōtei Kamo Mabuchi zenshū* [Collected works of Kamo Mabuchi, enlarged edition] (Tokyo, 1927–32), X, p. 359 (*Kokuikō*).
[30] Ibid., p. 369.

are once established they should be upheld by the people under heaven for ages to come."[31] Here the Sorai school's contention that the Way is a once and for all historical invention is the beachhead for an attack upon Confucianism in general.

Norinaga took it further. He defined the sages as follows: "The Chinese called sages men who won the support of the people by their authority and the profundity of their wisdom, who conquered other people's lands and had well-laid plans to prevent others from conquering their own lands, and who, for a time, governed their lands well and established patterns for later generations to emulate."[32] Thus, although, like Sorai, he defined the sages in political terms, he immediately reduced them from figures of otherworldly validity to political usurpers. He said of the Way of the Sages: "Now then, *what was invented and established by the Sages was called the Way*. Thus the ultimate purpose of the Chinese notion of the Way can be reduced to two points: conquer the land of others, and prevent others from conquering one's own land."[33] Like Sorai, he saw that the essence of the Way was its political purpose, but in content he turned Sorai's theory upside down. For Sorai, the fact that the Way is an invention (*sakui*) of the sages was what made it absolute, while for Norinaga the same fact was the reason for rejecting it. Of course, the scholars of National Learning had begun to question the value of Confucianism before they were exposed to the Sorai school. Ever since Keichū had begun his study of the Japanese classics, they had been becoming more and more conscious of the dichotomy between Confucian morality and the ancient spirit of Japan. But it was undoubtedly the Sorai school that influenced the direction their criticism of Confucianism took. This is one negative relation between the Sorai school and National Learning.

Another important negative relationship involves the intellectual purity of the Sorai school. At this point I must briefly review the relationship between Confucianism and Shinto from the beginning of the Tokugawa period. I have already noted that the independence acquired by Confucianism in the Tokugawa period

---

[31] Ibid., p. 370.
[32] *Zōhō Motoori Norinaga zenshū*, I, p. 54 (*Naobi no mitama*).
[33] Ibid.

was accompanied by a violent anti-Buddhism. This tendency encouraged a group of early Tokugawa Confucian scholars to attempt to free Shinto, which had had to compromise with Buddhism as Sannō Shinto and Ryōbu Shinto,[34] etc., from Buddhist influence, and to link it instead with Confucianism. The beginnings of such an endeavor can be seen in the writings of Fujiwara Seika, the founder of Tokugawa Confucianism. He wrote: "The ultimate objectives of Japanese Shinto are to rectify the heart [*kokoro*], to be compassionate towards everyone, and to perform acts of benevolence. The ultimate objectives of the Way of Yao and Shun are the same. In China, this Way is called Confucianism. In Japan, it is called Shinto. The name is different, but the spirit is the same."[35] It was Hayashi Razan, however, who envisaged a union of Shinto and Confucianism on a grand scale: "Some people ask what is the difference between Shinto and Confucianism. My reply would be that they are one in principle. They only differ in effect. . . . The Way of the Kings in another form is the Way of the Gods [Shinto], and the Way of the Gods in another form is the Way, that is, the Confucian Way. It is not the heretical Way. Buddhism is the heretical Way."[36] He established his own school of Shinto (*Ritō Shinchi Shintō*) with intentions that were openly antagonistic to Buddhism. In content Razan's Shinto is entirely dependent on Chu Hsi philosophy: "Shinto is *li*. Nothing can exist outside *li*. *Li* constitutes the truth in nature." Razan remained a Confucian all his life. Yamazaki Ansai went further. Although at first a Chu Hsi scholar, he ultimately abandoned Confucianism and became an outright proponent of Shinto. But in his Suika Shinto,[37] even he used categories clearly taken from Sung philosophy such as li, ch'i, yin and yang, and the five elements when interpreting, or rather distorting, the *Nihon shoki* (the "Chronicle of Japan," completed in A.D. 720).

[34] Sannō Shinto was affiliated with the Tendai sect, and Ryōbu Shinto with the Shingon sect. (Translator's note.)

[35] *Nihon rinri ihen*, VII, p. 40 (*Chiyomotogusa*).

[36] *Razan Hayashi sensei bunshū*, Book LXVI (*Kyōto shisekikaihon*, II, pp. 360–61).

[37] Also referred to as Suiga Shinto. The term was coined from two words that occur in a Shinto text: "Divine Grace (shin*sui*) depends first of all on prayer; divine protection (myō*ga*) has its beginning in uprightness." D. C. Holtom: *The National Faith of Japan* (New York, 1965), pp. 42–43. (Translator's note.) The preceding Razan quotation is from his *Shintō denju*.

At the same time, traditional Shinto moved closer to Confucianism. This is not difficult to grasp if we recall the commanding position of Confucianism in Tokugawa Japan. For example, Watarai Nobuyoshi (1615–90), who was responsible for the rebirth of Ise Shinto,[38] rejected the Buddhist and Taoist elements that had become attached to it but upheld the unity of Shinto and Confucianism: "The objectives of Shinto and Confucianism are the same so the teachings of these Ways should also be the same."[39] The term "Shinto of the Rationalist School (i.e., the Chu Hsi school)," applied to the Shinto school of Yoshikawa Koretaru (1616–94), who had emerged from Yoshida Shinto[40] to become the bakufu's official in charge of Shinto, amply demonstrates the compromising posture of Shinto towards Confucianism. But the rise and popularity of the Sorai school paralyzed this active trend towards a fushion of Shinto and Confucianism like an electric shock.

True to his logical conclusions, Sorai, who looked on the Way of the Sages discovered by the study of ancient words and terms as absolute and staunchly opposed its contamination by any "latter-day" distortions or heretical ideas, absolutely denied the very existence of Shinto. However, his historical awareness led him to acknowledge the historically specific emergence of the Way of the Sages, and therefore that "there is no such thing as Shinto, but these spirits and demons must be worshiped. The Way of the Sages expects those of us born in this country to revere the gods of the country" (see p. 99). But Dazai Shundai, having inherited the public aspect from Sorai, and confident that it represented the whole of Sorai's system, insisted upon the absolute validity of the Way of the Sages in such a mechanical fashion that he pushed Sorai's denial of the existence of Shinto to extremes. He held that Shinto was no more than "the Way of the Sorcerers." "For someone who is not a sorcerer, it is of no importance to know about it.

---

[38] Also called Watarai Shinto from the family name of the priests who propagated this school. The Watarai priesthood associated itself with the Shinto shrine at Ise, hence the name Ise Shinto. Holtom, op. cit., p. 41. (Translator's note.)

[39] *Nihon seishin bunken sōsho: Shintō* [Collection of literature on the Japanese spirit: Shinto] (Tokyo, 1938), I, p. 30 (*Yōfukki*).

[40] Also known as Yuiitsu Shinto and formulated by priests of the Yoshida family. Yuiitsu Shinto emphasized its purity and freedom from contamination by Confucianism and Buddhism. Holtom, op. cit., p. 39. (Translator's note.)

It is not a matter to be studied by gentlemen."[41] The religious observance of a gentleman, he argued, should consist "only of daily respect shown to Heaven, fear of crimes, upholding the proper rules of conduct, and performance of benevolent and virtuous deeds." He compared his faith in Confucius to that of members of the Ikkō sect (True Pure Land Sect of Buddhism), "who believe only in the one Buddha, Amida, placing no faith in any other Buddhas or gods."[42]

Once so coldheartedly rejected by the Ken'en school, which dominated the Confucian world, Shinto had no choice but to establish its own independent position. Taking advantage of this situation, the scholars of National Learning declared war on all the old Shinto sects. Thus, ironically, the scholars of National Learning, who upheld pristine Shinto, and the Sorai school formed a common front, but from wholly different standpoints, against the move to fuse Shinto and Confucianism. Norinaga remarked of Sorai's denial of Shinto's existence: "What the proponents of latter-day Shinto profess are all fabrications of Confucians and Buddhists. They simply substitute such terms as 'founding gods' and *Takamagahara* [the Land of the Gods] [for Confucian and Buddhist terms]. The substance of what they teach is no different from Confucian and Buddhist teachings. They have not established an independent Way of their own. *Ogyū is entirely correct when he says there is no such thing as a Way of Shinto.*"[43] On Shundai, he wrote: "In my opinion, Dazai's *Bendōsho* is very reasonable. . . . Many generations of Shintoists have propounded a Shinto that they have invented out of envy of the teachings of the Confucians and Buddhists. . . . It is not true Shinto. For this reason I agree with Dazai. *He is indeed a true Confucian.*"[44] Thus he praised the consistency of Shundai's position.

But Norinaga's approval of Sorai and his school, founded upon a viewpoint totally different from that of the latter, was, we might say, a paradoxical approval, and therefore in the next instant it turned into violent disapproval:

[41] *Nihon rinri ihen*, VI, p. 208 (*Bendōsho*).
[42] Ibid., pp. 291–92 (*Seigaku mondō*).
[43] *Zōho Motoori Norinaga zenshū*, VI, pp. 121–22 (*Suzunoya tōmon roku*).
[44] Ibid., X, p. 140 (*Kōgodan*).

Now although Ogyū and Dazai were correct in their judgements of Shintoists of later generations, they were ignorant of the obvious fact that there is a true Shinto other than that propounded by these so-called Shintoists. Moreover, these men deemed it wise to speak as if China alone were worthy of respect, to claim that it is superior in all things, and to hold our imperial land in extremely low regard, insisting that it is a barbarous country. . . . Although they too were fortunate enough to have been born in this imperial land and to have been exposed to the scripture of the Gods . . . they failed to comprehend and realize that the Way of the Gods [Shinto] is superior to the Ways of foreign lands, and that it is truly the grand and just Way. They even disparaged and vilified it. What could they have been thinking of?[45]

This criticism is not completely just. As we have already noted, Sorai did not look upon any particular country, in this case China, as the "most superior land." However, it is indisputably clear that the intellectual purity of the Sorai school had, through its views on Shinto, served to mediate negatively between it and National Learning.

III

The fact that from the beginning of the Tokugawa period Shinto had depended on Confucianism, particularly on the Chu Hsi school, for its theoretical foundations meant that its conception of the gods acquired characteristics common to those of Confucianism. Sung philosophy held li to be an ultimate reality inherent in each individual thing in the universe that, while transcending these individual entities, endows them with their value. When, therefore, the Sung mode of thought was made the foundation of Shinto, the latter acquired a more or less pantheistic, or rather panpsychic, structure. Razan, whose Ritō Shinchi Shinto held that "outside the heart [kokoro] there is no separate God or separate li"; Watarai Nobuyoshi, who said, "God is of course the master of our hearts, so clearly God is I and I am God; there is no distinction at all";[46] and Yoshikawa Koretaru, who believed that God "turns

---

[45] Ibid., VI, p. 122 (Suzunoya tōmon roku).
[46] Nihon seishin bunken sōsho, p. 36 (Yōfukki, Book I).

out to be without material substance when we seek to grasp His physical form, but since all things acquire their physical forms from Him, He structures all things without having a physical form of His own; this God is Kunitokotachi-no-mikoto, the founder of the earth, and his spirit inhabits even the minutest particle"[47]— all endowed their gods with pantheistic characteristics. Even when they spoke of gods in anthropomorphic terms, they conceived them as continuous with an impersonal li. Even Suika Shinto with its strong irrational and religious coloring was no exception. Although its conception of God was not clear-cut,[48] the fact that it explained the origin of the universe in terms of li, yin and yang, and the five elements and employed the term Yuiitsu Shinto (One and Only Shinto), not just to distinguish itself from Ryōbu Shinto (Dual Shinto)[49] but also to emphasize the oneness of heaven and man, testifies to this.

How does the theoretical structure of pristine Shinto compare with this? Insofar as Mabuchi rejected the "narrow rationalism" of Confucianism, he thoroughly resisted any attempt to provide the "Ancient Way" with a rational foundation, but, on the other hand, this led to an emphasis on inaction reminiscent of Lao-tse's "drifting with Heaven and Earth." As a result, the natural character of the Way was explained in terms of the cycle of the four seasons, and pristine Shinto began to acquire the qualities of an atheistic natural philosophy.[50] In other words, li was replaced by nature as the normative standard for the world. The foundation of the Way was still impersonal, however.

But with Norinaga there was a great transformation. Basing himself on faithful inductions from the examples in the *Kojiki* (the

[47] Ibid., p. 21 (*Shintō taiichū*).

[48] Cf. Takeoka Katsunari: *Kinsei-shi no hatten to Kokugakusha no undō* [The development of modern history and the activities of the scholars of National Learning] (Tokyo, 1927), pp. 221ff.

[49] Ryōbu Shinto arose out of an attempt to reconcile the Buddhism of the Shingon sect with Shinto. Ryōbu (Dual) refers to "the two phases of reality differentiated in Shingon metaphysics, namely, matter and mind, or the male and the female, or the dynamic and potential, aspects of observable things." Holtom, op. cit., p. 36. (Translator's note.)

[50] This definition is based on Muraoka Tsunetsugu's "Shisōka to shite no Kamo Mabuchi to Motoori Norinaga," in his *Nihon shisōshi kenkyū* [Studies in the history of Japanese thought] (Tokyo, 1940). Of course, to say that it was "atheistic" does not mean that it was directly so. It merely means that it was not theistic.

"Record of Ancient Things," the first Japanese historical work, completed in 712), he held that in addition to the many anthropomorphic gods found in the ancient Japanese classics, "such things as birds, beasts, trees, grass, seas and mountains, and everything else which is unique, possesses superior virtues, and is awe-inspiring"[51] should be classified as *kami* (gods or superior beings). He rejected any rational interpretation or ethical evaluation of these gods, but because he sought to make two gods, Taka-mi-Musubi (High Producing God) and Kami-mi-Musubi (Divine Producing God), the supreme source of all these gods and of the world, he had to change the basis of the Ancient Way completely. "When we inquire into the nature of this Way, we find that it is not the natural way of heaven and earth, nor a way established by man. This sacred Way was initiated by our ancestral Gods, Izanagi-no-Mikoto [Male who invites] and Izanami-no-Mikoto [Female who invites], in accordance with the wishes of Taka-mi-Musubi, and was received, preserved, and transmitted by Ama-terasu-Ō-mi-kami [the Sun Goddess]. That is why it is called the Way of the Gods."[52] The Way then is no longer Taoist nature, nor is it an invention (sakui) of the sages; it arose as a creation of the ancestral gods. According to Norinaga, "The term 'god' used *in China is merely an empty principle and does not refer to anything that actually exists*. But the gods of our imperial country are the ancestors of the Emperor who reigns today. They are quite different from gods founded on empty principles."[53] He thus made clear his thoroughgoing opposition to all abstract, idealized views of the gods.

Let us now consider how the fate of the Chu Hsi mode of thought, the foundation for the pantheistic structure of pristine Shinto, was affected by subsequent developments in Confucian thinking. In the preceding chapters, I have shown that the disintegration of Chu Hsi rationalism resulted first in the separation of heaven and man, and second in the downgrading of the lawlike character of heaven (the Way of Heaven) and the highlighting of its concrete anthropomorphic character (the Will of Heaven). This trend is already clearly discernible in Jinsai's system, but

[51] *Zōho Motoori Norinaga zenshū*, I, p. 135 (*Kojiki den*, Book III).
[52] Ibid., p. 61 (*Naobi no mitama*).
[53] Ibid., pp. 61–62.

although he rejected the li of Chu Hsi philosophy, he attributed the ultimate validity of the Way itself to "nature" and hence never fully developed the concept of the Will of Heaven. For Sorai, the Way's validity depends entirely on the personalities (the sages) whose invention it is. Moreover, these personalities are linked to heaven and given otherworldly status; the personified heaven completely excludes the impersonal li. Here there is a close agreement between the modes of thought of the Sorai and Norinaga schools. Not only was there an external link between the Sorai school and the Norinaga school through the former's rejection of Shinto, but by destroying the pantheistic structure of the Confucian thought on which Tokugawa Shinto had based itself, it gave internal assistance to the reforms Norinaga's school instituted in Shinto. But because Norinaga brought the sages down to earth, he consciously made a categorical distinction between the structure of a mode of thought for which the Way is a creation of the ancestral gods of Japan, and the structure of Sorai's mode of thought, expressed in the simple statement that the true way "is not a Way *founded by human beings.*"

For the Norinaga school, it was no longer necessary to ascribe an anthropomorphic character to heaven. Its view of heaven was therefore primarily spatial: "In the end Heaven is merely the country in which the heavenly gods live. It does not have a heart [*kokoro*], so there can be no such thing as the Will of Heaven. Revering and respecting Heaven without revering and respecting the Gods is like holding the palace in awe and respect without holding the ruler in awe and respect."[54] Here Norinaga clashed directly with Sorai, who had argued: "Is it not clearly evident that Heaven has a heart [*kokoro*]?" Nevertheless, if, instead of criticizing the Sorai school from on high like Norinaga, we try to understand it from the inside, we have to admit that the position of the sages or of heaven in Sorai's system of thought and the position of the gods in Norinaga's have much in common, inasmuch as Sorai, by linking the sages with heaven, endowed them with an otherworldliness that separated them qualitatively from ordinary men, and inversely, by linking heaven with the sages, turned it into a

[54] Ibid., VIII, p. 22 (*Tamakatsuma,* 1).

personalized entity underlying the way. The content of Norinaga's Way was indeed completely different from that of Sorai's, but he adopted the same method of thought in establishing its foundation. He adopted Sorai's criticisms of Chu Hsi rationalism in toto, using them as weapons for the destruction of Confucianism and all Confucian modes of thought (i.e., of what he called "*karagokoro*," or the "Chinese spirit").

According to Norinaga, the origins of everything—heaven and earth, nature and human affairs—can be traced to the gods: "All the actions of the Gods cannot be fully understood by man in terms of ordinary principles. Even the wisest man's intellect is restricted, minute. It cannot comprehend matters beyond the limits of its competence."[55] In spite of this, "*the Sages used their private intellects* to formulate all sorts of theories, such as *yin* and *yang*, trigrams and hexagrams, and propounded the principles of all things in the universe. But these are all fabrications based on blind guesses. When they speak of the Way of Heaven and the Gods, *they are merely using these terms on the basis of subjective assumptions in terms of* li. It is not clear to them whether these things exist or not."[56] This is clearly a perversion of the argument Sorai had used against the Sung Confucians: "Scholars of later ages delight in exercising their private intellects without any restraint. . . . They express opinions based on their subjective views, and confidently expound the theory that Heaven is the same as Principle (*li*). . . . They base their concept of Heaven upon their own subjective notions and claim to 'understand Heaven.' Is this not the extremity of irreverence?" (See p. 80, above). Norinaga even invoked Sorai positively in his criticisms of Ryōbu Shinto:

Ryōbu Shinto professes to adopt the strong points and eliminate the weaknesses of the three teachings [i.e., Confucianism, Buddhism, and Shinto]. . . . What standard did these scholars use in determining the strengths and weaknesses? Did they not rely entirely on their mediocre minds? . . . They assert that because all things can be understood in terms of an easily accessible *li*, we can quite clearly discern their strengths and weaknesses. But this assertion is all the

---

[55] Ibid., V, p. 460 (*Kuzubana*, Book I).
[56] Ibid., p. 486 (*Kuzubana*, Book II).

more mystifying to me. *What they call* li *is not something clearly fixed,* it is not something readily comprehensible to the human intellect. Hence *a Confucian should define* li *in terms of the theories of the ancient Confucian Sages,* and a Buddhist should do so by using the theories of Buddha. What should we call a Way that seeks to select the strengths and weaknesses of Confucianism and Buddhism? It is a Way based not on any objective criteria, but arbitrarily established by individuals.[57] (See pp. 92–94, above).

Thus the Sorai and Norinaga schools were on common ground in making otherworldly personalities the ultimate ground for their Ways and in rejecting the normative standards of an impersonal li. This gave rise to a further important relationship between them. The Sorai school had taken the manifold consequences that had been nurtured slowly during the course of the disintegration of Chu Hsi rationalism in Japan as far as was possible within the Confucian framework. The Norinaga school was able to take them much further, for it had eliminated the final restraints on the Sorai school, restraints that stemmed from the essential character of Confucianism itself.[58] On the other hand, of course, criticisms of Neo-Confucian rationalism had arisen with the development of National Learning under the leadership of Toda Mosui and Keichū, either independently or else partly under the influence of the Sorai school, in succession to Azumamaro and Mabuchi. Thus the Sorai and Norinaga schools encouraged the same results, but the fact that they maintained and developed these results on the basis of essentially similar systems of thought links them together in a unique manner. I shall now make a simple survey of these results, bearing in mind what has been discussed so far.

The first of these results was the inheritance or development of a philological and positivistic methodology. The influence of Sorai's study of ancient words and terms is clear in both Azumamaro and Mabuchi. *Of particular significance in the relationship between Sorai and*

---

[57] Ibid., X, pp. 141–42 (*Kōgodan*).

[58] However, the "discovery of politics," which is also a consequence of the disintegration of Chu Hsi moral rationalism and constitutes the most distinctive feature of the Sorai school, cannot be detected at all in Norinaga's system. The reason for this should become clear in the discussion of the place of National Learning in the history of Japanese thought that follows.

Norinaga is the fact that the desire to remove all subjective arbitrariness from philological analysis went hand in hand with the attitude that places absolute faith in personified entities, an attitude that was basic to both the Sorai and Norinaga schools. When Sorai stated, "The Way of the Ancients is contained in books and consists of sentences. If one is able to comprehend the sentences correctly and read the books *just as they are written, without injecting one's own ideas into them, the will of the ancients will be clear.* But one must realize that the meanings of words and sentences change with the passage of time. Confucians of later ages . . . *attempted to understand the Way of the Sages in terms of their own knowledge and beliefs,* and therefore produced arbitrary interpretations of the Way,"[59] his position is simply a counterpart to the attitude revealed in his statement that "my humble desire is to preserve a deep faith in the Sages and even if something may seem improper to me, I shall carry it out in the conviction that so long as it is the Way of the Sages, it could not be improper" (see p. 96, above). In the same way, when Norinaga argued, "It is indeed a sad thing when someone shows off his cleverness by distorting the writings of the Age of the Gods and tries to relate them to the Chinese outlook,"[60] and "There is no way of knowing things that have not been transmitted to us. We must be content to remain ignorant of things that cannot be known,"[61] and when, in interpreting the classics, especially the *Kojiki* and the *Nihon shoki*, he abandoned all a priori categories and accepted in toto all sorts of illogical and immoral features as part of the content of the ancients' consciousness,[62] his method of thought is intimately related to an irrational faith in the ancestral gods, a faith manifested in such expressions as "How can anyone be so presumptuous as to contest the actions of the Gods when he has only man's insignifi-

[59] *Nihon rinri ihen,* VI, pp. 189–90 (*Tōmonsho,* Book III).

[60] *Zōho Motoori Norinaga zenshū,* X, p. 110 (*Tama-hoko no momo-uta*). *Sakashira ni | kamiyo no mifumi | tokimagete | kara no kokoro ni | nasu ga kanashisa.*

[61] Ibid., p. 111. *Tsutae naki | koto wa shirubeki | yoshi mo nashi | shiraenu koto wa | shirazute o aran.*

[62] I am not concerned with how thoroughly this positivist methodology was actually put into practice, but with the significance, from the standpoint of the history of thought, of the fact that Norinaga adopted such an attitude. This holds true whenever I use the terms "positivism" or "from the standpoint of philological studies" in the discussion that follows. The individual cases in which Norinaga made subjective comments on the text of the *Kojiki* do not detract from the significance of this methodology for the history of thought.

cant strength?"[63] and "Although man is intelligent, there is a limit to his understanding. How can he comprehend what was accomplished in the Age of the Gods?"[64]

Sorai, who denied the a priori character of the Way and made it dependent on the sages, was able to carry out Confucian philological studies by removing the Neo-Confucian distortions embedded in Jinsai's "study of ancient meanings." But philological studies original to National Learning were first initiated by Norinaga when, going even further than Mabuchi, who had counterposed nature to Confucian "cleverness" (*sakashira*), he denied the ascendancy of all ideas, including that of nature. Just as Sorai placed "things" above "righteousness" and "facts and words" above "clever arguments," Norinaga argued that "the nature of all things in this world can be ascertained by investigating 'remnants' [*ato*] from the Age of the Gods."[65] He held that the primary object of ancient studies was the investigation of these "remnants," or vestiges, of the Age of the Gods. Moreover, while Sorai still viewed the Way clarified by the study of ancient words and terms as "teachings" or "skills" devised by the Early Kings, for Norinaga the vestiges were not merely steps in the investigation of the Way, but themselves constituted the Way and should under no circumstances be turned into normative teachings. The Ancient Way, he explained, "is merely, in an ordinary sense, *the way to reach things*. It is the practice of foreign countries to ascribe the principle of things and all sorts of teachings to different Ways."[66] He therefore concluded that "the fact that Shinto has no books containing [moral] teachings is an indication that it is the True Way. Basically all the ways which endeavor to teach and lead people are not just and proper ways. . . . The way that has no teachings is the one that should be valued. The way whose purpose is to teach [moralize] is a puny, man-made way."[67]

An approach that rejects all teachings and adheres only to facts

[63] *Zōho Motoori Norinaga zenshū*, X, p. 112 (*Tama-hoko no momo-uta*). *Ofuke naku | hito no iyashiki | chikara mote | kami no nasuwaza | arasoiemeya.*

[64] Ibid., p. 111. *Sakashikedo | hito no satori wa | kakiri aru o | kamiyo no shiwaza | ika de hakaramu.*

[65] Ibid., p. 112. *Yo no naka no | aru omobuki wa | nanigoto mo | kamiyo no ato o | tazunete shirayu.*

[66] Ibid., I, p. 53 (*Naobi no mitama*).

[67] Ibid., VI, p. 122 (*Suzunoya tōmon roku*).

(things) brings with it significant changes in the traditional concept of learning. Teaching presupposes a subject, the teacher, and an object, the disciple. When teaching is regarded as the essence of learning, the teacher's transmission of knowledge is of fundamental importance. Until then learning had been based more or less on this tradition. But the emergence of a philological and inductive method slowly undermined it. Scholars of National Learning had, since Keichū's day, criticized the court poets for accepting the transmission of knowledge from master to disciples, and the same tendency was reflected in Confucianism in Sorai's scathing attack on the system of education by lectures. When he rejected all norms that deviate to any degree from the facts, Norinaga clearly raised this revolution to methodological consciousness. Learning became learning the truth instead of studying teachings. The relationship between subject and object changed from a relation between master and disciple into one between a discipline and its object. Norinaga praised Mabuchi because he constantly admonished his students not to be bound by the theories of their teachers: "This is one of the reasons why my master was an outstanding scholar." "When, simply because what is expressed is the opinion of his teacher, someone remains silent, concealing and glossing over [its defects] in order to make it appear good even though he knows it is wrong, he is *showing respect only for his teacher, and giving no thought to the Way*." He therefore instructed his students: "If those who study under me encounter worthy opinions after my time, they must not be unduly influenced by my personal opinions. They should point out my mistakes and help disseminate better ideas. The sole reason for my teaching others is the clarification of the Way. . . . It is not my wish to have my students respect me to no purpose while they give no thought to the Way."[68] The better to appreciate the value of this attitude towards learning in a period of feudal education, let us compare it with the prevalent lecturing method, as it appeared to Sorai. "The students accept what their teacher holds to be correct and worthwhile. They transcribe the words of their teacher, without changing a single word in the explanation he presents. In extreme cases, some

[68] Ibid., VIII, pp. 61–62 (*Tamakatsuma*, 2).

will jot down, 'The master coughed at this point in the chapter,' or 'When he came to this phrase in this sentence, he struck his fan once,' and so on. They imitate their master's manner of speech, intonation, and even his facial expressions and manner of dress. . . . Can anyone be more misguided than this?''[69]

The second relationship between Sorai and Norinaga, after their common denial of the supremacy of impersonal ideas, is their historical consciousness. We have discovered that in practice Chu Hsi rationalism led to a rigid normative revivalism; for example: "Prior to the Three Dynasties, all things were derived from the Principle of Heaven. Since the Three Dynasties, everything has been derived from human desires." But with the rise of the school of Ancient Learning there came an awareness of the historical mutability of norms. We have seen that the moralistic Neo-Confucian interpretation of history was almost eliminated by Sorai, who made the Way dependent on the historical actions of the sages. Norinaga, who rejected any normative interpretation of the Way, could be expected to advance Sorai's historical consciousness even further; he certainly could not accept the Neo-Confucian approach to history. Not only did he reject the view that history should serve to reward good and punish evil (judged by human standards), he also opposed any rationalization of history in terms of suprahuman standards (e.g., the Will of Heaven, the Way of Heaven or the Gods). He deliberately cited historical examples in which good perished while evil prospered. The following statement reveals his completely positivist position on this question: "Now, it is said that it is the Way of Heaven to favor the good and punish the immoral. This is a well-known fact understood even by a child who does not know a single letter. It is certainly a reasonable notion. But although these words may *accord with rational principles, the actual facts do not bear out this theory*."[70] This fidelity to historical fact, together with the faith that led him to place all worldly things under the control of the gods, led him to oppose any ethical conception of those gods. In his opinion, the most typically evil god was Magatsubi-no-kami,[71] but even the good

---

[69] *Nihon bunko,* III, p. 20 (*Shibunkokujitoku*).

[70] *Zōho Motoori Norinaga zenshū,* V, p. 474 (*Kuzubana,* Book I).

[71] A god born of the pollution of the land of the dead. (Translator's note.)

gods did not always do good things. "It would be like Confucian or Buddhist learning to reason that there is not a tinge of evil in the actions of the good gods. We should realize that the gods are merely above ordinary people."[72]

As we have already seen, Sorai rejected the Sung scholars' definition of the sages as "identical with the Principle of Heaven and without even a speck of human desire," arguing that "the Sages, too, are no more than human beings. Men's virtues differ with their natures. Even Sages are not identical in their virtues" (see p. 95, above). Sorai's claim that "Sages, too, are no more than human beings" does not contradict his absolutization of them. On the contrary, the two claims are complementary. In the same way, Norinaga's refusal to make the gods ethical was the natural consequence of his intention to place them beyond human value judgements. It is amazing how close Sorai and Norinaga came in their modes of thought after their liberation from Neo-Confucian rationalism, despite the fact that Norinaga's gods and Sorai's sages are absolutely opposed in their positive definitions.

Despite his belief in pristine Shinto, Norinaga, who opposed the injection of any Ideas into historical studies, could not remain a theorist of apocalyptic decadence. Of course, he often pointed out that the advent of Confucianism and Buddhism had perverted the Ancient Way. But he never allowed his interest in antiquity to blind him to the reality of historical progress. "In all things and in all matters," he observed, "there are many instances when later ages have been superior to antiquity. . . . For example, there are many things which were inferior in ancient times but are excellent today. In the light of this it is natural to wonder how things might turn out in the future. No doubt many things that are finer than what we have today will come into existence."[73] "Because there are things which in later ages excel over those of antiquity, we cannot insist stubbornly that later ages are inferior."[74]

The same reasonable, objective attitude is revealed even more clearly in his discussion of Japanese poetry. "Nowadays those who are interested in Manyō-style poetry arrogantly and casually dis-

[72] *Zōho Motoori Norinaga zenshū*, VI, pp. 114–15 (*Suzunoya tōmon roku*).
[73] Ibid., VIII, p. 428 (*Tamakatsuma*, 14).
[74] Ibid., IX, p. 498 (*Uiyamabumi*).

miss the poems of Shunzei [1114–1204] and Teika [1162–1241][75] as if they were completely without artistic merit. . . . This is a serious mistake. The poems of these lords are not faultless but, *as is true of all things, some are superior to poems of other ages. This is truly a wonderful thing.*"[76] The antipositivist worship of the past manifested by his contemporaries in the school of National Learning, who decided "on the basis of fanciful reasoning that in all things the ancient age was superior to later ages, and insist on this in a forceful and overbearing fashion,"[77] was, in his opinion, no more than a metamorphosis of the "Chinese spirit" (*karagokoro*), despite its outward opposition to Confucianism. This brings into sharp focus the process by which, with Jinsai, who believed that "just as it is impossible that no virtuous person could exist in later ages, it is impossible that no insignificant man ever existed in antiquity. How can anyone contend that human desires became the basis of all things only after the age of the Three Dynasties?" (see p. 59, above), and then Sorai, who argued that "it is very simple to criticize all ages by judging them in terms of fixed scales of measurement. Anyone who does so considers himself to be right and does not weigh the circumstances of any era. Of what value then is history?" (see p. 100, above), the historical spirit gradually achieved independent growth, breaking through the crust of rigid Confucian rationalism.

As we have already seen, the disintegration of Neo-Confucian rationalism liberated the natural characteristics of man suppressed by Chu Hsi philosophy as "human desires." This leads us to the third relationship between Sorai and Norinaga. Norinaga's opposition to moral rigorism is well known, and I need not elaborate on it here. But the following point deserves attention: the severance of the continuity between norms and nature in Chu Hsi philosophy led to a double development: on the one hand, to the purification of normative standards, and on the other, to the liberation of natural characteristics. However, until Norinaga, all the emphasis was put on the former, the latter being interpreted negatively as a

---

[75] Fujiwara Shunzei and Teika, father and son, renowned poets of the late Heian and early Kamakura periods, and members of the family that had dominated the imperial court for generations. (Translator's note.)

[76] *Zōho Motoori Norinaga zenshū*, VIII, p. 350 (*Tamakatsuma*, 12).

[77] Ibid., IX, p. 497 (*Uiyamabumi*).

literal freedom from moral standards.[78] Even Sorai, who insisted most adamantly on this separation and made norms purely political, rejecting all moral rigorism, believed that the essence of the Way of the Sages lay in its public aspect. Norinaga rejected even the Sorai school's conception of the Way and founded the essence of his own Way precisely in the negation of everything normative. Only then did man's natural sentiments for the first time advance from negative toleration and acquire a positive validation.

According to Norinaga: "The Way is not basically something which can be known only after the pursuit of learning. It is the inborn spirit of man [*umarenagara no magokoro*]. The spirit with which one is born *is natural in the sense that it is beyond good and evil*."[79] Thus the Way is originally endowed in the hearts (*kokoro*) of all men. But "because men of later ages all turned their attention to Chinese ideas and lost their inborn spirit, they could no longer understand the Way without studying."[80] The inborn spirit was obscured by Chinese ideas (*karagokoro*), and therefore "excessive pretentiousness" prevailed. Replace "the inborn spirit" by "man's original nature" (*honzen no sei*), and "Chinese ideas" (or thought) by "the nature of the Specific Ether" (*kishitsu no sei*), and you have the Chu Hsi theory of human nature. The optimism of the Chu Hsi philosophy, which saw the Way as the naturalness of the "principle of Heaven," became in Sorai a pessimistic theory of the immutability of human nature. Norinaga then transformed it further by defining the Way in terms of the naturalness of "human desires." Thus he could say, "I cannot understand those who abhor and label as 'human desires' attitudes that conflict with the Way. . . . *Why should human desires not also constitute principles of Heaven?*"[81]

A truly sensitive optimism had finally come into being, as the negation of the negation of Chu Hsi philosophy. Norinaga extolled the age before Confucianism and Buddhism entered Japan for its happy life. "Even the lowliest person equated the will of the Emperor with his own will and wholeheartedly respected, revered, and worshiped the Emperor. . . . *Everyone did his best in his work and went*

[78] As noted above, Sokō did recognize the positive character of "human desires" but in his case "human desires" was interpreted in a very broad sense.

[79] *Zōho Motoori Norinaga zenshū*, VIII, p. 16 (*Tamakatsuma*, 1).

[80] Ibid., pp. 16–17.

[81] Ibid., I, p. 64 (*Naobi no mitama*).

through life tranquilly and happily. Thus, there was no need for a Way whose teachings had to be followed in carrying out one's tasks."[82] It is a well-known fact that Norinaga, by emphasizing the importance of "the inborn spirit," exposed the formalism and hypocrisy of the then predominant moral outlook. I need only add here that Norinaga's optimistic viewpoint was developed into a progressive philosophy by Tsuda Mamichi (1828–1903), an enlightened thinker of the early Meiji period, who wrote: "It was ridiculous for the Chu Hsi scholars to have concluded that the principles of Heaven and human desires are incompatible. *How can anyone say that human desires cannot constitute the principles of Heaven?* The passion to comprehend the nature of things, to pursue what is novel, to delight in freedom and crave for happiness, and so on, are the most attractive of human desires, and are a necessary part of human nature. They all contribute to our progress."[83]

The relationship between Sorai and Norinaga established by their common opposition to moral rigorism recalls their common opinions on literature. In this matter we find Norinaga first adopting and then slowly transcending Sorai's mode of thought.[84] In his early discussions of literature, Norinaga stressed the need to liberate it from ethics and politics. In this he was much like Sorai, who rejected Neo-Confucian interpretations of poetry and sought to confine literature to the private domain. For instance, in Norinaga's *Ashiwake-obune* [A little boat weaving through the reeds], believed to have been written while he was studying in Kyoto, he wrote: "Question: Poetry is a way to assist in governing the world. One should not consider it something one can casually amuse oneself with. . . . What do you think of this opinion? Answer: *It is not correct.* The essence of poetry does not consist in supporting politics nor in furthering moral discipline. It has no other purpose than

---

[82] Ibid., pp. 65–66.

[83] *Meiji bunka zenshū* [Collection of works on Meiji culture], ed. Yoshino Sakuzō (Tokyo, 1927–30), XVIII, p. 222 (*Jōyokuron*).

[84] Of course, the Sorai school was not alone in rejecting the practice of interpreting literature in terms of rewarding good and punishing evil. This rejection had gradually emerged along with the development of National Learning, ever since the time of Keichū. But since here I am concerned only with Norinaga's relationship with Sorai, the other moments have not been brought into consideration. Here, too, it would appear that it was Sorai who influenced the direction that this style of criticism took.

to enable one to say exactly what one feels in one's heart."[85]
"There are many other things better suited than poetry to provide
assistance in the task of government and in furthering moral discipline. *Why should it be necessary to rely on such a farfetched thing as
Japanese poetry?*"[86] This line of argument coincides exactly with
Sorai's. As the latter put it: "Among the Five Classics, there is one
called the *Book of Odes*. This is just the same as Japanese poems
[*waka*]. It does not explain the principles by which to govern one's
mind and body, nor does it explain the way to govern the nation
and the world. It consists only of words with which the ancients
gave expression to sorrow and happiness."[87] "It is a great mistake
to insist that the *Book of Odes* was written in order to reward good
and punish evil. If that had been its purpose, *it would have been
presented in a better form*" (see p. 107, above). As well as the direct
influence of Sorai upon Norinaga here, one should not overlook
the indirect influence through Hori Keizan.

While liberating poetry from ethics and politics, Sorai still believed in the "benefits" that accrue from it: "Although the study of
poetry is of no use for understanding the principle of things, it has
the power to develop one's heart and reasoning faculties naturally,
because it uses words artfully and expresses human feelings effectively. . . . It is further beneficial in that it naturally enables one's
heart to experience human feelings extensively; it enables those of
high standing to acquire knowledge about matters concerning
those of low standing; it enables men to understand the feelings of
women, and the wise to understand the thoughts of the foolish. . . .
It is of considerable benefit to those who stand at the head of the
people to understand elegant literary matters."[88] In the same way,
although as we have seen, Norinaga argued that "the *essence* of poetry does not consist in supporting politics nor in furthering moral
discipline. It has no other purpose than to enable one to say exactly what one feels in one's heart,"[89] he did concede the "uses" of
poetry: "There is no better way for the ruler of men . . . to gain

[85] *Zōho Motoori Norinaga zenshū*, X, p. 149.
[86] Ibid., p. 162.
[87] *Nihon rinri ihen*, VI, p. 179 (*Tōmonsho*, Book II).
[88] Ibid., pp. 179–80 (*Tōmonsho*, Book III).
[89] *Zōho Motoori Norinaga zenshū*, X, p. 175 (*Ashiwake o-bune*).

knowledge of the conditions of those under him than poetry."[90] Ordinary people, too, "cannot understand the intentions or feelings of anything unless they come into contact with the thing itself. The rich do not know the feelings of the poor, the young do not know the feelings of the old, and men do not know the feelings of women," but "the intentions and feelings of all things can be understood" through poetry.[91]

Both Sorai and Norinaga emphasized the importance of freeing literature from ethics and politics, mentioning its political and social uses only as matters of secondary importance. In this their respective modes of thought are exactly the same. But even at this time Norinaga was already beginning to go beyond Sorai. Sorai had argued that although waka (Japanese poems) and shi (Chinese-style poems) are the same, the former for some reason "have a feminine air to them. This is because they are poems from a country without Sages" (see p. 108, above). Norinaga, on the other hand, while agreeing that waka and shi are essentially the same, completely inverted Sorai's evaluation of the latter. "Because the three hundred verses of refined *shi* (in the *Book of Odes*) are unadorned expressions of human sentiments, *they are like the words of young girls and wholly ethereal*. This is truly the essence of *shi*."[92] The "masculine" shi of later periods, he argued, had deviated from the true nature of shi. This is a reflection of Norinaga's belief in the primacy of the emotions. "It is natural to man's inborn spirit to be moved emotionally. Those who boast that they cannot be moved are like rocks or trees."[93] The rigorous development of this viewpoint, which he had acquired from medieval literature, enables him to throw off the last remaining restrictions on Sorai's literary views—restrictions that derived from the nature of Confucianism itself—and at the same time to go beyond his teacher Mabuchi, who had disapproved of the cleverness of Confucianism, but insofar as he praised the "heroic masculinity" of antiquity at the expense of the "graceful maidenliness" of the medieval period,

---

[90] Ibid., p. 176.

[91] Ibid., p. 199 (*Isonokami sasamegoto*, Book III).

[92] Ibid., p. 178 (*Ashiwake o-bune*).

[93] Ibid., p. 114 (*Tama-hoko no momo-uta*). Ugoku koso | hito no magokoro | ugokazu to | iite hokorau | hito wa iwa ki ka.

he did not differ from Sorai, who derided waka for their "feminine air." In Norinaga's literary philosophy, on the contrary,

> when a writer depicts the heroic death of a warrior in battle, he should describe the warrior's actions so as to show him in a truly courageous light, thus invoking a sense of admiration. If the writer were accurately to describe the true inner feelings of the warrior without any fabrication, he would have to describe him as longing for his parents at home, desiring to see his wife and children just once more, and not wishing to lose his life. These are all natural human sentiments, and everyone would experience them. Those who do not possess these sentiments are worse than rocks and trees. If his feelings were honestly described, there would be many indecisive, foolish sentiments usually associated with young girls.[94]

In these inner feelings hidden behind a facade of "heroic masculinity" he revealed the *mono no aware* ("sadness of things") essential to the *Utamonogatari*.[95] If we can still detect a form of feudal-samurai consciousness latent in Mabuchi's contempt for "graceful maidenliness" here, Norinaga had finally made literature independent of all Neo-Confucian categories. However, as Norinaga's philosophy developed, this problem, too, developed in an even more significant way.

Literature, whose inherent value Norinaga had brought to consciousness, soon fused with the interest in antiquity he had inherited from Mabuchi, and gradually came to occupy a central position in the Ancient Way (National Learning). "The Way of the Gods," wrote Norinaga, "does not contain a single argument that annoyingly evaluates things in terms of good and evil, right and wrong, like the Confucian and Buddhist Ways. It is opulent, big-hearted, and refined. *The essence of Japanese poetry suits it well.*"[96]

Thus he elevated the sense of mono no aware, which was "the essence of Japanese poetry," to the level of the essence of Shinto itself. As a result, literature, which had been freed from moral discipline and the art of government, seems once more to have

[94] Ibid., p. 306 (*Shibun yōryō,* Book II).
[95] Romantic tales of the Heian period (A.D. 794–1185) in which waka constituted an important part of the work; for example, the *Ise monogatari.* (Translator's note.)
[96] *Zōho Motoori Norinaga zenshū,* IX, p. 494 (*Uiyamabumi*).

been burdened with political and social qualities. If this can for the time being be called a "politicization of literature," with Norinaga this politicization does not mean the transformation of the content of literature into political matters, nor—as with Sorai, and even the younger Norinaga—that literature has a political use, but rather that the principle of literature (that is, the sense of mono no aware) is to be validated as it stands as a political principle. Norinaga's optimism, which saw antiquity as an ideal era when everyone "went through life tranquilly and happily," found its methodological basis in this sense of mono no aware. However, from the opposite viewpoint, the fact that literature was politicized while remaining literature meant that politics was aestheticized. Paradoxically speaking, it meant the "depoliticization" (*Entpolitisieren*) of politics. This is not just a paradox. I am convinced that by pursuing this problem, it will be possible to discover the general significance of the various relationships between Sorai and Norinaga, and simultaneously to fix the place of Norinaga's school of thought, as the ultimate form of National Learning, in Japanese intellectual history.

IV

According to Chu Hsi philosophy, the preservation of order in the state and peace in the world depends on virtuous conduct, and virtuous conduct in turn depends on comprehending the Principle. As this "rationalism" disintegrated, politics gradually became independent of individual morality, until with Sorai, Confucianism was completely politicized. But this sublimation of normative standards at the political level led, on the other hand, to the liberation of man's inner nature and opened the way to its free development. National Learning then came onto the scene as the heir to this movement and denied all the inventions of Confucianism. In Sorai's philosophy, man's inner sentiments were granted a negative freedom as what may be called the private sphere, but they became the keystone of the philosophy of National Learning. *Thus National Learning inherited the Sorai school's private, nonpolitical side while completely rejecting its public side.* That is why Shundai, who took Sorai's political philosophy to extremes, became the object of its most violent criticisms, and why Mabuchi, who was infuriated by Shundai's *Bendōsho* [Discourse on distinguishing the Way], could maintain such friendly relations with Nankaku, the heir to the private side of Sorai's philosophy. Let us consider the above-discussed continuity of the Sorai school and Norinaga's school from this standpoint.

A positivistic methodology in philological studies and a historical consciousness were fundamental characteristics throughout the Sorai school. But concretely these characteristics were most in evidence where nonpolitical objects are concerned, that is, in the "extensive knowledge of the facts." Needless to say, an opposition to moral rigorism and a defense of the independence of literature fall into the Sorai school's private sphere. Just as Sorai argued that the Confucian's only duty was to preserve words and phrases and transmit them to future generations, while the task of putting the Way into practice should be "left to the Sages of the future," Norinaga defined the scholar's position in nonpolitical terms, e.g., "Scholars should make it their business to investigate and elucidate the Way. It is not their business personally to practice the Way."[97] Thus it is clear that the Norinaga school is linked to the Sorai school through the latter's private sphere. *However, although the Sorai school's private domain was, so to speak, a by-product of its politicization of Confucianism, National Learning, by contrast, gave inner sentiments purged of all normativity a positive role by identifying them with the Way itself.* Thus National Learning, unlike the Sorai school, linked something that was nonpolitical for the latter with politics itself.

Mabuchi had maintained earlier that "the spirit or intent of Japanese poetry" was to lay the groundwork for "order to prevail in the society and people to remain tranquil." "Generally speaking," he wrote, "the human heart is selfish. People argue with others and make distinctions on the basis of logical principles. But when the spirit of Japanese poetry prevails, tenderness is combined with logical principles, so order prevails in the society and people remain tranquil."[98] However, as long as "the spirit of Japanese poetry" was still defined as "heroic masculinity," it must be described as still politically and practically colored.

[97] Ibid., p. 486.
[98] *Kamo Mabuchi zenshū*, X, p. 374 (*Kokuikō*).

When Norinaga argued that "if the sense of *mono no aware* [the sadness of things] is broadly applied, it can be enlarged into a Way to discipline one's life and preserve order in the family and the country,"[99] and elevated the spirit of literature, now completely independent of any traditional standards of ethical, religious, political, or other norms, to an identity with the political, he completed the "depoliticization of politics" and for the first time firmly established the antithesis to the normative mode of thought. Hence even an attempt to make the spirit of mono no aware normative could not be permitted. If mono no aware were turned into a regulative principle in opposition to non-mono-no-aware positions, the purity of sentiments would be lost. It is unnatural to stress nature against norms. Thus, although Mabuchi praised Lao Tzu's naturalism very highly, Norinaga asserted that "what Lao Tzu regarded as nature was not true nature. In fact, he was more seriously in error than the Confucians. If one truly respects nature, one allows things in this world to follow their own course, regardless of what that might be. The actions of the Confucians and the actions of those who have deviated from the natural way of the ancients are all natural aspects of heaven and earth. To label them as erroneous and to insist that all actions must conform to the natural ways of antiquity would be a coercive action in itself, which is contrary to nature."[100] According to Norinaga, these errors of Lao Tzu were the product of speculation: "His views are restricted to ideas based on his own intellect."[101] Thus these views are distinguished from Norinaga's Way of the Ancients, which "does not include a shred of subjective cleverness but remains exactly as it appears in the literature of the gods."[102]

This shows us that Norinaga's respect for the purity of feelings is closely related to his objective and positivist attitude to scholarship. And this attitude of rejection towards "cleverness" (or intellectual pretentiousness) in matters of intellect and will is based on his conviction that "all things in this world, both good and

---

[99] *Zōho Motoori Norinaga zenshū*, VII, p. 513 (*Genji monogatari tama no o-gushi*, 2).
[100] Ibid., VI, pp. 128–29 (*Suzunoya tōmon roku*).
[101] Ibid., VIII, p. 209 (*Tamakatsuma*, 7).
[102] Ibid., p. 208.

bad, are products of the will of the gods."[103] He therefore asserted that "when one is propounding the Way, one should not concern oneself with the beliefs of the many meaningless ways or with whether or not one's ideas are being accepted by other people." And although he rigidly opposed any compromise in learning, insisting that it must "lean resolutely in one direction only," he was clearly opposed to the transformation of the Ancient Way of Japan, once it had been clarified by the removal of Chinese and Buddhist beliefs, into a political revival of the past: "When I propound the Way, I do not advise the people of *today* to behave like the ancients, unlike the Confucians and Buddhists. . . . Any attempt to compel people to practice the ancient Way of the Gods in opposition to existing circumstances is contrary to the behavior of the gods. It is an attempt to outdo the gods."[104] Going further, he pledged absolute loyalty to the Tokugawa Bakufu. "In today's world, the laws of today must be respected and subversive practices must not be adopted." "May the world that was pacified by the God Azumateru [Ieyasu] prosper for ten thousand generations."

This was not, as is often thought, a conscious sophism on Norinaga's part, nor is it a logical contradiction. It is a natural result of his position that what is given must be obediently accepted as what is given. It did not therefore serve in any special way to strengthen the foundations of the Tokugawa Bakufu. For since "in today's world, the laws of today must be respected," but "the laws of each era are based on the will of the gods. How can we violate them?" if there is any change in the existing political situation, the new politics must also be accepted as "the will of the gods." This is a thoroughly apolitical attitude (*unpolitische Haltung*), and for that very reason has the capacity to embrace political principles of all hues. This is not strictly speaking a conservative disposition, but rather the opportunistic relativism common to all romantic attitudes. Norinaga, who believed that "the rise and fall, prosperity and decay, of all things depends on the will of the gods,"[105] recognized the historical and, according to him, divinely

---

[103] Ibid., X, p. 112 (*Tama-hoko no momo-uta*). Yo no naka no | yoki mo ashiki mo | kotogoto ni | kami no kokoro no | shiwaza ni zo aru.

[104] Ibid., V, p. 513 (*Kuzubana*, Book II).

[105] Ibid., VIII, p. 41 (*Tamakatsuma*, 2).

ordained inevitability of the bakufu form of government, and yet, in doing so, whether consciously or not, he deprived the Tokugawa Bakufu of the possibility of obtaining an a priori and absolute foundation.

The consequences of Norinaga's Way reveal that its properties were self-contradictory. It was based on the rejection of all so-called bothersome teachings and all normative standards, whether these be abstract principles based on benevolence, righteousness, propriety, wisdom, and so on, or political ideologies. Thus he believed that "because the Way exists, there is no name for it, and though there is no name for it, the Way exists."[106] Sorai's Way was based on "facts and words" but "facts and words" were really the teachings of the Early Kings. Norinaga's Way, however, was "the vestiges of things." But these could not be converted into normative standards as teachings. It was Norinaga's firm conviction that "men do not become good because of any teachings, and they do not depend on teachings [to be good]."[107] He pushed the antithesis to Neo-Confucian rationalism as far as it would go. But once this negation of normative standards was a thoroughgoing negation, it inevitably changed into its opposite.

The very fact that Norinaga's Way was distinguished from the Confucian and Buddhist Ways resulted necessarily in the conceptual elevation of the "vestiges of things." The affirmation that accompanied the negation slowly began to develop independently as an affirmation. Hence the "Ancient Way" of the scholars of National Learning was bound to develop into a positive "norm." This tendency was already inherent in Norinaga's thought, but it was developed further by his disciple Hirata Atsutane after his death. Historical facts were no longer accepted simply as facts, but were subjected to the criticism of the Ancient Way, which was now a particular political ism. The political activities of one section of the Hirata school of National Learning during the Meiji Restoration were logically based on this kind of development. But at the same time, this development was also more or less the cause of the collapse of the scholarly character of the Norinaga school.

[106] Ibid., I, p. 55 (*Naobi no mitama*).
[107] Ibid., VIII, p. 430 (*Tamakatsuma*, 14).

In National Learning a positivist and objective spirit was inseparably linked to an apolitical outlook. This was its sad dilemma, a situation created by the fact that historically it emerged as the negation of Confucianism after the latter had been politicized. It could not defend its right to survive in the new era by raising itself to the level of an exclusive political principle, but only by preserving absolute purity in its scholarly methodology, i.e., by rejecting the "Chinese spirit" (karagokoro), and, on the contrary, by embracing ideologies of all hues in the political realm, arguing that "Buddha and Confucius are also gods, so their Ways are offshoots of the comprehensive Way of the Gods," and that "things that cannot be regulated except by Confucianism should be regulated by Confucianism. Things that cannot be regulated except by Buddhism should be regulated by Buddhism; in these instances they are serving as the Way of the Gods."[108]

---

[108] Ibid., VI, p. 129 (*Suzunoya tōmon roku*).

CHAPTER V

CONCLUSION

We have now completed our initially projected journey from Confucianism's attainment of independence at the beginning of the Tokugawa period. I must remind the reader here that my discussion has treated a system of thought as complex as National Learning in a highly condensed fashion, solely in terms of its relationship to my main consideration, the delineation of the internal disintegration of Tokugawa Confucianism. The result has been a somewhat unilateral view. I am afraid many problems could not be discussed adequately. However, my efforts will not have been in vain if I have shown more or less concretely, through the subtle changes that occurred in the style of thought, how in this process the Chu Hsi school, which had dominated the early Tokugawa intellectual world, lost its social relevance with the subsequent historical changes; as well as how the Sorai school recovered this relevance by completely politicizing Confucianism; how, because it thereby acquired an apolitical element, the rise of National Learning became inevitable; and how, as a result of this process, a modern consciousness gradually emerged.

But why is it that I have studied the emergence of a modern consciousness that resulted from the internal disintegration of Confucianism from the point of view of changes in method of thought? I touched briefly on this point in Chapter 1, but now that I have completed this part, let me consider it once more. Two points are

involved. The first is: Why have I looked for a modern consciousness deep in these methods of thought themselves rather than in
antagonistic tendencies in political thought? Insofar as conscious
resistance to feudal authority is concerned, the thought of Sorai,
who advocated bakufu absolutism, and of Norinaga, who believed
that the bakufu's policies were divinely ordained, was more feudal
than that of Ōshio Heihachirō (1792–1837),[1] or even that of Takenouchi Shikibu (1712–67)[2] or Yamaga Sokō. This latter approach might be the valid method of examination for modern
European thought, where changes in the fundamental mode of
thought have occurred more or less in parallel with changes in the
political thought based on them. But it cannot be applied in the
same way to Japan. During the Tokugawa period, the steady development of bourgeois social power in the womb of feudal society
was impossible, so only arbitrary results could be obtained by looking for evidence of a modern consciousness in political theory that
was governed largely by accidental conditions and lacked any
connection with the basic mode of thought. I am not interested in
the fragmentary modernity of this or that school of thought; my
aim is to uncover a consistent growth of modern consciousness in
the systematic framework of the thought itself.

The second point is: Why have I traced the growth of modern
consciousness only in the process of internal disintegration of Confucianism? My object has not been to present a comprehensive
history of the development of modern thought in the Tokugawa
period. Even scholars extremely distinguished as individuals and
highly modern in their outlook have been excluded from consideration if they happen to have been largely isolated from the
general framework of intellectual development. Arai Hakuseki
and Miura Baien[3] were such men. Naturally enough, scholars of

[1] Ōshio was a Wang Yang-ming scholar who staged an uprising in Osaka in 1837
against the established order for its indifference to the miseries and hardships of the
poor. (Translator's note.)

[2] Takenouchi Shikibu belonged to Yamazaki Ansai's school of thought. He held
proimperial, antibakufu views and was exiled for his beliefs. See pp. 276–77, below.
(Translator's note.)

[3] Arai Hakuseki (1657–1725) was chief adviser to the sixth shogun, Tokugawa Ienobu, and a distinguished Confucian scholar and historian with some knowledge of the
West. Miura Baien (1723–89) was a rationalist, a positivist, and a critic of Chu Hsi
philosophy. (Translator's note.)

the school of Dutch Learning (*Rangaku*), which gradually gained in importance from the Kyōhō era (1716–36) on, reveal a relatively well developed modern consciousness. But these men have also been excluded from my investigation. I have focused on the schools that constituted the mainstream of Confucian thought and those men who were in general pure Confucian scholars. I have adopted this approach in the belief that, insofar as Confucianism was the most powerful form of consciousness in the feudal society, an analysis of its rather unexpected disintegration from within, rather than of its destruction from without, would demonstrate most effectively that Japanese thought in the Tokugawa period did not merely "maintain itself in a vacuum"; in other words, it would illustrate its developmental character. In essence, the dual character inherent in "modern" Japan, that is, its backwardness (the first point) and its nevertheless nonstatic character (the second point), has determined the methodology that I have adopted.

One of the most important characteristics of the modern spirit is rationalism. The line that extends from Chu Hsi philosophy through the Sorai school to National Learning, however, developed in an irrationalistic rather than a rationalistic direction. What is the reason for this? This problem, too, must be considered from two angles: from the standpoint of world-historical development, and from the standpoint of the unique features of Chu Hsi philosophy.

To take up the first point, modern reason did not, as is often naïvely believed, develop in a straight line by the gradual elimination of the irrational. Modern rationalism has had a mutually constraining relationship with an empiricism based more or less on the natural sciences. Before cognitive intent can turn to the empirical and sensuous, it must abandon its leanings towards the metaphysical. In this process, the area open to rational cognition is considerably reduced, and instead, the irrational gains the ascendancy. This is reminiscent of the part played by late scholasticism in the history of medieval European philosophy. In their struggle with the intellectualism of the earlier scholastics, the Franciscan followers of Duns Scotus and then Nominalists like William of Occam set narrow limits to man's cognitive powers. By allotting to the realm of faith many items that had traditionally been the objects of rational cognition, on the one hand they made way for religious reform, and on the other cleared the way for the rapid rise of the natural sciences.[4] The irrationalism of Sorai and Norinaga represents a similar phase. Needless to say, just as Ancient Learning and National Learning are not identical with Nominalism, there are decisive differences between Chu Hsi rationalism and scholastic rationalism. But there is an undeniable similarity in the significance for the history of thought of later Scholasticism as opposed to Thomism and of Confucian Ancient Learning and National Learning as opposed to Chu Hsi philosophy.[5]

As we have discovered, the limited character of the Chu Hsi concept of "the exhaustive study of the Principle" led to Jinsai's separation of the way of man from the Way of Heaven and to Sorai's empirical observation of politics. Moreover, the growth of an irrational faith in the sages gave rise to a philological, positivist approach to the Confucian classics. This approach was adopted and developed by Norinaga, who simply substituted the ancestral gods of the imperial family for the sages. Norinaga's complete rejection of the "exhaustive investigation of Principle" has been the object of much discussion. But insofar as the principles that were the objects of Norinaga's criticism were the metaphysical categories of Chu Hsi philosophy, Buddhism, and Taoism—that is, yin and yang, the five elements, karma, and so on—this criticism

[4] Cf., e.g., Wilhelm Windelband: *Geschichte der Philosophie,* 9th and 10th eds. (1931), pp. 260–92, esp. p. 289; E. V. Aster: *Geschichte der Philosophie,* 2nd ed. (1935), pp. 164ff.; M. Grabmann: *Die Philosophie des Mittelalters* (Vol. III of the Goschen "Geschichte der Philosophie"), pp. 110ff.

[5] It has hitherto been commonplace to compare the rise of Ancient Learning in Confucianism and the progress of National Learning in Japan to the Renaissance in Europe. Recently historians have pointed out the differences in the social bases of the two, and the present trend is to deny the validity of this traditional analogy; e.g., cf. Hani Gorō: "Kokugaku no genkai" [The limitations of National Learning], *Shisō,* Vol. 169 (1936). This analogy is hard to justify not only in terms of the social foundation, but also with respect to the level of intellectual enlightenment. (Needless to say, the "modern"—Tokugawa—period in Japanese history is by no means identical with the "modern" period in Europe.) My choice for comparison of a period that preceded the Renaissance by a century or two is based purely on the criterion of the history of thought, but even in social background the period of my choice is more like the Tokugawa period than the Renaissance. See Part II, Chapter 4, section 2 below, for further comment on this point.

generally tended to nurture a receptive attitude towards natural-scientific cognition. It is clear that Norinaga's rejection of "cleverness" is related to the position that recognizes as certain only knowledge of the sensible world. We can see this in the method of criticism revealed in the following quotations. Pointing out the arbitrariness of the method of calculation that led Shao Yung[6] to conclude that the total cycle of the universe was 129,600 years, Norinaga observed: "To speak of *things hidden to the human eye,* as Buddhist writings do, is a simple matter; one can say anything one pleases . . . . [Shao Yung's] theory of the cycle of the universe is like the theories in Buddhist scriptures. *It deals with matters not visible to man. Anything can be fabricated when one speaks of principles in the abstract.* Unless one were present at the beginning and end of the universe and actually saw these events, how could one know whether one's theory was correct?"[7] When Ichikawa Tadasu[8] countered this argument by stating that "if only things visible to the human eye exist and everything else is nonexistent, are the gods, who are invisible to the human eye, all nonexistent?" Norinaga replied:

When I spoke of things as they appear to the human eye in that book [*Tamakatsuma*], I was speaking of such things as the moon, the sun, fire, and water, which are visible to the eye. I was speaking of one aspect of the situation. There are other things which are not visible but we know of their existence. Things that make sounds we can hear with our ears, things that smell we can smell with our noses. We know the existence of such things as the wind because we feel its pressure against our bodies although it does not affect our eyes, ears, or noses. . . . The same is true of the many gods. The gods of the Age of the Gods are not visible to our eyes now, but they were visible during that age. Among the gods, the Goddess Amaterasu is visible to everyone, even today.[9]

[6] Shao Yung (1017–73) was a Neo-Confucian of the Sung Dynasty who was influenced by religious Taoism. Among other things, he formulated a cosmological chronology. (Translator's note.)

[7] *Tamakatsuma,* 7.

[8] Also known as Tazumaro. He died in 1795. (Translator's note.) The quotation is from his *Maganohire.*

[9] *Kuzubana,* Book II. Norinaga, being completely faithful to the account in the *Kojiki,* regarded the Goddess Amaterasu as the sun that shines on the world today.

The far-fetched interpretations of the "principles of the Way" used by Confucians, Buddhists, and Taoists had acquired such authority since the middle ages that the reactions of Sorai and Norinaga were extremely radical, encouraging in them a strong mystical tendency to the point of undermining their positivist attitude. But it is undeniable that Sorai—who held that "not only the wind, the cloud, the thunder, and the rain, but all the secrets of the universe are impenetrable for the human intellect. Rationalist scholars (i.e., the Sung scholars) have merely used such terms as *yin* and *yang* and the five elements to construct superficial explanations. *Even if we are acquainted with their explanations, it does not necessarily follow that we really know the why and how of things.* . . . After all, the impenetrable mysteries of the universe cannot be known. *Hence thunder should be accepted as thunder*"—and Norinaga—who maintained that "fire is hot and water is cold. The principles responsible for their being hot and cold cannot be known. *But to feign knowledge about these things, concepts called* yin *and* yang *were formulated,* a thing called the Supreme Ultimate was established in the inner sanctum, and methods of divination like the *li-k'an*,[10] which provided an avenue of escape to the left and right, were constructed. These were all foolish fabrications of the Chinese Sages"—occupied positions which provided progressive tools for the destruction of the concrete contemporary content of the "exhaustive investigation of Principle."

As Fukuzawa Yukichi declared later in his *Bunmeiron no gairyaku*: "The road to the 'exhaustive investigation of Principle' cannot be entered without sweeping away the misguided notions of *yin* and *yang* and the five elements." A modern approach to the "investigation of principle" could not be developed without first eliminating the nonmodern approach. Thus, while the scholars of National Learning belonging to the Hirata school, which had elevated Shinto into an exclusive ideology and tried to enforce a revival of the past, suddenly lost the position of absolute preeminence that they had held just after the Meiji Restoration, becoming no more than a group of reactionaries fulminating against Westernization, the positivist spirit of National Learning made an active contribu-

---

[10] In the Book of Changes, *li* means fire and *k'an,* water. (Translator's note.) The quotations are from *Tōmonsho,* Book I, and *Kuzubana,* Book II.

tion, through a few enlightened, but not necessarily prominent, Shinto priests, to the dissemination of European bourgeois culture, and certainly fused with modern rationalism.[11]

In discussing the factors that endowed the irrational principles of Sorai and Norinaga with modernity, we must not ignore the second point, namely, the contribution of the unique features of Chu Hsi philosophy. Because Chu Hsi rationalism was strongly moralistic, its disintegration made various cultural values independent. I have already discussed the concrete aspects of this process, and there is no need to repeat this. The essential point is that the various domains such as politics, history, literature, and so on, which had been completely bound to ethics by the continuative mode of thought of the Chu Hsi system, began to break their fetters and demand cultural "citizenship." Thus politics ceased to be a mere extension of the "cultivation of personal life and regulation of the family," history ceased to be a "mirror" for moral pre-

---

[11] Here, for example, are some quotations from a collection of essays by Shinto priests entitled *Bunmei kaika* [Civilization and enlightenment], to be found in the *Meiji bunka zenshū*:

> The Way of the Gods of our divine land is quite different from what is taught by the Buddhists. It came into being naturally, without being sought and without being forced. Our Way of the Gods is truly an exalted Way. Some men propound fantastic theories. What is called Ryōbu Shinto is an example. It arose from the theories of the Buddhists and is all mixed up with Buddhism. There is nothing fantastic about the Gods at all. Of course, strange things are written in the books of the Age of the Gods. But those who claim that because of this strange things can happen today are applying the past to the present. This is a grave mistake. The Age of the Gods was the time when heaven and earth were created so it is reasonable that strange things should have happened then. . . . *But there is no reason for strange things to occur once heaven and earth had been fixed in their proper places.* (*Meiji bunka zenshū*, XX, pp. 14–15.)
>
> Generally speaking, someone who is fascinated by strange happenings. . . cannot be regarded as a man who is civilized and enlightened. In all matters, one must investigate thoroughly the principles of things which are not completely clear to one. And one should believe or disbelieve things only after one has become competent to judge whether they accord with the principles of things or not. (Ibid., p. 17.)
>
> All things in this world, whether they have feelings or not, are governed by certain principles. It is impossible for things to happen that are contrary to principle. There is a saying that "there are reasons that lie beyond reasoning" but this was first mouthed by someone who had not sufficiently investigated the principles of things. . . . He used it as an alibi for his failure to understand certain things even though he had used his brains to the utmost. And he failed to understand because he did not investigate the principle of things thoroughly enough. (Ibid., pp. 17–18.)

These opinions are already based on modern rationalism. Although the terms "investigation of principles" and the "principle of things" are the same as those used by the Chu Hsi school, they belong to different categories in the history of thought.

cepts, and literature ceased to be an instrument rewarding good and punishing evil. Each acquired intrinsic normative standards, the first as "giving peace and security to the people," the second as "positive proof," and the third as "mono no aware." This autonomy of cultural values is the emblematic form of the modern consciousness as a "divided consciousness" (Hegel).

As my final point, let me consider a very basic doubt that may be raised against this approach. That is to say, what is the value now of looking in this way for a modern consciousness in the internal disintegration of Confucian thought? Is it not this modern mode of thought that arouses the present cry of "crisis"? If we trace back the confusion and disorder that supposedly prevail in the modern spirit, shall we not find its origin here? To these doubts I can only reply as follows: What you say is true. But the question is, can the perplexities of modern thought be resolved by a return to premodern thought? Just as the citizen cannot revert to serfdom, the internally divided consciousness can no longer accept the innocent premodern continuative consciousness. Of course, each of these varied cultural values, although aware of its autonomy, cannot remain wholly unrelated to the others. For instance, it is undeniable that, deep down, art is linked with ethical values, but if these connections are held to be direct and immediate links, art ceases to be art. History, too, cannot be confined to a mere description of past events. But so long as history remains in any way the slave of moralistic standards, it cannot in any sense be called true history.

True history or modern historiography only begins after what Hegel called "pragmatic historical writing" (*pragmatisches Geschichtsschreibung*)[12] has been completely overcome. "Cultivation of personal life, regulation of the family, order in the state and peace in the world" (*The Great Learning*). What beautiful words! How harmoniously they strike the ear! But we must not forget that even in Sorai's day the complexity of political affairs had made this simple continuative mode of thought, which links private morals with politics, completely ineffective. The problem of historiography left for us today is the task, while recognizing the meaning of historical facts that are free from any normative judgements, of

[12] G. W. F. Hegel: *Die Vernunft in der Geschichte,* op. cit., pp. 173ff.

objectively describing these facts and relating them to normative standards without being influenced by any value judgements. Regarding the relationship between morals and politics, the real difficulty lies in conceptualizing a new link between the two while remaining aware of the autonomous nature of politics.

I should like to close this part by quoting Windelband's concluding remarks in an essay in which he compares Greek and German philosophy:

> We need not lament the fact that the harmonious simplicity, the naïve beauty, the unaffected harmony of thought with which Greek philosophy stormed the universe, are no longer possible for us. It is not for us to choose any longer, but only to conceive: we must be clear that this innocence has been lost, and that in reflection we have a substitute for what was represented to the Greeks in a beautiful illusion. For it is surely foolish to demand that the same tree bloom and bear fruit at the same time.[13]

---

[13] W. Windelband: *Präludien,* 7th and 8th eds., I, pp. 145–46.

PART II

NATURE AND INVENTION
IN TOKUGAWA POLITICAL THOUGHT:
CONTRASTING
INSTITUTIONAL VIEWS

CHAPTER I

THE PROBLEM

During the Tokugawa period, learning broke free of its previous reliance on religion and became independent, in respect both to its content and to its protagonists, and there arose a series of different schools of thought with a deep concern for reality and society. No other period in the history of Japanese thought is so colorful. But because, with the rare exception of men like Andō Shōeki, who will be discussed later, these points of view or schools all accepted the feudal social order absolutely as a *conditio sine qua non,* politically and socially their content is undeniably flat and monotonous. Commenting on learning in old Japan, Fukuzawa Yukichi remarked:

In our country learning has meant learning belonging to the world of the rulers; it has been no more than a branch of the government. Look for instance at the 250 years of Tokugawa rule. No one founded schools in the country except the central government or the various *han* [clan] governments. There were undoubtedly famous scholars and massive works, but these scholars were all other men's retainers and their works were all official publications. There were unemployed scholars and private publications too, but these were scholars who had sought to become retainers and failed to find employment, and private publications were those that had been rejected for official publication. . . . To make an analogy, it is as if the scholars

were locked in a cage called government, and having made this
cage their universe, they struggled and worried in this microcosm.[1]

He summed up Confucianism, by far the most influential current
in Tokugawa intellectual history, as follows: "Who was it that
propounded the principle of despotic government? Even if the
elements of despotism were to be found in the nature of the government itself, was it not the learning of Chinese, Confucian
scholars which nurtured and fostered it?"[2] Where their immediately political positions are concerned, the major intellectual currents of the Tokugawa period cannot escape such criticisms. If we
take the ideology called *sonnō* (revere the emperor), the majority
of its proponents during the Tokugawa period approved of the
bakufu system as a system entrusted with the powers of government
by the imperial court. Even when the deteriorating political situation in the Bakumatsu period (the period of the "downfall of the
bakufu" at the end of the Tokugawa period) made the sonnō
position into a clear-cut antibakufu ideology, its proponents did
not fully consider the possibility of overthrowing the feudal social
order itself. Anyone who follows theoretical literature chronolog-
ically from the Bakumatsu period to the beginning of the Meiji
period will be surprised at the sudden eruption of criticism of the
feudal system from a modern standpoint that occurs after the
Restoration, or more specifically around the fourth and fifth year
of Meiji (1871–72), simultaneously with a series of reforms: the
abolition of the feudal domains (*han*), the establishment of prefectural administration, the liquidation of the old system of estates,
the granting of freedom of occupation, the removal of the ban on
buying and selling land, and so on.

But simply because all Tokugawa thought arrived at a common
political conclusion in this way, it would be wrong to say that the
diversity of the schools of thought was due merely to sectarian
disputes and to see in it only intellectual stagnation. Changes in
thought, like social changes—indeed, even more than social
changes—do not take place suddenly. No matter how suddenly
these changes seem to occur superficially, they have been preceded

[1] Fukuzawa Yukichi: *Bunmeiron no gairyoku* (Tokyo, 1875), Book V.
[2] Ibid.

internally by the gradual disintegration of the old. The direct intellectual genealogy of so-called enlightened thinking may have
been its foreign derivation, but foreign ideas could only enter
because the existing factors "within" had changed sufficiently in
nature to admit them without serious opposition. The fact that
Tokugawa thought did not attain a clearly defined antifeudal
consciousness is related to the restricted character of the growth
of bourgeois social power, but just as the immaturity of industrial
capital did not hinder the disintegration of feudal relations of
production, the fact that modern political thought did not emerge
did not mean that there was not an internal process of decay in
the feudal system of ideas. In fact, if we do not focus on the conclusions that appear on the surface alone but examine the systematic structure that led to those conclusions, we can find in the
development of Tokugawa thought many logical strands common
to the modern thought of the period after the Restoration, a period
from which, superficially at least, it seems to be divided by a wide
gulf. In the light of this, I have tried in Part I of this book to trace
the process of the internal disintegration of the structure of Confucian thought, following the development of Tokugawa Confucianism up to the emergence of the Sorai school. But because I
put the main emphasis there on immanent changes in the mode
of thought as a whole, I did not examine the problem of how this
mode of thought related to the existing society.

In this part, I shall shift my perspective and analyze the following problems: how this development of Confucian thought from
the Chu Hsi school to the Sorai school was mirrored in differences
in attitudes towards the feudal social order and in its justification,
the universal significance of these differences, and the lessons
derived from these differences by schools of thought after Sorai.
The Chu Hsi and Sorai schools were identical in regarding feudal
relations of authority as absolute. However, the logical bases for
their belief in this absolutism were directly opposed. In this study
I shall attempt to pinpoint this conflict in terms of two concepts,
nature (*shizen*) and invention (*sakui*),[3] and then demonstrate that

---

[3] Sorai's term *sakui* means, as a concrete noun, something like "artifact." However,
it does not have the pejorative connotations that the adjectival form "artificial" has
attained in English. It is therefore often translated as "creation." But in both its religious and aesthetic uses, "creation" has implications of spontaneity and naturalness

this issue is not simply a technical problem inside the framework of feudal society, but that it implies the world-historical problem of the conflict between the medieval view of social and state institutions and the modern bourgeois view. I shall trace the pattern of development of the logic of the concepts "nature" and "invention" to the early Meiji period and try to explain how far Tokugawa thought was able to cope with the problem.

Remember that although I speak of the attitudes to the feudal social order and its justification, the thinkers of the Tokugawa period hardly dealt with the problem of justifying the existing system in terms of their own empirical observations of the political and social environment. After the middle of the Tokugawa period there were some efforts in this direction, but in the early years, when feudal authority boasted invincible strength, there was no social incentive for such efforts. Moreover, the prevailing tradition, generally speaking, was to regard scholarly investigation as the acquisition of knowledge from the ancient classics rather than the examination of social reality itself. It must be realized, however, that many scholars of the period did interpret and understand existing society via the knowledge they acquired from classical texts. In most cases they were unaware of the real gap between what was in the classics and existing society. They regarded the various Confucian categories as "frames of reference" (*Aspektstruktur*) and observed the feudal social order only through these frames of reference.

This is well illustrated by a quotation from Nakae Tōju:

There are five grades in the status of men. They are the Emperor, the feudal princes, the ministers and high officials, the gentlemen-scholars, and the common people. The Emperor rules all under heaven and has the status of *mikado*; the princes govern their own provinces and have the status of daimyo. The ministers and high officials manage the governmental affairs of the country and the provinces according to the commands of the Emperor and the

---

that make it impossible to oppose it to "nature" as Sorai and Professor Maruyama do. Hence I have chosen "invention" (and its adjectival forms, compounds, and so on). The reader should bear in mind, however, that *sakui* certainly does not mean "thinking up" an institution, as "invention" can in English; it definitely implies constructing, putting into practice. (Translator's note.)

princes. The gentlemen-scholars accompany the ministers and high officials and perform different functions of government. They have the status of samurai. Those who farm are called peasants [*nō*], the workmen are called artisans [*kō*], and the tradesmen are called merchants [*shō*]. These three, the peasants, the artisans, and the merchants, all have the status of common people [*shojin*].[4]

The essential differences between the princes discussed by Confucianism and the daimyo of Tokugawa feudal society, or between the Confucian gentlemen-scholars and the samurai, are simply set aside. The so-called Five Relationships (between ruler and subjects, father and son, husband and wife, elder and younger brother, and between friends) were the sum total of the social relations known to the Tokugawa scholars. When they encountered the words "righteousness in the relationship between ruler and subjects" (*kunshin no gi*), they did not see it as referring to the relations between ruler and subject in the Chou period of ancient China, but to the feudal relations between the lord and his followers in the world they had before them.

Although there is value in detecting and criticizing from the modern standpoint the discrepancies between the thought and the social reality of the time, we should not conclude that Tokugawa scholars were completely engrossed in debates about classical texts and totally removed from political and social realities. The connection between their cognitive intentions and the existing social system simply had to be established via an intermediary known as the "Five Relationships."[5] Thus, even in early Toku-

[4] *Okina mondō* [Questions and answers of an old man], Vol. I.

[5] Given the structural peculiarities of Tokugawa feudal society, it was not unreasonable that all existing social relations should have been summed up in the Five Relationships. Tokugawa feudal society can be said to have moved closer to modern society insofar as there was a somewhat clearer division of the public law of taxation on the one hand and private property rights on the other than was the case with medieval land tenure rights, and political authority was becoming increasingly abstract and centralized and further removed from relations of economic exploitation based on land. But inasmuch as hierarchic relations between estates were perfected in this period, we are justified in saying that, as a social system, feudalism reached its apogee in the Tokugawa period. This is most clearly visible in the universalization of the pattern of feudal ties based on a master-servant relationship. If the fact that the Laws of the Military Households (i.e., the laws of the Tokugawa family) completely overwhelmed the laws of the imperial court and the laws issued by the owners of *shōen* (the tax-free manors that emerged in the late Heian period) and had become the general law of the land

gawa thought, which hardly concerned itself with the nature of the feudal social order, we can discover the feudal social outlook, indirectly to be sure, by examining how the Five Relationships were justified.

---

can be called the lateral extension of the master-servant relationship, the fact that hierarchic divisions within the samurai class became finer and social relations among the common people came in most instances to be modeled on master-servant bonds is no more than its extension in depth. Moreover, the family system that, together with the master-servant relationship, was the fulcrum of the feudal legal system acquired a clear-cut political significance and began to emerge as an important element in feudal authority relations, owing to the indissoluble link between the family and the feudal stipend among the samurai and the establishment of Five-Man Groups (groupings of five to ten heads of households who were held jointly responsible for the payment of taxes and violations of the law) among the common people. Thus the master-servant relationship, which had spread to all social levels, and the relations of control exercised by the family head over the other family members became the basic and universal models for social ties in Tokugawa society. Hence conditions in that society were favorable to the facile acceptance of the Confucian mode of thought, which reduced all social relations, except for those between friends, to those between ruler and subjects, and between family members (father and son, husband and wife, elder and younger brother). In this way, a morality based on the Five Relationships came to constitute the "basic normative standard" of Tokugawa feudal society.

CHAPTER II

CHU HSI PHILOSOPHY
AND
THE IDEA OF NATURAL ORDER

It is logical to begin our examination with Chu Hsi philosophy, which was in the forefront of the intellectual developments of the Tokugawa period and became the official position in feudal education under bakufu protection. The Chu Hsi school more or less completely dominated the intellectual world of the early Tokugawa period. For this reason, by studying the early Tokugawa Chu Hsi scholars' conception of the social order under which they lived, we should be able to find out the prevailing attitude to the feudal social order and the hierarchical relations of authority. And if we have to select the most representative of the many Chu Hsi scholars of this period, the one who stands out, both in the breadth of his scholarship and in his social influence, is Hayashi Razan. The thought of this scholar, who served three shoguns, Ieyasu, Hidetada, and Iemitsu, and became the founder of the official school of the bakufu, can be seen as a microcosm of the intellectual trends of the period.

First, let us see how Razan justified the Five Relationships. "The Five Relationships," he wrote in *Santoku shō*, "between ruler and subject, father and son, husband and wife, older brother and younger brother, and between friends, have prevailed past and present between heaven and earth. This way never changes, so it has been called the 'universal way.' In man's relationships there are no more than these five." In other words, he emphasized that the Five Relationships encompass all social ties and that they are eternal and immutable. What guarantees the immutability of these relationships?

> The Way of the ruler and the father is the Way of Heaven, and the way of the subject and the son is the way of the earth. When a man brings order into the world outside his house, he behaves like heaven. He stands for *yang*. When a woman keeps order in the house, she behaves like the earth. She stands for *yin*. The nobility of the ruler and the father and the baseness of the subject and the son can be compared with the fact that the places of heaven and earth are fixed and cannot be disordered. But the hearts of those above reach those below, and the feelings of those below extend to those above. The ways of ruler and subject, and father and son, are mutually upheld, the righteousness that governs the relationship between the high and the low, and the noble and the base, are closely related, and the principles of *yin* and *yang,* in the house and in the outside world, are harmonious. That is why the Way of Heaven prevails above, and the principles of human relationships are clear below.[1]

In other words, "the righteousness that governs the relationships between the high and the low, and the noble and the base," i.e., the ruler's relation to his subjects, the father's to his sons, and the husband's to his wife, is justified by the authority that heaven exercises over the earth, and yang over yin, i.e., by principles of the natural world.

An approach that deduces social relationships from observations of natural phenomena and projects human affairs onto the natural world is often found in the early stages of human thought, but in China in particular it was a prominent feature of ancient thought, embodied in the maxim that "heaven and man are mutually related." This tendency was, of course, also inherent in early Confucian thinking, but Confucius and Hsun Tzu were concerned exclusively with practical ethics and were in fact opposed to metaphysical speculation. The idea that "heaven and earth are mutually related" came to dominate the foreground only after the Ch'in and Han eras, after the Book of Changes had been

---

[1] *Razan Hayashi sensei bunshū,* Book XXX.

added to the Confucian canon, and the theory of yin and yang had been combined with Confucian ethics. The idea that a hierarchical order can be deduced from nature is clearly visible in the Book of Changes and the Book of Rites. For example: "Heaven is noble and earth is base. In this manner their places are fixed. The high and the low are placed in order and the noble and the base are properly positioned"; "Heaven above, the lake below: the image of Treading [conduct]. Thus the superior man discriminates between high and low, and thereby fortifies the thinking of the people" (Book of Changes);[2] "Music establishes harmony in heaven and earth. Rites establish order in heaven and earth. Because of harmony hundreds of things are transformed, and because of order all categories of things have differences. Music creates in heaven and rites exercise their control on earth" (Book of Rites).

Needless to say, these statements constitute the theoretical background to Razan's positions as described above. But these positions have a more obvious methodological foundation, for Razan was a Chu Hsi scholar. Sung philosophy synthesized a promiscuous mixture of pristine Confucian thought, as manifested in the classical learning of Ch'in and Han, the theories in the Book of Changes, and yin and yang into a gigantic metaphysics. It thereby laid a solid theoretical foundation for the principle that "heaven and man are mutually related."

According to Chu Hsi philosophy, all things in heaven and earth are made of a combination of li (Principle) and ch'i (Ether). Li as the ultimate basis of the universe endows all things with universal qualities, but individual things are endowed with their own unique characteristics by the action of ch'i. All things in heaven and earth are infinitely variable in their external forms, but ultimately they are all offshoots of the same li. The li of the natural world (*tenri*, the Principle of Heaven) lodges itself in man and becomes his innate character (or Original Nature, *honzen no sei*). At the same time, it is the basic standard (the Five Constant Virtues, namely, benevolence, righteousness, propriety, wisdom, and faithfulness) governing social relations (the Five Relation-

---

[2] Translation from the *I Ching*, trans. Cary F. Baynes (New York, 1950), II, p. 73. (Translator's note.)

ships). The ultimate li is called the *t'ai chi* (Supreme Ultimate) or
ch'eng (sincerity). Thus Razan wrote:

> In heaven and earth, past and present, all things truly share in one
> common thing. [All things are governed by li.] Because of this,
> among larger things, heaven covers and earth upholds all things.
> The sun rises in the East and sets in the West. It has never risen in
> the South or North. Water seeks a lower level and fire burns. Day is
> bright and night is dark. The cold weather comes and the hot
> weather goes. The four seasons come round and all things are born.
> Among little things, a single blade of grass, a single tree, a single
> bird, a single insect, all have their li. . . . With man, the righteousness
> that prevails between the ruler and the subject, the intimacy between
> father and son, the distinction between man and woman, the order
> between the elder and younger, the association between friends, are
> all based on true principle.[3]

The imperative implied by the Five Relationships is based on the
same "true principle" as the natural inevitability by which
"heaven covers and earth upholds all things" and "the cold
weather comes and the hot weather goes." Moreover, "the reason
for the Five Relationships is the Five Constant Virtues. The Five
Constant Virtues are rooted in the heart. The principle which
resides in the heart is the nature of man."[4] Thus Razan equated
li with human nature. The Chu Hsi mode of thought naturalized
the ethical standards of Confucianism in two ways. First, it rooted
normative standards in the order of the universe (the Principle
of Heaven); and second, it held these standards to exist innately
in human nature as man's "*original* nature" (*honzen no sei*). This
implies the most typical form of the theory of natural law. This
natural-law character of Sung philosophy was clearly perceived
by Fabian Fukansai,[5] the author of the *Myōtei Dialogue*, a well-
known work of early Tokugawa Christianity. "The Confucian
scholars," he observed, "uphold the teaching of *nature*, and adhere
to the Five Constant Virtues of benevolence, righteousness, pro-

---

[3] *Razan bunshū*, Book VIII.

[4] Ibid., Book LXVIII.

[5] Fabian Fukansai became a Japanese Jesuit brother and a staunch champion of
Christianity, but in 1607 he renounced Christianity and became one of its bitter foes.
(Translator's note.)

priety, wisdom, and faithfulness, which are characteristics man
is born with in his soul. These virtues are highly commended in
the Christian religion also."[6] (Of course the book ultimately rejected Confucianism.)

What was the relationship between this natural law and the
actual social order? Generally speaking, as soon as natural law is
related to the actual social order it encounters an "either-or"
(*Entweder-oder*) characteristic. Either by rigid adherence to pure
doctrine it becomes a revolutionary principle directed against the
concrete social order, or by its complete identification with the
actual social relations it becomes an ideology guaranteeing the
permanence of the existing order.[7] It is not impossible to draw
revolutionary conclusions regarding the existing reality from the
Chu Hsi school's ideas about natural law. According to the Chu
Hsi theory of li and ch'i (Principle and Ether), the actual existence
of the ruler and the subject is under the sway of ch'i, so it is distinct
from the righteousness of ruler and subject, which is under the
sway of li. Since li takes precedence over ch'i, existing relations
between ruler and subjects must be changed if they conflict with
the righteousness of ruler and subject. But this naturalism, which
had penetrated deep into the theoretical structure of Chu Hsi
thought, had greatly weakened the pure, transcendental doctrinal
character of li, and hence of natural law, too. In fact there is in
Sung philosophy a tendency for the gap that exists between the
"Way" and "things," between norms and existing reality, to be
bridged from the side of the norms. For example, according to the
Chin-ssu lu [Reflections on things at hand],[8]

A thing cannot exist outside the Way, and the Way cannot exist
apart from things. That is, there is nothing in heaven and earth that
is not part of the Way. In the relationship between the father and
the son it is present in their intimacy. Between the ruler and the
subject it exists in the strict and correct relationship between them.

---

[6] *Myōtei mondō,* Book II.

[7] On the political and social role of natural law, see, for example, H. Kelsen: *Die
philosophischen Grundlagen der Naturrechtslehre und des Rechtspositivismus* (1928), pp. 37ff.
Kelsen, however, denies the revolutionary character of natural law.

[8] A collection of the works of the Sung philosophers, edited by Chu Hsi and Lü Tsu-
ch'ien. (Translator's note.)

... Thus, in dealing with the world, the superior man does not have a preconceived notion as to what should be adopted and what should be rejected. He simply follows the path of righteousness. If he had preconceptions about what to adopt and what to reject, he would have to believe that there are gaps in the Way, that heaven and earth are not perfect.

Our concern here, of course, is not Chu Hsi philosophy itself but only early Tokugawa Chu Hsi philosophy, with its iron authority over the hierarchical principles permeating all levels of the society, hierarchical principles established by the Tokugawa Bakufu, which had brought under complete control the turbulent conditions of the Sengoku era when underlings fought their superiors, had established a hierarchical order within the samurai class extending from the shogun down to the samurai servants, and had progressively diffused the feudal master-servant relationship down into the subjugated classes. Razan held that:

> It accords with the proper rules [rei] of heaven and earth that heaven is above and the earth below. Man is born with the proper rules of heaven and earth in his heart, so there is rank (high and low) and order (first and last) in all things. If we extend this spirit throughout heaven and earth, there will be no disorder between ruler and subject, high and low, or in any human relationship.[9]

And also that:

> *It is natural that heaven remains above and earth remains below.* Once the positions of high and low have been fixed, the nobility of the former and the baseness of the latter have been established. *The existence of order in the principle of nature* can be seen in the existence of high and low. The same can be said of man's heart [kokoro]. When [the distinction between] high and low is not violated, and noble and base are not confused, human ethics are in order. When ethics are in order, the state is well governed. When the state is well governed, the Way of the King has been realized. All this indicates that the rules of propriety [rei] are in full sway.[10]

---

[9] *Santoku shō*, Book II.
[10] *Keiten daisetsu.*

Thus, for Razan, the ultimate significance of natural law lay predictably in the recognition of the existing feudal hierarchy as the *"natural order"* itself. And this logic of "natural order" was the very thing that made Chu Hsi philosophy the most general and widespread mode of social thought in the ascendant feudal society.

Of course, all scholars did not use exactly the same method in justifying the social order as an a priori natural order. Razan himself, besides justifying it in terms of heaven and earth, that is, in terms of a spatial, static nature, sought to explain it in terms of a dynamic nature, as a subdivision of the li: "The fact that man and things emerge from heaven and earth is in accordance with the one and only *li*. The existence of myself, the people, things, elder and younger brothers, sages, the untalented, the filial son, the outlaw, the rich and noble, the poor and base, are all subdivisions of the *li*."[11] Nakae Tōju[12] justified the existing social order in terms of inherited refinement and coarseness. As he put it in *Okina mondō*:

> Under the sky, nothing that has form lacks the distinction of refinement and coarseness. The sun, the moon, and the stars are the refined aspects of heaven. Dragons are the coarse aspect of heaven. Productive mountains and wet and dry fields are the refined aspects of earth. Bare mountains and unproductive fields are the coarse aspects of earth. Sages and superior men are the refined aspects of man, while stupid and unworthy people are the coarse aspect. . . . Now, in all things the refined element becomes the vital force and the master of the thing. The coarse aspect submits to the refined aspect. Therefore sages and superior men, endowed with the refined aspects of mankind, become the rulers of the stupid and unworthy, and govern and instruct them. *The stupid and the unworthy, possessed with the coarse aspects, become the subjects of the sages and superior men, and follow their commands; this is the true nature of the command of heaven.* By the very nature of things, there are few rulers and many subjects. Thus there are few sages, who are to be the rulers, and many stupid and unworthy men, who are to be the subjects. *This is an obvious principle.*

[11] *Razan bunshū*, Book XXX.

[12] Tōju leaned towards Wang Yang-ming philosophy in later life, but when he wrote his *Okina mondō*, his thinking was definitely in line with Chu Hsi philosophy. Of course, for the problem under consideration, it is not very important whether he belonged to the Chu Hsi or the Wang Yang-ming school.

Whatever their differences, the ultimate logic of these explanations lies in the Sung philosophy's theory of natural law and its twofold justification of the Five Relationships in terms of nature: on the one hand through the laws of the universe (the Principle of Heaven), and on the other, as human nature (*honzen no sei*). Thus we can summarize the situation by saying that after the establishment of Tokugawa feudal society, the mode of thought that first arose in justifying it took the standpoint of the natural order.

At the beginning of the Tokugawa period, the intellectual world was uniform in tone, because of the Chu Hsi school, but soon signs of differentiation began to appear. Nakae Tōju advocated Wang Yang-ming philosophy later in life, and this school made more spectacular advances under the leadership of his disciples Fuchi Kōzan (1617–85) and Kumazawa Banzan. Schools of Ancient Learning were established simultaneously in Edo and Kyoto by Yamaga Sokō and Itō Jinsai respectively. These new theories made notable internal changes in the systematic structure of Chu Hsi philosophy. Banzan and Sokō in particular made significant progress in the empirical observation of political and social realities, where early Tokugawa Chu Hsi philosophers had been so weak. But where the justification of social relations in terms of nature was concerned, these men were still unable to move beyond the bounds of the Chu Hsi mode of thought. For example, Banzan said:

> The Four Virtues of Heaven [mentioned in the Book of Changes: spring representing benevolence; summer, propriety; autumn, righteousness; and winter, wisdom] and man's propriety, benevolence, righteousness, and wisdom are the same things with different names. Heaven's five elements and man's Five Relationships are the same *ch'i* with different forms. In heaven and earth, when the four seasons occur in accordance with the Four Virtues of Heaven, then heaven and earth are properly positioned and all things grow. When man adheres to the qualities of benevolence, righteousness, propriety, and wisdom, and the Five Relationships are clearly upheld, then the family will be regulated, the state will be in order, and there will be peace in the world.[13]

[13] *Shūgi washo*, Book VI.

Here the founding principles of the preservation of order in the state and peace in the world are still the Five Relationships and the Five Constant Virtues. The latter are, in turn, founded ultimately on nature, on yin and yang and the five elements. Propriety (rei), the ethical principle of the hierarchical order, is described as follows:

> Propriety corresponds to the *virtue of the principle of heaven* called *hsiang*,[14] which is a marvelous thing, flourishing and popular. However, when applied to matters of this world, it induces a spirit of respectfulness and modesty. *When the status of high and low, noble and base, have been fixed, rank and quality can be distinguished and there is no conflict or rivalry. Hence there is peace in the world.* When there is peace in the world, material things become available. *This is analogous to the fact that heaven produces summer and all things grow in abundance.*[15]

Sokō, too, argued as follows:

> What should be the basis for the education of the people? We should adhere to *the truth [makoto] of heaven and earth and nature,* and not pursue a different path. What is the truth of heaven and earth and nature? It is intimacy between father and son, righteousness between ruler and subject, distinction between husband and wife, the order of elder and younger brothers, and faithfulness between friends. These are called the five teachings.
>
> *The space between Heaven and earth* [is filled by] *the two forces [ch'i] of* yin *and* yang. They are the rites and music employed in the world of man. . . . In extending the principles of *yin* and *yang* to the everyday world, we say that rites [li] prevail when proper principles are

[14] *Hsiang*: to receive, to enjoy, to make or receive sacrificial offerings. (Translator's note.)

[15] *Shūgi washo,* Book VI. However, Banzan clearly distinguished between the Way and laws. The Way, he argued, "belongs to heaven and earth, and man. It also belongs to the five elements. Even when there was no such word as virtue, and there were no teachings of the sages, the Way was in effect. Even when man had not yet come into existence it was in effect in heaven and earth. Even when heaven and earth were not yet separated it was in effect in the universe" (*Shūgi gaisho,* Book III). That is, the Way is clearly seen as having a natural existence. But laws "were instituted by the sages to fit the circumstances of the times. Thus in those days they belonged to the Way" (ibid.). Hence he held that laws, that is to say, institutions, were produced by sages; he classified them as historical entities. This is one of the transitional systems of thought between the Chu Hsi school's naturalistic standpoint and the Sorai school's position of "invention." A similar viewpoint can be seen in Kaibara Ekken.

preserved in accordance with differences in status; and we say that music [*lo*] prevails when all things are friendly, in harmony and happy.[16]

He thus attempted to found the normative standards of the Five Relationships and rites and music on nature. This attempt to base the social hierarchy on "the general law of Heaven" rather than on "human capacities and arbitrary intentions" naturally led him to argue that:

> The distinction between high and low is the general law of heaven and earth. The reason why heaven is overhead and the earth beneath our feet is evident in itself.

> What is one's proper place? There are natural differences between high and low, noble and base. There is a fixed division which must not be overstepped. It is not caused by human capacities or arbitrary intentions.[17]

Jinsai did, however, make a significant change in the theoretical basis for the Chu Hsi school's concept of natural law. He separated the Way of Heaven and the way of man, distinguished yin and yang and the five elements from benevolence, righteousness, propriety, and wisdom, and criticized the Sung philosophers for equating social norms with natural law on the one hand and the intrinsic nature of man on the other, on the grounds that the terms benevolence, righteousness, propriety, and wisdom are "names of moral principles and not of human nature." But Jinsai's arguments were limited to questions of pure philosophy, so these changes did not affect his social and political thought. Moreover, in his opinion the Way (that is, normative standards) has its own internal justification, so he had no need to go further into the question. Although he did not attempt to base norms on the natural world (*Naturwelt*), he did believe that "the Way does not depend on the existence of man. It is sufficient unto itself."[18] That is, it retains its a priori validity so far as human existence is concerned. "The Way is the path of human relationships that must be adhered to every day.

16 *Gorui*, Book VII.
17 Ibid., Book XI.
18 *Dōjimon*, Book I.

It was not preceded by any teachings. And its perfection was not achieved by corrections and reforms. *It is naturally the way it is.*"[19] Its existence and its characteristics are thus natural after all. For Jinsai, the ethics of the relationships between ruler and subject, father and son, and husband and wife are part of an eternal order: "If there is a universe other than our universe, if men exist and children are born there," then these ethical standards will prevail there too.[20] The basic norms of the feudal society may not have been a natural order in the substantial sense, but for these men norms still endured, constituting a natural order in themselves.

[19] *Gomō jigi,* Book I.
[20] *Dōjimon,* Book I.

CHAPTER III

THE SORAI SCHOOL REVOLUTION

The Overthrow of the Theory of Natural Order. Its Practical and Political Purpose.

I

Certainly the justification of a given political and social order in terms of natural law should provide a most powerful guarantee for the immutability of that system. But the very fact that it is the most powerful guarantee possible restricts the range of its ability to uphold any existing order. Paradoxical though it may seem, if the people living under a certain social order are to accept it as a natural order, it must look like the natural order as far as they are concerned. Once the political stability of the society has been noticeably undermined and social disorder is clearly in evidence, the justification of the basic standards of the society by natural law ceases to be generally acceptable. To base the social order on natural law presupposes a certain degree of stability in the society even while helping to give society that stability. This is true whether natural law is equated with the actual laws that govern nature, as in the case of the Chu Hsi school, or whether it is consciously given a normative character, as is the case with Jinsai.

Laws assume the recurrence of similar situations, and norms only take into account normal conditions. When social relations lose their natural balance and become less predictable, the authority of the society's norms or laws collapses. The norms can no longer be justified by any inherent rationality. The questions then arise: Who is to validate the norms? Who is to restore balance and stability to the social order? In such a critical situation a body of thought is bound to emerge that stresses the idea of an autonomous personality (*shutaiteki jinkaku*) whose task it is to strengthen the foundations that uphold the social norms and to bring the political disorder under control. In the Genroku era (1688–1704), the contradictions inherent in contemporary feudal society suddenly intensified, and this led to the Kyōhō Reforms of Yoshimune (the eighth shogun), the first measures designed to remedy the Tokugawa feudal system. As a result, the naturalistic concept of the social order that had been firmly entrenched since the beginning of the Tokugawa period was completely overthrown. And Ogyū Sorai became the first man in the Tokugawa period to raise the issue of "*who* created the Way?" when he proclaimed his famous thesis that "the Way is not a principle which things adhere to, *nor is it* the natural way of heaven and earth. It is a way that was founded by *the Sages*."[1]

For Sorai, the Chu Hsi mode of thought, which based social relations on nature, was excessively optimistic and ineffective as a justification for feudal authority relations, because it was too far removed from reality. Moreover, as it held the existing social order, already showing signs of deterioration and decay, to be natural, it was obstructing what he called the "reconstruction of institutions" necessary to restore stability to society. For example, discussing a manifestation of the feudal hierarchy such as the rank and status system, Sorai remarked: "At present there is roughly a 'proper status' for everyone, and ignorant people think that this constitutes a form of regulative institution [*seido*]. But the 'proper status' of these days is not 'rites' or rules of propriety [*li*] handed down from antiquity, nor has it been definitely laid down by those in authority. Although some aspects of it have been subject to regulation by the authorities, *it has grown up naturally out of the manners and customs of the time. . . . It does not constitute what we can really call a system of regulative institutions*."[2] And yet it was accepted by society as its system of rank and status because "as time passed,

---

[1] *Tōmonsho*, Book III.
[2] *Seidan*, Book II.

Confucians, too, *forgot the real intentions of the Sages and began to say that the 'rites' [li] were cultural expressions of the Heavenly Principle, as if they existed naturally in Heaven and earth*. And thus they justified the concept of 'proper status' which had in fact emerged haphazardly as a result of the course of historical events."[3] In other words, the concept had its origin in the Chu Hsi mode of thought. Hence, in order to rescue feudal society from the critical situation confronting it and to rebuild it on a firm foundation, it was first necessary to transform completely the Confucian theories on which it was conceptually based. The latter had assumed a "natural order" of things; this assumption had to be supplanted by the assumption that social institutions are autonomously invented. This was the task Sorai undertook, and he carried it out with audacity and thoroughness.

The theory of natural order had arisen because Confucian norms link cosmological nature, called the Heavenly Way or Principle of Heaven, with human nature, called "original" or "inborn nature" (*honzen no sei*). First, Sorai excluded cosmological nature from the matters that were relevant to the Way of the Sages. In his opinion, concepts such as the Heavenly and Earthly Way are merely analogies with human systems projected onto the natural world. Consequently, he firmly rejected the practice of importing into the social system the concepts of yin and yang, which are categories of the natural world. He remarked:

> *Yin* and *yang* were established when the Sages invented the principle of divination. They were made the Heavenly Way, that is, the ultimate principle. When scholars use *yin* and *yang* as conceptual standards in the analysis of the course of the Heavenly Way and of natural phenomena, they may achieve some understanding in such matters. But where human affairs are concerned, this is not the case. For the Sages did not establish *yin* and *yang* as the Way of man. Only by loose thinking and loose use of words have the latter-day advocates of *yin* and *yang* imposed them on the Way of Man.[4]

Do not forget that the Chu Hsi school always used yin and yang to buttress hierarchical class relations based on natural law. This can

[3] Ibid.
[4] *Benmei*, Book II.

be seen in Razan's writings in such statements as "the ruler is Heaven, the subjects are *yin* and *yang* and the Five Elements," or "When a man brings order into the world outside his house, he behaves like heaven. He stands for *yang*. When a woman keeps order in the house, she behaves like the earth. She stands for *yin*."[5]

In Sorai's interpretation, the five elements (water, fire, wood, metal, and earth), too, which, according to the Chu Hsi school, are the basis of the Five Constant Virtues (benevolence, righteousness, propriety, wisdom, and faithfulness) and are usually coupled with yin and yang, are merely symbolic categories invented by the sages as convenient devices for the enumeration and arrangement of the countless things in the world. This he compared to the "rich merchant who classifies his stock by means of certain signs" merely as a "device to control complexity."[6] These symbols have no intrinsic value in themselves. "They are not principles," observed Sorai.[7] Categories such as the eternal law of heaven and the righteousness of the earth occur frequently in the works of thinkers who subscribed to the ideology of natural order. Sokō, for instance, said, "the distinction between high and low is the eternal law of Heaven and earth."[8] Sorai, on the other hand, held that these were "words extolling 'rites' [*li*]" and "to refer to heaven and earth is merely to eulogize them."[9] He thus stripped them of all substantive significance, reducing them to the level of allegories.

Sorai rejected all attempts to justify the Way in terms of cosmological nature, treating instead the various categories of the Confucian philosophy of nature as mere devices to maintain order in the state and peace in the world, and hence as a subordinate part of the Way of the Sages. He could not, however, make light of the concept of heaven, which undeniably held a significant place in pristine Confucianism. Instead, he made a clear distinction between the two meanings embodied in the concept of heaven, namely, heaven as the principle of natural regularity (the Way of Heaven), and heaven as a personalized entity (the Will of Heaven). He denied the independent existence of the former and gave

---

[5] *Keiten daisetsu; Razan bunshū*, Book XXX.
[6] *Benmei*, Book II.
[7] Ibid.
[8] *Yamaga gorui*, Book XI.
[9] *Benmei*, Book I.

full support to the latter. In Part I of this work, I have already discussed the place the theory of the Will of Heaven occupied in the philosophical structure of Sorai's teachings and elaborated on the part it played in the disintegration of the Chu Hsi mode of thought; there is no need to repeat these arguments here. It is sufficient to note that the shift in conceptual emphasis from the Way of Heaven to the Will of Heaven was one manifestation of a general tendency in Sorai's thought to give precedence to the autonomous personality over impersonal forces.

Second, Sorai asserted that the Way (the normative system) was independent of and superordinate to the innate qualities of human nature, and he confined the concept solely to external, objective systems, that is, to rites and music: "There is no Way apart from rites, music, law enforcement, and political administration," he said in *Bendō*. Needless to say, Sorai did not regard rites and music as abstractions, unlike the Sung scholars, who held them to be "literary expressions for the Principle of Heaven and the laws of human affairs." Nor was he concerned, like Hsun Tzu, with the reform of man's inner nature. By making them means of political control, he placed them completely outside human nature.[10]

But these maneuvers merely removed the naturalistic elements from the constituents of the Way, which was to take only a little further a moment that had already begun to emerge in the thought of Sokō and Jinsai. Sorai did confine the Way to human norms and held it to consist of the objective realities of rites, music, law enforcement, and political administration; but so long as the basis for the validity of the Way remained within the Way itself, it would not differ from Jinsai's Way, remaining a "self-validating" natural order. If the theory of natural order was to be completely overcome, no normative standards of any kind could be present in the background as the premise; instead, the starting point had to be human beings who, for the first time, invented norms and endowed them with their validity. This role of absolute inventors

[10] The fact that they were located outside human nature does not mean that they are in conflict with it. Unlike Hsun Tzu, Sorai emphasized the fact that the Way is in harmony with human feelings (this relates to his insistence on the immutability of human characteristics and his rejection of the view that man is by nature evil).

of the Way was precisely the role Sorai assigned to the Early Kings. "The Way," he said, "was established by the Early Kings. It does not exist naturally in heaven and earth."[11]

Needless to say, the Early Kings were Fu Hsi (who first domesticated animals), Shen Nung (the god of agriculture), and political rulers of ancient China such as Yao, Shun, Yu, T'ang, Wen, Wu, and the Duke of Chou. The Way, i.e., rites and music, first came into existence when these men invented them by "fully exerting their minds and utilizing their knowledge and skill to the utmost."[12] The Way is not something that exists "of itself, whether man exists or not." The inventors of the Way, then, were the sages, and, in turn, the term "sages" means those who have invented the Way. That Sorai restricted the concept of the sages exclusively to the historical figures known as the Early Kings is the element that decisively distinguishes Sorai's system from all previous schools of Confucian thought. Before him, "sage" was a general category meaning primarily a perfect embodiment of virtue, a model to be emulated in moral cultivation. The Early Kings such as Yao and Shun were of course included in the category of sages, but only insofar as they were the possessors of perfect moral virtues. In other words, they were sages because of an Idea inherent in them. But when this aspect, the Idea, is stressed in the notion of the sage, the concrete human aspect readily dissolves into an ultimate and impersonal concept. The Sung philosophers provide the typical examples of this: "The virtue of the Sage is identical with that of heaven and earth, his brilliance is the same as that of the sun and the moon, his course is in harmony with that of the four seasons, and in his good or bad fortune he is in harmony with the spirits" (Chou Tun-yi); "The Sages constitute the whole of the Supreme Ultimate" (Chu Hsi).

Hsun Tzu is often regarded as the source of Sorai's ideas; consider, for example, his contention that "the Sages transformed man's nature and developed acquired characteristics. When acquired characteristics had been developed, propriety [li] and righteousness emerged, and when propriety and righteousness had emerged, laws and systems were instituted. Hence propriety,

[11] *Benmei*, Book II.
[12] *Bendō*.

righteousness, laws, and systems were all created by the Sages."[13]
There is some truth in this, but while Hsun Tzu did regard the
sages as the inventors of propriety, righteousness, laws, and systems, he also held them to be models for moral training, that is,
he too believed in the significance of the sages as Ideas. "The
Sage," he once wrote, "is the quintessence of the Way. Hence the
goal of every scholar is to become a Sage"; and again, "The status
of a Sage is acquired through accumulated effort."[14] So long as the
concept of the sage has the significance of a universal Idea, the
sages as concrete persons who invented propriety, righteousness,
laws, and systems must ultimately derive their authority from an
Idea that exists *before* they do. Thus in the book of *Hsun Tzu,* the
Early Kings are still not absolutely autonomous. Sorai, in contrast, restricted the term "Sages" to refer to the Early Kings, who
had existed as actual historical personalities, and in *Bendō* he
stated that "one cannot hope to become a Sage by studying." This
prevented their conversion into impersonal (abstract) concepts.
Only thus could the Early Kings acquire the logical status of
absolute inventors of the Way.

Giving the sages (i.e., the Early Kings) the status of absolute
inventors of the Way also implies that they preceded the establishment of all political and social institutions. In theories based on
the natural order the sages were placed within that order. The
rejection of these naturalistic assumptions meant that the sages
had to be removed from the natural order and given the role of
producers of order out of absolute disorder. Before the sages' invention there was nothing [normative]; after it, everything. An abyss
separates the age that preceded and the age that followed the
sages' invention.

It follows that before the advent of the sages, society was without
norms of any kind, in a state of nature like that conceived by
Hobbes. It was no longer possible to regard the Five Relationships
and the Five Constant Virtues as had earlier Tokugawa Confucians such as Razan: "The Five Relationships—between ruler and
subject, father and son, husband and wife, elder brother and
younger brother, and friend and friend—have always existed *in*

[13] *Hsun Tzu,* Chapter XXIII.
[14] Ibid., Chapters XIX, XXIII.

the past as in the present, since heaven and earth began";[15] or Banzan: "The Way consists of the Three Bonds [between ruler and subject, father and child, husband and wife] and the Five Constant Virtues. It is coterminous with Heaven, Earth, and Man, and with the Five Elements. Even before there was a term for virtue, and *before there were teachings of the Sages, the Way already existed.*"[16]

According to Sorai, the only naturally existing aspect of the Five Relationships was the love between father and son. The ethical relationship between man and wife might seem natural and innate, but in fact it was established for the first time as a normative standard by Fu Hsi. "In the wild chaotic age, men behaved like beasts," said Sorai. "This being the case, the ways of ruler and subject and friend and friend were known to men only *after* they had been established by the Sages." Similarly, the sages had invented the modes of production: "For instance, Shen Nung introduced the cultivation of the five grains, and the Yellow Emperor established the way of building palaces and weaving clothes." Sorai argued that today it is generally believed that these norms and modes of production had existed from the beginning or had sprung into existence naturally without the sages' intervention because the sages "in their profound and comprehensive wisdom *invented in harmony with human nature.*" This harmony with human nature provides a refutation of Hsun Tzu's thesis that human nature is evil and norms mere artifices (*wei*) designed to correct it, but it does not constitute evidence, said Sorai, "that these things were present naturally in heaven and earth *before the Sages were born.*"[17]

Of course, the notions that Fu Hsi taught man the ethical principles of the relationship between husband and wife and that Shen Nung is the father of agriculture were not in themselves new ideas at all. They were commonly held notions among Confucian scholars. Sorai's originality lay in the fact that he appreciated and rigorously developed methodological implications of these ideas to the point where they posed a clear challenge to the theories of natural order. Sorai was thorough and consistent in applying his

[15] *Santoku shō,* Book I.
[16] *Shūgi gaisho,* Book III.
[17] *Tōmonsho.*

principle. It led him even to ascribe to the invention of the Early
Kings the system of the four estates (*shih*—gentlemen-scholars in
China, samurai in Japan—peasants, artisans, and merchants) so
fundamental to Tokugawa society. In his *Tōmonsho* [Questions
and answers], he remarked: "The principle that the entire world
should be organized into the four classes of gentlemen-scholars,
peasants, artisans, and merchants was also established by the Ancient Sages. *The four classes did not exist naturally in heaven and earth.*"
And in *Taiheisaku* [A policy for great peace], he wrote: "Neither
the Five Relationships, nor the division into gentlemen-scholars
or samurai, peasants, artisans, and merchants is a product of
nature. These Ways were invented by the Sages in order to bring
peace and security to the people." Compare this with the most
detailed accounts of the matter offered before Sorai's time. Banzan,
for example, wrote:

> *Man's first concern was with agriculture. Without anyone clearly appointing*
> *him, someone who happened to be skilled in agriculture* came to be gen-
> erally consulted. When his directions were followed, everything
> turned out well. So people began to get together to do his agricul-
> tural work for him, and he was given the task of serving as a general
> judge. This is the origin of the gentleman-scholar. Then gradually
> the superior individuals among the gentlemen-scholars from various
> places came to be consulted by all the other gentlemen-scholars.
> Thus these superior men were acclaimed as feudal princes. Among
> the feudal princes there was one man who was far superior to the
> others. His virtues were known in the four corners of the earth. He
> offered principles to explain those things which other men found
> beyond their powers of comprehension. Thus people united under
> him and looked up to him as the Emperor. Then the chief ministers
> and high officials were appointed from among the gentlemen-
> scholars, and the artisans and merchants emerged from the peas-
> antry. In this way, all things under heaven were established. The
> Five Relationships and the Five Constant Virtues came into being
> in compliance with the Five Elements of heaven and earth.[18]

And according to Yamaga Sokō:

When people came into existence by obtaining the *ch'i* of heaven

[18] *Shūgi washo,* Book VIII.

and earth, and receiving the *li,* they had first to fill their stomachs; they needed food and drink. If man lacks nourishment even for a day, he grows weak, and finally dies. For this reason, *the practice of agriculture naturally came into being.* But man's four limbs alone are not sufficient for successful agriculture, so wood and bamboo tools were used. But they were not well formed. So the shape and size of the wood and bamboo were fixed, and iron was melted for use as agricultural implements. That is why, even though the arts of agriculture were known, without artisans there would not be enough tools to practice them. . . . But although the artisans began to produce tools and sell the products themselves, it was difficult to trade with distant places and far lands. So middlemen emerged who earned their living by providing these services. They are called merchants. Hence the three popular classes came into existence. There were now three classes, but they were all concerned with their own needs and desires. The peasants worked to ensure their own food supply but neglected the care of the mountains. . . . The merchants made inordinate profits and devised dishonest schemes. Everyone allowed his desires free rein, and remained in ignorance of proper conduct. Banditry and strife knew no bounds. Everyone behaved according to his natural urges, and the great rules of human conduct were unknown. For this reason it was decided to set up a ruler and obey his commands. He became the basis for the education of the people and the source of their manners and customs. That is how the classes of gentlemen-scholars, peasants, artisans, and merchants arose, and the institutions and practices of the old world were perfected.[19]

Thus both Banzan and Sokō explained the origin of gentlemen-scholars (samurai), peasants, artisans, and merchants as a gradual development arising from the necessities of human life. If we examine this problem solely from the standpoint of historical explanation and ask which theory is closer to the historical truth—that proposed by Banzan and Sokō, or that of Sorai (who held that the four classes were entirely an invention of the ancient sages)—few would hesitate in choosing the views of Banzan and Sokō. But if it is assumed that social, human existence is in direct continuity with natural existence, assertions of historical origin automatically become assertions of natural origin, and to that extent the question

---

[19] *Yamaga gorui,* Book V, *Minsei,* Part I.

of *who* makes history is never raised. Looking at the matter from the standpoint of the history of thought, Sorai's "inaccuracies"—the result of his consistency in maintaining the absolute primacy of the Early Kings' act of invention—were, in baseball jargon, "sacrifice flies": minor points thrown away in the interests of a wider aim—in Sorai's case, the complete transformation of the ideology of natural order.

II

From this analysis we can see that, although they are both described as Confucian, the Chu Hsi school (which held the essence of the Way to be an a priori li existing in heaven and earth and nature) and the Sorai school (which believed that actual historical personalities, the Early Kings, invented the Way originally out of nothing) were based on fundamentally opposed forms of thought. Ultimately this opposition stems from a fundamental philosophical problem: Do Ideas precede persons and are persons the embodiment of these Ideas, or do persons first exist in reality and are Ideas made into realities by persons? It is not my purpose to attempt a general logical resolution of this problem or to make a value judgement as to the relative merits of the two theories. As I have already suggested, my task is to determine how this opposition was expressed concretely in the social and institutional conceptions of these schools.

As the frame of reference (*Aspektstruktur*) of feudal society was Confucian based, the Confucian conception of the Way had a direct bearing on social institutions. As we have seen, it was possible to derive from Chu Hsi teachings the view that feudal society is part of the natural order. Social norms were justified by the ideal character inherent in them. How, then, are the principles of the Sorai school expressed in its institutional views? For the Sorai school, Ideas are no longer allowed a priori, absolute status. They can only exist as subordinate to actual human personalities. Hence validation of social norms cannot be based on an ideal character inherent in them, but only on the political personalities who invented them. These political personalities were primarily the Early Kings of the Three Dynasties (Hsia, Shang, and Chou). We have already seen that, according to Sorai, the Five Relationships and the estate system of gentlemen-scholars, peasants, artisans, and merchants were invented by the Early Kings. In *Tōmonsho*, Sorai wrote of the Early Kings, or sages, the inventors of this Way, as follows: "This ignorant old man [i.e., himself] does not believe in Shākyamuni Buddha, but he does believe in the Sages," and "This ignorant old man has deep faith in the Sages. Even if he felt in his heart that a certain dictum might not be correct, he would accept it and practice it, reasoning that precisely because it is the Way of the Sages it could not possibly be harmful." Thus by raising the sages to the level of religious absolutes, he sought to give absolute validity to the basic standards of feudal society. But Sorai also went further than this.

According to the Sorai school, the Way, concretely speaking, is the specific historical institutions and cultural products of the era of the Three Dynasties, and the inventors of these were the first historical rulers Yao, Shun, Yu, and T'ang. Once established, this logical connection between the sages and the Way could be applied to the relationship between the political rulers and the institutions of all ages, not just to that of the Three Dynasties. Sorai frequently pointed out that Chu Hsi rationalism ignored historical particularities, and he emphasized the need to be aware of the uniqueness of the institutions of each era, even after the ages of Ch'in and Han, when the Way of the Sages was already in decline. The institutions of every era can be justified in terms of the autonomous inventions of the founding ruler (who invented at his own "discretion"). "*The entire structure of the world* [the country] *changes at the discretion of the founding father of each era*. Hence institutions and laws also change."[20] Here, then, is the most significant social and political theory implied by Sorai's mode of thought.

As noted earlier, Sorai was confronted with two political problems. First, a new basis was needed for the ultimate standards of feudal society. Second, he had to formulate forceful political measures that would overcome the prevailing social disorder. The first problem could be solved merely by justifying the ultimate standards in terms of the sages' work of invention, by making the

[20] *Tōmonsho*.

sages into absolutes. But if the logic of invention were confined to the ancient sages and the historical past, this would not meet the intellectual preconditions for the solution of the second problem. In other words, if, after its invention by the sages, the Way is cut off from the inventing agent and justified in itself as an objectified Idea, this means after all a return to the concept of natural order. But this approach could not provide any *political decisions* capable of dealing with existing reality. By extending the analogy of the logic of "invention by the Early Kings" to all ages, the ascendancy of persons over ideas was firmly established for the first time. This made it possible for political rulers to engage in inventive activities, *directed towards the future*, in order to overcome the crisis confronting them.

In Sorai's case, the Way of the Sages had a universal validity that transcended time and place. However, the Ideas embodied in the Way did not come into existence by themselves but emerged through the inventive acts of the founder-king of each era. In theories of natural order, the Idea is realized immanently and continuously, but in Sorai's case, the realization of the Idea is discontinuous, in that institutions must be invented anew by the ruler of each new regime. It was on the basis of this reasoning that Sorai proposed large-scale reforms "from above" in his books (*Seidan, Taiheisaku, Rinroku*, etc.). Sorai had directly experienced the social changes of the Genroku and Kyōhō eras, and the existing feudal society seemed to him to be in a chaotic age and its stratified social system to have completely broken down. It was an age when, "if he has but sufficient money, the basest of the common people can imitate a daimyo with impunity. How sad it is that if a person does not have money and is in straitened circumstances, even if he is a man of high status and superior virtue, he must debase himself and suffer contemptuous treatment."[21]

The reason for this chaotic situation was that "institutions are everywhere lacking." The existing estate system had not been invented in the manner described earlier; it was nothing more than "the manners and customs of the society and had emerged naturally."[22] Sorai argued that the Tokugawa founder, Ieyasu,

---

[21] *Seidan,* Book II.
[22] Ibid.

had been entrusted with the basic task of establishing institutions (seido)[23] in accordance with the Way of the Sages. But "his was an age when peaceful conditions were restored by military force after a long period of civil war, and because a long time had elapsed since the period of antiquity it was impossible to restore the ancient institutions. Moreover, since it was a period following the civil war, all existing institutions had been destroyed. But he did not reform the manners and customs of his age, and left them as they were."[24] As a result, the society had remained without regulative institutions to Sorai's day. Sorai wanted the eighth shogun, Yoshimune, to invent the institutions as Ieyasu should have done. It would be no exaggeration to say that these political and practical considerations were the true motives for his lifelong intellectual effort to expel from Confucianism the ideology that held that norms (the Way) were naturally valid.

What then was the nature of the institutions that Sorai wanted to establish with the help of Shogun Yoshimune? His proposals for reform of the social structure are among the most famous presented in the Tokugawa period. There is no need to discuss them in detail here, but in simple terms, their basic tone is summed up in the phrase "restoration of the past." Sorai was perceptive enough to see that the crisis confronting the feudal society of his age stemmed from the rapid growth of a money economy and the concomitant rise of commercial capital; and that the latter had its origin in the fact that the samurai class had severed its ties with the soil and gathered in castle-towns, falling into the state he described as "living in an inn." He therefore aimed for a return of the samurai to their fiefs, a registration system to prevent the population from moving about, rigidly enforced status distinctions, and the restriction of desires within limits set by social standing. These measures would, he hoped, ensure the smooth functioning of the feudal mode of production.

Sorai was a passionate advocate of pristine feudalism. The men he really admired were the warriors of old who ate and dressed very simply and roamed the mountains, forests, and fields in

---

[23] *Seido* means literally "regulations and degrees." Cf. J. R. McEwan: *The Political Writings of Ogyū Sorai*, op. cit., p. 38. (Translator's note.)

[24] *Seidan*, Book II.

normal times, while in emergencies they hurried to the service of their lord. The men he most detested were those "retired merchants" "who have no one below them whom they must govern, nor retainers, nor rules of conduct and obligations as the samurai do, but are as extravagant as a daimyo in their clothes, food, and houses."[25] The ideal social relationship, in Sorai's opinion, was that of the lord and retainer "resting on the benevolence and gratitude of the superior and inferior with only simple rules of conduct."[26] The life least to his taste was that of "the castle-town, where everything is easygoing and convenient" and the "slothful custom" of "going through life selling for profit" prevailed.[27] But in his own day, the sort of warrior he admired was becoming more and more a figure of ancient tales, while the unruly activity of merchant and money-lending capital was becoming more intolerable day by day. Purely status-based social relationships were being rapidly overrun by contractual ones. In Book I of *Seidan*, Sorai gave the following vivid description of a typical example of this, the process whereby purely feudal hereditary servants were being replaced by free, contractual, temporary servants:

> In recent years there has been a great increase in the number of servants hired on short-term contracts, and there are no longer any hereditary servants in the service of the members of the military class, while very few are left in the service of peasants in the countryside. The reason is that hereditary servants give too much trouble. Since they are born into the household of their master, the latter has to care for them during childhood, and after they have grown up, he must continue to look after them, providing them with food, clothing, and other necessities because he uses them strenuously and harshly. They are a part of their master's household and since they have no other home, their master is responsible for them and must continually look after them. . . . But now that all members of the military class live crowded together in castle-towns, their first concern is to avoid the occurrence of incidents involving their servants. Servants hired on short-term contracts serve for only one year, and

[25] Ibid.
[26] *Tōmonsho.*
[27] *Seidan*, Book II.

even if they are unsatisfactory they can be put up with for a year. If they commit an offense they can be handed over to the *ukenin* [guarantor] and then cease to be the responsibility of the master. Since the hired servant is responsible for the supply of his own clothing and other needs, the master does not have to look after him. . . . Hired servants are used to the ways of the world and perform their duties intelligently when they accompany their master, run errands, and so on. For all these reasons, hired servants are preferred to the original hereditary servants, all of whom have now been dismissed with the pretense that this is an act of benevolence or is motivated by a concern for their posterity on the part of the master, and now there are none left in the service of the military class.

These substantive changes in social relations were bound to influence the spirit sustaining the master-servant relationship:

Besides the fact that this is a time of peace, *no affection or sympathy is felt towards retainers* simply because only hired servants are employed. *As the period of employment is limited to one year, master and servant look on one another as strangers they have met on the street.* . . . For the servants, *Edo has become a city of* [potential] *masters*; this attitude has become part of the social mores, and it is naturally spreading from the lower to the upper levels of society—the masters themselves are losing their loyalty to their own masters. All this points to a change in social customs. And whether he is raised by a hereditary or hired servant will affect the way a child grows up. Hereditary servants are well aware of the family tradition inherited from the ancestors, and being in the family for many years, they will know the relatives. And though they are of low status they have a sense of honor. Having been raised through the kindness of their master, their attitude and behavior in raising their master's children will be exceptional. A hired servant has none of these qualities. *He works only for the time being, to fend for the time being.*[28]

These passages describe nothing but the decline of *Gemeinschaft* consciousness and the growth of *Gesellschaft* consciousness. This was a natural consequence of the fact that the feudal master-servant relationship, which was originally based on a natural economy,

[28] Ibid., Book I.

mediated by land and realized within a very restricted circle, was now being widely extended in the heart of a commercial economy in which "not a single day passes without something being bought for money." Sorai lived at a time when the poison that was to corrode and dissolve away feudal society was spreading rapidly through the system, and he devoted all his intellectual powers to the elimination of this poison. Insofar as the spread of this poison was historically inevitable, he was undoubtedly a reactionary thinker. The *content* of his system consists of the natural elements that constituted primitive feudalism: an agricultural livelihood, a natural economy, a family-based master-servant relationship, and so on. Hence the structure of the Sorai school's position is, really, in the last analysis, an attempt to produce nature by the logic of invention. This is by no means a verbal game. It is one of the ironies of history that a reactionary may be forced to use the theoretical weapons of his opponents. While Sorai abhorred Gesellschaft social relationships, the Gesellschaft logic was embedded in his theory of invention. A closer analysis of this point will reveal to us the full historical implication of the opposition between the naturalistic and the inventive viewpoints.

CHAPTER IV

THE HISTORICAL SIGNIFICANCE OF THE TRANSITION FROM NATURE TO INVENTION

The Modernity of the Logic of Invention. The Problem of the Absolutization of the Autonomous Personality.

I

What do I mean when I say that the theory of autonomous invention contains within it a Gesellschaft logic? There are in human society two fundamentally opposed modes of social bonds. One is the bond that exists before the individual as a necessary "given." The other is the association that the individual forms out of his own free will. In the former, the pattern of the bond has a fixed, objective form, and the individual fits into this pattern as if he were destined to do so. In the latter, the individual has a plan, and as a means to attain his objectives, he enters into new social relations. Thus there is no fixed, objective pattern in this mode of association; it varies according to the objectives sought. Of course, the many social relations that exist in real life are not limited to these two types. They are merely ideal types that constitute the two extreme forms of bonds in human society, and actual social relations lie in an infinitely nuanced range between them. The family is a comparatively pure form of the former, while associations such as political parties and academic societies generally belong to the latter, though with different degrees of *Geschlossenheit* (exclusiveness).

These two contrasting types of bonds are of course universally present in the social systems of all ages. But in Europe scholars who have traced historically the rise of modern society, both from the legal and from the sociological standpoint, have found that in the course of the historical changes that led to the formation of modern bourgeois society within the declining medieval feudal system, social bonds of the latter type began to displace those of the former, and they have made various suggestions to explain this transition. Such schemata as "From Status to Contract" (Henry Maine) and from Gemeinschaft to Gesellschaft are notable attempts of this kind. In particular, the latter scheme, presented by Tönnies,[1] who described in great detail the opposition and transition between the two types of social bond described above, has had a remarkable influence within the academic world.

However, this scheme has been applied indiscriminately as a cure-all; in reaction to this its scientific rigor has recently come into considerable doubt. The concept of Gemeinschaft in particular presents a problem. The generalization of Gesellschaft bonds can clearly be allocated to a historical stage, roughly that of modern society, but the historical scope of Gemeinschaft predominance is not at all clear. It seems vaguely to include all the epochs prior to modern bourgeois society. As a result, it ignores the historical changes that occurred around the time when the primitive communal system dissolved and a *Herrschaftsgebilde* (pattern of authority) was established, changes that are just as important as those in the transition from the medieval to the modern period. For this reason, Freyer[2] divides Tönnies's Gemeinschaft into two stages to give a three-stage division of *Gemeinschaft, Ständesgesellschaft,* and *Klassengesellschaft*.[3] Here, feudal society is placed in the category of Gesellschaft as a Ständesgesellschaft, that is, as a society based on hereditary status (*mibunshakai*). It would certainly be ahistorical when discussing actual social structures to include both the kinship-based communal system, in which class divisions (in the broad sense) have not yet arisen, and feudal society, in which estate and class relations run through the entire social structure, under the term Gemeinschaft. Perhaps Freyer's classification is

---

[1] Ferdinand Tönnies: *Gemeinschaft und Gesellschaft* (1887; 8th improved ed., 1935).

[2] Cf. Hans Freyer: *Einleitung in die Soziologie* (1931), pp. 131ff.

[3] *Ständesgesellschaft* is feudal society stratified according to hereditary estates, and *Klassengesellschaft* is modern society stratified according to the distribution of property. (Translator's note.)

more valid than Tönnies's. But if we do not just examine social relations from the standpoint of their socioeconomic structure but focus primarily upon the consciousness, not the individual or subjective consciousness but the social consciousness, the so-called objective spirit, that permeates the social structure, Tönnies's schema still retains fresh significance and value.

For example, if we take the different social bonds in a feudal society—such as the important feudal master-servant relations, as well as the church and guilds (in Europe), and the *za* (guilds), *kabunakama* (merchant guilds), and Five-Man Groups (in Japan) —they tend to be closer, in the process of their formation and in their structural patterns, to the social relations of bourgeois society than to those of primitive, kinship-based communal systems. But considered in terms of the spiritual props supporting these bonds, that is, in terms of the *images* that their participants have of them, the difference between these and kinship-based communal systems is only a matter of degree. On the other hand, there is an unbridgeable gap in this respect between feudal social bonds and, say, those in a joint-stock company. For instance, although there is undeniably a contractual element in feudal master-servant relations, under normal circumstances the consciousness found in them is more analogous to that found in the relations between father and son in the family than to that in a modern bilateral contract. So far as the content of the prevailing images of social relations is concerned, the changes that occurred during the formative period of modern society can be said to be much more drastic than the changes that had occurred during all the historical stages up to and including feudal society.

At the end of the Middle Ages and the beginning of the modern period in Europe, social bonds of the second type rapidly began to overshadow those of the first type. This was more evident in social consciousness than in social reality. Medieval man considered the prototype of all social relations to be natural and inevitable bodies (*societates necessariae*) like the family. Modern man, on the other hand, believes that whenever possible, social relations should be founded on the free will of the individual (*societates voluntariae*).[4]

[4] On *societates voluntariae* and *societates necessariae* and the process whereby the ideas of the former were applied to an increasing number of social bonds as the modern pe-

Herein resides the real significance of the "discovery of man" in the modern period. In the Middle Ages, man and the individual were by no means ignored. In fact, the duties and functions of the individual were frequently discussed. The discovery of man does not mean recognizing the existence of man as an object, but that man began to be conscious of his autonomy. Until then man had fatalistically accepted the various social systems into which he had to fit. But now he found himself in a position to establish or abolish these systems freely according to his own will and ideas. Man, who used to act according to the social order, now began to act upon it. Tönnies wrote in explanation of the opposition between *Wesenwille* (natural will) and *Kürwille* (rational will):

> Natural will is the psychological equivalent of the human body, or the principle of the unity of life, supposing that life is conceived under that form of reality to which thinking itself belongs. . . . Rational will is the product of thinking itself and consequently possesses reality *only with reference to its author, the thinking individual.*[5]

> Natural will derives from and can be explained only in terms of the past, just as *the future in turn evolves from the past.* Rational will can be understood only from the future developments with which it is concerned. Natural will contains the future in *embryo* or emergent form [*Keim*]; rational will contains it as an *image* [*Bild*].[6]

In these passages Tönnies is pointing out the inversion of the relationship between the social system and man that occurred in the transition from the medieval to the modern period. The situation in which what exists in reality was generated in the past, and the future is contained embryonically in the past, is typical above all of the organism. For an organism, an agent that stands outside it and invents it is inconceivable in principle. An organism is a self-sufficient whole, and all its components arise naturally inside it. The form that stands at the completely opposite pole is, of course, the machine. A machine presupposes an agent who makes

---

riod progressed, finally penetrating the family system itself, see Otto von Gierke: *Das deutsche Genossenschaftsrecht,* IV, p. 402.

[5] *Gemeinschaft und Gesellschaft,* op. cit., 8th ed., p. 87; trans. Charles P. Loomis as *Community and Association* (London, 1955), p. 119.

[6] *Community and Association,* op. cit., p. 120.

it and operates it from the outside. As a means, it is subordinate to the goal established by the agent. "An aggregate or form of the rational will is related to an aggregate of the natural will in the same manner as an artificial tool or machine built for definite ends or purposes compares with the organic systems and the various organs of the animal body," wrote Tönnies.[7] Hence we can say, with Gierke, that "medieval thought proceeded from the idea of a single Whole; an organic construction of Human Society was as familiar to it as a mechanical and atomistic construction was originally alien."[8] Thus the process that established man's autonomy with respect to the social order began with the decline of organicism and culminated in the formation of mechanical thought.[9] The first glorious page of this modern view of institutions was written by Thomas Hobbes when he began his *Leviathan* with these words:

NATURE, the art whereby God hath made and governs the world, is by the *art* of man, as in many other things, so in this also imitated, that it can make an artificial animal. For seeing life is but a motion of limbs, the beginning whereof is in some principal part within; why may we not say, that all *automata* . . . have an artificial life? For what is the *heart*, but a *spring*; and the *nerves*, but so many *strings*; and the *joints*, but so many *wheels* giving motion to the whole body, such as was intended by the artificer? *Art* goes yet further, imitating that rational and most excellent work of nature, *man*. For by art is created that great *Leviathan* called a *Commonwealth*, or *State*, in Latin *Civitas*, which is but an artificial man.[10]

Even from the general observations made here, I believe it can be inferred that the shift from the Chu Hsi mode of thought, which considered political and social systems to exist naturally in heaven

[7] Ibid., p. 155.

[8] Otto von Gierke: *Political Theories of the Middle Age,* trans. William Maitland (Cambridge, 1938), p. 22.

[9] For modern man, who has witnessed the contradiction of control, the fact that man does not control the machine but is instead enslaved and driven by it when it is supposed to be a means, the notion that the image of a machine could be a symbol of man's autonomy may sound strange, but that is precisely the historical significance of the appearance of the image of the machine in opposition to organicist thought. The contradiction of control only became apparent after the Industrial Revolution.

[10] Thomas Hobbes: *Leviathan,* ed. Michael Oakeshott (New York, 1947), p. 5.

and earth, to the Sorai school's logic, which held that they are invented by men as agents, corresponds roughly to the changes that occurred in the "medieval"[11] social consciousness described above. (The significance of the fact that men as agents first appeared as the sages and then by analogy with the latter as political rulers will be discussed later.) For example, if we consider the apprehension of the estate system of samurai, peasants, artisans, and merchants, the backbone of the Tokugawa feudal system, we find (see pp. 214–216) that in the ideology of natural order, it is understood as the gradual growth of estates that "naturally came into being" "without anyone clearly appointing them." On the other hand, Sorai conceived it as a system invented by the Early Kings, who "fully exerted their minds" and "utilized their knowledge and skill to the utmost" in order to achieve the goal of bringing "peace to the people." Compare this with Tönnies:

A fellowship [*Genossenschaft*] is an organization of *Gemeinschaft*; a special-interest group [*Verein*] is a phenomenon of *Gesellschaft*. Consequently, a fellowship is, so to speak, *a product of nature* and can be comprehended only as something which has grown up [*ein Gewordenes*], only from the condition of its origin and development. . . . In contradistinction, a special-interest group is a fictitious being which serves its authors, expressing their common rational will in certain relationships. It is, therefore, of prime importance to find out the *end* for which it is intended.[12]

It is undeniable that early Tokugawa thought, based on the concept of natural order, corresponds both in its subjective intentions and in its objective content to a Gemeinschaft. In contrast, although the conscious aim of Sorai's concept of invention was a Gemeinschaft, this concept is clearly permeated with the logic of a Gesellschaft (ultimately of a Verein!).

I have argued above that when any really existing order is justified by the idea of a natural order, that existing order is in its stage of ascendancy or stability, whereas when, on the contrary, if justified in terms of autonomous personalities, it is in its period

---

[11] The word "medieval" is used here in its universal and substantive sense and is not restricted to the Japanese historians' use of the term "medieval" (*chūsei*).

[12] *Community and Association,* op. cit., p. 248.

of decline or crisis. I reached this conclusion by examining the temporal relationship between the Chu Hsi school (or the Chu Hsi mode of thought) and the Sorai school solely in reference to a certain formal rule.[13] Now we have reached a point where it is possible to go on and consider the actual historical and social positions these two schools occupied.

The Chu Hsi school succeeded in becoming the dominant mode of political and social thought with the establishment of Tokugawa feudal society not only because the concept of natural order it contained was appropriate to the rise of feudal society but also because it was particularly suitable given that it was a rising feudal society. It is easy to see why a form of consciousness that regards social relations as naturally and necessarily given would incline toward universality in the feudal society of Japan during the Tokugawa period, a feudal society regarded as a "model example" in world history because of its stable and orderly estate relations and its life-styles modeled along the same lines. The importance of the family, a natural order in the strictest sense, in public law, the de jure or de facto inheritance of social status, the extensive authority derived from status and family background, joint responsibility for taxation and crime, were all moments that made existing social relations appear natural and necessary, inalterable by man's free will. The following description by Tönnies is doubly true if applied to the ideology of Tokugawa feudal society:

> It is only important to note to what a great extent in the culture of the village and the feudal system, which is based upon it, the idea of *natural* distribution and of a sacred tradition which determines and rests upon this natural distribution *dominates all realities of life* and all *corresponding ideas of its right and necessary order,* and how little significance and influence attach to the concepts of exchange and purchase, of contract and regulations.[14]

The Chu Hsi system, which identified the basic norms of feudal society, i.e., the Five Relationships, with *ontological* nature at two levels (as intrinsic human nature and the natural order of the uni-

---

[13] In this sense, this society does not necessarily have to be feudal. For instance, in the opinion of the Physiocrats of the eighteenth century, it was precisely capitalist society that was the *ordre naturel*.

[14] *Community and Association,* op. cit., pp. 67–68.

verse), most effectively represented and provided the theoretical basis for such a notion of the social order. Moreover, the most deep-seated metaphysical roots of Chu Hsi philosophy undoubtedly lay in organic reasoning (*organisches Denken*). That is, the Supreme Ultimate, the fundamental principle of the order of the universe, is the unitary root of the world, and at the same time it is a particularizing force inherent in all things and endowing them with ultimate value. As Chu Hsi said in *Chu Tzu ch'üan-shu*: "Speaking from the point of view of the whole, the myriad things constitute one Supreme Ultimate. Speaking from the point of view of the individual things, each individual thing possesses the Supreme Ultimate in its entirety." A thinker of the Tokugawa period ingeniously compared this relation to "the moon reflected in each rice field." The image of the moon is reflected in an infinite number of rice fields, but the moon transcends all the individual images as well as their sum total. In *Shunkan shō*, Razan explained this theory, known as *li-i fen-shu* (*Li*, the whole and the particular), in simple, concrete moralistic terms:

> The sole purpose and task of creation by heaven and earth was to nurture and foster the growth of the myriad of things. Because of this the four seasons begin and end, and end and begin. From the past to the present, without a moment's rest, it has had as its purpose and task the production and nurturing of all things over and over, around and around. . . . The heart of heaven and earth can be seen clearly in this. Because it is the task of heaven and earth to create and nurture things, *all things—grass and trees, birds and animals—grow because of the benevolent, nurturing will of heaven and earth. Thus the Principle of Heaven is inherent in all things.* And certainly there is no question that man, who is spiritually superior to the myriad things, possesses the Principle of Heaven. *All men must accept as their own heart the heart of heaven and earth which nurtures all things, and must possess the spirit of benevolence and righteousness.*

The organic activities of the all-embracing Being, Heaven, and Earth are repeated in miniature in the ethical behavior of one of the beings in heaven and earth, man. Otto von Gierke remarked of the ideas of medieval European society:

> To every being is assigned its place in that Whole, and to every link

between Beings corresponds a divine decree. But since the World is One Organism, animated by One Spirit, fashioned by One Ordinance, the self-same principles that appear in the structure of the World will appear once more in the structure of every part. Therefore every particular Being, insofar as it is Whole, is a diminished copy of the World; it is a *microcosmus* or *minor mundus* in which the *macrocosmus* is mirrored.[15]

If Razan's phrase "the nurturing will of heaven and earth" is substituted for the term "divine decree," Gierke's statement could be read directly as an interpretation of the Chu Hsi school. Moreover, in Chu Hsi philosophy, any concept of a personal god outside and transcending even the all-embracing world known as heaven and earth is totally lacking. In this sense its organic mode of thought, essentially an immanentism, is more thoroughgoing than that of scholasticism.

II

While the Chu Hsi school almost purely and completely embodied the Gemeinschaft mode of thought, there are obviously certain historical limitations to a similar accord between the Sorai school and the Gesellschaft mode of thought. No matter how much a thinker's subjective intentions may differ from the objective meaning of his thought, it is impossible for a believer in feudalism to adopt a mode of thought that is completely modern and bourgeois. Hence it is necessary to measure the extent of the modernity contained in Sorai's concept of autonomous invention. The first point that comes to mind is the restrictions on the personalities who can invent the social order. In a completely modernized Gesellschaft mode of thought, the theory that men as agents with free will invent the social order applies to every individual. The theory of social contract is the inevitable consequence. But for the Sorai school, the personalities who invent the social order are above all the sages, and then by analogy political rulers in general. Moreover, these sages are raised virtually to the level of religious absolutes. The Chu Hsi school saw the essence of the Way in the prin-

---

[15] *Political Theories of the Middle Age,* op. cit., p. 8.

ciple of heaven and earth and in the principle of the true path for everything. Sorai's most violent criticisms were directed at the point that its "reasoning on its own that this should be so and that should be thus" was "an attitude which seeks to put the stamp of approval on the Sages and is truly the height of presumptuousness."[16] Surely such an attempt to endow mystical qualities to the sages weakened the modernity of the Sorai school's logic. If not, is there some sort of objective necessity in the fact that as the logic of natural order was transformed into the logic of autonomous invention the autonomous personality first appeared as the absolutized sage? For guidance on this question we must once again turn to the history of ideas in Europe. What kind of logical and historical path did the transition from medieval to modern notions of institutions take in Europe?

In Europe, too, the idea of natural order and the organic theory were not replaced overnight by the complete form of the idea of invented order, that is, the social contract theory or the mechanistic outlook. The discovery of the individual, as noted earlier, meant the individual's awareness of his own autonomy with respect to the social order, but this autonomy was not generally conceded to every individual straight away. This only became possible with the diffusion of democractic political concepts. Historically, the absolute monarch, the representative of the modern unified state, was the first to appear as a person endowed with this awareness. The absolute monarch was the first historical individual to stand as an autonomous inventor with respect to every normative standard, because he was emancipated from the normative restrictions that preceded him. The medieval monarch certainly did not occupy such a position. In the Middle Ages, the *organic community itself*, the embodiment of divine reason (*ratio divina*), was the supreme authority, and the monarch had a particular place with a particular function within the order of the community. Thus the conflicts between papal rights and state authority characteristic of medieval history were actually, as Troeltsch states, "not conflicts between Church and State but rather struggles over the share each should have in the leadership of a combination of state and church

---

[16] *Tōmonsho*, Book II.

activity that *both accepted in principle.*"[17] And the legal norms, in their most basic aspect, were seen as the self-expression of this combination of activities. In a sense the Middle Ages are the age of the rule of law. Ernest Barker states:

> The *lex* which was *rex* to medieval thinkers was a law which did not proceed from a human legislature. So far as it was revealed, it was the stern daughter of the voice of God; so far as it was natural, it was the inevitable outcome of the reason in man, whereby he discovers the mind of God. From either point of view, it was universal and eternal. It permeated all human society; it knew no end of its validity. It followed that *all human actions took place in a preexisting and all-determining atmosphere of law, and that they were valid when they conformed to its rules and invalid when they did not.*[18]

This is the inevitable logical conclusion of the theory of natural order. Because natural law (*lex naturalis*) takes precedence over man, the authority of the monarch is strictly and rigidly limited. Political control entails first of all duties and responsibilities. A rule that violates these duties and neglects these responsibilities loses its legitimacy and becomes mere brute force. Medieval thought therefore drew the conclusion that the people have the right to resist a tyrant and in certain instances even to kill him.[19] As the pluralistic hierarchical power relations of the Middle Ages declined, the feudal aristocracy and the church took this theory of the right to resist tyrants in particular as their theoretical weapon against the emergent nation-states. Hence once the absolute monarch had succeeded in establishing a centralized, unified state, by a long struggle against the "vested interests" (*Wohlerworbenesrecht*) of the feudal estates, he was inevitably freed from all the immanence of the normative order and appeared instead as the personality who establishes the normative order of his own free will and endows it with ultimate validity. The image put forward as a model for this relationship between the monarch and the order

[17] Ernst Troeltsch: *Aufsätze zur Geistesgeschichte und Religionssoziologie,* in *Gesammelte Schriften,* IV (1925), p. 131.

[18] Ernest Barker: "Medieval Political Thought," in *The Social and Political Ideas of Some Great Medieval Thinkers,* ed. F. J. C. Hearnshaw (New York, 1923), p. 19.

[19] Cf. Gierke: *Genossenschaftsrecht,* op. cit., III (1881), pp. 563–65; *Johannes Althusius* (1913), p. 275.

that he had invented and governed was none other than the relationship between God and the world. Carl Schmitt's thesis that "all the important concepts of the modern state are secularizations of theological concepts"[20] finds its first historical confirmation here.

It is paradoxical but true that the history of philosophy from Thomas Aquinas, representing the high point of scholasticism, to Descartes, the founder of modern philosophy, is the history of a reinforcement of God's absolute, transcendental nature. Of course, in the Christian world-view it is universally recognized that God holds absolute and transcendental authority over the world order that he has created. However, in medieval theology, based on Aristotelian philosophy, the natural and supernatural were seen as continuous. The world order was conceived as an organic body stamped in every part with divine reason and one in which goodness is inherent. In their rational action, all men cooperate with the action of divine grace. There is thus a necessary inner connection between the otherworldly God and the this-worldly society. The intellectual currents of later scholasticism and religious reform, however, severed this inner connection between God and the world and ascribed to God absolute freedom. Duns Scotus rejected theories such as Thomism, whose value system was based on the purposes of things in themselves, as placing limitations on the divine will. The world is God's absolutely arbitrary creation, and all values are established *after* God's creative decisions. Later, the nominalist William of Occam took Duns Scotus's theory of the supremacy of the divine will further and, freeing God from the limitations of all Ideas, concluded that the relationship between the divine will and the content of moral law is completely fortuitous and arbitrary.

Needless to say, the staunchest advocate of the absolute sovereignty of God was Calvin, whose position was clearly anti-Catholic. Doumergue writes: "Calvinism is a theocentric theology in the most profound sense. For the Calvinists, the doctrines of God are doctrines among doctrines, in a sense they are the *only* doctrines. The glory of God, the sovereignty of God, God as God absolutely

---

[20] Carl Schmitt: "Soziologie des Souveränitätesbegriffes und politische Theologie," in *Erinnerungsgabe für Max Weber*, II, p. 26.

—truly, Calvin always starts from here and returns to here."[21] Unlike Occam, however, Calvin did not hold the relationship between God and moral law to be arbitrary. He held that God's goodness is inextricably bound up with his divine essence. But this merely means that anything wrought by God's absolute free will is of necessity good in itself. It does not mean that his actions are bound by any normative restrictions. God may favor the world with his divine grace, but the divine substance and essence have nothing in common with things of this world. For Calvin, "it is sheer madness to speak of dividing the substance of the Lord of Creation and allotting to each of His creatures a portion of it." His renowned theory of predestination was based on his intention to secure this absolute authority for God.

This tendency to make God transcendental, which began in the late Middle Ages, was taken to its logical conclusion by Descartes. For Descartes, God is "an infinite, autonomous being who possesses the maximum of intellect and power." God is not only the creator of all things, but the source of all moral standards and even of the laws of nature. According to Descartes, all values pertaining to good and evil, true and false, were first established by God's decision. Consequently He is totally indifferent to the actual substance of those values. If God so willed, he could have made good, just, and true what is now the opposite of good, just, and true. God does not make Ideas real that exist naturally in themselves. God is an actuality who does not contain within himself any potentialities. The real existent, God, as an omnipotent sovereign, invents a value system out of nothing. In a letter written to his friend Marin Mersenne on April 15, 1630, Descartes remarked:

> In my physics I shall not neglect to touch on several metaphysical problems, and in particular the following: that mathematical truths, which you call eternal truths, have been established by God and are completely dependent on God, like all other creatures. . . . *It is God*

[21] Much of the discussion that follows is based on Buddeberg's *Gott und Souverän* and his "Descartes und der politische Absolutismus," in *Archiv für Rechts und Socialphilosophie*, XXX, part 4, a work commemorating the three-hundredth anniversary of Descartes's *Discourse on Method*. The Doumergue quotation is from his *Jean Calvin*, Vol. IV; K. T. Buddeberg: "Gott und Souverän," in *Archiv des öffentlichen Rechts*, N.F., XXVIII, part 3, p. 291.

who has established these laws in nature, just as a king establishes laws in his realm.

Note the last sentence.[22] This political ruler, who occupies a position comparable to that of the Cartesian God and who, as an absolute agent without any normative Idea behind him that he has to obey or realize, establishes all normative systems on the basis of his own free will and concentrates into his own hands the political decisions that distinguish between the legal and the illegal, is clearly the ideal absolute monarch of the beginning of the modern period. The image of a God who transcends the world in his absolute indifference was the precondition for the idea of a political personality possessing absolute autonomy with respect to the social system.

It must now be obvious that in the transformation of the ideology of natural order, the role played by God in the West was played by the sages in the Sorai school in Japan. In order to give man, who had been contained within the social order and presupposed the social order, autonomy with respect to that order, the supremacy of all impersonal Ideas had to be eliminated, and a personality free from all value judgments, whose existence itself is the ultimate source of all such values, making it unnecessary to trace them further back, had to be made the starting point for the mode of thought. Endowing this first personality with Godlike attributes was the almost inevitable consequence of the formulation of the theory of an invented social order. To the extent that the Chu Hsi school, with its theory of natural order, was firmly established, Ideas had strong precedence over persons. Hence the inevitability of the absolutization of a personality in order to reverse this situation. In this respect, the task of the Sorai school in the

[22] Cf. his statement in the *Discourse on Method*: "Thus also, those ancient cities which, from being at first only villages, have become, *in course of time,* large towns, are usually but ill laid out compared with the regularly constructed towns which a professional architect has *freely* planned on an open plain. . . . In the same way I fancied that those nations which . . . have had their laws *successively* determined, and, as it were, forced, upon them simply by experience of the hurtfulness of particular crimes and disputes, would by this process come to be possessed of less perfect institutions than those which from the commencement of their association as communities, have followed the appointments of *some wise legislator*" (*Contemporary Civilization in the West* [New York, 1954], 2 vols., I, p. 592). Here we see a belief in autonomous invention, standing in clear-cut opposition to natural growth, linked with absolutism.

history of thought was far more difficult than that of its counterparts in Europe, for there the Christian concept of a creator God
had constantly prevented the universalization of the organicist
mode of thought and the theory of natural order.[23] Consequently
Sorai eliminated the notion that the sages were Ideas and instead
made them real people; he objected violently to any attempt to
explain the Way of the Sages in terms of li (Principle) as a debasement of the sages; he denied the existence of any a priori right and
wrong: "Following the Way of the Early Kings, this is what is
right. Not following the Way of the Early Kings, this is what is
wrong,"[24] a thesis reminiscent of Hobbes's "*Autoritas, non veritas, facit legem.*" Now that we can grasp their objective significance, these logical constructions of Sorai's take on fresh value and
compel our renewed admiration.

When an analogy is drawn between the position of the sages and
the Tokugawa shogun, it inevitably produces political absolutism.
"Unless the entire land of Japan is put completely under the free
will of the ruler [the shogun], at times the way of government will
be obstructed," wrote Sorai.[25] "All the people of the world . . .
must be brought under the control of the ruler and made to submit to his wishes."[26] Of course, the difference between the historical
circumstances that gave rise in Europe to the absolute monarch,
a secularized version of the God of Duns Scotus and Descartes,
and in Japan the Tokugawa shogun, seen as an analogy to the
sages by Sorai, made it inevitable that, as we have seen above,
many more feudal characteristics intruded into the content of the
latter's absolutism. But the "feudalism" of Sorai's system was no
longer the result of values inherent in the system itself, but merely
a feudalism arising as an invention according to the "discretion
and wishes" of whoever happened to be the existing political
ruler. Thus, in another era, a new ruler would be able to change
completely "the entire structure of the world" according to the

[23] In medieval Europe, an organic mode of thought was applied to the static structure of existing organizations, but in considering the developmental processes of these
organizations, the concept of natural growth is not so apparent. Instead, we find that
the concept of divine creation, and its replica, the concept of human invention, constituted the underlying mode of thought in this field (cf. Gierke, op. cit., III, p. 556).

[24] *Benmei,* Book I.

[25] *Seidan,* Book IV.

[26] Ibid., Book I.

same "discretion." This was the inevitable conclusion of the logic of invention. In order to solve the crisis of feudal society, Sorai set out to destroy the theory of natural order, but instead brought forth a demon whose actions he was unable to control. In what way and to what extent was this creature managed in the history of ideas after Sorai?

CHAPTER V

THE LOGIC OF INVENTION AS DEVELOPED BY SHŌEKI AND NORINAGA

Conclusions in Political Thinking Derived from the Logic of Invention. Nature and Invention in Andō Shōeki. Nature and Invention in Motoori Norinaga.

I

Let me review the path we have taken thus far. The theory of natural order, which, with the establishment of late feudal society, gained general currency as its ideological foundation, found it increasingly difficult to preserve its inherent optimism as the society began to experience large-scale disturbances for the first time from the Genroku to the Kyōhō eras. A new position was needed to deal with the existing crises. The Sorai school appeared on the scene to fulfill this task. It rejected the precedence of Ideas fundamental to the theory of natural order and argued that the Way was the invention of real but absolutized personalities, the sages. Out of political necessity it upheld the absolutism of the Tokugawa shogun. Sorai's ultimate plan was to bring order to the prevailing social confusion through inventions by the Tokugawa shogun, and thus to construct an estate system based on a purely natural economy.

Although plausible at first glance, these proposals contained serious contradictions. The logic of autonomous invention on which his theory depended was none other than that found in the ideology of a Gesellschaft social order. He had enveloped feudal social relations in a logic wholly alien to them. How did the envelope affect its contents? In other words, what conclusions in political thinking followed from the fact that the feudal social order or its basic norms were justified by the logic of invention? This problem was briefly hinted at at the end of the last chapter, but an accurate understanding of the significance of the opposition between nature and invention for the history of thought in the later Tokugawa period requires a more detailed analysis of this question, and this analysis is the theme of this chapter.

The most radical of these conclusions was the Sorai school's thesis that since man had preeminence over the social order, all social institutions were subject to arbitrary change according to the will of men. The political character of such an opposition between the natural and the invented is lucidly demonstrated in an essay included in one of the journals of the early Meiji Enlightenment, *Bankoku sōwa* [Anecdotes from myriad nations]:[1]

> Throughout history there has been a large number of schools of political theory, but they can all be divided into two: the theory of creation by heaven, and the theory of invention by man. Those who believe in the former argue that government and politics are not invented by man; nature creates them. The customs and traditions of a country form the basis for government and follow the natural course of events, so they must not be tampered with recklessly. Innovations in political institutions would result in chaos and would conflict with the natural course of things. Those who believe in the theory of human invention argue that political institutions are man-made, just as machines are man-made. Man may invent these institutions as he pleases. He should construct the best, most perfect form of government and, convincing the people of its perfection, should put it into effect. It makes no difference whether it is to be a government by one man or a republic. They can all be established by man.

Of course, Sorai would never have approved of such a conclusion.

[1] The *Bankoku sōwa* was published in 1875 by a group of scholars interested in Western studies (among them Yoshida Kensuke, Mizukuri Rinshō, Suzuki Tadakazu, Kawamoto Seiichi, and Kawamoto Seijirō). Its content consisted mainly of translations and presentations of European and American essays on government, society, and culture. The passage cited here is taken from an essay translated by Suzuki Tadakazu entitled *Seitai shusha yūgen-ron* [On the limitation of selecting political forms]. The original source is not identified, but it may have been based on the early sections of John Stuart Mill's *Representative Government* (1861) (*Meiji bunka zenshū*, XVIII, p. 366).

And his system of thought did contain a protective device against it. While on the one hand maintaining that "the entire structure of the world" can be changed at the "discretion of the founding ruler of each age"—as we have said, this was the logical premise of his theory to reform the feudal society—on the other he attributed to the invented Way (rites and music, law enforcement, and public administration) a universal validity transcending time and space, by raising the sages to the level of religious absolutes. The Five Relationships and the fundamental estate system of samurai, peasants, artisans, and merchants, that is, the basic norms of feudal society, were raised above the level of institutions merely invented by the Tokugawa shogun and incorporated into the Way, which was absolute. So it would appear that the necessary measures had been taken to ensure that all institutional changes would occur only within the framework of feudal society. But a closer examination immediately reveals the weakness of these measures. The moment Sorai shifted the ultimate value from the Idea to the Person, everything absolutely permanent in the world was put at the mercy of fluctuating time. For a mode of thought based on the supremacy of the Idea, history is the *field* in which this Idea is realized. Hence historical changes are merely variations in the aspect of the Idea. But when the Person as agent transcends these intrinsic values, historical continuity is inevitably disrupted.

This induced Sorai to rebel against the attitude that "is ignorant of historical changes and, believing all ages to be uniform, discusses history as Chu Hsi does in his *T'ung-chien kang-mu*."[2] It also led him to an awareness of historical individuality. "It is essential to understand the characteristics of each era," he wrote in *Shibun kokujidoku*, "and changes in an era mean changes in the language and institutions." However, a consciousness that has turned from continuity to discontinuity, from the universal to the particular, knows no limits. It was a logical precondition for overcoming the static rationalism of the Chu Hsi school and hence for the birth of this historical consciousness that the sages and the Way they invented had to be placed beyond rational comprehension and value judgment. But the very Way of the Sages, which was sup-

[2] *Keiji shi yōran*, Book II.

posed to be absolute, was suddenly found to be stamped with the imprint of historical relativity by what it had itself brought into being. As an illustration, while Sorai said, "Unless the Way of the Ancient Sages and their teachings are valid through past and present they cannot be described as such," and "The Sages are the founding princes who, taking careful consideration of the future, established rites, music, and institutions, making them as perfect as possible," did he not admit at the same time that "although rites, music, and institutions have been established, defects are bound to develop after several centuries, *even though they were instituted by the Sages*, and because of this society falls into disorder"?[3]

If this is to be regarded as a concession or retreat on Sorai's part, it can be said that this retreat began when he wrote in his *Benmei*, "If, as it is said, rites exist naturally, how can one explain the differences in the rites that prevailed during the Three Dynasties [i.e., Hsia, Shang, and Chou]?" and attempted to attack Chu Hsi philosophy with the weapon of historical impermanence as opposed to natural uniformity. Ultimately, despite Sorai's attempt to make sharp distinctions, there are no qualitative differences between the rites and music invented by the sages and the institutions invented by other "founding princes." Bitō Nishū (1745–1813), a Chu Hsi scholar, criticized the Sorai school precisely on this point when he said in *Seigaku shishō*: "In the last analysis, [Sorai's] Way is the laws employed by the Sages to order the world which have come down to the present. It is much like the regulations of today. The Six Classics, then, are seen by him as similar to the Penal Codes of the Kamakura period [*Goseibai shikimoku*]. . . . [According to the Sorai school] the Early Kings mean only the founding princes. They are no different than the founders of the Han and T'ang dynasties." If the Five Relationships and the basic ordering of feudal society into samurai, peasants, artisans, and merchants are not regarded as "the principle of heaven and earth," they too ultimately fall under the sway of time like all other institutions, however remote the Early Kings, by whose invention they are supposed to have been founded. What man can make, he can also destroy. The Sorai school, which arose as an

---

[3] *Tōmonsho*, Book III; *Taiheisaku*.

antithesis to the theory of natural order, had to accept this conclusion like every other theory of human invention. There was
thus no absolute assurance in the logic of the Sorai school that
changes for the sake of feudal society would not turn into changes
against feudal society.

However, this was by no means the only effect of the demon
lurking in the logic of the Sorai school. It did not just threaten
feudal social relations as a whole from the outside but also corroded
their intrinsic values from within, leaving them an empty shell.
How did this come about? One of the major characteristics of a
feudal society is the preservation of the ordered unity of the total
structure by linking together in layers closed, self-contained social
spheres (centered on the master-servant and father-son relationships). Politically, this takes the form of the *principle of indirect control*.[4] The economic basis for the politics corresponding to this indirect control is distributed separately inside each social layer.
What we have here is a typical case of what Max Weber called a
combination of *der personliche Verwaltungsstab* (personal administrative staff) and *das sachliche Verwaltungsmittel* (material administrative means).[5] The right to establish and administer the law was

[4] For example, Tokugawa feudal society is often referred to as a centralized feudal
society, but the real possessor of supreme authority in it, the shogun, did not exercise
direct political control over the entire authority structure. Formally, the shogun was
simply one of the feudal lords (*primus inter pares*). Except in his demesne lands, his relations with the daimyo, the *hatamoto* (bannermen), and the *gokenin* (housemen) were
those of principal lord to vassals, and he exercised political control only through these
intermediary powers (*pouvoirs intermédiaires*). The authorities possessing these intermediary powers did not, like the local officials of a modern state, represent the authority
of the central government; they were autonomous authorities with their own economic
bases. The supremacy of the Tokugawa Bakufu over the other feudal lords rested ultimately on the quantitative superiority of its material foundations, its demesne lands
(*tenryō*). Otherwise there was no qualitative difference in the status of the bakufu and
the other feudal lords.

[5] Cf. Max Weber: *Politik als Beruf*, in *Gesammelte politische Schriften* (1921), p. 400.
Thus the basic principle here is that the head of each closed social sphere defrays his
own political expenses. The spirit of this practice is seen in Shogun Yoshimune's pro-
nouncement, issued to the daimyo when, unable to pay his housemen's stipends, he was
compelled to ask them for rice contributions (*agemai*), which said: "This request is
made regardless of shame." (Sorai's absolutist ideas clashed violently with this sort of
attitude; cf. part I, p. 133 above.) In the Tokugawa period, the secondary lord and
vassal relations within the bakufu and the daimyo's fiefs reveal a high level of political
centralization. Many samurai received rice or monetary payments instead of subfiefs,
and in this respect approached the status of modern bureaucrats; however, each samurai was still required to maintain a fixed number of men, horses, and weapons, depend-

allocated broadly to each status level.[6] Moreover, the principle of the closure of social spheres governed not only the social relations of the samurai, but also those within the common people.

To characterize this aspect of the feudal society in a phrase, we might call it a *hierarchic structure of immanent values*. The values of the total social system are diffused and embedded in each closed social sphere. As a result, each of these social spheres plays an indispensable part in the preservation of the total structure. It should be unnecessary to elaborate on how vital the preservation of the hierarchical and regional immanence of these values and of the exclusiveness of these social spheres is to the survival of the feudal social order.[7] The instant this closure is breached and the values that have been distributed between the different social spheres condense at the top of the pyramid, the feudal structure collapses. When control ceases to be indirect and *pouvoirs intermédiaires* are absorbed by the supreme authority; when the material facilities necessary for administration (such as buildings, horses, military equipment, etc.) are removed from the private ownership of the administrators and concentrated in the hands of the state; when

---

ing on the size of his stipend, at his own expense. Thus there was still a considerable dispersion of the material means of administration.

[6] Needless to say, the laws of the daimyo and the *jitō* (fief holders among the shogun's immediate retainers) together with the laws of the bakufu formed the basis of the national legal system. Law enforcement was more widely dispersed. The article in the bakufu's legal provisions that permitted every samurai, "even if he is only a foot-soldier [*ashigaru*], if townspeople and peasants insult him" to punish them with impunity (*kirisute gomen*) meant that each individual samurai on his own responsibility was given the authority to enforce the law. The same thing holds for the master's right of private punishment over his servants and the father's over his children.

[7] The notions that everyone must adhere to his status (*bun*) and know his place (*mi no hodo*) form part of the highest ethical ideals of such a society. From this arises the principle that any problem that occurs must be solved at the place (*ba*) in which it occurs. For example, the strict ban against submitting petitions directly to the shogun or the daimyo and the policy of settling disputes locally by mutual settlement decrees were designed to prevent the vertical extension of incidents. On the other hand, edicts such as the following were intended to prevent the horizontal extension of incidents: "In case of the outbreak of extraordinary disturbances, those involved must stay where they are, whether in their residences or districts, and report the matter to the authorities immediately. . . . If an emergency takes place in the Palace, those present must take care of the matter. The others must keep to their places and not act in a hasty manner" (1630 Laws Governing the Military Households). Similar rules are contained in edicts issued in other years. For example, the Laws of 1635 stated that "if a fight or an argument breaks out, people are prohibited from congregating where the disturbance is taking place." All these decrees reflect the desire to keep social spheres closed.

the broadly distributed legislative and judicial powers are unified under a central authority—then we have the birth of a modern nation-state. These illustrations should clarify the meaning of the statement that the Sorai school corroded the feudal order.

The Chu Hsi school's organic schema of macrocosm and microcosm, which I have already discussed, accords precisely with the above-mentioned "hierarchic structure of immanent values" in feudal society. In the Chu Hsi philosophy, the ultimate value (the Supreme Ultimate) is immanent in each tree and each blade of grass, becoming its li; it is inherent in every social relation, taking the form of the Five Relationships and the Five Constant Virtues; and it is inherent in man in his original and innate nature (*honzen no sei*). Because Sorai denied the ultimate value of these ideas and subordinated them to the sages, the values that had been distributed among things were all to be absorbed into absolutized personalities, the sages. Thus the validity of social norms was no longer based on the natural principle of heaven and earth essentially inherent in them, but solely on the fact that they had been invented by absolute personalities. Just as the arbitrary right to determine the content of moral law was deduced from the Cartesian concept of a God who transcends all things in the world in an absolutely undiscriminating manner, and just as legal positivism resulted from Hobbes's thesis that "authority, not truth, makes laws," the justification of the feudal social order by invention deprived it of its intrinsic value, and founded it simply on arbitrary formalism.

The fact that the institutional content of Sorai's political absolutism was the restoration of a pure natural economy and the completely hierarchical order based on it does not mean that it was less of a threat to Tokugawa feudalism than European absolutism was to European feudalism. For these theories of completely autonomous invention were in accord in their indifference to the actual content of institutions. Moreover, Sorai not only *ritualized* norms in this way but also *externalized* them. If the Way does not exist naturally in heaven and earth, but only comes into existence after its invention by the sages, social norms such as the Five Relationships and the Five Constant Virtues can no longer be rooted in human nature itself. Of course, as we have said, Sorai emphasized that the Way is in harmony with human nature, but this was possible only because the norms were completely sublimated in public, political values and did not come into contact with the private, inner life of man. Looked at in another way, it means that these norms had lost the power to invoke a sense of moral obligation in man from within his conscience. Sorai argued that any attempt to control anyone's heart (kokoro) through his heart is like an insane man trying to bring his own insanity under control, and he therefore scoffed at the Chu Hsi school's theory of the "original nature of man."[8] And although the methodological purity characteristic of Sorai was on the contrary obscured in many points by Dazai Shundai, in this matter of the externalization of norms he faithfully took his master's views to their ultimate logical conclusion:

> Now, in the Way of the Sages, the good and evil at the bottom of someone's heart are never discussed. The teachings of the Sages are devised to enter from without. Anyone who, in his personal conduct, upholds the rites of the Early Kings; in dealing with everything follows the righteousness of the Early Kings; and has the *outward* decorum of a Gentleman, is to be considered a Gentleman. *What is inside his heart is not in question.*[9]

> Regardless of what is inside his heart, if someone adheres outwardly to the rules of proper conduct and does not violate them, he is a Gentleman.[10]

> According to the Way of the Sages, even if an evil intention arises in someone's heart, so long as he abides by the rules of proper conduct, and, not cultivating this evil intention, does not commit an evil act, he remains a Gentleman. The stirring of an evil thought inside one's heart is not regarded as a crime. . . . For instance, to see a beautiful woman and to be attracted to her sexually in one's heart is a natural human feeling. But if someone allows his feelings free play, violates the rules of proper conduct, and wantonly indulges himself with women, then he deserves to be called a puny man. . . . The right and wrong of the matter depends on whether he indulges himself or not. That his feelings are aroused is not to be condemned.[11]

[8] For a discussion of Sorai's ideas about norms and human nature, and his separation of the public and private, see part I above.
[9] *Seigaku mondō.*
[10] Ibid.
[11] *Bendōsho.*

Pushed to this point, Confucian norms no longer have any connection with man's inner self. Once internal and external matters have been so thoroughly separated, it seems to be easier to abide by the norms, but in fact their moral imperative has been weakened. As we shall see later, it leads to the total dominance of a naturalism founded upon man's sentiments.

The possible political functions of the theory of autonomous invention introduced by the Sorai school vis-à-vis feudal society can be divided into two. First, it could serve as a logical weapon to transform the feudal order and establish a new one. Second, it could deprive feudal social relations and their ideological cement (the Five Relationships and the Five Constant Virtues) of any real raison d'être, reducing them to a skeleton. The former is the positive implication, and the latter the negative. If on the other hand we ask which of these two really affected the history of thought in the latter part of the Tokugawa period, in the main the answer would have to be the latter. The thesis that the social order is an invention first acquired positive significance in the so-called man-made theory of *Bankoku sōwa* mentioned above, and as its date of publication indicates, it was in the main a post-Restoration phenomenon. Fortunately or unfortunately, the "demon" accidentally conjured up by Sorai did not become a force to destroy the feudal authority from the outside but ate into its vitals, steadily corroding it from within. This process will be discussed later. First, I shall consider why the logic of invention developed along these lines. The answer can be found in the specific character of the historical development of Tokugawa society.

Earlier, I noted that the difficulties of the feudal system, which first came to the surface during the Genroku era, were caused by the rapid emergence of commercial and usury capital, punctuated by the recoinage of money. This was the situation that led Arai Hakuseki to worry about the fact that "not everyone from the top to the bottom of society lacks financial means. It is the military class in particular that lacks financial means."[12] It also induced Sorai to warn: "If a money economy is allowed to predominate, financial power will certainly fall into the hands of the mer-

[12] *Shoseikengi.*

chants.''[13] Finally it compelled the eighth shogun, Yoshimune, to institute the Kyōhō Reforms.[14] But the fact that commercial capital failed to advance beyond commercial capital indicates its historical limitations as a force for change vis-à-vis feudal society.

Needless to say, at that time agriculture was the dominant form of production. Industry never went beyond the stage of rural cottage industries, craft-guild industries, or at most wholesale handicrafts. During the Tokugawa period, industrial capital never managed to escape the domination of premodern commercial capital and subordinate the latter to it instead. The isolation from overseas markets produced by the seclusionist policy removed any social stimulus for a change in the mode of production. Certainly wealthy townsmen (*chōnin*), such as official warehouse managers (*kuramoto*), financial agents (*kakeya*), and brokers (*fudasashi*), had economic control over the existence of the military class. On the one hand they made great profits by loaning money to the samurai class while, in their capacities as commercial capitalists (in the rice trade and transport), eroding the pattern of feudal property by trade. But as long as they derived their income from the traditional mode of production and only influenced that mode of production externally, then their existence was a parasitic one, basically dependent on the feudal authorities. Against the encroachments of the ruling class, by legal and illegal means, such as nonpayment of debts, imposition of forced loans and mandatory contributions, the merchants only had purely economic means of defense, such as blacklisting, to deny offenders further loans. But even this was wholly ineffective in the face of the ultimate weapon of the ruling authorities, sequestration.

On the other hand, it is true that the penetration of the commercial economy into the farming villages had led to class differentiation among the peasantry, but this too was circumscribed by the fact that capitalist production had not developed sufficiently to absorb the labor force it thus deprived of land. It merely corroded the internal life of the villages by producing an intermediate ex-

---

[13] *Tōmonsho*, Book II.

[14] Yoshimune issued sumptuary laws to discourage waste and encourage frugality. He also devised means to increase government revenues, encouraged the reclamation of waste lands, and so on. See pp. 121–122 above. (Translator's note.)

ploiting class in forms such as urban contractors working reclaimed lands. This merely helped to increase the misery of peasant life. In short, on the one hand the feudal power structure was weakened economically by the incursions of commercial and usurious capital and undermined politically by rice riots in the cities (beginning in Edo in 1733) and peasant uprisings (*ikki*) in the villages (these became increasingly frequent in the Kyōhō era: e.g., the Echigo land forfeiture disturbances of 1724, the Mimasaka ikki of 1726, the Iwashiro uprising of 1729, and the Echigo ikki of 1736). But on the other hand, the forces for the development of a new mode of production failed to mature socially during the Tokugawa period. The historical roots of the development of the logic of invention along the lines described above can be found here.

As feudal society entered its period of decline beginning with the Kyōhō Revival, intellectual currents that were in any way opposed to the existing order, lacking the strength to raise Sorai's philosophy to the level of a modern theory of human invention, subordinated it to the feudal authorities and instead sought to take advantage of the decadence it gave rise to as a buttress of the existing order. In other words, by conceiving the feudal social order (or its conceptual cement) as the product of invention, they sought somehow to avail themselves of nature, necessarily alienated from the feudal system by such a conception, for their intellectual resistance to this order and its theoretical cement.[15] We can see two thinkers, Andō Shōeki and Motoori Norinaga, as the most typical representatives of this tendency. Each of them, one from an agrarian and the other from an urban standpoint, tried in his own way to solve the problems posed by the Sorai school. In the next sections I shall examine each of them in turn.

II

Andō Shōeki has come to the attention of historians of thought

---

[15] These positions should not be confused with the *natural law* of the Enlightenment, which was used as a theoretical weapon by the rising bourgeois classes in Europe. Insofar as the logical core of the natural law of the Enlightenment was the "theory of social contract," it belongs clearly to the category of invention in my classification. In this respect, the natural law of the scholastics and that of the Enlightenment lead to diametrically opposed conclusions. Cf. Tanaka Kōtarō: *Sekai-hō no riron* [Theory of world law], 3 vols. (Tokyo, 1932–37), I, pp. 119–20.

only recently. In his lifetime he seems to have traveled throughout Japan and to have had friends and disciples who shared his views in various places, but because his ideas were highly unorthodox they failed to win wide acceptance. After his death his school of thought vanished, and until a handwritten copy of his chief work, *Shizen shineidō*[16] [The way of nature and true vocation], was discovered by Dr. Kanō Kōkichi, he remained a completely forgotten thinker.[17] Even today, little more is known of his life than that he was born in Akita, later practiced medicine in Hachinohe in northern Honshu, and was active in the Hōreki era (1751–64). I have selected this isolated scholar for consideration here not only because he was almost the only thinker of the entire Tokugawa period who thoroughly criticized the feudal social order and its various ideologies and rejected them all but also because his criticisms were constructed around the problem we have been examining, namely, a more advanced application of the opposition between nature and invention, and because his position thus constitutes an indispensable step in the development of my argument. The following discussion of his system of thought will therefore focus on those aspects of his theoretical system that are relevant to that development.

Shōeki's system of thought is especially comprehensive and detailed in its fundamental natural philosophy. But like all other serious thinkers, his grandiose system was ultimately sustained by

---

[16] According to E. Herbert Norman, this is a title "I despair of translating adequately, but will render as 'The Way of Nature and Labour.'" E. H. Norman: "Andō Shōeki and the Anatomy of Japanese Feudalism," *Transactions of the Asiatic Society of Japan,* Third Series, II (December, 1949), p. 8. Incidentally, the present study of Shōeki was made in 1940, before Norman's analysis. Norman's and the author's common interest in Shōeki fostered a close friendship between them. (Translator's note.)

[17] Cf. Kanō Kōichi: *Andō Shōeki* in *Sekai shichō* [Intellectual currents of the world], Iwanami Lecture Series, II (Tokyo, 1928). The ninety-two-volume manuscript of *Shizen shineidō* that Dr. Kanō had acquired came into the possession of the University of Tokyo Library, but, soon afterwards, the bulk of it was destroyed in the great earthquake of 1923. Only fifteen volumes survived. Other works by Shōeki extant today are three volumes of *Shizen shinei-dō* and five volumes of *Tōdō shinden* [A true account of the supreme way]. The former is included in Volume IX of *Nihon tetsugaku zenshū* [Collected works of Japanese philosophy] (Tokyo, 1936). The original sources consulted by the author in composing this essay include the twelve manuscript volumes of *Shizen shineidō* in the University of Tokyo Library and the published volumes under the same title. As for other sources, I have utilized *Andō Shōeki to shizen shineidō* by Watanabe Daitō, who examined most of Shōeki's works before they were lost and described them in detail. The translations given here are based on a corrected version of Shōeki's idiosyncratic *kanbun*.

a deep interest in the society existing in his own day. His metaphysical speculations may at first glance seem abstract, but in fact they were preliminary stages on the way to his political and social conclusions. The confusions and contradictions of feudal society that had also confronted Sorai he observed a generation later, but in a much graver form. And although the two men observed the same object, their perspectives were entirely different. Sorai saw the crisis of the feudal order at Edo as the adviser to Shogun Yoshimune, whereas Shōeki observed the same crisis from his home in the distant northeastern region, where he was never employed by any lord and lived in the midst of the peasantry.

What was it that Shōeki saw from his standpoint? He saw that the feudal society looked to the peasants for the solutions to all its social contradictions, shifting the whole burden onto their shoulders. Under Yoshimune, the major efforts to reinforce the financial position of the bakufu turned out to be heavier taxes and more stringent tax collection. Naturally, the burden of the "rice contributions" (*agemai*) imposed on the daimyo was immediately transferred to the shoulders of the peasants, since each han had economic difficulties of its own similar to those of the bakufu. While the peasants groaned under the burden of feudal taxes, they also suffered from the penetration of the commercial economy into the countryside. Foreclosures on land were frequent (in 1721 there was a ban on the foreclosure of mortgaged land). There were also famines, volcanic eruptions, and earthquakes (in 1721, 1722, and especially 1732). The cold response to the desperate uprisings into which the peasants were driven was a series of edicts like the *Sonmin shirubeshi* [Notice to the villagers] of 1721,[18] the official circular to *daikan* (deputies) of 1734,[19] and the instructions to the *jitō* (district magistrates) on peasant disturbances of 1741.[20]

[18] The second article states: "Regardless of the purpose, it is strictly forbidden to assemble the common people together, use holy water, or swear an oath to join together in an association or faction" (*Tokugawa rizai kaiyō*, Book XXIV, in *Nihon keizai taiten*, LIV, p. 201).

[19] "If there are any trouble-makers in the area within the jurisdiction of the *daikan*, they should be reported. Since consultation with Edo would mean delay, minor incidents should be reported to the daimyo in the vicinity and his aid should be obtained. Feudal lords with holdings over 10,000 *koku* have been instructed to provide the *daikan* with the necessary warriors. Bear this in mind" (*Ofuregaki kanpō shūsei*, op. cit., p. 701).

[20] Cf. *Tokugawa kinreikō goshū, dai-ni-chitsu*, published by the Ministry of Justice, p. 149.

These edicts were all the peasants obtained from the Kyōhō
Reforms of the eighth shogun, who is renowned as a wise ruler!
The situation failed to improve under the ninth shogun, Ieshige;
in fact it became worse. As an index of this, the number of peasant
risings and riots increased dramatically throughout the country.[21]
The edicts issued to deal with these disturbances became even
more stringent (e.g., the extra strictness of the regulations of 1750[22]
and 1762[23]). And famines still went on tormenting the peasants.
Especially in Shōeki's home country, the Ōu region, famines
broke out in succession in 1749, 1755, and 1757. It was in this
period that infanticide came to be widely practiced in the Kanto
region and the entire northeastern part of Honshu.[24] Thus the
population, which had been slowly increasing from the beginning
of the Tokugawa period to the Kyōhō era, not only ceased growing but began to decline absolutely. For every 100 of the population in 1726 there were 98.51 in 1744, 98.16 in 1756, and 97.25
in 1762.[25] This is a clear indication of the deterioration in the
living conditions of the peasantry, who constituted more than 80
percent of the population.

Shōeki was very bitter at this situation. The peasants, he reflected, were the producers of the "five cereals" without which no
one could survive even for a day. And yet their living conditions
had become so desperate that they had to abandon their own new-
born babies. What had created this situation? Was it not the fact
that there was an unproductive class of consumers who expropri-
ated the products of the peasants' labor without themselves doing
any work, that is, engaging in what Shōeki called "direct cultiva-

[21] Cf. tables on pp. 258 and 263 in Kokushō Iwao: *Hyakushō ikki no kenkyū*, op. cit.

[22] *Ofuregaki kanreki shūsei* [Laws of the bakufu compiled in the Kanreki era], ed.
Takayanagi Shinzō and Ishii Ryōsuke, p. 355.

[23] This was a new regulation for the peasants designed to restrict "illegal appeals
made by large numbers of people gathering in front of the mansions of the lords of
fiefs." It is noteworthy that they are to be punished "regardless of the merit" of their
causes. (*Nihon keizai taiten*, LIV, p. 242.)

[24] A memorial submitted by Ashi Tōzan (1696–1776) of Sendai han stated: "Fifty
or sixty years ago each peasant couple used to raise five, six, seven, or eight girls and
boys, but recently, perhaps because they do not inherit anything or because they have
got used to luxurious living, they have no more than one or two. Claiming that they
are returning the babies, they abandon them as soon as they are born." This was in
1754. (*Nihon keizai taiten*, XI, p. 477.)

[25] Honjō Eijirō: *Nihon shakai keizai shi* [Japanese social and economic history]
(Tokyo, 1928), pp. 494–95.

tion" (*chokkō*)? Chief among these were the samurai. "The gentle-men-scholars [*shi*] are the warriors. The ruler has under him the warriors. They greedily consume the grain the people produce by direct cultivation. If anyone resists, the overwhelming force of the warriors is used to arrest him. They behave in this way because they are robbing the world of nature and fear that they might be the objects of attack by others." Suppose there were no warriors in the world. The peasants would survive as peasants as before. (There was a saying *Nō wa nō ni shite nō nari* ["agriculture is not possible without peasants"].) All peasants establish the basis of their living by means of their labor, and would live in eternal peace generation after generation. But what if the tables were reversed? Without peasants, clearly the samurai, who depend on their taxes, would instantly fall into desperate straits. The peasants are thus, for the warriors, "the fathers who support them." And yet, the samurai is not only unashamed to treat his "fathers" dis-respectfully, he also calls what he does "benevolent rule" and behaves as if he were the benefactor of the people. "Greedily ex-propriating what the people produced by direct cultivation, the warriors give part of it back to the people and call this benevo-lence. This is false and evil. Can a reduction in taxes be called charity and benevolence to the people? This is treachery."

What he found more amazing was the fact that not one of the Confucian scholars or religious figures who talked about "saving the world" and "aiding the people" had pointed out this glaring contradiction. This was because these Confucian scholars and religious figures were themselves, like the warriors, "greedy con-sumers who do not cultivate the soil."[26] Going even further, Shōeki wondered if their teachings themselves might not have contained ideological elements tolerating this nonproductive consumption from the start. With this question in mind he examined the thought of past Confucians, Buddhists, Taoists, followers of Chuang Tzu, Shintoists, and others. Despite the great variations these schools of thought exhibited, he found they had something fundamental in common: they all accepted as their basic premise a relationship between laborers who are governed and governors who live off

---

[26] *Fukō donshoku-sha.* Norman translates it "idle and gluttonous people." Norman, "Andō Shōeki and the Anatomy of Japanese Feudalism," p. 178. (Translator's note.)

their labor; in other words, they agreed with Mencius that "he who is governed must support others. He who governs must be supported by others." Having been inundated with these teachings for several centuries, people had come to accept this premise unquestionably as natural. In consequence, even when confronted with the clearly perverted state of affairs described above, they could no longer see any contradiction in the situation. Thus the problem had a remote origin. That these teachings had prevailed for centuries implied that the perverted relations of Shōeki's time had existed for centuries too. If the existing situation was a perversion, then, in the past, at a specific time in human history, somebody must have changed the normal state of affairs into the perverted one; that is, the original human condition, in which everybody worked for his living, "the world of nature" (*shizen no yo*), was replaced by the relations in which some men are allowed to expropriate the products of other men's direct cultivation and to subjugate the others to themselves, "the world of law" (*hōsei*).

Who then was responsible for this historical transition from the world of nature to the world of law? It could be no one but the sages. Were not the sages themselves the original inventors of relations of authority between high and low, relations that had persisted uninterruptedly until Shōeki's day? "In the natural principle of human relations," he argued, "heaven and earth are one and all men are one. There is no distinction between noble and base, as there is in the relationship between the prince and his subjects. The term prince came into being *after* the Sages came into being, robbed the entire world, and established *their own private laws*." "The Five Relationships of ruler and subject, father and son, husband and wife, older and younger brother, and between friends were instituted by the sages as they established their teachings." "The four classes of gentlemen-scholars [samurai], peasants, artisans, and merchants were also established by the sages."

This being the case, "the emergence of the sage-ruler was the beginning of extravagance, and the cause of all evil." Thus ultimately the sages were entirely responsible for all the social ills of the age. "From Fu Hsi to Confucius," said Shōeki, "there are eleven men called sages. They all violated the true way of nature.

Their desire to rob the world and the state have plunged the world into war." "All men came into being naturally. If people called sages had not come into the world, mankind would not have heard of 'order and disorder,' and their greed would not have been aroused. It is indeed lamentable that the sages, being ignorant of nature, established private laws." Whereas Sorai made invention by the sages the basis of all values, Shōeki saw precisely in this the beginning of all decay and degeneration. For Shōeki, then, there was only one possible solution to all problems, a return to the situation before the sages' invention, that is, a return to the world of nature.

But for this there had to be a basic transformation in the way of thinking of the people as a whole, since they had lived under the rule of the world of law for several thousand years and had therefore completely forgotten the state of nature. First, the Way of the Sages, which had built its nest in the consciousness of the people, and all the other teachings mentioned above had to be cleansed away. It had to be proven that their function was ultimately "to make excuses for the thieves," who extorted the product of the common people's direct cultivation. While making such an ideological critique of the contents of traditional teachings, Shōeki brought his own philosophy into the foreground. He argued that "beginning with Fu Hsi, Shen Nung, the Yellow Emperor, Yao, Shun, Yu, T'ang, Wen, Wu, the Duke of Chou . . . and all the sages, saints, and Buddhas down the generations . . . all the scholars down the generations in Japan, including Hayashi Razan *and Sorai,* were nontillers and violated the way of heaven by robbing the common people who engage in direct cultivation. They have gluttonously devoured the people's surplus grain, ignoring the excellent principle of 'reciprocity and completeness.' "[27] Thus when Shōeki counterposed his philosophy of "reciprocity and completeness" to all earlier schools of thought, the final stage of the ideological succession he set out to refute was occupied by none other than the Sorai school.[28]

[27] *Gosei gusoku* is probably best translated literally as "completeness is achieved by the reciprocity of all things." (Translator's note.)

[28] Elsewhere in the same volume (*Shihōsei monogatari*), Shōeki wrote, "The Ch'eng Tzu school imitates the shrike, the Chu Hsi school the lark, *the Sorai school the wren,* the T'ang, Sung, and Ming men write literature and poetry in imitation of the

Since Shōeki's primary task was the destruction of the ideology of "gluttonous consumption without tilling the soil," it is easy to see why "direct cultivation" was the constant leitmotif of his philosophical speculation. The nature he had discovered by eliminating the sages' invention was what he called "direct cultivation." By deeply probing the significance of direct cultivation he was able to construct a unique logic and with it transcend and incorporate (*aufheben*) both Sorai's concept of autonomous invention and the Chu Hsi philosophy of nature. What did Shōeki mean by "direct cultivation"? Needless to say, he meant working the land by one's own labor. Man is to obtain the food to keep him alive by producing it himself. Hence direct cultivation is what makes man man. Man's existence is direct cultivation. Man exists because he works. Concretely, there can be no personalized entity called "man" apart from the activity called "work." In fact, this is true not only for man. Is not nature in this universe constantly engaged in active work to produce the myriads of things? This is nothing but the direct cultivation of heaven and earth.[29] The beginning of the activities of heaven and earth cannot be determined. The universe busily revolves without beginning or end. The true picture of heaven and earth is the birth of all things out of themselves by the "forward and backward motion of nature" (*shizen no shintai*). If anything really exists in a truly natural fashion, it is only *self-induced motion*. (Shōeki used the term *katsushin jikō* to express this idea, that is, the self-induced motion of all matter.) The notion that there are personal or impersonal entities behind all motion as its origin is merely a product of an abstract mode of thought.

However, all traditional views, Shōeki observed, presuppose some basic entity of this kind: for example, the Will of Heaven, the Supreme Ultimate, yin, yang, and the five elements, etc. This

---

quail. All literature and poetry are written by imitating the chirping of the birds." This, too, indicates his special interest in Sorai.

[29] Shōeki always used the characters 転定 (*ten-chi*) to write "heaven and earth," instead of the usual 天地 (*ten-chi*). This was based on his notion that heaven revolves and transports (*hakobu,* 転ぶ) things, and earth moves (*nagaruru,* 定るる) with the ebb and flow of the sea. He employed these peculiar phonetic equivalents to accent the ideological nature of traditional writing. He argued that Chinese characters were the inventions of the sages, who wished to "rob the people of the marvelous way of the truth of heaven" (here again 転俔 [*tenten*] instead of 天俔 [*tenten*]).

proves that these schools of thought are the ideologies of gluttonous noncultivators, for those who consume without laboring represent man's form of existence as immobile and cut off from the activity called work. A mode of thought that does not interpret everything in terms of its concrete activity, but envisions an abstract, fixed entity behind everything, is the form of thought corresponding to such a form of existence. For example: "to found the difference between heaven and earth in an empty circle and to establish a hierarchy of high and low, noble and base," like the *Diagram of the Supreme Ultimate,* "is based on the selfish desire to stand above the people and extend one's personal laws throughout the world. This is responsible for the distortion of the way." "Heaven and earth know no distinctions of beginning and end, superior and inferior, base and noble. Nothing precedes or follows anything else. This is the natural way of things as they are. But it is the greatest of mistakes, simply in order to further one's selfish interests, to transgress and violate the way of nature and to establish a hierarchical order in heaven and earth, placing the Supreme Ultimate to the fore and heaven and earth behind, arguing that heaven and earth emanate from an abstract principle called the Supreme Ultimate. Nature, which is without beginning or end, should be accepted as such. It is the beginning of error and the source of great disorder to establish a hierarchy in heaven and earth."

Of the concepts of yin and yang and the five elements in the Book of Changes, Shōeki wrote:

The five elements are one and the same and cannot be divided, nor can anything be added to them. They are all one element. The five elements are of one spirit. But [the scholars] take the five elements, which are one and the same and cannot be made the private possessions of anyone, and value only the element fire, rejecting the other four elements, which belong to the same group and have the same functions. Using cleverness founded on self-interest, they ascribe to fire a princely character, and for the mass of humanity who are one and the same, without distinctions of high and low or other differences, they establish the Five Relationships of ruler and subject, father and son, husband and wife, older and younger brothers, and between friends, and institute the four classes of gentlemen-scholars, peasants, artisans, and merchants. Why have they done this? Because they wished to place themselves above the people as the possessors of princely character, and to live and eat in comfort without cultivating the soil. In order to be respected by the people they equated the fire of the sun with the symbol of the prince and the fire on earth with the symbol of the ministers. Heaven is equated with the principle of *yang* and is held in high respect, while the earth is equated with *yin* and is held to be base. In this way, they distinguish between the high and the low, and proclaiming this to be the law, they claim to possess princely characters and place themselves above others.

This sort of practice, Shōeki pointed out, is not limited to Confucian thought. The Taoists claim that their way is in harmony with nature, but Lao Tzu also separated nature from its concrete activities and made it static. "Man, earth, heaven, and the Way are all the same spirit (*ki*).[30] They are all nature in motion. [Lao Tzu] believed all these to be separate entities, thus insisting on these words [that the Way *abides by* nature]." "Lao Tzu said: 'There is something that existed before heaven and earth.' This proves that he did not understand nature. There is no first or second in heaven and earth. . . . Again, Lao Tzu said, 'The names that can be given are not absolute names, the nameless is the origin of heaven and earth.'[31] He spoke of the origin of heaven and earth when they have no beginning or end. Such remarks prove that Lao Tzu did not understand heaven and earth or nature." Shōeki saw the same fallacies in the Buddhist mode of thought. "Lin Chi[32] said, 'When the reflection of the moon falls into the water and is shattered into a myriad ripples, the moon in the sky remains unaffected. Similarly, though the deeds of all beings may descend into hell and be castigated without limit, the truth that one's soul aspires toward Buddhahood remains unaffected.' This is a mistake. It is a mistake based on ignorance about nature. How could the moon exist apart from its reflection? Without the moon there

[30] The character for *ki* is the same as *ch'i*, and Shōeki was obviously influenced by the Chu Hsi concept of *ch'i*, but his *ki* is "the all-embracing essence of nature." (Translator's note.)

[31] The translation of this sentence is from Lin Yu-tang: *Wisdom of China and India* (New York, 1955), p. 583. (Translator's note.)

[32] Chinese Buddhist monk of the ninth century who founded a Zen sect known in Japan as the Rinzai sect. This sect was introduced into Japan by Eisai at the end of the twelfth century. (Translator's note.)

is no reflection, without the reflection there is no moon. The reflection and the substance of the moon constitute one reality." There is clearly a common logic in Shōeki's method in these criticisms, a kind of functionalist logic. The battle on behalf of direct cultivation against gluttonous noncultivation inevitably found its philosophical expression in a battle for functionalist concepts against substantive concepts. The concept of *gosei* (relativity or reciprocity) played a crucial part in this struggle.

Gosei denotes the interrelatedness of everything. When everything is understood only in terms of self-induced motion (katsushin jikō), all absolute, fixed oppositions are relativized as a matter of course. When the all-embracing essence (ki) of nature advances, there is life. When it retreats, there is death. Without life, there is no death. Without death, there is no life. "Because of death there is life; because of life there is death." Life implies death and death implies life. Thus life and death symbolize gosei. "Life and death are therefore identical with *gosei* and are embodiments of self-induced motion." Oppositions such as those between heaven and earth, male and female, good and evil, right and wrong, high and low, order and chaos, are all gosei, like life and death. "Heaven and earth have no beginning or end and are a unity. Without heaven there is no earth; without earth there is no heaven." "The nature of man implies that of woman; the nature of woman implies that of man. Male and female are *gosei* and are in self-induced motion." "Without the male heart there is no female heart; without the female heart there is no male heart. Men constantly think of women, and women constantly long for men. This is due to the all-embracing essence [ki] of nature which advances and retreats." (From this principle, Shōeki deduced the concept of monogamy.) "Without evil there is no good; without good there is no evil. . . . If we say that the left hand is good and the right hand is bad and cut off the right hand, the left hand alone will be unable to take care of our needs. . . . If we say that the day is bright and good, and the night dark and bad, and get rid of night, there will be no day either."

These oppositions are oppositions but at the same time they are unities. Hence just as it is wrong to confuse them, it is one-sided— "*henwaku*" (confused and biased)—to separate and fix them abstractly. "Neither destroy the heart by insisting on its singular nature, nor fix it rigidly as a duality. Neither insist on the division of the heart and the body, nor mix them together." "Neither insist on the division of good and evil nor insist on their being the same. Neither insist on the duality of right and wrong nor confuse them by asserting that they are one and the same." But the traditional modes of thought that comprehend things by separating their substance from their concrete functions necessarily fall into this kind of fallacy. "A myriad books, starting from the Ancient Sages, Buddha, Lao Tzu, Chuang Tzu, and Prince Shōtoku,[33] all speak only of illustrious virtue, illustrious heart, and illustrious intellect, but they are ignorant of reciprocal [*gosei*] arrangements." As a result, they "fail to make clear the excellent principle of direct cultivation, which is the essence of the true way of nature, and allowing this principle to remain unknown, they establish teachings that are based on separating everything into two—heaven and earth, the sun and moon, male and female, prince and people, Buddha and the masses, high and low, noble and base, good and evil. They deprive the world of the true way in which the true essence [*ki*] is a duality and a unity." Thus, "the excellent way of *gosei*" corresponds to the "world of nature," of direct cultivation, just as the "teachings that are based on separating everything into two" correspond to the "world of law," of gluttonous noncultivation.

The transformation of human society from the world of nature to the world of law occurred when the principle of reciprocity was discarded and concrete unity was transformed into the abstract oppositions of "reasoning by distinction" (*funbetsuchi*). For example, while originally "heaven and earth were a unity, there was no high and low, and all was governed by *gosei*," the sages appeared, separated heaven and earth, and fixed them, insisting that heaven is superior and noble, while earth is base and vulgar. The hierarchy of prince and subject, high and low, was then established (cf. the natural order of Chu Hsi philosophy). As soon as the existence of man and woman as "two persons and one person at the same time" was divided and they were distinguished in terms of

---

[33] As regent to the Empress Suiko, he introduced political reforms and also sought to disseminate Buddhism (574–622). (Translator's note.)

yin (female) and yang (male), the natural state of monogamy disappeared, and Confucianism came to permit polygamy while Buddhism encouraged celibacy. As for talk of governing the world,
government only came into existence after "the sages had appeared and placed themselves above the people, bringing about
disorder. In nature there is neither disorder nor order. There is
only direct cultivation and comfortable living." Shōeki described
his ideal society in detail in the twenty-fifth volume of his *Shizen
shineidō* in a section entitled "Treatise on the World of Nature"
[*Shizen no yo-ron*]. Here too he based his discussion on the rejection
of the abstract "duality" of the sages' invention. Here are some of
the essential points of this essay:

> The duties of the men of the plains consist of producing the ten
> grains in abundance; the duties of the men of the mountain villages
> consist of gathering firewood to supply the flat lands; the duties of
> the men of the sea-coasts consist of fishing to supply the flat lands. The
> firewood, the ten grains, and the many fishes are all exchanged.
> People in the mountain villages can consume firewood, cereals, and
> fish, and build houses. People in the sea-coasts can also build houses,
> eat cereals, and fish. The same is true of the people in the plains.
> There is no surplus in the plains, no shortages in the mountain vil-
> lages or in the sea-coasts. There is neither affluence here nor poverty
> there. There is no distinction between high and low in any place. . . .
> There is no one above, there is no exploitation of those below for
> luxury and greed. There is no one below so there is no flattery and
> deception of those above. Hence there are no malice or quarrels,
> and no rebellious armies. Since there is no one above, no one makes
> laws to punish those below. Since there is no one below, there is no
> one to violate the laws of those above and be punished by them. . . .
> Since there are no selfish teachings about the five constant virtues,
> the five relationships, and the four classes, there are no distinctions
> between the sages and the foolish. There are no samurai who criti-
> cize the misconduct of the common people and strike them on their
> heads. . . . Since there is no teaching about filial piety, no one
> flatters or hates his parents and no one commits parricide. Since
> there is no artificial teaching about benevolence, there are no fathers
> who drown themselves emotionally in the love of their children, nor
> parents who hate their children. . . . All this results from the motions
> of nature and the five elements. The world is a unity. There is no

duality. Each man energetically and industriously cultivates the soil, supports his parents, and raises his children. Just as one man acts in this manner, myriads and myriads of men act in the same manner. No one exploits others, so no one is exploited. There is no distinction between heaven and earth and human relations. Heaven and earth create and man cultivates the soil. Aside from this there are no personal interests. This is the state of things in the world of nature.

This is a society of barter based on all the people directly cultivating the soil as equals. In other words, it is Sorai's ideal society, without his ruling class, that is, without the samurai. For Shōeki, this was definitely not an imaginary dream world. It had existed everywhere before the emergence of the world of law. What is more, it prevailed in his own day in Ezo land (Hokkaido) and Holland![34] He expected this state of nature to be restored in Japan too. "The fact that someone like myself," he argued, "who understands the errors of the sages and Buddha, and clarifies nature, has been born in Japan is proof that we shall be returning to the world of nature." Thus, 150 years after the founding of the Edo Bakufu, Tokugawa feudal society heard a dissenting voice for the first time, raised by a thinker born in the outlying region of Ōu. A small voice, to be sure, but what it said was more thoroughgoing in its opposition than the ideas of any other thinker of the entire Tokugawa period. In the early part of the period, the Chu Hsi philosophy and the mode of thought based on it saw the feudal hierarchy itself as a part of the natural order that "existed between heaven and earth, past and present." Sorai, however, saw it as a system invented by the sages. As a result the natural order was alienated from the feudal society. Now Andō Shōeki used this alienated nature to condemn the feudal society, which was assumed to have been invented by the sages.

[34] He had visited Nagasaki often and had a high regard for the Dutch and their culture, which he had encountered there. It would be interesting to know how much his thought was influenced by Dutch learning, but this is a task that must be left for the future. He described the world of nature in Holland as follows: "From the beginning of its history, Holland has had no rebellions or wars. The people engage in direct cultivation, are naturally skilled in handicraft work, excel in shipbuilding, sail around the world, and half the population is engaged in the business of trading goods. This is how that country provides for its needs. The way of agriculture then is the marvelous way that conforms to the duties of men of all nations and naturally results in plenty. It is the basic principle of the world; it is not a thing that is dependent on the teachings of others."

For Sorai and Shundai conditions before the advent of the sages were like a world of beasts. Only after the sages had invented rites, music, and institutions did the world governed by proper human relationships arise. But according to Shōeki, "man is created by the impartial and common essence [*ki*]. It is therefore natural that there should be equality and direct cultivation without dualities of great and small, high and low. Only after the sages arrived did distinctions between great and small come about. Then the great began to devour the small. This is exactly the way of the birds, beasts, insects, and fish. This is the crime of the sages, who transformed the world ruled by proper human relationships into a world of birds and beasts." For Shōeki, then, the change from the natural to the invented society is responsible for man's degeneration to the level of the birds and beasts. The negation of the natural order of Chu Hsi philosophy gave rise to the invention of the Sorai school, and the negation of this negation led to Shōeki's world of nature. Shōeki doubtless arrived at his political conclusions after observing first-hand the wretched conditions of his society. But the logical path that led him to these conclusions had already been prepared for him by earlier intellectual developments.

But the fact that this unrelenting foe of feudal society was someone who simply denied the values of the logic of invention could not but limit his antifeudalism. For all Shōeki's conceptual rejection of feudal society and his hopes for the advent of the world of nature, he was so opposed to any "dogma of human invention" that his theory lacked the active element necessary to bring about the transformation from the world of law to the world of nature. True, there is in his theory the logic *representing* the natural world that he called direct cultivation, but the idea of bringing about the world of nature was wholly lacking from his theory. Instead of discussing ways to restore the world of nature by destroying the world of law, he treated in detail the way to obtain the same effects as those of the world of nature *while living in the world of law*. Shōeki was a pacifist (as he put it, "I do not want to discuss military affairs") and expected his theories to be realized "in a hundred years' time." This was not a temporary tactic, but rather an attitude deeply embedded in his mode of thought. This, and the fact that

despite his interest in Holland, his description of the world of nature contains many features characteristic of a prefeudal rather
than a postfeudal society, clearly reveal to us the extent to which
even such a radical thinker was conditioned by his historical and
social circumstances. With Motoori Norinaga, whom I shall examine next, these limitations are still more visible, though they
take a different form.

III

It is not my object here, of course, to investigate the role in the
history of thought played in the Tokugawa period by the school of
National Learning, which culminated in Motoori Norinaga. In
Part I, I discussed its intellectual significance as an antagonist to
Neo-Confucianism, the dominant ideology of the Tokugawa period, and referred to its close structural relationship to the last
phase of Tokugawa Confucianism, the Sorai school, an affinity
which arose as a result of that conflict. Here, too, I shall concentrate on the area where National Learning came into contact with
the existing social and political order. My object is thus to find out
how feudal society was seen in the structure of the mode of thought
of National Learning.

It would not be an overstatement to say that its ideas concerning
the political and social realities constitute the weakest link in the
content of the complex structure of National Learning. In the
early period, National Learning was mainly concerned with the
study of Japanese poetry, but even with Mabuchi and Norinaga,
who came little by little to adopt consciously a fixed theoretical
position that they called the Ancient Way (kodō), considerations
truly concerning the real political and social circumstances of their
lives did not strictly speaking have an adequate place in the ramifications of their work. Norinaga's *Tamakushige* [Precious comb
box] and *Hihon tamakushige* [Secret book of the precious comb
box] are the most important works in this regard, but there is little
in them of the fertile originality and penetrating criticism revealed
in his other works. The opinions they express hardly rise above the
level of the commonsense political theory of the time. That this is

so had a great deal to do with the profoundly apolitical character of National Learning.

Mabuchi sneered at the Confucian theory of maintaining order in the land and peace in the world, saying in *Kokuikō*, "Those who have only a little learning are anxious to become the teachers of others and are loquacious about governing the country." Norinaga repeatedly emphasized the need to distinguish sharply between theory and practice. "The Way of Antiquity expects all those below to obey and to follow exactly the existing laws issued by those above, regardless of whether these laws are good or bad. The sole task of the scholar is to investigate and clarify the Way. It is not his task to try to practice the Way according to his own standards."[35] In his *Kogaku-yō* [Essence of Ancient Learning], Motoori Ōhira (1756–1833) said that "unlike in China, in the Land of the Emperor [Japan] learning is not equated with political affairs. Whether the society is well governed or not is not the concern of learning." This conception ran through National Learning from beginning to end.[36] What enabled National Learning, despite its notion of *sonnō* (revering the emperor), to avoid discord with bakufu rule to the very end and kept it from turning into a fundamentally oppositional ideology was precisely this apolitical character.

All we hear from the main thinkers of National Learning about feudal relations of authority is praise or calls for unconditional acceptance of that existing order. Mabuchi warmly extolled the ancient period of Japan, when the nation was governed "smoothly and peacefully in complete accord with heaven and earth," and bemoaned the fact that the Ancient Way disappeared during the

---

[35] *Uiyamabumi.*

[36] On the other hand, Norinaga wrote: "The manner in which people have treated the Way [the Way of the Gods] is like the way they have treated other useless things. People only constantly say they cannot abandon the Way of the Gods because it has been inherited from the distant past. I have yet to encounter a man who realizes that this Way is of the utmost importance and is *essential in governing the world and in governing the nation.* Is this not indeed a sad thing?" (*Tamakatsuma,* 14). But here I am not concerned with the content of his learning, but rather with the way in which he approached learning. Moreover, I am not concerned with the conscious behavior of the scholars of National Learning. My claim is that the spiritual inclinations that conditioned their thought processes are *unpolitisch.* Why these inclinations emerged will become clear later.

middle ages because of the infiltration of "petty political institutions established by noisy people," that is, Confucian institutions.[37] Nevertheless, he composed a poem praising Tokugawa political hegemony: "So long as the Gods guard Mount Futara [Nikko], the land of Shimotsuke, it is not likely that the Tokugawa regime will ever be disturbed."[38] Going further, he wrote: "May the world governed by the mighty Shogun, as far as the clouds can reach, and as long as the frogs jump around, remain peaceful and have not a single inhabitant who is discontented. . . . May the life of the Bakufu last for ever and ever, so that it may be known as the longest regime that has ever existed. And just like the pine tree and the bamboo, may it survive and prosper for a myriad generations. And may its branch families also extend their power wider and further and flourish forever."[39]

Norinaga also legitimized the feudal hierarchy on the grounds that "the present era is one in which the Great Shogun governs the land, since the days of the founding father of the Bakufu, *Azumateru-no-kami Mioyanomikoto* [Ieyasu], in accordance with the designs of the Sun Goddess Amaterasu and by the authority vested in him by the Imperial Court. The Shogun has divided the administration among the different provinces [*kuni*] and counties [*gun*], entrusting to the daimyo the task of governing them. . . . The rules of the founder of the Bakufu and the regulations of the succeeding great Shogun are all the rules and regulations of the Sun Goddess Amaterasu."[40] During the An'ei (1772–81) and Temmei (1781–89) eras, floods, droughts, and famines one after another cast their shadows throughout the land, causing ghastly conditions. There were riots and uprisings on an unprecedented scale. But with these terrible facts staring him in the face, Norinaga was able to compose the following poems: "Having been born in a peaceful era in a peaceful country, and living in tranquillity, nothing worries me"; "The land pacified by Azumateru-no-kami [Ieyasu] as a land of tranquillity will endure for ten thousand

---

[37] *Kokuikō; Kamoō-kashu*, Book III.
[38] *Shimotsuke ya | kami no shizumeshi | Futarayama | futatabi toda ni | mi-yo wa ugokaji. Kamoō-kashu*, Book III.
[39] *Kamoō-kashu*, Book IV.
[40] *Tamakushige.*

epochs."[41] Even Hirata Atsutane (1776–1843), who constructed a kind of positive theology from Ancient Learning, and whose following produced some of the "men of high purpose" (*shishi*) of the Meiji Restoration, regarded the delegation of authority from the emperor to the bakufu, and from the bakufu to the daimyo, as an "eternal" political system.[42] He was so realistic a supporter of the existing order that he did not hesitate to say: "Dazai Shundai said that the nation is governed peacefully because of the Way of the Sages. The last phrase should be corrected to read: because of the military capabilities and virtues of Tōshōgū [Ieyasu]."[43]

If we accept its political thought at face value, we must conclude that from beginning to end, National Learning never stepped outside the limits of feudal society. But does this mean that the revolutionary significance of the thought of National Learning was strictly limited to the realm of pure learning, that it contributed nothing new to the changes in mode of observation in the political and social spheres, the focal point of my essay? Certainly not! Paradoxical as it may sound, it was precisely because National Learning was essentially apolitical, that is, its affirmation of feudal society was made from an apolitical position, that it was able to acquire a certain political significance. The apolitical character, which prevented National Learning from developing into a revolutionary ideology, also to a certain extent limited its politically conservative function. I shall inquire further into the meaning of this thesis by analyzing the structure of the theory of Norinaga, the purest exponent of the mode of thought of National Learning.[44]

National Learning began as a philological study of ancient

---

[41] *Yasukuni no | yasurakeki yo ni | umare aite | yasukekute areba | mono omoi mo nashi. Azumateru no | kami no mikoto no | yasukuni to | shizumemashikeru | mi-yo wa yorozuyo. Tama-hoko no momouta.*

[42] *Shishi* is a term used for activists concerned about developments at the end of the Tokugawa period, particularly after Perry's arrival. They tended to be opposed to the bakufu and to favor the restoration of political power to the imperial court. By and large they were also anti-Western. (Translator's note.) *Tama dasuki,* Book IX.

[43] *Ibuki oroshi,* II.

[44] The author believes that the work of National Learning in the history of thought was completed by Norinaga. Atsutane made some advances in a new direction methodologically, but in some respects he reverted to Confucianism. This is a major question that cannot be discussed in detail here, but I shall proceed as if this premise had been established.

literature. This gave rise to the discovery of unadorned human sentiments, free of the intellectual reflections and ethical compulsions of later eras, and soon there arose a passionate yearning for the way of life of antiquity, when people supposedly enjoyed the free expression of their natural inclinations and sentiments. As a result, in its initial phase National Learning stood for Taoist nature in opposition to all human invention (sakui). This can be most clearly expressed in Mabuchi's words in *Kokuikō:* "Things made by human designs are frequently defective. If we consider the inventions of the knowledgeable men of the past (the Chinese sages), we find that no age ever used their way because it does not conform to the intentions of heaven and earth. *Rather, the teaching of Lao Tzu, which stressed living in harmony with nature, conformed to the way under heaven.*" Here, then, Sorai's theory that Confucian standards were invented by the sages served as a negative factor.

Earlier I traced the externalization and ritualization of Confucian standards that occurred between Sorai and Shundai. The scholars of National Learning used the alienation of these standards from human nature to proclaim the inviolability of the world of inner sentiments. These alienated standards were not merely private ethical standards but, just as they were for Sorai, public political institutions. This is clear from Norinaga's statement in *Naobi no mitama* that "the Confucian scholars criticize the laws of later ages as being contrary to the Way of the Early Kings. But why was the Way of the Early Kings not identical with the laws of antiquity?" Thus, if this resistance of inner nature to external standards is taken positively to its logical conclusions, it must lead to a denial of the limitations inherent in the feudal estates. It did in fact lead to such a conclusion in the case of Andō Shōeki's naturalism.

As a rule, whenever naturalism is raised to the level of an Idea, as it was by Shōeki, Lao Tzu, and Rousseau, its political conclusions include a denial of the restrictions of the society of the thinker in question. But one naturalism, that of National Learning, failed to follow this path. This was so because National Learning evaded its logical conclusions, not primarily as a concession to the times, but because its naturalism had at its core the poetic spirit, the spirit of *waka* (*uta no kokoro*), which sought to adhere consistently to the fundamental characteristic of human sentiment; as Norinaga put it in *Tama-hoko no momouta*, "To be moved emotionally is man's inborn nature."[45] That is, the moment the natural standpoint becomes an ism, rising above the existing reality, it is bound to confront inner sentiments as a new imperative, reimposing rigid ideas on fluid sentiments, and thus stifling the pure expression of these sentiments. Norinaga recognized this fact more clearly than anyone else. Like Mabuchi, he generally accepted Taoist naturalism. "The thinking of Lao Tzu and Chuang Tzu resembles the Way of the Gods in many respects. This is so because they abhor cleverness and respect nature. Things natural are similar regardless of time and place."[46] However, he immediately qualified this by stating that "motivated by their dislike of cleverness, they attempt to establish the way of nature *by deliberately opposing what is artificial*. Their nature is therefore not truly natural. If it is best to allow things to follow their natural course, then in a cleverly artificial age, the cleverly artificial should be allowed to prevail. Ironically, in such an age, to abhor and dislike what is clever itself becomes a labored argument."[47] Therefore in order to maintain the primacy of inner naturalness over human invention, while avoiding any ideal absolutization of nature itself, there was no alternative but to posit a superhuman, absolute personality behind the inner nature as its foundation. Thus Norinaga introduced the theory of *"nature as the invention of the Gods."*

According to Norinaga in *Naobi no mitama*, the way of life of the ancient Japanese, who were free of all normative restrictions and lived in accordance with "the true spirit [*magokoro*] they were born with" and "went through life tranquilly and happily," was as such the Way of the Gods. And the creation of the foundations of this Way of the Gods could be ascribed to the imperial ancestor gods: "What is the Way of the Gods? It is not the natural way of heaven and earth [this should be understood and not be confused with the views of the Chinese Taoists, added Norinaga], nor is it a way made by man. This Way was originated by the Gods Izanagi and

---

[45] This is nothing but the psychological basis for the apolitical attitude of National Learning. See part I, chapter 4.

[46] *Kuzubana*, Book II.

[47] Ibid.

Izanami in accordance with the spirit of the august deity Takami-
musubi-no-kami, and was received, preserved, and handed down
by the Sun Goddess, Amaterasu." In later ages, Norinaga argued
in *Kuzubana,* the true or inborn spirit was obscured by the Chinese
spirit, and the Way of the Gods was prevented from revealing
itself in all its purity by the many norms "created by the sages . . .
on the basis of their own private intellect." Of this turn of events,
he observed in *Tamakushige,* "it is commonly said that it is the
natural course of things for the conditions of society and the spirit
of the people to change in this way with the changing times.
However, these are not natural developments but are also *brought
about by the actions of the gods.*" This decline was directly the work
of the evil god, Magatsubi. But even an evil god is a god. Magatsubi, too, descends from the "spirit" (*mitama*) of the two gods,
Takamimusubi and Kamimusubi, so man is helpless in the face
of his actions. Hence

> if we were to seek to return to the Way of antiquity and attempt
> *forcibly* to make the government and the people *conform to the Way of
> antiquity,* we should be going against the present intentions of the
> gods, and departing from the true purpose of the Way. The inten-
> tion of the Way is for the government of today to conform to the
> conditions of today. Contemporary officials should govern by ad-
> hering to the contemporary laws established by the ruler, retaining
> the structure that has come down from the past, and preserving the
> vestiges of the past. This would truly conform to the spirit of antiq-
> uity, when the country was still governed in complete accord with
> the Way of the Gods.[48]

Thus even the Ancient Way, which he had illuminated by a lifetime's study, was not allowed to act upon the existing situation as
an imperative. To allow it to do so would mean the exertion of a
form of compulsion upon the natural activities of the human spirit,
and would contradict the attitude to life that naturally follows the
Way of the Gods. In the last analysis, to accept docilely all historical givens as givens necessarily follows from the spirit of National Learning, which has as its essence "the spirit of Japanese

[48] *Tamakushige.*

poetry," which is "abundant, big-hearted, and refined."[49] The theoretical foundation for this is an absolute devotion to the inventions of the gods: "All things in the world, good and bad, are the products of the spirit of the Gods."[50] "Can we audaciously challenge the actions of the Gods, with our insignificant power as human beings?"[51]

This clears up the mystery of the attitude that the scholars of National Learning adopted toward the bakufu-han political system. The feudal hierarchy was a real historical given of their time, and as such it was also an invention of the gods. It was to be accepted because, according to Norinaga in *Tama-hoko no momouta*, "the laws issued in each age are the commands of the gods issued in that age." "*When all is said and done,* to obey the laws of the day is to follow the true way of the Gods." Could the feudal society rest easy with this kind of justification? No. Although resistance to the existing order cannot be justified by it, neither does it provide any guarantee for the absolute validity of that order. "In the present era, one has to respect the laws of the present," but once times change and a new form of rule emerges, it too will be acknowledged as the "will of the gods" at that particular time. Of primary importance here are "the acts of the gods" themselves, not the content of those acts. Hence the feudal system, as one content of the acts of the gods, is affirmed, but at the same time it is denied.

This dialectic of Norinaga then turns out to be none other than Sorai's dialectic of autonomous invention. National Learning began as the champion of nature against man-made standards, but in order to prevent nature itself from becoming a normative standard, it made nature dependent on the invention of the gods. Thus it had ultimately to accept the logical conclusions of the theory of autonomous invention. Although Norinaga made every effort to distinguish terminologically between "the way originated by the Gods" and "the way established by the sages," it is impossible to deny the similarities between the positions of Norinaga's gods and Sorai's sages in their respective systems, however different the

[49] *Uiyamabumi.*
[50] *Yo no naka no | yoki mo ashiki mo | kotogoto ni | kami no kokoro no | shiwazu ni zo aru.*
[51] *Ofuke naku | hito no iyashiki | chikara mote | kami no nasuwazu | arasoieme ya.*

content of those systems. Both gods and sages are the ultimate
sources of the authority of all institutions and culture in the world.
(In Norinaga's view, the immediate inventor of institutions was
the actual political ruler, but in the last analysis he believed that
the ruler merely acted as a puppet of the gods; see the comments
on "invisible things" and "visible things" in his *Tamakushige*.) And
both are absolute personalities beyond ordinary ethical value
judgments. Just as Sorai considered it an insult to the sages to try
to make them conform to li, Norinaga argued in *Naobi no mitama*
that "the Gods are not to be judged in terms of whether they conform to *li* or not. Our duty is only to fear their wrath and revere
and worship them single-mindedly." Thus both Norinaga and
Sorai denied any superiority of ideas over their gods and sages
and instead subordinated them to these personalities.[52] But we
should note that in their *motives* for adopting such a system of
thought, Norinaga's starting point was the complete opposite of
Sorai's. Sorai's logic of autonomous invention was intended from
the outset to strengthen feudal society; it was inherently public
and political in nature. As a result, he argued solely from the point
of view of political authority. Norinaga, on the other hand, following the tradition of National Learning, was interested first of all
in the world of inner sentiments (magokoro, or inborn spirit, and
mono no aware, or a sense of the sadness of things). The logic arising as a result of attaining this purity of thought is the system
called *kami no shiwaza,* or the "actions of the gods." Thus, even
when his logic had political society as its object, Norinaga was always aware of his position as a private individual and considered
the problem primarily from the standpoint of a political subordinate. After all, Norinaga's theory of autonomous invention can
be said to be the viewpoint of the governed, who see the other side
of Sorai's absolutism, in which the ruler acts as he pleases, beyond
good and evil.

---

[52] The supremacy of these personalities was the theoretical basis that later enabled
Atsutane to inject into ancient Shinto the Christian concept of a creator god. With a
clear, logical consciousness, Atsutane said: "This God is timeless and of course created
heaven and earth and all things for a divine reason. Just as the founder of a regime
becomes the prince of that country, He too reigns supreme" (*Honkyō gaihen,* Book I).
Notice the remarkable similarity between this reasoning and Descartes's as expressed
in the latter's letter to Mersenne discussed above.

Earlier, I noted that one of the effects of making the logic of invention the justification for given institutions was to empty those institutions of their inherent values. When Norinaga took his stand on an apolitical inner nature and put all political institutions under the will of the gods, the historical relativism of the values ascribed to these institutions was openly revealed. By advocating submission to feudal authority relations, because "in the present world, we must respect the commands of the present," he did not uphold these authority relations as based on any substantive value such as "the natural principle of heaven and earth," but only because "the Way of Antiquity expects all those below to obey and to follow exactly the existing laws issued by those above, *regardless of whether these laws are good or bad.*"[53] The phrase "regardless of whether these laws are good or bad" aptly expresses a Hobbesian positivism that believes that the validity of the political order depends purely on the formal positive character of the sovereign and is wholly indifferent to intrinsic values such as truth or justice.

That this was no careless phrase tossed out on the spur of the moment, but one Norinaga carefully thought out, is clear from the fact that he said the same thing in his *Tamakatsuma*: "Those below must submit to the intentions of those above, *regardless of whether they are good or bad.*" This indifference to the intrinsic value of norms is an unexpected implication of Sorai's thought, but in Norinaga's, which stands in inverse relation to Sorai's, it becomes clearly visible. In its apolitical optimism, National Learning lauded the existing regime with the words "The land pacified by Azumateru-no-kami as a land of tranquillity will endure for ten thousand epochs," but the entire structure of its mode of thought was already beginning to be ominously agitated by the logic of invention.

[53] *Uiyamabumi.*

CHAPTER VI

FURTHER DEVELOPMENTS AND STAGNATION IN THE BAKUMATSU PERIOD

The Political and Social Situation and the Intellectual World in the Latter Half of the Tokugawa Period. Various Theories of Institutional Change. Theoretical Limitations of the Doctrine of Invention. Conflict between the Two Views of Institutions after the Meiji Restoration.

I

Gustav Radbruch remarked: "If the wish is father to the thought, so is an interest the mother of the idea; like other mothers, the interest cannot prevent her daughter from growing up, coming of age, and leading her own life. The moment an interest appeals to the idea, it delivers itself up to the logic of that idea which henceforth develops according to its own laws, possibly even against the interest which invoked it to act for it."[1]

The concept of "autonomous invention" formulated by Sorai can be said to have undergone such a fate. Originally it was a logic invoked to reestablish feudal society on an unshakable foundation. But the outcome, as we have seen in the two thinkers who inherited this mode of thought in its most typical form, Andō Shōeki and Motoori Norinaga, was a clear rejection of feudal society in one and a passive affirmation of it in the other. In both cases there were no longer any theoretical grounds for feudal society to be as immutable as heaven and earth and as eternal as human nature. Nature as an absolute value had been detached from the feudal hierarchy and had either become a political utopia or been implanted in the inner sentiments of man. In parallel with

---

[1] Gustav Radbruch: *Kulturlehre des Sozialismus,* 2nd ed. (1927), pp. 8–9.

this trend towards an ideological weakening of feudal society went a rise in the activity of the *real forces* threatening its stability. The number of riots and uprisings indisputably increased spectacularly during the Hōreki, Meiwa, An'ei, and Tenmei eras (1751–89). In 1786 and 1787 there were fifteen uprisings in the country each year. The so-called Tenmei riots of 1787 started in Osaka and broke out almost simultaneously in Kyoto, Nara, Fushimi, Sakai, Yamada, Kōfu, Suruga, Hiroshima, Nagasaki, Ishimaki, and then spread to most of the country. The riots in Edo were so violent that they were called "the worst disturbance and disaster since the founding of Edo."[2]

It was during this year that Norinaga wrote the *Hihon tamakushige* in response to questions submitted to him by the Lord of Kishū.[3] He prefaced his responses with a statement typical of him: "For a lowly person like myself to dare to discuss the affairs of government is indeed an audacious and disrespectful thing." However, he went on: "*In past times of peace, one never heard* of a great number of peasants and townspeople banding together to make forceful demands and behave riotously. Such incidents were rare even in the recent past. *But lately these incidents have been breaking out all over the place and they are no longer unusual occurrences.* . . . After reflecting on the causes of these incidents, I believe they are all caused by the wrong-doing of those above, not by that of those below." He judged the basic cause to be excessive taxation and warned that such extortion would "result in great losses for those above in the future" because it would eventually obstruct the reproduction of labor power. But the feudal authorities were not only threatened "from below." They had begun to feel pressure from outside around the same period. This threat came first from the north.

The Russian absolute monarchy, with the support of domestic commercial capital, was gradually extending its authority over the Siberian plains. As early as the middle of the seventeenth century it had reached the Amur River region; by the end of that century it had occupied the Kamchatka Peninsula, and was

---

[2] Cf. Tsuji Zennosuke: *Tanuma jidai* [The Tanuma period] (Tokyo, 1936), p. 157.
[3] Kishū, in the modern Wakayama Prefecture, was the domain of one of the three collateral houses of the Tokugawa family. (Translator's note.)

reaching out for Sakhalin, the Kuriles, and Hokkaido. In 1738–39 Captain Spanberg surveyed the coastlines of Honshu and dropped anchor off Hokkaido. In 1771 a Russian vessel was ship-wrecked at Awa in Shikoku. A group of fur traders landed on Kunashiri Island in the Kuriles in 1778 and sought to establish commercial relations. In 1786 another Russian ship arrived off Hokkaido. In the same year the bakufu decreed that the defenses of the northern regions be strengthened. In 1792 Laxman, an en-voy sent by Catherine II, arrived at Matsumae in Hokkaido and formally requested the establishment of commercial intercourse between the two countries. The island country that had rigidly cut itself off from international society, leaving only a tiny outlet at Nagasaki, now had to recognize that European capital was knocking louder and louder at its doors.

Faced with such an internal and external situation, the feudal authorities naturally sought to strengthen their political control. After 1762 bakufu decrees to deal with peasants rebelling or fleeing the land were issued one after another in 1767, 1769, 1770, 1771, 1777, 1783, and 1788.[4] At the same time the bakufu gradually began to keep a sharp lookout for the development of oppositional intellectual movements. The incidents in the Hōreki (1751–64) and Meiwa (1764–72) eras, in which Takenouchi Shikibu (1712–67), Fujii Umon (1720–67), and Yamagata Daini (1725–67) were involved, are significant as early instances in which a proimperial (sonnō) theory caused offense to the feudal authorities. Objec-tively, rather than full-fledged antibakufu movements, these inci-dents were exaggerated by the over-sensitivity of the bakufu itself so that they seemed to be heralds of the royalist movement of the Bakumatsu period. According to the record kept by Takenouchi Shikibu on the investigation conducted by the bakufu's deputy in Kyoto (the *shoshidai*), he responded courageously to the question: "Do you believe that the entire country at present shows outward signs of being in danger?" "Indeed," Shikibu replied, "*I believe that these are precarious times.* In my lectures I have restrained my-self, but because, in this place of judgment today, you ask me about my real feelings, I have no reason to tell any lies. I sincerely

[4] Cf. Kokushō Iwao, op. cit., pp. 340ff.

believe that society is in a precarious state." On hearing this, Shikibu writes, "The magistrate was unable to speak for a moment, and all the public officials present at the examination seemed to be highly upset."[5] This suggests that there was a rather widespread sense of impending crisis. In the same text, Shikibu also wrote: "I was asked if I had regretted the decline of the Imperial Court and had spoken ill of the prosperity of the military class. I replied that . . . I did not recall having *talked* about the decline of the Imperial Court and the prosperity of the military class, but that I had *thought* these things, so although I am not aware of it *such thoughts may have slipped out unintentionally.*" This suggests that the objective circumstances were, if only embryonically, beginning to arouse the political consciousness of some royalists, as well as a certain guilt about the increasing gap between their outward actions and their inner convictions.

Whatever may have been his ability to put his ideas into practice, the royalism (*sonnōron*) in Yamagata Daini's *Ryūshi shinron* [New ideas of Ryūshi] had an unprecedentedly violent critical tone. At the beginning of the book, he extolled the period of imperial rule for its flourishing rites and music, and glittering culture. He then noted that "imperial rule began to decline after the Hogen [1156–59] and Heiji [1159–60] eras. After the troubles of the Juei [1182–84] and Bunji [1185–90] eras, the center of power shifted to the east and all state affairs came to be decided by the military." As a result, he complained, "the rites and music of the Early Kings lamentably declined."[6] He then argued that "once the government moved to the Kanto, rustics seized its authority and lowly subjects monopolized its power. This situation has lasted 500 years. People value only military affairs and do not value learning. As a result of this lack of concern for learning, rites and music have degenerated and the gentlemen-scholars [shi] are overshadowed by rustic and vulgar ways. Because military affairs are cherished, [the authorities] concentrate only on the enforcement of punishments, and the people are burdened by their

---

[5] Hoshino Hisashi: "Jinmonshidai," in *Takenouchi Shikibukun jisekikō furoku* [Appendage to a consideration of Takenouchi Shikibu's record] (Tokyo, 1890).

[6] *Seimei*, Part I.

severity."[7] "I find nothing worthwhile in the government of the east since the Juei and Bunji eras."[8] Thus his argument reached the point of a virtual rejection of the Tokugawa Bakufu. It is noteworthy here that despite his philosophical affiliation to the Chu Hsi school, the method of thought underlying his criticisms of the period is amazingly close to Sorai's.

Daini wrote of man in the state of nature: "It is the nature of man to be born naked into the world. No one is noble, no one base. Everyone is preoccupied with the search for food and the quest to fullfill his desires. Man is no different from birds and beasts." While the human race is in this primitive state of life, "a great man" appears and "teaches man agriculture, weaving, and spinning, and provides for his needs and well-being." After winning the people's hearts in this way, he establishes order in society on the basis of the Five Relationships and the four classes, namely, gentlemen-scholars, peasants, artisans, and merchants, thus bringing the state of nature to an end. "As rites are fixed, distinctions come into existence; as occupations are designated, the structure of the government is established; as apparel is made, court dresses come into existence. *The men who invented these things are called sages.*" Hence social classes exist "not because these distinctions are in the nature of heaven [*tensei*]." They came into being only "after institutions were established."[9] This is more or less Sorai's theory of the invention of the order of things. Daini extolled the origin of Japanese history: "When our land was founded in the East, the Imperial Gods established the foundations, and gloriously and reverently *labored to make the way in order to fulfill the needs and well-being of the people.* Their virtue shone brilliantly in the four directions for over one thousand years. *They established a system of court apparel, and introduced the teaching related to rites and music,* in the manner of Chou, Chao, I Yin, and Po Shuo. The people have all been under their influence to this day."[10] This is the practical application to Japan of his theory of the origins of society.

[7] *Bunbu,* Part V.

[8] *Rigai,* Part XII.

[9] *Jinbun,* Part III.

[10] The Duke of Chou (died c. 1105 B.C.) and the Duke of Chao (died c. 1053 B.C.) were kinsmen and supporters of Wu Wang, the founder of the Chou dynasty. I Yin was an adviser to the founder of the Shang dynasty, and Po Shuo minister to Emperor Kao Sung of the Shang dynasty. (Translator's note.) *Seimei,* Part I.

According to Daini, then, the degeneration and distress of his day resulted from the fact that the rites and music invented by the Imperial Ancestors had decayed, and yet no new institutions had been invented to replace them. "Those conducting the affairs of government today are incapable of formulating their own plans and producing their own ideas. They are generally wrapped up in things of the past and, regardless of the merit of a thing, they exclaim, "it is a historical tradition, it is a historical tradition.' "[11] But what were these historical traditions?

> Yu and T'ang were sages of antiquity. Hsia and Yin were sagacious eras of antiquity. Still there are things that cannot be managed if we rely solely on these men and these ages. The value of a thing should be assessed before deciding whether or not it should be established and institutionalized. The present age follows a period of civil war and is separated from the age of invention by over one thousand years. This age is not that age and this country is not that country. There are no rites that we can rely on. There are no laws that can be followed. *Those things referred to as historical traditions are nothing more than customs inherited from the age of the civil wars and vestiges of the age of barbarism.*[12]

As we know, Sorai had already said: "At present everyone in society appears to have his status [*kaku*] fixed so those who are ignorant of the principle of things believe this to be a fixed institution. But the existing statutes are . . . all part of the society's *customs and developed naturally. . . . They are not what we can call true institutions.*" Institutions had vanished, he explained, because "his [Ieyasu's] was an age when peaceful conditions were restored by military force after a long period of civil war, and since a long time had elapsed since the period of antiquity it was impossible to restore the ancient institutions. Moreover, since it was a period following the civil war, all existing institutions had been destroyed. But he did not reform the manners and customs of his age, and left them as they were."[13] These statements leave no doubt about the similarity of the methods of thought used by Daini and Sorai.[14]

[11] *Daitai*, Part IV.
[12] Ibid.
[13] *Seidan*, Book II.
[14] There are many other similarities between the arguments of *Ryushi shinron* and those of the Sorai school, but I cannot cite them here.

Daini complained that the statesmen of his day were "generally wrapped up in things of the past" and were "incapable of formulating *their own* plans and producing *their own* ideas," or in other words that their norms of conduct presupposed the validity of institutional standards inherited from the past, thus making them incapable of acting freely upon the existing order. We can see the vigorous pulsation of the theory of autonomous invention in its basic form here.

For Shōeki and Norinaga the theory of invention had a negative value, that is, they stressed the implications of degeneration in it, but for Daini, as for Sorai, it had a positive significance, giving the tone of his theory a noticeably political active character. But now this political orientation was not in favor of the bakufu; rather it acted as a criticism directed against the bakufu. Like Sorai, Daini suggested the establishment of institutions as the ultimate solution to the contradiction of the society of his day, institutions whose content was the stringent enforcement of status distinctions between noble and base; the suppression of commercial capital; the encouragement of a return to the land; the establishment of census records, and so on. In other words, he agreed almost completely with Sorai in this respect. (As a result, his criticism of the bakufu did not, like Shōeki's, extend to the structure of feudal society itself.) But he no longer looked to the Tokugawa shogun as the supreme agent to invent these institutions; his eyes were turning hesitantly westward.[15] Here, then, we find another prominent metamorphosis in the goal of the logic of invention. In August, 1767, Shikibu was exiled to Hachijō Island, and Daini and Umon were executed.

The Kansei Ban on Heterodox Studies (*Kansei igaku no kin*) marks an epoch in the enforcement of thought control in the face of such political and social disturbances. Outwardly it was simply a decree directing the head of the Hayashi school to enforce orthodoxy in government schools, but the bakufu's policy automatically affected the other han (domains) too, and non-Chu Hsi scholars were barred from government posts, so its real significance was, needless to say, one of general thought control. The fact that

---

[15] I.e., from Edo, the seat of the bakufu in the east, to Kyoto, the seat of the imperial court in the west. (Translator's note.)

this edict was issued because of the unprecedented factional disputes and consequent intellectual confusion that followed the rise of the school of Ancient Learning is attested by the opinions of Shibano Ritsuzan (1736–1807), Rai Shunsui (1746–1816), Nishiyama Sessai (1735–95), et al., men who had recommended it to Matsudaira Sadanobu, chief adviser to the shogun.[16] At any rate, it is significant that a powerful effort was made to revive the Chu Hsi school, even when Sung positions had lost their influence in Confucian circles because of the rise of the Jinsai, Sorai, and Eclectic schools.

As we have noted, its inherently optimistic method of thought[17] made Chu Hsi philosophy an ideological system suitable for periods of ascendancy or stability. It therefore proved unsuitable in the Genroku and Kyōhō eras when feudal society was beset by violent disturbances. Thus, hegemony fell to the more practically effective Sorai school. But because of this adaptation to crises, the Sorai school had only limited value to the authorities. The unrelenting realism of its interpretations and its decisiveness in *Entweder-oder* debates could be welcomed so long as feudal authority was still as a whole on a firm foundation and could afford to recognize the existing contradictions as contradictions. But once social disturbances had broken out and the ruling class was busy concealing and patching up its difficulties, these qualities could not be tolerated. The more so because, as I observed earlier, there was a conflict of intentions and consequences in the Sorai school,[18] and the rebellious implications of its mode of thought had finally been recognized.

As a result of this, Chu Hsi philosophy, with its essentially static structure, was brought back into play by the feudal rulers, anxious to allay the people's frustrations, not because of its adaptation to the society but for its ideological utility. Norinaga had already pointed out to "those who govern" the explosive character of the Sorai school as opposed to the stabilizing function of the Chu Hsi

[16] See *Nihon Jurin sōsho* [Series of Japanese Confucian writings], 13 vols. (Tokyo, 1927), Vol. III, "Kansei igaku-kin ikensho."

[17] For the uniqueness of the Chu Hsi mode of thought, see part I, chapter 2.

[18] This kind of contradiction between subjective intentions and objective results is a common feature of the thought produced in times of crisis. Cf. for example Machiavelli and Hobbes.

school: "If those who govern wish to engage in learning, *the Sung School is suitable in times of peace, for although it is somewhat removed from reality, it is complete and without defects. The learning of recent students of ancient words and writings could, without proper care, lead to serious mistakes.*"[19] But now even Norinaga was reprimanded by Nishiyama Sessai, who said: "Norinaga constantly writes works critical of the Confucianism of the Duke of Chou and Confucius. In his discussions he includes information about the ancient Sage Emperors of our Imperial Court and *covertly attempts to arouse public feeling*. This is indeed something hateful."[20] This alone is sufficient to indicate the social atmosphere surrounding the prohibition of heterodox studies.

What direct relationship does this prohibition have to the thesis of this treatise? It was in effect an attempt at a compulsory revival of the ideology of natural order. It was an attempt to impose feudal standards as a natural law by force, when they had already lost such self-evident validity. Scholars who upheld the traditional position in face of the rising theory of invented order had not been idle even before this. I need not mention all of the voluminous anti-Sorai writings here. There were among them vilifications that missed the point completely, but the majority simply asserted the ideology of natural order's "right of self-defense." For instance, Takaizumi Mei in his *Jigaku shinpei* [Remedying and clarifying the current state of learning] (1747) wrote, "The Book of *Music* states: 'he who invents is called a Sage, and he who explains is called enlightened.' This means that there must be the virtues of enlightenment and wisdom before there can be any invention or explanation. *It does not mean that enlightenment and wisdom follow invention and explanation*." In his *Bendō kaihei* [Unmasking Sorai's Bendō] (1755), Ishikawa Rinshū (1705–57) also argued that a person is called "a Sage because of his virtues, not because of his inventions. . . . The *Po Hu T'ung*[21] mentions the invention of the

[19] *Tamakatsuma*, 14.
[20] Based on Yoshida Tōgo: *Ishinshi hakkō to Tokugawa seikyō-kō* [Eight lectures on the Meiji Restoration and considerations of Tokugawa politics and thought] (Tokyo, 1924), pp. 277–78.
[21] Based on the discussion on the classics held by Chinese scholars in A.D. 79 and traditionally ascribed to the historian Pan Ku. (Translator's note.)

Eight Diagrams and the art of divination, and the inventions of Shen Nung, the Yellow Emperor, and Yao and Shun. Whenever invention is mentioned in literature, it clearly refers to the Sages. This would seem to substantiate Sorai's words. But it only means that we know they were Sages because of their ability to invent. It does not mean that they were called Sages only after they had invented things." That is, they both rejected Sorai's concept of the sages as the ultimate reality and emphasized the supremacy of ideas over persons.

Another scholar of the Chu Hsi school, Hei Yu, began his book *Hibutsu* [Anti-Sorai] (1783) by saying: "Sorai states that 'the Way of the Early Kings was invented by the Early Kings. It was not the way of heaven and earth.' Yu would say, 'These words of Sorai will lead people under heaven along the wrong path. . . . If this idea prevails, everyone, high and low, will seek after profit and benefit without hard work, and the country will be in danger.' " Moreover, "Sorai argues that the Way is an invention of the human intellect, and that what is useful is virtuous. *This is to turn virtue into something outside human nature.*" Thus he called attention to the inimical effects of Sorai's thought, the externalization of norms. All these statements indicate the fundamental point of conflict between the theses of natural and invented order. Needless to say, the heated arguments about the Sorai school that reverberated in intellectual circles were many and various; they became more complex with the advent of the Eclectic school, but the basic and decisive issue involved was suggested by Miura Atsuo, a follower of the Sorai school, in *Kansō jiteki:* "Is the Way, as the Sung philosophers say, a part of heaven and earth and nature? Or is it the invention of the Early Kings as Sorai claims? He who says it is of heaven and earth and nature is a follower of Sung philosophy no matter how intelligent he may be. He who says it is a Way invented by the Early Kings is a disciple of Sorai."

The prohibition of heterodox studies was designed to give official support to the view that the Way is, "as the Sung philosophers say, a part of heaven and earth and nature," to put an end to the many splits in the intellectual world since the Kyōhō era (1716–36), and to restore to feudal society the ideological unity it had long lacked. Did the theory of natural order regain its former universality? Rather than enter into a detailed discussion of this point, let us examine the following statement:

> The Way was established by the Sages in accordance with the nature of man. It is not the natural way of heaven and earth and nature. All things such as clothing, food, and housing were originated by the Sages. The reason people think they are natural aspects of heaven and earth is because the Sages invented them in harmony with the nature of all things.

No one could have any difficulty deciding whether this is closer to the position that the Way is, "as the Sung philosophers say, a part of heaven and earth and nature," or to the position that it is "the invention of the Early Kings as Sorai claims." This is indistinguishable in method of argument from a passage in Sorai's *Tōmonsho* in which he wrote:

> The cultivation of the five grains was instituted by Shen Nung. The way to build houses and weave clothes was originated by the Yellow Emperor. They established these things in harmony with human nature so they have now spread throughout the world, and people look on them as if they were natural aspects of heaven and earth.

But who was the author of the first of these two statements? It was none other than Matsudaira Sadanobu, the man directly responsible for the edict against heterodox studies! In his *Seigo* [Political discourses] (1788), he shows how deeply he was influenced by the theory of "invention by the Early Kings." But only two years later he branded it as heretical. Can we not see here again the inexorable infiltration by the "cunning scheme of historical reason" of the theory of invention?

II

Around the same period, new proponents of a radical reconstruction of institutions, as proposed by Sorai, came to the fore one after another. They were scholars more or less influenced by Dutch Learning (*Rangaku*). Yuasa Genzō in his *Kokuiron* [Doctoring to the nation], written in 1793, argued that the "national disease" of his day was due to the fact that no sound institutions had been established since the time of Ieyasu. He complained that Sorai's reform proposals had not been put into practice:

> The Eighth Shogun, Yoshimune, was able to understand the general conditions of the country and adopted a policy of austerity suitable to the times. This remedy was effective and the acute disease of the country was cured. But he did not get at the basic cause of the national disease that induced the decline in agriculture, which is the foundation of our country, and the rise of commerce and industry, which are only minor sectors [of the economy]. He commanded Sorai to submit his advice, which the latter did in his *Taiheisaku* and *Seidan*. But I have not heard that his suggestions were ever put into practice. Yoshimune was a wise ruler who brought about a revival [of Tokugawa rule], and Sorai was a heroic figure of his age. *If his advice had been put into effect at that time, nothing would have been impossible even though it might have been done later than it should have been. It is certainly a lamentable matter.*

But by then the times did not permit a return to the pristine feudalism proposed by Sorai. What with destructive erosion by commercial capital at home (*Chirizukadan*, a work describing conditions from the Hōreki [1751–64] to the Bunka [1804–18] eras, argued that "properly, the military should govern the people and the merchants should be the ones governed, but today we seem to be living in a world in which the townspeople are governing"), and a growing threat from the forces of Russia and England abroad (in 1797 a British warship came to Hokkaido; in 1804 a Russian envoy, Nicholas Resanov, bearing the permit issued to Laxman entitling him to enter Nagasaki, arrived at that city asking for the establishment of commercial intercourse and was refused; in 1806 and 1807 Russians encroached upon the Kuriles and Sakhalin; in 1812 the British frigate *Phaeton* created a disturbance at Nagasaki; and in 1825 the bakufu issued a decree ordering the repulsion of all foreign ships by force), the difficulties confronting feudal Japan at this time were far graver than the troubles of the Kyōhō era. Thus in their theories of institutional reform, those minds astute enough to perceive the nature of the age soon extended the range of their vision internationally, and as a result could not fail in some measure to overstep the bounds of feudal society in the content of their theories. Representative names here are Honda Toshiaki, Satō Nobuhiro, and Kaiho Seiryō. I do not have the space to discuss their thought in detail, but given that it can be regarded as a concrete development of the logic of invention, I shall briefly touch on the general direction of their proposed institutional reforms.

Honda Toshiaki (1744–1821) was a mathematician of the school of Seki Kōwa.[22] He interpreted the period as follows: "Today all wealth and money have been concentrated in the hands of the merchants. Their prestige and authority overwhelm the other three classes. If we divide the national production of the country into sixteen parts, fifteen of these are acquired by the merchants and one by the samurai and peasants."[23] "Never in the history of Japan have the samurai and the peasants been reduced to such hardship and misery. Unless reforms are carried out we shall certainly court disaster." It follows that the root cause of these unprecedented social difficulties is "the mistake of entrusting shipping, transport, and trade solely to the merchant class."[24] He proposed that shipping be managed by the central government. This would correct "inequalities in the prices of commodities" from place to place. He also proposed Japanese involvement in overseas trade and colonization to strengthen the economy.

Thus Toshiaki ascribed the ills of the time to the uncontrolled activities of commercial capital, or, in his own words in *Keisei Hisaku,* they had arisen *"because the system or institution [seido] that should have been established has not yet been established."* But for Toshiaki, the "system that should be established" was not, as Sorai and many other theorists before this had advocated, the simple suppression of commercial capital. Rather, he proposed the state administration of its functions. In *Keizai hōgen* he discussed Banzan and Sorai in connection with his proposals:

During the two hundred years since peace was established . . . a large number of learned men have arisen, but Banzan and Sorai

[22] Seki Kōwa (1642–1708) invented a system of calculus and knew the principle of determinants. (Translator's note.)
[23] *Shizen chidō no ben.*
[24] *Keisei hisaku.*

are the only two who have won recognition as experts in *keizai* [government and political economy].

But the two concerned themselves only with how best to improve the situation by persistently considering different ways to get the greatest benefit from the products of a given piece of land. . . . But it is impossible to extract a surplus from crops produced in a limited piece of land, after first meeting the need for food, clothing, and housing of the people, who continue to increase in number without limit. There is a limit to the crops that can be produced from land that is fixed in size. The people who procreate each year increase in size each year without limit. Finally there will be more people than the national product, and the national product will be less than the number of people in the country. This is a process which knows no end.

This is what has often been cited as Toshiaki's "Malthusian" perspective.

But Toshiaki's theories of reform leaped far ahead of anything before them in their rejection of the "political economy which seeks to deal with things within Japan alone" and their advocacy of "the enlightened method of overseas expansion." He had acquired this point of view as a result of his travels and observations in Hokkaido and the knowledge of the rest of the world he had obtained from Dutch learning, particularly geography. He was especially struck by the wealth and power of the British Empire. "There are no oceans in the great world without British territories." But England itself was basically "an isolated island and very cold. It is a wasteland, poor in national production and with nothing of value." How, then, did it become such "a great and wonderful nation"? Kamchatka to the north "is a great country extending from 51° north to 70° or more north." That is, it has more or less the same latitude as England and the climate is similar. Yet one was immeasurably strong and wealthy, while the other remained a wasteland. Recently it had become the possession of "Moscovia" (Russia). This showed that *"the wealth and strength of a country depend, not on the quality of its land, but on its institutions and teachings."*[25] Britain was not the only great country. "The greatest countries in the world are in Europe. How did this

[25] *Seiiki monogatari.*

come about? First of all, those countries have been in existence for five to six thousand years. Their institutions were established after all the ways had been perfected, the foundations of the art of government developed, and the principle that naturally enriches a nation studied. This is the reason."[26]

In comparing the prosperity of European countries with the poverty of Japan, Toshiaki attributed the differences to the fact that they had a system of "overseas expansion" (colonization) and "encouragement of industry and development of resources," while Japan did not. The negligence in inventing such institutions in Japan was responsible for domestic disasters such as "the crop failures and famines that beset this country for three years after 1783, when over two million people starved to death in northern Japan alone." "Because Japan lacks the system of 'developing enterprises,' government is not extended to the various islands [of Hokkaido]. As government does not prevail there, the blessings of the ruler are unknown. As the blessings of the ruler are unknown, they will quickly submit to the rule of Moscovia."[27] Thus Japan would suffer international disgrace. On the other hand, "If this system were to be established as I have mentioned before, there would be a great island of Japan in the East comparable with the island of England in the West. In the great world under heaven there would be two most wealthy and powerful nations."[28]

Toshiaki did not probe deeply into the theoretical foundations of his position. But he did see the qualitative difference in values *before* and *after* the establishment of these institutions, so it can be inferred that his method of thought was not related to any naturalistic continuism. He did not see the natural order as inherent in the existing feudal society, but expected it to emerge only after the invention of such institutions. "After these institutions (that is, colonization, shipping, and trade) have been established," he wrote in *Shizen chidō no ben*, "even though a drastic crop failure may occur, the people will not starve to death. This is the kind of good government that will endure immutably forever. These institutions represent the natural way of government."

[26] *Keisei hisaku.*
[27] Ibid.
[28] *Seiiki monogatari.*

The plans for an astonishingly well organized and elaborate ideal society produced by Satō Nobuhiro (1769–1850) were also motivated by his intimate experience of domestic hardship and international threat. He was particularly concerned about the decline in agriculture, a subject that his family had traditionally been concerned with. He made frequent investigatory trips to the northeastern and southwestern parts of Honshu and was especially distressed by the tragic practice of *mabiki* (infanticide) common in the rural villages. As he observed:

> I have heard that long ago in the Western world there was a great nation whose king killed 3,300 children every year to use their livers to make medicine for the kidney which would give him power over women. Everyone who hears this story is shocked and condemns this inhumane practice. When I first heard it, I too was highly astonished. But later I reflected over the matter carefully and thought, "to be sure, his behavior was inhumane, but he restricted the number of children he killed to 3,300; the number is not stupendous. At present in the two provinces of Mutsu and Dewa [northern Japan] alone, no less than 60,000 to 70,000 infants are killed annually. And yet I have not heard of anyone who is shocked at this and condemns the practice." Is not this indeed an astonishing matter?

> When the Imperial Ancestral God Takami-musubi created this world and commanded the God Izanagi to consolidate this heaven and earth, he did so because he sincerely loved the people and desired to have them prosper and increase.[29]

But in his day this prosperity and growth were being curtailed by infanticide. This situation was for Nobuhiro a result of the fact that the rulers who were divinely assigned the task of aiding and giving security to the people were ignorant of the "way of *keizai*" (governing) and neglected to practice the "art of *tenkō kaibutsu*" (cultivation of natural products and development of resources). In Nobuhiro's definition, *keizai* means "the art of saving the people of the world by putting into practice the divine will of heaven and earth," and *kaibutsu* means "the art of managing the land, increasing the production of goods, enriching the homeland, and further-

[29] *Keizai yōroku*, Books XIV, III.

ing the prosperity and growth of the people."[30] The Way of the Early Kings is no more than this way of governing. "The reason the founder of the Shang Dynasty, T'ang, was wealthy, although he was the prince of only seventy ri,[31] was not because gold rained from heaven in the land of Shang, but because I Yin, the minister, *meticulously refined the institutions, enforced the laws strictly, and eased the circulation of currency.* The refinement of institutions, clarification of laws, and regulation of expenditures are what we call the establishment of the national foundation. A country that has not established its national foundation is bound to suffer from a lack of funds, regardless of the size of its territory."[32]

Thus, for Nobuhiro, like Toshiaki, the wealth or poverty of a country does not have a natural basis in such things as the fertility or extent of the land but is founded on the kind of institutions established in order to make use of the natural conditions. For example, a comparison of the conditions of the different Japanese han illustrates this point. The fief of Aizu (in the modern Fukushima Prefecture) is "a very inconvenient land, located in an out-of-the-way place among mountains . . . where there is no sea or river that can be used to transport things." But "*because its institutions are excellent* . . . a variety of industries have arisen in large numbers, the state of the *han* is extremely healthy, and its customs are simple and wholesome. In all these things it ranks at the top of the country." In contrast, the land of Nobeoka in Hyūga (in the modern Miyazaki Prefecture) occupies a spacious area, the climate is mild, and it is blessed with the means of water transport. And yet, "because it entrusts all its farm lands, forests, mountains, valleys, and plains to the peasants and permits them to buy and sell them as they please, the lord is often unable to have his way concerning the resources of the mountains and woods, and even rice. The only thing the lord does is collect the annual taxes."[33]

Although there were such differences between the various han in the country, nowhere in Nobuhiro's time was there any sign of basic institutions of the kind established by I Yin. A survey of

[30] Ibid., Books XV, I.
[31] One *ri* equals 2.44 miles. (Translator's note.)
[32] *Satsu-han keiiki.*
[33] *Keizai yōroku,* Book II.

Japanese history showed, according to Nobuhiro in *Sai shikai konkyū kenpaku,* that these institutions had not existed even in antiquity, but people had been able to get by somehow in those days. "I have not heard that Japan has ever had a system that governed everything, not even in antiquity. But in antiquity the rulers were modest and respectful, and the customs were simple, so the country was naturally wealthy." The natural order of antiquity, however, collapsed with the rise of the *shōen* (tax-free manor). The ensuing chaos and disorder were temporarily brought under control with the rise of the samurai, but "all the samurai did was grasp the political reins of the country; *they did not establish any worthwhile institutions.* Thus money slowly concentrated in the hands of the merchant class, and the samurai became desperately impoverished." Needless to say, with each passing year it became less and less desirable to allow things to follow their natural course, and more and more necessary to invent institutions on a large scale. (This is why Nobuhiro praised the three reforms of Kyōhō [1716–36], Kansei [1789–1801], and Tenpō [1830–44].)

Thus in Nobuhiro's opinion, the unprecedented domestic troubles and foreign threat could not be met with reforms carried out at the local level in each feudal domain. It was necessary to establish an overall system that would unite all of Japan into one integral unit. And the content of this system could no longer be a mere reproduction of the institutions of the Early Kings. Nobuhiro's understanding of his age had progressed beyond a mere "sense of crisis." "By careful observation of the conditions of the world," he explained in *Hōtei shōtō hikidakun hōji,* "I have become aware of the fact that the end of a historical epoch is near at hand. There are signs pointing to drastic changes in the course of events." Because he was harried by this acute sense of an impending world revolution, the system he devised turns out to be unprecedentedly broad in scope and serious in conception. There was to be a national political organization with three departments, six ministries, and five bureaus, by means of which the functions of production, distribution, and currency were to be concentrated in the central government, while the state was to be actively responsible for the care of the poor and the education of the people. All this is explained in his *Suitōhō* [Method of social control]. Unfortunately, I lack the space even to give a general description of his plan.

Nobuhiro's plan is often described, aptly or not, as "state socialism." He himself admitted its utopian character when he said in *Suitō hiroku*, "The so-called *Suitōhō* is an incomparably excellent system, but it is an enormous undertaking designed to transform the world completely, so unless conditions in heaven and earth are propitious, it will be difficult to put it into practice." It was obviously far removed from the social realities of his day. If the Tenpō Reform of 1841–43, introduced by Mizuno Tadakuni (1793–1851), was the last and most radical reform actually put into practice to preserve the feudal system, then Nobuhiro's *Suitōhō*, formulated around the same time, put a period to the series of theories of institutional reform that had been devised since Sorai's day and was the most elaborate of such ideological systems.

It is worth noting that, in its philosophical basis, Nobuhiro's thought was heavily influenced by Hirata Atsutane's National Learning. "As I respectfully examine the classics of the Age of the Gods," he remarked, "I find that *when heaven and earth were not yet formed*, the three gods Amenominaka-nushi (the Supreme God in the Center of Heaven), Takami-musubi, and Kami-musubi already existed. These three gods constitute the fountainhead of all creation."[34] Thus he clearly adopted the position that the gods created the world "out of nothing." "Wherever there is land," he observed, "there are always the products of the land. This is so because Takami-musubi created land so that mankind might prosper and grow. . . . All men are children of Takami-musubi, who loves them deeply and preserves and fosters them. . . . From heaven above, he commanded the myriad gods to bring forth from the land metal and stones, grass and trees, birds and beasts, and so on, and from the water, fish and turtles, shellfish and seaweeds, and so on. These he intended for man's use to make his life rich and abundant, to preserve his life, and to have his descendants increase and flourish."[35] In other words, Nobuhiro saw in political economy itself a creation of the two *musubi* gods for the benefit of

[34] *Yōzōkaiku-ron*, Book I.
[35] *Keizai yōroku*, Book XIV.

mankind. Political rulers govern all things in this world as deputies of the creator gods of this world. (This is what Nobuhiro meant when he said that the rulers have a duty to aid the poor in accordance with the will of the gods.) This supremacy of personal creators that lay at the bottom of his thought led him to endow the supreme ruler in his ideal state with the attributes of absolutism, empowering him "to do as he pleases with the entire country of Japan as if it were his hands and feet."[36]

Sorai's "absolutist" invention, which would enable the shogun to rule "all Japan" "as he pleases," implied a planned return to pristine feudalism, following the suppression of commercial capital. But Nobuhiro's absolutism is much closer to the European variety. "In the various countries of the West," he wrote, "trade is the monopoly of the king, and this function is not entrusted to the common people. This is because the profits to be gained from trade are enormous and far exceed income from the taxation of land and miscellaneous commodities. For this reason, in my plan . . . there is the secret of political economy. Thus, the goods of the whole country will move busily about, and the great profits to be gained from this will all fall into the hands of the ruler." What he meant here in *Nōsei honron* is not entirely clear, but the passage provides adequate evidence of the similarities between his ideal state of "social control" (*suitō*) and the European mercantilistic states with centralized power. (Of course, unknown to Nobuhiro, Europe was by this time already undergoing the Industrial Revolution.) Just as the absolutist states of Europe expanded overseas, so, once "social control" had been enforced, Japan had the great duty of "fusing" together the nations of the entire globe, turning them into Japanese counties and prefectures, and transforming "all the rulers of the world" into Japanese subjects (cf. *Udai kondō hisaku*). In effect, Nobuhiro's ideal state was simply a perfect inversion of the realities of Bakumatsu Japan, gasping under the strain of internal cleavage and international pressure.

In contrast to the plans for reform devised by Toshiaki and Nobuhiro, the so-called system of "hoisting-up" (*makiage*) formulated by Kaiho Seiryō (1755–1817) was designed primarily to

---

[36] *Kondō hisaku.*

provide relief for the samurai class. Moreover it was a plan for one han in particular and was therefore much more limited in scale. But Seiryō did tend in the same direction as the others in his advocacy of a plan for han government management of commerce, and he also explained all existing social relations in terms of the principle of commercial exchange (*urikai*). This makes his theory unique and worthy of consideration. Seiryō studied under a disciple of Sorai, Usami Sensui, and inherited all of Sorai's realism. In *Keikodan* he denounced the Confucian scholars as "parasites of the world, perverted men of the world," but admitted that "among the Confucian scholars of recent years, Hakuseki and Sorai *discussed things with real facts in mind,* so they differed greatly from the other Confucian scholars." In other words, he praised Hakuseki and Sorai for their empirical and inductive observations.

Seiryō's relief plan for the samurai was also based on such empirical observations of social reality. How did he characterize the realities of the period? "This is not an age of parricide and regicide. It is not an age of strife. One cannot get by even for a day without buying and selling. This is not a world in which gold and silver are held in contempt, nor is it an age that scoffs at commerce." Despite this, "it is the custom of the entire samurai class to laugh at those who value money and call them 'men wrapped up in commerce.' " Does this mean, then, that the samurai do not engage in commerce? "First of all the daimyo with large domains sell their rice every year to obtain money which they use to carry out their public functions and put everything in good order. Selling rice is nothing but commerce. Everyone from the daimyo of large fiefs down thus engages in trade. And yet they laugh at commerce while they themselves are engaged in it. Hence there is a contradiction between their status [*mibun*] and their actions. No wonder they have become impoverished."[37]

In effect, the samurai class was reduced to poverty because, although they lived in the midst of a commercial economy, they deliberately shut their eyes to this reality. Given that one is living in a commercial economy, it is only natural to profit from commercial exchange; there is nothing disgraceful about it. On the

[37] *Zenchūdan.*

contrary, it is those who ignore the principles of the exchange of equivalents

> and neglect to return the money they borrow from the merchants who are really disgraceful. . . . Those who do not return the money they borrow are like those who take away someone's property without paying for it and refuse to return it. . . . What should we call such people who take things away from others without paying and refuse to return them? . . . People burst out laughing when told that the King of Holland engages in trade. But they themselves buy and sell things. To buy and sell things is a principle [li] of the world. There is nothing laughable about it. Rather, it is disrespectful to laugh at a principle of the world. It is contrary to the principle of the world to take things away from others without paying. The lord in heaven despises this sort of behavior. While openly doing things that are contrary to the principle of the world without any sense of shame, they do not hesitate to insult and laugh at the principle of the world. Alas, how terribly misguided are such people![38]

The only way to relieve the difficulties of the samurai class, Seiryō believed, was for them to engage actively in "profit raising." "Profit raising is what the merchants call money making."[39] In accordance with the principle stated in the *Hung Fan*[40] that "water sinks to the bottom and fire burns upward," all things with forms in the universe move downward and all formless things move upward. Thus, if money is allowed to follow its natural course, it must flow downward to the common people. The ruling class therefore needs an invention (sakui) to reverse this flow and "hoist it up." Profit raising is simply a means to this end. One way to raise profits, but a crude one, would be to take the people's money away by force. For the samurai to engage actively in commerce and make money within the framework of the commercial economy is the "skillful way of raising profits." Seiryō suggested encouraging the samurai by secret awards to engage in supplementary work in their homes, opening ports for trade as in the

[38] *Keikodan.*
[39] Ibid.
[40] The Great Norm, a section of the Book of History. (Translator's note.)

province of Aki (modern Hiroshima), and establishing mutual loan associations for commodities (*shiromono mujin*), and so on, as such methods. He went so far as to propose trade in titles of nobility and the substitution of fines for punishments in order to increase government revenue.

In other words, "to take away money skillfully is to do it without people even being aware of it."[41] We can detect a touch of Machiavellianism here. Seiryō himself was aware of this and said: "It is only natural for people to become extravagant in times of peace. When they fall into extravagance, they necessarily become clever. When they become clever, those above cannot take from those below at will, and those below will not allow those above to take from them at will. Clearly, then, in this age, when there is a struggle for profits, it is pointless to continue talking about the Way of the King." As he boldly and forthrightly stated: "In the Way of the King there is no victory or defeat; no friend or enemy. If there is victory and defeat, and friend and enemy, it is [the Way of] the Overlord.[42] *Thus in the present age, we must be well trained in the Way of the Overlord.* . . . Although we prefer the peaceful Way of the King, this is unavoidable, because we live in an age of the Overlord."[43]

Needless to say, this thoroughness of Seiryō's method of thinking relates to his sense of crisis. In the Bunka era (1804–18), when the people outwardly enjoyed great tranquillity under the carefree rule of the eleventh shogun, Ienari, Seiryō issued a warning in *Keikodan*:

> In time of peace people become careless because they are comfortable for the moment. . . . They say, "Now, now, leave everything alone. Even if the laws have deteriorated, leave things as they are. It is difficult to change things. It cannot be done. It is better to carry on as usual without changing things." Thus lacking courage . . . they have got used to temporizing and become expedient. This is the picture of an age of peace. In this way they put this off and put that off. Because of such procrastination *the sickness soon develops into*

[41] *Keikodan.*
[42] *Pa* (Chinese) or *ha* (Japanese). "Machiavellian" power politics in which might rather than right prevails. (Translator's note.)
[43] *Yōjindan.*

a major one. Hence it is necessary to act with courage and decisiveness as if we were walking in deep water. We must roll up the bottom of our clothes. We must be as mentally prepared as when we are about to embark on a *difficult maneuver*.

That he opposed the attitude that would "leave things as they are even though the laws have deteriorated," and "carry on as usual without changing things," and argued the necessity to approach reforms with the resolute attitude of one "walking in deep water," reveals once again the ground gained by the idea of autonomous invention.

Be that as it may, it is highly significant that Seiryō placed the logic of commercial exchange, "buying and selling" (urikai), at the root of all social relations. Since he held that "all things in heaven and earth are commodities," that is, values that produce profits, and that buying and selling is "the principle of the world," he naturally concluded that "since everyone, high and low, engages in buying and selling, everyone is a merchant."[44] Hence he regarded the feudal master-servant relationship as purely the buying and selling of labor power. "From antiquity, it has been said that the relationship between the lord and his subject is that of the marketplace. The lord gives his subject a fief and compels him to work. The subject sells his labor to the lord and receives rice. The lord buys from the subject, the subject sells to his lord. It is simply a matter of buying and selling. Buying and selling is all right. Buying and selling is not a bad thing."[45] For Seiryō, of course, this was a natural conclusion. All he did was provide a rational theory for the existing master-servant relation. But now this relationship, which had once been regarded as an inherent natural order that human beings have to enter, was clearly seen as a union based on the free will of those concerned. Let me recall Tönnies's words: "Where truly mercantile individuals . . . confront one another in the international or national markets and exchanges, the nature of the *Gesellschaft* is represented as in an extract or concave mirror."[46]

[44] *Keikodan; Zenchūdan.*
[45] *Keikodan.*
[46] *Gemeinschaft und Gesellschaft*, op. cit., 8th ed., pp. 52–53. Loomis translation, p. 87 (modified here). (Translator's note.)

III

As Tokugawa society went on decaying internally and the external crisis deepened, intellectuals, as we have seen, produced various proposals for institutional reform. The content of these proposals could no longer be confined within purely feudal categories, but on the other hand, it is also true that none of these proposals discussed the possibility of completely transforming feudal authority relations. Even Kaiho Seiryō, whose perceptive *understanding* of the nature of feudal society was so amazingly modern, offered only a "device" (*karakuri*) with which the samurai class could take (*makiage*) money away from the common people. His thesis that "everyone, high and low, is a merchant" merely meant that the daimyo in his capacity as a daimyo and the foot soldier (*ashigaru*) in his capacity as a foot soldier fulfill the same functions as does the merchant. It is not at all a call for the transformation of the daimyo into a merchant. On the contrary, he still believed in the ignorance of the common people (*gumin*): "The [common] people are all extremely stupid." "It is all right for the people not to know what kind of behavior constitutes filial piety, or what constitutes loyalty to the lord. The only important thing is for the people to be punished if they do not obey the commands of their superiors. There will then be no difficulties for myriads of years. Those who obey the commands of their superiors should be rewarded. There will then be no difficulties for myriads of years."[47] Toshiaki, too, whose proposals for the establishment of a system of commerce, colonization, and encouragement of industry were clearly incompatible with feudal autarchy, expected the samurai class to serve as the agent inventing these institutions.[48] Basic to

---

[47] *Kaiho giheisho.*

[48] Toshiaki himself was fully aware of the dangers inherent in his thought and was very careful about what he said in his published writings. Towards the end of the first volume of his *Keisei hisaku* [Secret plan for managing the country], he wrote: "The above secret plans all trace the customs of the day to their roots and clearly choose between good and evil, right and wrong, so it may sound as if the present administration is being criticized. I am over-awed by this thought. But when one is too cautious, and emphasizes reverence and respect alone, important principles may sound shallow. For this reason, I have committed the crime of speaking beyond the limits of propriety and have written as I have." In the preface to his *Seiiki monogatari* [Tales from the West], he remarked: "To call what is right, right, and what is wrong, wrong, may seem to be

his scheme was a desire to "*maintain strict class distinctions between the four peoples,* to eliminate idle vagrants, and to pacify society."[49]

No doubt because he was writing at a later period, the institutions proposed by Satō Nobuhiro were more radical in content than those of Seiryō and Toshiaki. He remarked in *Suitō hiroku:*

> The institutions of Chou and T'ang governed the people by dividing them into four branches: gentlemen-scholars, peasants, artisans, and merchants. I have reflected over the matter carefully and concluded that the four-peoples system leaves some areas untouched by the government and hinders the perfecting of the many industries. . . . Thus, in order to conduct the affairs of government, a matter within the purview of heaven, we should, after considering the activities of all men, reclassify and group together those engaged in similar work and divide the industries of the world into eight categories: thus there would be people engaged in cultivation, forestry, mining, manufacturing, trading, hired labor, shipping, and fishing. The people classified into these eight groups would be assigned to the six ministries. . . . They will be strictly prohibited by law from engaging in any other occupation.

Thus he consciously opposed his six-ministry, eight-class system of social control to the traditional samurai-peasant-artisan-merchant estate system. As we have seen, his plan denied the independence of the han and had strong implications of centralized authority. But even here the daimyo's feudal domains were to remain, and the positions of authority in the six ministries were to be occupied by members of the traditional samurai class. The common people were merely to have the chance of "promotion." Elsewhere he argued that those who occupied the position of daimyo in this

---

directly criticizing, slandering, or vilifying [the bakufu]. If this is true, it is impossible to avoid the charge of having plotted against the rulers from below. I have always feared this." And in his *Chōkiron* [Useful tools], he wrote: "The various points discussed above are accounts of the exact conditions of Japan today. It may sound as if I am criticizing the present system and I feel guilty about this. Nevertheless, I have described exactly the way things are without holding anything back, feeling that it is important to do so. *I have taken strict precautions to prevent other people from seeing this.*" For these reasons, he was especially careful not to make his writings public and only showed them to a few people. That is why he was able to avoid the fate of Hayashi Shihei (1738–93) (who was imprisoned by the bakufu for seeking to arouse public opinion against the threat from Russia).

[49] *Keisei hisaku.*

world had performed good deeds in the previous world, won the favor of the gods, and had been born into this world as daimyo. "Those who behave disgracefully towards the lords, even though they do so in the dark without anyone seeing, will be punished by the gods." By the same token, ministers, high functionaries, and all "worthy officials" "have patron gods who constantly watch over them and protect their spirits." Thus he admonished the people "to consider the principle of heaven carefully and to beware not to commit any disrespectful acts and suffer the punishments of the gods," hence to respect the existing hierarchical order.[50] The limits of this antifeudalism are obvious.

In effect, the common feature that limited the revolutionary character of the theories of social reform of the later Tokugawa period was the fact that all the proposed systems were to be imposed *from above*. The common people were assigned no active role in the implementation of the changes. If we consider the significance of this in relation to my thesis, we see that the theorists discussed here echoed Sorai's call for the reconstruction of institutions, although their reform proposals are immensely richer in content and even incorporate some modern elements. In this respect they were concrete developments of the theory of invention. But at the same time, they reveal little theoretical progress in that position. The theoretical limit of Sorai's philosophy of invention, the fact that the inventing agent could only be a special personality such as a sage or a Tokugawa shogun, still remained. This limitation clung obstinately to all the adherents of the theory of invention whom I have discussed, from Sorai on. In other words, there is no indication that these theorists were inclining toward the concept that it is the people who make institutions (such as the social contract theory). For this reason, even those with the most progressive tendencies among them, like Toshiaki and Nobuhiro, saw the traditional ruling class as the source of the motive power behind their institutional reforms. When they realized that this would not be easily accomplished, they degenerated into fantasy, appealing to "an unprecedented hero ruler" (Nobuhiro) or "a national hero" (Toshiaki). This qualitative stagnation of the logic

[50] *Keizai yōroku*, Book I.

of invention naturally meant that its quantitative diffusion in the society was confined within fixed bounds. So long as the ability to invent is made dependent on a special status, the great majority of the people are denied the right to transform the existing order as autonomous beings. For them the existing social and political order remains in fact a predestined arrangement. Thus a real basis remained for these people to hold to the theory of natural order.

I have noted that the social foundation for this stagnation of the logic of invention was the weak development of industrial capital. Let us look a little closer at this relationship. The economic activity symbolically most appropriate to the theory of natural order is fundamentally agriculture. Agriculture is highly dependent on natural conditions and leaves little working room for active human freedom. For instance, Miwa Shissai (1669–1744), a Confucian scholar, wrote in his *Shōkyō mondō:* "Question: According to the Way of the King, one year's surplus should accrue from three years' farming, but this seems wholly impossible in Japan today. Is there any way to make this possible? Answer: . . . This practice was not established by man but is the natural way of heaven. . . . *All these things are based on the natural Way of heaven and earth and are not man-made. If all things are left to the Way of heaven, everything will turn out well without our having to worry about it.*" Thus agriculture has always been the stronghold of belief in the natural order.[51]

[51] In this respect the *sui generis* theory of invention proposed by Ninomiya Sontoku (1787–1856) is worthy of note. His famous doctrine of *hōtoku* or "recompense virtue" was designed to stimulate the economy of the agrarian communities and han lands. "Few people distinguish between the principles of heaven and the way of man. It accords with the principle of heaven that there should be greed where human beings exist. It is the same as the fact that grass grows in the farm lands. It accords with the principles of heaven that dikes crumble, moats get filled, and bridges rot. But the way of man upholds the principle of curbing individual greed. Its way is to weed the farm lands, build dikes, dredge moats, and rebuild bridges. Because the principles of heaven and the way of man differ in this way, the former remain unchanged forever, while the latter decays immediately if it is neglected even for a day" (*Ninomiya-ō yawa,* Book I). This shows that, methodologically, he was clearly aware of the distinction between norms and nature. He went on to emphasize the necessity of invention in the Way of Man. "The way of man is like specially prepared food or a special sauce. It was made by sage rulers and wise subjects who prepared and adjusted it for many generations. As a result it has a tendency to deteriorate. It was therefore necessary to establish government, teachings, penal laws, and rules of etiquette. And by strictly and constantly watching over things, the way of man was preserved. To think that it is the same as the principles of heaven and the way of nature is a grave mistake. Ponder this well" (ibid.). This was the logical basis for his philosophy of labor. "Forget about the affairs of the world," he advised. "It is more important to regulate one's own family

On the other hand, there is a fundamental symbolic link between industrial production and autonomous human invention.
The social rise of "manufacture" is accompanied by a simultaneous rise of man's awareness of himself as a "tool-making animal"
(Franklin). Thus, when agriculture was still the dominant form of
production in the society, that is, when industrial goods had not
yet become the major means of livelihood and were still mostly
specialized luxury craft products, there was bound to be only
limited appreciation of the value of human invention. A book
written in the Bunsei (1827–30) to Tenpō (1830–44) eras, Nakamura Seishō's *Chimeiki* [An account of knowing one's destiny],
stated:

> The various countries of the West concentrate on machines and
> develop remarkable arts. They develop queer utensils and diverse
> skills to an inconceivable level. Because of this the Chinese people
> seem to conclude that foreigners are especially shrewd and intel-
> ligent. But this is foolish. To employ all one's intellectual faculties
> and deliberations *for the manufacture of useless utensils* and to *invent
> trivial crafts,* thus losing sight of one's spirit and fixed purpose, are
> matters motivated by caprice. They should be intensely despised.

This rejection of "queer utensils and diverse skills" corresponds
perfectly to a typical adherence to the theory of natural order.
This is demonstrated particularly in the author's defense of polygamy:

> Father is heaven; mother is earth. Heaven provides and earth
> produces. There is one sun in heaven. From it the moon and the
> stars receive their light. There is one prince. All the people receive
> his commands. There is one husband. Wives and concubines are under
> his control. This is the true principle of heaven and earth. When
> *yin* and *yang* are in harmony, all things come into existence. When
> the prince and his subjects are in harmony, government is main-
> tained. When husband and wives are in harmony, their descendants

---

authority and to clarify the family rules." Because of the basic narrowness of this
economic individualism, Sontoku does not fit directly into the framework of my study.
Nevertheless, it is interesting to note that the desperate state of agriculture in the
Bakumatsu period led him to see man's role as that of an inventing agent.

thrive and the way of the family is perfected. Western people are meticulous in investigating the principle of things but they are ignorant of the Way of Heaven, and do not know how to comprehend the principle of things. . . . To respect women and degrade men, to adhere rigidly to the rule of one husband, one wife [monogamy], and allow the family line to end cannot be in accordance with [true] principles.

Toshiaki, on the other hand, said: "It is clearly evident that the basic way to make our country rich and fertile is *to establish institutions which will produce a large amount of expertly made novel objects and speciality goods.*" "All the countries of the world are big and spacious but none can surpass the European countries in excellence of manual skill and produce as many expertly made rare objects and speciality goods. How has this come about? It is due to the system of encouraging industry."[52] These two views conflict in their attitudes to social institutions and are diametrically opposed in their evaluation of industrial production. But even for Toshiaki, industrial goods are no more than "novel objects." We can see from this that at that time Japan had not reached the stage of using industrial goods in everyday life. That is to say, existing conditions were such that the industrial structure had not developed sufficiently internally to enable anyone to see novel objects as useful things. This is undoubtedly the historical secret behind the failure of the logic of invention to develop smoothly and unimpededly.

Moreover there was another real factor in favor of the stagnation of the logic of invention and the revival of the theory of natural order. This was the demand for national unity in the face of the threat posed by the foreign powers. I have already argued that the international crisis aggravated the contradictions of feudal society, producing various proposals for institutional reform. These proposals were based on the belief that if the social contradictions at home were not solved, the threat from abroad could not ultimately be eliminated. This was the position of those thinkers more or less influenced by Western learning. But it was not until just before the collapse of the bakufu that this point of view gained unquestioned ascendancy. Before then the opposite view prevailed:

[52] *Keizai hōgen.*

unconditional acceptance of the existing national order was seen as the theoretical weapon against the barbarians. In particular, an intuitive sense of the structure of European bourgeois society made the ruling military class fear that egalitarian ideas might seep into the country.

"Barbarians," Aizawa Seishisai (1782–1863) said in *Tekiihen*, "call everybody in the world a friend and fail to distinguish between lord and subject, father and son, husband and wife, older and younger brothers. It is their pernicious custom to regard them as friends. I hear that students of Dutch Learning in our country blindly and thoughtlessly believe their words." This was soon followed by the opinion that "*to begin with, the barbarians do not distinguish between the gentlemen-scholars* [or samurai] *and the merchants*. Those holding official positions engage in overseas trade with other nations. This is so because they are barbarians and have no conception of righteousness and shame. It is their way to concentrate solely on profits. It is different in Japan. Here, there are proper distinctions between samurai and merchants. The samurai value most highly righteousness and shame. As a result, Japan has become the most respectable country in the world. If Japan were to become like the other nations, she would lose her most precious aspects, and we should fall to their level and become completely degenerate."[53] This led to the theory of *jōi* or "repel the barbarians," which saw the feudal hierarchy as the characteristic way of Japan and its preservation as the precondition for Japan's protection against foreign foes.

On the other hand, the slogan *sonnō* or "revere the Emperor," which swiftly grew in strength as a psychological support for national unity, was linked with this jōi theory. Thus, rather than calling for any transformation of the feudal order, it arose at first as an ideological reaffirmation of it. Typical of this trend was the Mito school of the late Tokugawa period.[54] For instance, one of its leading theorists, Aizawa Seishisai (1782–1863), wrote in his *Tekiihen* [On the way to proceed]:

---

[53] Ōhashi Totsuan: *Kaei zuihitsu.*

[54] The Mito school emerged around the middle of the Tokugawa period in Mito han, the domain of one of the collateral houses of the Tokugawa family. It is the later phase of this school that is discussed here. (Translator's note.)

The Emperor, representing the activities of heaven, spreads the deeds of heaven. The Bakufu aids the Imperial Court and governs the whole country. The local rulers are all supporters of the Imperial Court and promulgate the decrees of the Bakufu throughout their provinces. That is why *the people who obey the commands of the local daimyo are in effect obeying the decrees of the Bakufu and this is precisely the way to revere the Imperial Court and repay one's debt to the heavenly ancestors. The principle is simple and the way is clear.*

The subjects of today are the descendants of those who were favored by the benevolence of the heavenly ancestors and heavenly descendants. *They must obey the decrees of the Bakufu and the local daimyo.* During thousands and thousands of generations the conditions of society may change ten thousand times, but the cardinal principle of lord and subject and the great obligation of father and son have not changed a whit since the beginning of the universe and remain perfectly clear. As human beings we cannot depart from the ethics of the Five Relationships. . . . We must obey the great precepts revealed by the gods, *hold the commands of the Bakufu in awe, and uphold the laws of the local daimyo.*

This shows that Seishisai's sonnō (royalist) philosophy is not only not in contradiction with the feudal hierarchy but, on the contrary, supports it. The theoretical basis on which he provided this support, again in *Tekiihen*, is a belief in the natural order in its purest form.

In ethics, the existence of the Five Relationships of lord and subject, father and son, husband and wife, elder and younger brothers, and between friends accords with the natural creation of heaven.

That the prince employs his subjects, and the subjects serve their lord, is based on the fact that each is behaving righteously. *This is the great way of nature, it is not the invention of man.* . . . He who engages in manual labor is destined to support others and be governed by others. He who uses his mind is destined to be supported by others and govern others. The warriors, peasants, artisans, and merchants assist each other in different ways by their efforts. These are known as the four peoples. That there are princes and subjects in this manner is *the natural way of heaven and earth.* We cannot for a day do without the righteous principle of lord and subject.

By placing the relations between the imperial family and its subjects on the same plane as the relations between feudal lord and
subject, Seishisai sought to extend the former's eternal immutability to the latter. This shows the historical significance of the
revival of the theory of natural order. Moreover, what we can call
a theoretical "union of the Imperial Court and the military" (*kōbu
gattai*) of this kind was not confined to the Mito school and other
ultraroyalists.

Sakuma Zōzan (1811–64) had the following grasp of the world
situation on the one hand:

> In the present world, the traditional knowledge of Japanese and
> Chinese is not sufficient. It will not do [without a study of] the way
> of governing and managing the five continents. Considering general
> world conditions, after the three great discoveries—namely, Colum-
> bus's discovery of the new world, assisted by scientific investigation;
> Copernicus's discovery of the true principles of the motion of the
> Earth; and Newton's discovery of the true principles of gravitation
> —the foundations of all the sciences have been firmly established
> and have become accurate, without any evidence of superstitious
> dogmas. Owing to these discoveries, conditions in Europe and the
> United States of America have gradually shown a remarkable im-
> provement. Steam-ships, magnetism, telegraphs have all been in-
> vented. It is as if the art of creation had been captured by man. A
> truly amazing situation has come about.[55]

But on the other hand, even he could say:

> The distinctions of noble and base, superior and inferior, are *laws of
> etiquette based on the natural way of heaven and earth.* . . . Above all in
> our imperial land, there is a profound reason for strictly upholding
> the distinctions of noble and base, superior and inferior.[56]

He asserted that Japan's "national polity" (*kokutai*) was different
from that of the "foreign barbarians" and for this reason opposed
reducing the number of attendants who accompanied the daimyo
on their travels, and the wearing of cheap clothing. His famous

[55] Letter to Yanagawa Seigan, March 6, 1858.
[56] Memorial to the bakufu, September, 1862.

slogan "Eastern morals and Western science" (*tōyō dōtoku, seiyō geijutsu*)[57] symbolizes the great obstacles modern European culture was to meet as it filtered into Japan at the end of the feudal period.

As the international situation became increasingly tense, a fanatical jōi movement erupted, eliminating even the small area of freedom previously allowed the Western scholars. As a result, Ōhashi Totsuan (1816–62) even rejected Zōzan's opinion of Western science and technology, arguing that "this is the opinion being spread by Confucian scholars who favor Western learning. It may sound reasonable, but it is a false doctrine. . . . To say 'trust in their technology' while attacking Western moral teachings is like saying, 'although the source of the river contains poisonous water, there is no poison in the lower tributaries so it is all right to drink their water.' Is this not indeed ridiculous?" He criticized the science of anatomy: "Medicine in the barbarous countries of the West considers the dissection of the human entrails to be of the utmost importance. This suffices to show what brutal customs prevail there." He regarded photography and electricity as magical arts designed to stir people up and expressed a violent hatred for all things Western. Inversely, he extolled the system "that properly distinguishes between samurai and merchants" and advocated a policy of absolute isolationism. Beneath this hysterical defense of everything traditional, the logic of the natural order is unmistakable: "Now, in things under heaven there are fixed laws that say, 'basically it should be this way by nature and it would not do unless it were like this.' *These laws are endowed by heaven and are not inventions of man.* This is called the Principle of Heaven, and when all these laws are grouped together they are called the Way."[58]

But history advanced remorselessly, brushing off the desperate resistance of this Chu Hsi scholar from the Shōheikō (the bakufu's Confucian school). All the conflicts and contradictions inherent in the feudal structure between daimyo and peasant, samurai and merchant, upper and lower samurai, imperial court and bakufu,

[57] *Seikenroku.* Zōzan used the word *geijutsu* (art), but what he actually meant was something more like *gijutsu* (technology).

[58] *Hekijya shōgen.*

bakufu and major han, worsened despite every effort to conceal them, and converged towards the fall of the bakufu.

At the same time, dispassionate and serious observers of the situation all began to realize that the way to save Japan from the international threat did not lie in obstinate attempts to preserve the traditional relations of authority. Around 1855 Hirose Kyo-kusō (1807–63) wrote:

> The most serious problem today is the impact of foreign nations. In considering the outlook of the people of the entire country, the officials [of the bakufu], the feudal lords, the retainers of the Shogun, the subjects of the feudal lords, the peasants, the artisans, and the merchants, we find that each has his own mind [*kokoro*]. *In this situation, each group is content to stay in its assigned place in society. This may seem like* a good thing, but if there are a hundred million people and each *has his own mind, they will fail to overcome the enemy.* . . . At present the [bakufu] officials do not wish to engage in a war; the feudal lords prefer to do so; some among the Shogun's retainers wish to do so; some do not. Those above are concerned about the lack of money, while those below dislike letting go of their money. The samurai prefer years of poor harvest, while the artisans and merchants prefer years of abundant harvest. The peasants prefer one or the other depending on whether they are rich or poor. . . . This is how the people's outlooks differ. Only a few share the same worries and the same pleasures. If we engage the foreign powers in a war while such conditions prevail, we shall clearly fall into danger. The most urgent task today is to inform the people of the grave threat from abroad and have everyone unite to perfect the art of [national] defense.[59]

In this way he faithfully and fearlessly revealed that what was preventing the spiritual unity of the people in the face of the foreign threats was the system of feudal estates itself. Given such a penetrating assessment, the bourgeois social order could no longer be the object of senseless fear or hatred. "In the past," he commented, "agriculture was considered to be important. So there were peasant soldiers. Recently in the West, commerce has come to be highly regarded. As a result, everyone, from the Emperors

---

[59] *Kyūkei sōdō zuihitsu*, Book VI.

down, is a merchant. And there are merchant soldiers [mercenaries]. *This too accords with the times, and has its proper reasons.* Han Fei-tzu stated: 'Where profit is involved even women and girls become courageous heroes like Ming Pen and Hsia Yu [of the period of the Warring States in China].' This is true of the people's attitude today. Since people are willing to sacrifice their lives for profits, we too can start using mercenaries."[60]

Yoshida Shōin (1830–59), a friend of Kyokusō, agreed with his diagnosis of the necessary relationship between "domestic troubles" and the "foreign menace." In a letter written to Sugi Umetarō on September 14, 1853, he remarked: "Everyone says 'coastal defenses, coastal defenses,' but I have yet to hear anyone say '*minsei, minsei*' [government for the people]! Because foreign threats and domestic troubles are inevitably interrelated, coastal defenses and *minsei* must be considered together." As a result, his jōi position was not simply a swaggerer's self-inflated antiforeignism. "Concern for the four hardships,"[61] he argued, "is an important aspect of royal government. I favor the establishment of good institutions to take care of all of them. Even Western barbarians have poor-houses, hospitals, orphanages, and practice the way of charity to the lower classes. Is it not a serious defect that we lack such institutions in this auspicious land of Yamato?" Thus Shōin too was honest and forthright in assessing the realities of Japan.

This critical attitude made it impossible for him to accept feudal authority relations complacently. "It is the function of the samurai," he remarked, "to stand above the three [common] classes. They do not perform the tasks of these classes. They remain beneath the ruler and, representing his will, perform the task of preventing disasters and calamities and assist in the management of things for the good of the people. But the samurai of today ignore this principle, squeeze sweat and blood from the people, and steal their stipends from their rulers. Indeed they are outlaws who defy heaven."[62] Shōin thus no longer agreed with Seishisai and Totsuan that class distinctions constituted the traditional and

---

[60] Ibid., Book IV.
[61] The aged man without a wife, the aged woman without a husband, the orphan, and the aged person without children.
[62] *Bukyō zensho kōroku.*

unique way of Japan; nor did he accept the opinions of his teacher Zōzan any longer. On the contrary, he said:

> People throughout the country must all *regard the affairs of the entire country as their business and serve the Emperor by sacrificing their lives if necessary. In this respect there should therefore be no distinctions of noble and base, superior and inferior, segregating the people. This is the Way of the Land of the Gods.*
>
> Relations with the barbarians have so far been the business of the ruler and ministers, but everyone in the country born in the Land of the Gods must consider them to be his business too.[63]

This is but a step from Fukuzawa Yukichi's demand for individual independence and self-respect in his *Gakumon no susume* [Encouragement of learning], written soon after the Meiji Restoration:

> In order to defend our nation against foreign powers, it is necessary to fill the entire nation with the spirit of freedom and independence. Everyone throughout the nation, without distinctions such as noble and base, high and low, must be personally responsible for the nation. And the wise and the stupid, the blind and those with good eyes, must all do their duty as members of the nation.

If the people lack an awareness of their autonomy with respect to the social order to which they belong, merely accepting it as given them by fate, they can hardly be expected to defend the nation vigorously against a foreign foe. The growth of this awareness necessarily changed the doctrine of *sonnō-jōi* ("revere the emperor and repel the barbarians") from its hierarchical form into one that levels "all the population under one prince" (*ikkun banmin*). Around 1859 Shōin was already writing: "It must be made clear that the present Bakufu and feudal lords are incapable of serving the Emperor and expelling the barbarians."[64] "This great country of Japan has maintained its independence and has been free from conquest for three thousand years. If it were ever conquered by others, no red-blooded person could endure it. Unless a man like

---

[63] *Heishin yūshitsu bunkō; Kōmō yowa.*
[64] Letter to Nomura Yasushi.

Napoleon emerges and calls out for *vrijdom*,[65] the internal sickness will not be cured. . . . The Bakufu and feudal lords of today are like drunken men. They lack the ability to preserve the nation. There is nothing else to do but hope for a leader to rise suddenly from among the people."[66] Thus Shōin was fully aware of what was happening. Only seven years after his execution came the Great Command proclaiming the restoration of imperial rule, and the new Meiji government emerged from the deep chaos of the Bakumatsu period shouldering the historical task of realizing Shōin's hoped-for vrijdom.

IV

With the Meiji Restoration, the theme I have developed so far in this book entered an entirely new phase. Japan's social and political structures were modernized at a breathtaking pace by a whole series of general reforms such as transferring the feudal domains to the imperial government, pensioning off the samurai, replacing the han by prefectures, promulgating national conscription, abolishing such class privileges as the right to wear swords and to cut down members of the lower classes with impunity, emancipating the lower classes from their estates, establishing freedom of occupation, adopting a new form of land tax, and so on. Existing realities proved beyond doubt that the feudal class system was certainly not a natural order that "has prevailed past and present between heaven and earth." That being so, it was only to be expected that the wave of "civilization and enlightenment" (*bunmei kaika*) that inundated the country was directed first at the class distinctions of the old society. In his *Kaika mondō* [Questions and answers about enlightenment], Ogawa Tameji, a popularizer of the Enlightenment ideals, remarked: "When heaven created man, it did not discriminate, saying, 'this man is a daimyo so he must have four eyes and eight limbs' and 'this man is an *eta* [outcaste] so he can have only one eye and two limbs.' When we see that all human beings have two eyes and four limbs, is it not clear that in human relations a man with the rank of Junior Grade

[65] I.e., "freedom." Shōin was a student of Dutch Learning.
[66] Letter to Kitayama Ansei.

Fifth Order and a plain old peasant called Gombē or Hachibē are equal in status?" This theory of natural equality led Tameji to a concept of invented order. "Now there is the question of man's actual situation. This involves such classifications as noble and base, rich and poor, family background, rank, and status. Among men there are nobles, members of the samurai class, rich families, and the poor. *But these differences are not based on the commands of Heaven.* They are all *rules ordained by human beings themselves.* They are merely situations that prevail in the world of men."

Moreover, a clearer methodological consciousness prevented the identification of laws of nature and social norms so characteristic of the theory of natural order. According to Tsuda Mamichi (1829–1903): "In all these things—natural phenomena, conditions on earth, human affairs—there are fixed rules. *These rules are natural in the sense that they are beyond the control of man.*" But, in contrast: "When people possess land and myriads of things, and come together to assist each other, a state is formed. In order to preserve order and maintain peace, the state establishes regulations. *These are man-made, not heaven-made, laws.* They are called public or civil laws."[67] Furthermore, it was the emergence of the Movement for Freedom and Popular Rights[68] that established the supremacy of the theory of invention in the post-Restoration period. *Here the doctrine of invention was at last able to develop its implications to their conclusion in a clear-cut theory of man-made institutions.*

There is no need here to bring in the vast literature dealing with the institutional views of the Movement for Freedom and Popular Rights. They were first introduced in systematic fashion in Fukuzawa Yukichi's *Seiyō jijō* [Conditions in the West] in 1866–69. In this work, he wrote: "As civilization developed, the weak and helpless consulted together and established ways to ensure the people's rights and to protect their lives. These are called national institutions. . . . This is the origin of government. The function of the government is to unite the people spiritually and ensure by force the fulfillment of the will of the people." Ueki Emori (1857–92) was their most radical exponent. He began his *Minken jiyūron*

[67] *Seiron,* II; *Meiroku zasshi,* Vol. XI.
[68] *Jiyū Minken,* a movement that was in force from roughly the early 1870s to the mid-1880s. (Translator's note.)

[Discourse on popular rights and freedom] with the words: "Pardon me, may I speak to all of you together, you, the honorable farmers of Japan, you, the honorable merchants of Japan, and you, the honorable artisans and craftsmen of Japan; and also you, the honorable ex-samurai [*shizoku*], you, the doctors, you, the boatmen, you, the pack-horse drivers, you, the hunters, you, the candy salesmen, you, the wet-nurses, you, the new commoners [the *eta*]." "Because liberty is so precious in this way, in order to preserve and protect it fully, *the state was constructed, and a place of assembly called the government was established,* laws were instituted, and officials were employed. In this way the freedom and rights of the people are protected, and their happiness and well-being are preserved." In *Minken inaka-uta,* the appendix to *Minken jiyūron,* he wrote: "When heaven created man, it made everybody equal under heaven. There is no man above other men, no man beneath other men. That is why all men have equal rights. Insist on your rights, fellow countrymen! *Governments are established by the people. Laws are meant to protect liberty.*"

Let us stop here long enough to note that the theoretical basis for this doctrine of liberty and popular rights is the natural law of the Enlightenment. Since the latter taught that the rights of men are natural rights, it would seem superficially that we should classify it as a theory of natural order. But a more careful examination shows directly that the opposite is true. The "rights of man" in question are not rights embedded in any actually existing social order. On the contrary, they are concrete embodiments of the autonomy of man, who can establish a positive social order. Thus the theory's insistence on the a priori character of natural law necessarily implies the view that any positive law derives its validity from its original establishment by man. The famous debate between Katō Hiroyuki (1836–1916) and the advocates of popular rights about the former's *Jinken shinsetsu* [New theory of human rights][69] clearly demonstrates this point. Hiroyuki had insisted that rights were fixed by the sovereign only after the state had been established in the course of human evolution; the theory of natural rights was no more than a fantasy. Baba Tatsui (1850–88),

[69] The literature on this debate can be found in *Meiji bunka zenshū,* Vol. V (*Jiyū minken-hen*).

a leading thinker and activist of the popular rights movement, pointed out that the rights Hiroyuki was referring to were "rights established by positive laws, not the natural rights that we are discussing." "Positive laws come into existence only if there is a sovereign. When the sovereign instituted them, no matter how oppressive and restrictive his commands may be, they are all referred to as laws."[70] This is strictly in the tradition of Hobbes's and Austin's theory of invention; Tatsui based the validity of positive law on its formal positive character, i.e., solely on the fact that it was enacted. Yano Fumio (1850–1931) also remarked that "it should be determined whether the word 'rights' used in Mr. Katō's book refers to moral rights or legal rights. . . . If it refers to legal rights, that is, *rights based on man-made laws* as explained by Austin, and these rights can be properly described as rights in the sense of jurisprudence, then they have their origin in law and of course come into existence after the establishment of government. There is no need even to discuss the fact that they do not derive from nature."[71] Thus he too accepted as obvious the man-made character of positive laws.

In spite of the heated argument between the two factions, the thesis that existing norms are valid because they were initially invented by man was accepted by both sides as a basic premise. Compared to the slow advance of the theory of invention during the Tokugawa period, this is a spectacular leap forward. But this leap forward did not take place overnight. Just as the enormous energy of a river as it breaks out of a dam is the product of the slow accumulation of hydraulic power during the containment, the irresistible spread of the theory of invention after the Meiji Restoration could not have occurred without these hidden developments beneath the surface of the feudal system. For example, another advocate of popular rights, Kojima Shōji, explained the "right of liberty" as follows:

Faith is a matter that belongs to the conscience of each individual, and even the government cannot control it. Even if it seeks to control it by force, the people will continue to hold to their faith silently,

---

[70] *Tenpu jinkenron.*
[71] *Jinken shinsetsu bakuron.*

and there is nothing that can be done about it. . . . For instance, even if you desire to overthrow the government or assassinate an official, *as long as you keep this intention concealed in your heart and do not express it overtly in word or deed,* the government does not have the right to arrest you. This is called the right of freedom of intentions.[72]

This is simply a more modern form of Sorai's and Shundai's externalization of norms (the separation of what is within from what is without, of the private sphere from public institutions) expounded in the statement that "regardless of what is inside his heart, if someone adheres outwardly to the rules of proper conduct and does not violate them, he is a gentleman."

In his *Bunmeiron no gairyaku* [Outline of the theory of civilization], Fukuzawa Yukichi also remarked: "In China and Japan the relations between the prince and the subject are described as a part of the nature of man. The relations between the prince and the subject are seen as like those between husband and wife or father and son. It is believed that the positions of the prince and the subject have been fixed in advance before birth. Even Confucius was unable to avoid indulging in such conventional thinking." He continued:

The relations between prince and subject are those of man and man. There are some principles involved in these relations, *but they came into being only after princes and subjects came into existence. Hence one cannot regard relations between prince and subject as inherent in human nature.* . . . If the principles of heaven were pursued with an open mind without prejudice, one would be sure to discover that these relations are nothing but the product of a fortuitous agreement. Once this is understood, the convenience or inconvenience of this agreement is bound to become a matter of debate. When the convenience or inconvenience of something can be discussed, it is a proof that it can be reformed and transformed. *Something that can be reformed and transformed is not a Principle of Heaven.* Thus, although the son cannot become the father, and the wife cannot become the husband, and the relations between father and son and husband and wife cannot be changed, a prince can be turned into a subject. The expulsion of their rulers by T'ang of Shang and Wu of Chou are cases in point.

[72] *Minken mondō,* Vol. II, Part I.

Rulers and subjects can sit in the same place and act as equals. The replacement of the han with prefectures in Japan is an example of this.

This rejection of the a priori nature of the feudal "relation between prince and subject" is undoubtedly based on the same logic as the criticism of "what the Sung philosophers call [the way of heaven and earth and nature" from the standpoint of "what Sorai calls invention by the Early Kings." The menacing aspects of that "fateful" result of the Sorai school that Norinaga had foreseen were now fully revealed.

But despite this overwhelming success of the theory of autonomous invention, the concept of natural order had not completely vanished from the scene. The decisive reforms of the restoration, the transfer of feudal domains to the imperial government, and the replacement of han by prefectural administration provoked a violent resistance by the feudal forces, with the natural-order theory as its ideological weapon. The opinion submitted to the lord of Yonezawa (now in Yamagata Prefecture) by Kumoi Tatsuo (1844–70) is a typical version of this point of view:[73]

> As this subject humbly reflects upon the question, he finds that the feudal counties and prefectures all came into existence *gradually in the natural course of events.* It is like the change brought about by the creator of the universe. Even if there were a man with great foresight, capable of making wise decisions, *these institutions could not be changed overnight by human efforts, however diligent.* As for the origin of the feudalism that came into existence during the Keichō [1596–1615] and Genwa [1615–24] eras, it can be traced back, first, to the system of *Kuni-no-miyatsuko* [provincial governors] and *Agata-nushi* [estate masters] in the ancient period, and, second, to the system of ranks for local officials. Powerful independent local lords eventually entrenched themselves throughout the country and [the central government] could no longer bring them under control. Even such a unique hero as Lord Tokugawa was unable to change this situation and was compelled to institute feudalism. Therefore, however much the Satsuma clan and others may exhaust themselves to change the situation today, they will be unable to do so.

[73] Cit., Kada Tetsuji: *Meiji shoki shakai keizai shisōshi* [History of social and economic thought of the early Meiji period] (Tokyo, 1937), p. 499.

After the decline of the forces representing feudal reaction in this pure form, the philosophy of the natural order found its social support among the opponents of the growing Movement for Freedom and Popular Rights. For instance, Yoshioka Noriaki (1813–74), who evidently wrote his *Kaika honron* [True discourse on enlightenment] as a refutation of Fukuzawa Yukichi's *Bunmei-ron no gairyaku*, stated:

> The advocates of enlightenment mistakenly equate the freedom of savages with human nature endowed by heaven. . . . They therefore argue that everything that restrains this freedom, regardless of what it is, is man-made and unnatural. Thus, of the three principles of human relations, they assert that the relation between prince and subject is not a natural one. But they are wrong, because the prince is the man who establishes the government and exercises political authority. And this political authority is law. *This law actually originates in the fixed principles of nature.* It prohibits greed and evil actions, and prevents savage liberty from prevailing. This is at any rate very inconvenient. So [the advocates of freedom] say that these laws restrain natural liberty and argue that they are only agreements made among men for reasons of social intercourse and are not eternal rules of nature. . . . As long as they maintain that laws and governments are temporary institutions established by man, they are driven to claim that the positions of the prince who governs the society and the people who are governed by him are not fixed by nature either but are man-made.

That is, he analyzed and criticized the theory of "man-made institutions" proposed by the advocates of popular rights from the standpoint that laws "originate from the fixed principles of nature." This is a good illustration of the new historical role assigned to the doctrine of natural order. In November, 1881, in the midst of heated agitation for a national assembly, there appeared a small book entitled *Seijiron-ryaku* [Outline of political theory], an adapted translation of Edmund Burke's works by Kaneko Kentarō (1853–1942).[74] It contains the following statement:

[74] This translation is based on Edmund Burke's *Reflections on the Revolution in France* and *An Appeal from the New to the Old Whigs*. Kaneko summarized the ideas in these two works, organizing the material as he saw fit. This work was welcomed by government leaders as an effective weapon against the Rousseauan logical foundations of the theses

To fix the nation's constitution and perfect its political form, the policy to adopt should be to follow the pattern of nature, *to abide by the natural climate of heaven and earth,* and bring about changes *gradually.* Thus we receive from our ancestors, we hold, we transmit to our descendants our government and our privileges, thus maintaining our polity eternally, in the same manner in which we enjoy and transmit our property and our lives. . . . Thus, by preserving the method of nature, *by abiding by the natural principle of heaven and earth,* in the conduct of the state, no matter how often the government is reformed an unusual and unique political form will not appear, and *the traditional practices will not be regarded as useless, obsolete customs.*[75]

Given that this booklet was published by the *Genrōin* (Council of Elder Statesmen), we may surmise that as the Meiji government's fear of the popular rights movement began to increase it came to recognize these uses of the theory of natural order.

The theory of natural order also spread to the people as an anti-popular-rights ideology, and it seeped into the party programs of parties opposed to the Liberal Party (*Jiyūtō*) and the Constitutional Reform Party (*Rikken Kaishintō*). Torio Koyata (1847–1905) and his faction of the Conservative Party (*Hoshutō*) formulated the fundamental differences between the two institutional outlooks in the first issue of their party organ, *Hoshu shinbun* [Conservative news]:

---

of the advocates of freedom and popular rights. Cf. Osatake Takeki: *Nihon kenseishi* [Japanese constitutional history] (Tokyo, 1930), pp. 302–4. In March, 1882, Ueki Emori published a long polemic entitled *Boruku o korosu* [Kill Burke] in the *Dōyō shinbun* and *Kōchi shinbun.* His arguments cover many matters, but at one point he did assert: "*States do not belong to the group of things created by heaven but are man-made. . . .* States exist in a temporary fashion, in accordance with the conditions of the times. They are not eternally immutable and forever invincible. States are made for the good of the people and are instruments to serve the people. *So the people are the masters of the state, and the government is nothing more than a machine to be used for the benefit of the people.*" This shows that the crux of the theoretical conflict between the two outlooks falls within the boundaries of my theme.

[75] The basis of this passage is from Burke, but Kaneko has interpolated paraphrases of Burke's terms and comments of his own. Cf. the original passage: "By a constitutional policy, working after the pattern of nature, we receive, we hold, we transmit our government and our privileges, in the same manner in which we enjoy and transmit our property and our lives. . . . Thus, by preserving the method of nature in the conduct of the state, in what we improve we are never wholly new; in what we retain we are never wholly obsolete." *Reflections on the Revolution in France,* ed. C. C. O'Brien (Harmondsworth, 1969), p. 120. (Translator's note.)

The politicians of individualism are concerned with nothing but the ordinary principles of man, the interests of the individual only. Regarding the state, *they hold that it was constructed by the people who happened to come together to attain their goals, and view it as if it were the ideal invention of man.* . . . In effect, they insist that, because it was created by human will, or human desires, it is subject to the control of man. *If the state is subordinate to man, it can be changed arbitrarily by human will.* To attain a certain goal, a certain state is constructed. When the goal changes, the state can be abolished or reconstructed.

In contrast, Torio and his faction believed that:

The state developed *in accordance with the natural character of mankind. It is not the ideal product of man.* It did not come into existence after men discussed and decided the benefits and ill effects, the advantages and disadvantages of establishing it, nor after they had chosen what to retain and what to abandon and arranged things among themselves. In all cases, the state had existed majestically before mankind sought to impose its ideals upon it. . . . When man first leaves his mother's womb, he enters the womb of the state, is nurtured by it and influenced by its will. In this manner his nature and sentiments are formed and passed on to his descendants. Thus succeeding generations naturally possess the attributes acquired from the state through eternity. One must understand this. *States are not subject to the control of man; rather man is subject to the control of the state.*

Apparently on the verge of recapturing his freedom as an autonomous personality with respect to the social order, having eliminated the restrictions of the estate system in the Meiji Restoration, man was to be swallowed up again by the new Leviathan, the Meiji state. Just as the theory of invention came to the end of its long and painful journey and was about to enjoy its success, it suddenly found it still had a thorny path ahead of it. This was the fate that awaited all modern elements in Japan. Just as the thought of the Tokugawa period was not feudalistic from first to last, never in the Meiji era was it completely bourgeois and modern. The problems of the post-Meiji period, however, are very complex and demand detailed analysis elsewhere. At this point we shall terminate our examination of one aspect of Tokugawa political thought.

PART III

THE PREMODERN FORMATION
OF NATIONALISM

CHAPTER I

INTRODUCTION:
THE NATION AND NATIONALISM

It has been said that a nation is something that wants to be a nation. The objective fact of belonging to a common state entity and sharing common political institutions does not constitute a nation (*kokumin*) in the modern sense. What obtains in this case is at best a people (*jinmin*) or members of a state (*kokka*), not a nation. Before a people can become a nation they must actively desire to belong to a common community and participate in common institutions, or at least consider such a situation to be desirable. In other words, we can say that a nation exists only if the members of a given group of men are aware of the common characteristics that they share with each other and that distinguish them from other nations as a special nation and possess some desire to preserve and foster this unity. Of course this sense of unity can have a variety of nuances. There are instances where a people is clearly aware of its cultural unity, founded on a common language, religion, customs, habits, and other cultural heritages, but lack any political consciousness as a nation. (Typical examples are the German and Italian nations until the early nineteenth century.) But when such a cultural nation[1] is forced to defend its

---

[1] It was Meinecke who introduced the category "cultural nation" as distinct from "political nation" (F. Meinecke: *Weltbürgertum und Nationalstaat,* 7th ed. [1928]). However, I have used the term cultural nation here in a narrower sense than that defined by Meinecke. It does not refer broadly to something stamped historically by a unique cultural legacy or tradition, but to the situation in which the culture is *consciously*

cultural unity, its existence is immediately raised to the political level, and it is faced with the necessity of forming a common state unit.

Thus national consciousness, insofar as it is a self-awareness, sooner or later congeals into a consciousness of political unity. National consciousness in this sense is what sustains modern nation-states in general. If we broadly label as *kokuminshugi* (nationalism, or the principle of nationality)[2] the demand for national unification and national independence that develops against the background of this national consciousness, then nationalism is indeed the spiritual motive force that is indispensable for the modern state to exist as a modern state. Moreover, since the world-historical situation of each nationality is different, the manner in which each nation-state forms or develops differs accordingly. Likewise nationalism itself develops in a unique way in each nation. As Vossler said: "There is no such thing as nationalism *in general* [*der Nationalismus*], the one and only nationalism throughout the world. Rather there are many different nationalisms [*Nationalismen*]."[3] By their very nature, the tenets of nationalism must of necessity be unique for each nation. The peculiar manner in which a given nation-state was formed is stamped most vividly on the pattern of historical development of its nationalism.

It is clear that the nation as a political category and national-

---

shared in common by the nation. Meinecke's category includes both the "vegetative" peoples of antiquity and peoples who have awakened to modern spontaneity. But I am primarily concerned with the latter whether I am speaking of the cultural or the political nation. The fact that this is the product of a certain stage in history will be discussed below.

[2] Nationalism has also been translated into Japanese as *minzokushugi* (sense of racial identity), but this term is appropriate to a people with the status of a minority race in another nation-state, or a colonized people, that gains its independence, or when a race that has been split into several groups under different nation-states unites to constitute an independent nation. But its use is questionable in the case of Japan, where racial homogeneity has been preserved from the past and where there have never been any serious racial problems. When the term minzokushugi is used in Japan, it sounds as if it involves only external problems, but nationalism, as will be shown below, is indeed a matter of external problems, but also one of internal problems. The term *kokkashugi* (*étatisme*) is frequently used as a concept in opposition to individualism, so it too is not an appropriate term. At a certain stage in its development, nationalism is inextricably linked to the tenets of individual autonomy. To cover all these nuances, the term kokuminshugi is used here.

[3] O. Vossler: *Der Nationalgedanke von Rousseau bis Ranke* (1937), p. 13.

ism as the nation asserting itself are products of a given historical stage. Before nations became conscious of themselves as political unities, or came to desire such unity, there was a long period in which they simply followed a natural, vegetative existence. Since people are attached to a given place for generations, they naturally develop a love for their land and way of life. No doubt this love arose in the distant past. This instinctive love of the homeland may be the source of national consciousness, but it cannot function directly as the force that creates a political nation. A love of one's homeland is in effect a love of one's surroundings. A love of one's surroundings means a traditional dependence on things outside of oneself, while the formation of the nation-state must be expressed in an active commitment by every individual. Moreover, love of one's surroundings spreads like a ripple from the one self at the center, and its intensity weakens as the distance increases; so the state environment, which is abstract to some degree, naturally evokes less sense of intimacy than the immediate surroundings of the village or family. As a result, in some instances, love of the surroundings impedes rather than fosters national consciousness.[4] In such cases modern nationalism can make headway only by removing the traditional love of the homeland.

On the other hand, even if a state system encompassing the entire nation exists, this does not automatically and inevitably give rise to an awareness of political unity in the nation. When the internal structure of the system prevents the people from congealing politically into a state, the state system will fail to grasp them from the inside, and the great majority of the people will continue to exist in a natural, impersonal (vegetative) fashion.[5] In such a

---

[4] It is well known that in China provincialism, and the feeling of local solidarity based on it, impeded the growth of a sense of popular unity until the present. Sun Yat-sen said: "The Chinese people have only family and kinship solidarity; they do not have a national spirit" (*Son bun zenshū* [The collected works of Sun Yat-sen], 7 vols. [Tokyo, 1939–40], I, p. 10). Of course, he states that family and kinship solidarity can be "extended" so as to transform kinship solidarity into a national spirit (kokuzoku-shugi) (ibid., p. 110). Perhaps he was as optimistic as this statement suggests; perhaps he was more interested in the psychological effect of this statement on the people themselves; but there is no doubt that kinship solidarity does not of itself develop into national solidarity, just as nationalism does not automatically develop into internationalism. The need for a common effort to resist foreign forces evoked among the Chinese a sense of unity extending beyond kinship solidarity for the first time.

[5] A typical example of this can be found in imperial China before the Revolution of 1912.

situation nationalism seeks above all to eliminate the force or structure that intervenes between the nation and the state, preventing the direct union of the two. At any rate, the fact that nationalism is willing to risk contradictions and collisions with the nation's traditional mode of existence in the interests of its own development indicates that a political national consciousness is not a natural, self-generating entity; its growth is dependent on certain historical conditions. At a certain stage in its historical development, a nation is spurred by some external stimulus and more or less consciously transforms itself from simple dependence on the surroundings into a political nation. Ordinarily the external stimulus that induces this decision to change is some foreign power, some external threat.

CHAPTER II

NATIONAL CONSCIOUSNESS
UNDER TOKUGAWA FEUDALISM

Despite our long and glorious national tradition, the birth of a
national consciousness in the sense described above, and a nationalism built around such a national consciousness, did not occur in Japan until the Meiji Restoration. Of course, ever since the
foundation of the country, the minds of the people had always
contained the idea of Japan as the Land of the Gods and a sense
of racial (minzoku) self-confidence based on the uniqueness of the
Japanese state system. But this did not automatically rise to the
level where the nation possessed a sense of political solidarity, nor
did it lead directly to national unity. The internal social conditions necessary for this were still undeveloped and international
contacts were few and far between (of course, there were the Mongol invasions, but these were accidental interventions from out of
the blue). The question of national independence and national
unity first became a significant issue in the Bakumatsu period with
the arrival of the foreign powers, which was no accidental, passing
event but rather the consequence of the historical necessity that
the world market then being formed absorb the last remaining
areas outside it. In this situation, Japanese nationalism was compelled to confront the system and spirit that were a major obstacle
to political coalescence into a nation-state. This obstacle was
Tokugawa feudalism itself.

In order, then, to understand the historical problem Japanese nationalism had to solve, it is necessary first to understand Tokugawa feudalism and the social consciousness that prevailed under it. Why was the development of a sense of national solidarity possible only after it had freed itself from this historical environment?

First of all, in Tokugawa feudalism, which was established by the complete separation of the military and the peasantry, the world of the rulers was sharply distinct from the world of the subjects. Not only did the ruling military (*bushi*) class monopolize all political authority, but socially and culturally too it clearly distinguished its pattern of life from that of the common people. And it sought to preserve this closure of estates by all sorts of legal devices. The bourgeois class, the bearer of modern society, sought to make itself the "whole," and only unwillingly became a "class" with the emergence of the so-called fourth estate, the working class. The feudal rulers, on the contrary, wanted to be an estate distinct from the other classes of the nation, and took pride in this fact.

The common people, that is, the peasants, the artisans, and the merchants, were permitted to exist only to serve the samurai and to feed the samurai. In particular, the peasants, who constituted the vast majority of the common people, were to exist merely to pay taxes.[1] (There was a saying, "*nō*," agriculture, means "*nō*," paying taxes.) The sole social duty of the peasantry was to pay their taxes in full. There was no need for the peasants to concern themselves with the fate of the state and society, nor did they have any responsibilities in these matters. In this sense we can say that the words of the proclamation of the Keian era (1648–52) that "as long as he pays his taxes, no one's life is as carefree as that of the peasant" contain some historical truth—if we ignore the cynicism of the words "as long as he pays his taxes" at a time when the

---

[1] This did not at all contradict the frequent pronouncements and admonishments urging that the peasants be treated with love and kindness; rather the two attitudes were complementary. Yamaga Sokō explained this relationship as follows: "The people are extremely ignorant and are unable to reflect upon the past or weigh the future. They are unable to reason things out or plan things carefully. They are busy with occupations such as agriculture and sericulture which fully occupy them during three seasons of the year. *They do not think of anything else,* so they cannot develop any intellectual ability. The way to love the people is thus to allow them to labor as much as they wish and pay taxes to the government, and have the government exercise complete control over their lives" (*Takkyo dōmon*).

burden of taxation endangered even the peasants' physical survival. This duty of taxation was not strictly speaking justified as
a political obligation by appealing to their sense of political responsibility. The description of the carefree nature of their conditions of existence outside the area of taxation was intended to
make their duty of taxation seem an inevitable fate. The peasants
themselves had no alternative but to accept taxation as an unavoidable evil descending from on high into the carefree world in
which they had no political concerns or responsibilities. The political order was imposed upon them from the outside. They submitted to that order because "there is nothing to do but give in to
a crying child or an official of the lord," not as a conscious inner
acceptance of the order based upon an awareness of political obligations. Hence they were always ready to try to remove this imposed order by violent uprisings (*ikki*).

What about the urban merchants, who, among the common
classes, were next in importance to the peasantry? While the
peasants were at least superficially valued as the producers of the
feudal society, the merchants, as we know, were ranked the lowest
among all the subject classes. Yamaga Sokō remarked that they
"only know about profits and not about righteousness; they are
only concerned about how to enrich themselves."[2] That is, they
were seen as living outside the ethical realm, supposedly devoid
of all sense of public responsibility, pursuing only their personal
economic interests. Naturally enough, politically they were held
to be "*rien*" (Abbé Sieyes). Feudal ideology tolerated them at
best as a necessary evil, and when the samurai class was threatened economically by their upper strata, they were cursed at and
their elimination was proposed. The townspeople themselves accepted the status assigned them in the social order and, arguing
that because they had been driven outside the ethical realm they
were justified in adopting any means at all to satisfy their personal
greed, they freely adopted the mentality of the outcaste.[3] Thus,

[2] *Yamaga gorui*, Book VI.

[3] The playwright Chikamatsu Monzaemon (1653–1724) has a merchant in his play
Nebiki no kadomatsu [Uprooted pine tree] say: "A samurai's child is reared by samurai
parents and is taught the code of the warrior [bushidō], so he becomes a samurai. A
merchant's child is reared by merchant parents and is taught the ways of commerce
so he becomes a merchant. A samurai forsakes profits and seeks to preserve his good

rather than seeking to raise the social power they had acquired through their wealth into political power, many townsmen sought refuge in a world of sensual pleasure. And in the dark corners of "indecent gay quarters" (*akusho*) they found petty satisfaction in ephemeral private freedom, or else merely sneered cynically at the existing relations of political authority. Here too there was no sign of any conscious will to take an active responsibility for the political order.

In this manner, Tokugawa feudal society remained divided into two parts. On the one hand the samurai class functioned as the sole political agents vis-à-vis the common people and took all political responsibility upon themselves. In contrast, the common people, who constituted more than 90 percent of the total population, were forced to "depend" (*yorashimu*) passively on the given order as no more than the objects of political control.[4] How could one speak of a unified nation when rulers and subjects were rigidly separated socially? This is what led the renowned historian Take-koshi Yosaburō to conclude, "When one [part of] society controls another, and one class controls another, we merely have a society, not a nation, even though many millions of people and perfect laws may exist in that society. Only when man-made classes are completely abolished and a country is organized into the two

---

name, *while a merchant forsakes his good name and seeks profits, accumulating gold and silver.* These are the ways appropriate to each. . . . To value gold and silver as if they were Gods or Buddha until his death, that is the way of Heaven so far as a merchant is concerned." This clearly complements the upper class ideology expressed in Muro Kyūso's statement that "the samurai teaches righteousness to the three common classes, while it is the business of the merchant to seek profits" (*Shisetsu*). In a word, the merchant possessed no basic sense of values; as the *Tekuda shamisen* has it: "Although I am a townsman, I can buy a prostitute, have my legs twisted by a bald-headed masseur, make cynical sounds with the drum, and drink sake lying down. I could wear a four-layered robe, burn perfumed sticks, and warm my bottom. As long as I do not violate the laws of the land I cannot be reprimanded." This is simply an unrestrained self-will that seeks a full enjoyment of every personal pleasure with an outward submission to the "laws of the land."

[4] The Tokugawa Bakufu governed with the philosophy that the people have to depend on the ruling class, and must not be informed about political matters. *Tami wa yorashimubekushite shirashimubekarazu*: "The people should be made to depend upon [the Way] but not be informed about it." This is based on a statement in the Confucian Analects (Book VIII, Chapter 9) that actually says that "the people can be made to follow [the Way] but they cannot be made to understand it." The Tokugawa rulers adopted the former interpretation. (Translator's note.)

great elements, the people and the government, can we speak of
the existence of one nation."[5]

In addition to the division of feudal society into two basic estates, the samurai and the common people, there were various
stratified status distinctions even within the samurai class and the
common people themselves, whose rigidity also hindered the development of a sense of national unity. Moreover, because, in accordance with the nature of feudalism, this hierarchy of status
entailed corresponding regional distinctions, vertical status divisions became intertwined with horizontal geographical divisions,
producing a distinctive sectionalism. Tokugawa feudalism is often
referred to as a centralized feudalism. To be sure, compared with
previous governments, the Tokugawa Bakufu had a strong strain
of centralized authority. It directly controlled all the chief cities
and mines in the country, exercised a monopoly in coinage, and
had the power to move all the daimyo around at will. But in essence the Tokugawa remained just another house of feudal lords.
In areas outside its demesne, the traditional pattern of indirect
authority through daimyo directly responsible to the shogun prevailed. Each of the 270 han constituted an insulated political unit
and the daimyo exercised independent legislative and judicial authority in their own domains. Communications between the separate han were deliberately made extremely difficult. Within each
han the samurai were ranked into twenty, thirty, or more strata,
each with a generally fixed status. Moreover, this kind of social
cohesion based on status and rank prevailed among the common
classes too, so that, as Fukuzawa Yukichi put it, it was as if the
"many millions of people throughout Japan were sealed up in
many millions of separate boxes or separated by many millions of
walls."[6]

The consciousness that arose in this kind of environment naturally inclined towards a narrow conservatism, lacking in public
spirit and open-mindedness. Matsudaira Sadanobu lamented the
fact that "generally speaking, the people of Japan tend to be narrow in outlook. For instance, people living in the downtown areas
[of Edo] are ignorant of the foothill areas. Few people go beyond

[5] *Shin Nihon shi,* Vol. II (1892).
[6] *Bunmeiron no gairyaku,* Book V.

Kawasaki [just outside Edo], so most people think the sea is like Shinagawa Beach and all the rivers are like the Sumida and Tama. In their thought, too, they deem it wise to concentrate on what is immediately at hand, ignoring the need for profound and long-range planning. This tends to make them even more narrow-minded."[7] But Sadanobu himself had no more foresight than to punish Hayashi Shihei for harboring "fantastic and unorthodox views" because he pointed out that the water at Nihonbashi (a bridge in Tokyo) extended as far as Europe and warned against the menace from abroad.

Even the samurai, who monopolized political responsibility, directed their sense of responsibility primarily towards their immediate lords. The meaning of the word *kō* (public) in *hōkō* (public service) is most revealingly expressed in the *Hagakure*.[8] "Shākyamuni Buddha, Confucius, Kusunoki Masashige,[9] and Takeda Shingen[10] were never employed by the Nabeshima House [the lord of Saga han]. Hence what they preached does not fit in with the traditional ethos of the House of Nabeshima." That is, public service was nothing more than a personal relationship with the lord of Nabeshima, bound by a feudal stipend. The mutual barriers and sense of rivalry that thus divided the different han are difficult for us to imagine today. The Satsuma and Chōshū han, which have been lumped together as one since the Meiji Restoration, were implacable rivals until the very moment they decided on a policy of cooperation. As the history of the Bakumatsu period shows, men such as Sakamoto Ryōma (1835–67) and Nakaoka Shintarō (1838–67) had to work desperately to make this alliance possible. Because of this narrow han-centered outlook, the *shishi* ("men of high purpose") of the restoration were often compelled to sever their ties with their han in order to carry on their political activities freely.

The social structure of Tokugawa feudalism itself, then, func-

---

[7] *Hima-naru amari.*

[8] A Saga samurai's (Yamamoto Tsunetomo) views on how a Saga samurai should behave; recorded by his disciple during 1710–16. (Translator's note.)

[9] Kusunoki Masashige was a royalist hero who fought on behalf of the imperial court against its foes during the Kenmu Restoration (1333–35). (Translator's note.)

[10] Shingen (1521–73) was a major warlord of the period of civil strife. (Translator's note.)

tioned as the decisive obstacle to the formation of a unified nation, and the corresponding sense of national unity. It was also the actual policy of the Tokugawa Bakufu to use this structure to the utmost to prevent the development of such a sense of national unity from below. To begin with, the policy of seclusion was the most important of the methods used to this end, but it would be no exaggeration to say that the other policies adopted by the bakufu for the internal control of the nation were designed to serve its goal of divide and rule. That is, on the one hand it sought to promote absolutism, the so-called will of he who is above, and to suppress the spontaneous political tendencies of the nation by condemning "criticisms of the government" as manifesting "a lack of deference for public authority, the extremity of disrespect" (the words used to condemn Watanabe Kazan). On the other hand, it cleverly took advantage of the jealousies and suspicions arising from feudal regionalism, by divising a system of mutual checks and controls.

This was the method used to control the society from the daimyo down to the common people, who were organized into Five-Man Units (*goningumi*). In this respect, the term for the official bakufu post of *metsuke* (one who keeps an eye on things, a censor) expresses in one word the principle of the whole bakufu system of control. This system of control was automatically adopted inside each han. Thus came into being what one foreign official of the Bakumatsu period called in amazement "the most elaborate system of espionage ever attempted."[11] This nationwide espionage system was remarkably successful, and until the collapse of its policy of seclusion the bakufu managed to nip in the bud all social and intellectual movements that might have developed into oppositional political groups (the Keian conspiracy of Yui Shō-setsu in 1651, the Hōreki and Meiwa incidents involving Take-nouchi Shikibu and others, the Siebold incident of 1828,[12] and

---

[11] Rutherford Alcock: *The Capital of the Tycoon*, 2 vols. (New York, 1863), II, p. 250.

[12] Philipp Franz van Siebold, a German doctor, came to Japan in 1823 and taught Dutch and Western medicine to some Japanese. When he was about to leave the country he was found to possess a map of Japan. It was illegal to take a map of Japan out of the country, so those who had given him the map were arrested and punished. (Translator's note.)

Ōshio's uprising of 1837 were all quickly uncovered with the help of informers).

Having been subjected to this pattern of control for 260 years, the national spirit had been completely eroded. As Fukuzawa Yukichi complained:

> The people desired only to ensure their own safety, and lacked the spirit to debate the difference between forming a secret faction [totō] and assembling to discuss public affairs [shūgi]. They all depended on the government and did not concern themselves with national affairs. Among a million persons, there were a million different minds. Each person shut himself up in his own house and ignored the outside world as if it were a foreign country. They failed even to consult each other about the best way to clean their wells, let alone ways to repair the roads. If they chanced to come upon someone stricken by the wayside, they sped away in haste. If they came upon dog's excrement, they went around it. They were so preoccupied with trying to avoid getting involved in anything that they had no time to discuss things together. This long-engrained habit became a custom and produced the present sad state of affairs.[13]

The attitudes that spread through the nation were mutual fear and suspicion; self-protection according to the maxim "A gentleman stays away from danger"; and the brazen egoism that says "It's no concern of mine." The day was bound to come when the feudal authorities would have to reap what they had sown.

When, in June, 1853, Commodore Perry's four warships arrived at Uraga and presented President Fillmore's letter asking Japan to open her ports, the bakufu was completely disconcerted and had no idea what to do. On the one hand it reported the matter to the imperial court and consulted all the daimyo present in Edo in order to obtain the advice and cooperation of the whole country in "this national crisis" and "extremely troublesome matter." On the other hand, it lifted restrictions that had prevailed in its traditional system of domestic control, permitting the construction of ships larger than five hundred koku, and the casting of large cannon, and encouraged the many han to strengthen their military forces,

---

[13] *Bunmeiron no gairyaku*, Book II.

while the bakufu itself hurriedly devised ways of defending Edo
Bay. But the generally low level of the productive forces and technology of the country could no longer be concealed. Advising the
government on national defense, Takashima Shūhan (1798–1866),
an authority on gunnery, stated: "What worries me first of all is
the fact that there is not enough gunpowder in the entire country
to fight a war for even one year." Shortage of munitions was not
the only problem. "Once we get involved in a war . . . it will
probably last at least four or five years. In that case, not only will
there be a shortage of nitrate, but there is also the problem of food
supplies. I have heard that there is probably no lord with as much
as three years' supply of arms and food."[14]

Earlier, in 1842, Shūhan himself had fallen under suspicion and
been imprisoned for calling attention to the urgent need to mod-
ernize Japanese gunnery. As this shows, what impeded the development of modern production and technology was the insular
"frog-in-a-well" outlook, which had been responsible for the suppression of scholars of Dutch Learning such as Watanabe Kazan
(1793–1841) and Takano Chōei (1804–50), who had the vision to
see that "neither the traditional Chinese way of curbing the barbarians nor a divine wind will help us. The most important thing
is to study the conditions of the enemy carefully."[15] As late as 1850
Sakuma Zōzan's request for permission to publish a Japanese-
Dutch dictionary was refused.[16] "To drive off the barbarians," he
argued, "the first thing that must be done is to understand their
ways. To understand their ways, the most important thing is to
become familiar with their language. . . . Coastal defense is the
business of the whole country. . . . To enable the entire population
to understand the ways of the barbarians there is no better method
than to make it easy for them to read barbarian books. To make
it easy for them to read barbarian books it is necessary first of all
to publish a dictionary of the barbarian language." The bakufu,
however, was determined to continue the policy of keeping the
nation ignorant of foreign affairs.

[14] Memorial of October, 1853.
[15] Watanabe Kazan: *Shinkiron; Seiyō jijō gotōsho*.
[16] The particulars can be found in his memorial to the bakufu of September, 1862.
Cf. *Zōzan zenshū* [Collected works of Zōzan], 5 vols. (Tokyo, 1934–35), I, p. 223.

It is therefore not surprising that with a few exceptions the memorials submitted by the many daimyo and han officials in response to the bakufu's request for advice on how to deal with Perry betray the frog-in-a-well outlook. Even the lord of Mito, Nariaki (1800–60), the most respected leader of his day, stated:

> Warships and cannon are useless in hand-to-hand fighting. Even if the barbarians succeed in attacking the coastal regions, they will not satisfy their greed unless they land troops ashore. Then we will hand-pick outstanding warriors and organize a company of spearmen and swordsmen. They will maneuver with agility and dexterity, taking advantage of every opportunity. If we utilize our advantage to strike them at their weak points, attack them from the sides, move behind them to cut them down, maneuvering as quickly as lightning, and engage them in a struggle to the death, there is no question but that we will succeed in annihilating all the barbarians.[17]

Thus, he expected to confront the enemy's warships and cannons with "the superior skill of our Land of the Gods," that is, with spears and swords. Other high-spirited suggestions as to concrete methods by which to drive the foreign powers away were no better than this. In his memorial, Takashima Shūhan sharply criticized such idealism:

> Never have the sword and the spear been utilized as much as they were in the Korean War [1592–98]. All the warriors were veterans of hundreds of battles; not a single one, not even a foot-soldier, was a poor warrior. Everyone gave the full measure of his loyalty and courage, and fought desperately. But for seven years we were stuck in the mire of Korea, and, sad to say, we failed to cross the border into Ming [China]. The Ch'ing Empire today combines both the lands of Han and Manchu; it is twice as large as the Ming Empire. But when they were attacked by England, they were forced to sue for peace in less than three years. What enabled England to gain this victory? . . . Reflecting upon this, we cannot say that they were superior in swordsmanship. Today anyone who engages the barbarians in battle without superior firearms and men trained in their use faces a dangerous situation.

[17] Memorial of July, 1853, *Bakumatsu gaikoku kankei monjo* [Documents relating to foreign affairs in the Bakumatsu period], 30 vols. (Tokyo, 1910–55), Vol. I.

When the bakufu realized that it could not help but open the ports of Japan, it found, ironically enough, that it had to exert all its efforts to subdue this blind antiforeignism (*jōiron*) in the country. (I shall discuss later the fact that there was a variety of jōi theories.) Even if this jōi position did have the outlook of a frog-in-a-well, it would have served some purpose if it had united the country and concentrated its attention on the foreign menace. But unfortunately by this time mutual distrust and jealousy were too deeply rooted in the country. A member of the Sendai han, Ōtsuki Heiji (1801–78; also known as Bankei), remarked: "The most urgent thing today is the need to *induce harmony among the people*."[18] According to Sakuma Zōzan: "The opportunity to expand our national authority is present. However much the government may desire to institute great changes, the problem of public sentiments remains. *Unless the people's spirits can be harmonized* it is difficult to predict the kind of internal and external troubles that might break out."[19] Yokoi Shōnan (1809–69) feared that "if we engage in a war when, as is the case at present, *the people are in disharmony* and there is a shortage of matériel, we shall undoubtedly suffer hundreds of defeats."[20]

The bakufu and the lords of the han closest to it feared that opening the Japanese ports as requested by Perry would reveal the decline in its political strength, and some daimyo and the common people might take advantage of the situation to stage uprisings against it. This attitude is represented in a memorial submitted to the shogun on August 7, 1853, by the lord of Fukui han, Matsudaira Yoshinaga (1828–90): "If such a humiliation [the opening of Japan's ports] is accepted and the decline in the Bakufu's military virtues becomes apparent, *aside from the foreign powers, what would be the reaction of the daimyo and lesser lords throughout the country?* It would be impossible to continue governing the land in the same manner as heretofore. I am afraid that conditions *similar to those which prevailed during the last years of Ashikaga rule* [that is, nation-wide civil strife] will come about."[21] The lord of Mito

---

[18] Memorial of August, 1853, ibid., Vol. II.

[19] Submission to the bakufu of April, 1858, *Zōzan zenshū*, I, p. 196.

[20] Submission to the bakufu of 1863, Yokoi Tokio: *Shōnan ikō* [Manuscripts left behind by Shōnan] (Tokyo, 1942), p. 100.

[21] *Bakumatsu gaikoku kankei monjo*, Vol. I.

han, Tokugawa Nariaki, also stated in his memorial: "If the Shogun does not adopt the policy of driving away the foreigners by force and adopts lenient and weak measures, the people will misunderstand his true intentions. *Evil schemers among them will cease to fear the Shogun's authority and might begin to harbor disloyal thoughts. It might become difficult to keep the daimyo and the people under control.*" Clearly the feudal authorities feared domestic rather than foreign difficulties. We could even say that they feared troubles from abroad precisely because they feared internal troubles. The entire feudal ruling class, from the bakufu to the lords of all the han, feared and suspected the common people, the subject classes.

When in 1842 Mizuno Tadakuni (1793–1851), a member of the bakufu's Council of Elders (*rōjū*), struck by the swift defeat of China in the Opium War, relaxed the decree of 1825 to fire at all foreign vessels on sight, Nariaki objected and advocated the adoption of a strong jōi policy. He defended his position by arguing: "The common people of this country are simple-minded and the crude fishermen are the worst. Even while the order to expel the barbarians is in effect, *there is a danger that they will secretly come into contact with the barbarians at sea.* If the decree is now rescinded, it will be impossible to prevent the inimical practice of foreign trade. I therefore request that the decree of 1825 be retained for the time being in order to keep the simple-minded people under control."[22] The literature of this period testifies to the fact that distrust of the common people because of their alleged stupidity and fear that they would collaborate with the foreign powers grew among the ruling class as international relations grew in significance.[23]

[22] Quoted from Fujita Tōko: *Kaiten shishi* [A history of poems that have transformed the world].

[23] There are many examples of this in *Bakumatsu gaikoku kankei monjo*. To cite two: "When the cunning foreigners take advantage of the weaknesses of the ignorant and stupid common people and lead them astray with money, valuable goods, and favors, *we cannot say that there is no danger, for their straitened circumstances may result in their becoming attached to the favors of the cunning foreigners, unaware that they are falling into a trap*" (Memorial of August, 1853, by the lord of Hizen, Matsudaira Iemasa). "Regarding the arrival of foreign vessels in the past few years, recently members of the baser classes have been suffering particular hardships and their mental outlook has been poor. Many have taken to drinking sake in despair, getting into arguments and squabbles, and assaulting women. It is said that some are bitter about the existing state of affairs. Now, the foreigners are *especially adept at attracting the ignorant people to their side.* If the foreigners were to take advantage of this situation in which *there is bitterness about the times and existing conditions* and to shower the common people with favors, serious diffi-

As if reacting to this kind of distrust, some merchants dodged the rigid controls and engaged in illegal trade with the foreign ships that came to Japan. In his memorial to the bakufu, Taka-shima Shūhan remarked: "All merchants are led astray by profits. Many knowingly break the law and undergo severe punishments. But it is not likely that they will change their ways. In a crisis, we cannot predict what they might not do in league with the enemy." It is possible that such base motives did lead these merchants to the unscrupulous employment of any means whatsoever for profit. But this is no justification for Nariaki's opinion that the people were stupid. As noted earlier, this unscrupulousness simply reflected the fact that the feudal system and its morality placed the merchants at the bottom of the scale of values. How could the common people suddenly be expected to display a sense of national responsibility when they had been cut off from any political activity and driven into the narrow confines of their private lives as simple objects of political control?

How did the common people react in August, 1864, when the Chōshū han, the leading proponent of the expulsion of the foreigners, was easily forced to surrender its fortifications at Shimonoseki by the combined fleet of England, the United States, France, and Holland? According to Ernest Satow, who witnessed the entire incident from an English warship: "The Japanese had shown themselves very friendly to the working party, and had themselves carried down the guns for delivery. They were not improbably glad to be rid of the toys that had brought them into so much trouble."[24] What a spectacle! Lack of confidence in the common people above and lack of political concern below complemented each other in this fashion. This was the unpleasant situation created by the long years of feudal rule. In 1860 Yokoi Shōnan summed up the situation as follows:

The entire nation of Japan is divided into separate sections without any

---

culties would ensue" (statement submitted in January, 1854, by an official at Uraga where Perry arrived).

[24] Ernest Satow: *A Diplomat in Japan* (London, 1921), p. 118. This is confirmed by a French officer, Alfred Roussin. Cf. his *Une campagne sur les côtes du Japon* (1866; Japanese translation, p. 183). See also Osatake Takeki: *Meiji Ishin* [The Meiji Restoration], 3 vols. (Tokyo, 1948), II, pp. 366, 456.

system of uniform control. So when Perry arrived in Japan in 1853, he concluded that it was a country without government. Indeed he possessed insight and perceptivity. To speak frankly, even at the risk of displeasing the Bakufu, we must say that in the beginning of its rule, in dealing with the feudal lords, it adopted measures designed to liquidate their military forces. That is why it adopted the policy of *sankin-kōtai* and required them to assist in construction projects, to participate in fire prevention work in the Bakufu's domains and mountains, to guard strategic passages, and, lately, to assist in the defense of the border areas. All of these assignments required a great deal of effort and man-power. But the Bakufu ignored the burden that was being imposed on the common people. Moreover it exercised its authority as overlord to retain the right to coin gold and silver and the authority to proclaim and institute many measures throughout the land. *It used its authority for the convenience and private interests of the Tokugawa family only. We see no evidence of the government putting into practice the political philosophy of bringing peace to the world and loving the common people as parents love their children.* Perry was indeed correct in regarding this country as a country without any government.[25]

Shōnan's statement may be regarded as the final balance-sheet of 260 years of Tokugawa rule.

[25] *Kokuze sanron* in *Shōnan ikō*, p. 39.

CHAPTER III

VARIETIES OF PREMODERN NATIONALISM

Advocates of Coastal Defense, of Enriching the Nation
and Strengthening the Military, of Revering the Emperor
and Repelling the Barbarians. Their Historical Limitations.

I

In the last chapter I showed that the feudal system and the form
of consciousness it fostered stubbornly impeded the consolidation
of the people into a nationstate system founded upon a sense of
national unity. Perhaps I have probed more deeply than necessary
into a commonsense thesis. But unless this is clearly understood, it
is difficult to comprehend the magnitude of the historical problem
that confronted Japanese nationalism and to appreciate the thorny
paths the champions of this movement had to follow. The Meiji
Restoration with its concept of *ikkun banmin* ("one prince, all the
people," i.e., equality under the emperor) was an epoch-making
change, removing as it did the obstacles between the people and
the state political order, and opening the way for the development
of nationalism. However, it was not itself the solution to the problem; it merely established the preconditions for that solution. Nationalism began its forward movement from this point. But these
preconditions had been slowly laid down within Tokugawa feudalism itself.

The development of these preconditions was the same thing as
the disintegration of the Tokugawa social structure. Ideologically
it was the maturation of a theory that to a certain extent tran-

scended[1] feudal patterns of thought. The formation of a truly modern nationalist thought had to await the changes wrought by the Meiji Restoration, but beneath the weight of the old regime the groundwork was slowly being laid. I shall now take a look at what might be called the premodern nationalist current of thought as the stage before nationalism. In a broad sense, every mode of thought that is opposed to or transcends feudalism constitutes, by that very fact, a basis for modern nationalism, but here I shall examine the problems inherent in the feudal system not for their own sake, that is, as purely political or social, cultural or economic problems, but only insofar as they relate to my thesis, that is, to the problem of national unification or state independence.

The arrival of foreign vessels, which glaringly exposed the separatist divisions in the national consciousness, was also what sowed the seeds of the idea of a national unity transcending these divisions. Of course, the conception of Japan as the Land of the Gods and the reverence to the emperor inseparable from it persisted throughout the Tokugawa period. On the other hand, the development of internal means of transportation and the extension of commerce and trade gradually gave rise to a national market. Thus, the internal conditions for a unified nation-state were in preparation during the Tokugawa period, but the swift growth of these internal conditions and the politicization of the sense of reverence for the emperor, which had previously had religious and ethical overtones, were unquestionably a result of the confrontation with the foreign powers. The following remarks of Tokutomi Sohō (1863–1958)[2] may be something of an oversimplification, but they are accurate as to the historical sequence of events: "A threat from abroad immediately directs the nation's thoughts outwards. This leads immediately to the rise of a spirit of nationalism. This directly induces national unification. . . . The concept 'foreign nations' brought forth the concept 'Japanese nation.' The day when the concept 'Japanese nation' arose was the day when the

---

[1] I say "transcended" (chōshutsu) here because a clear-cut antifeudal system of thought hardly existed throughout the Tokugawa period.

[2] Sohō was an advocate of liberal, Christian ideals in the earlier stages of his life but later became a supporter of military expansionism. Aside from his activities as a social and political commentator, he produced a multi-volume history of Japan. (Translator's note.)

concept '*han*' vanished. The day when the concept '*han*' vanished was the day when feudal society was overthrown."[3] Needless to say, the path Japan actually trod was far more complex and roundabout. Before the "threat from abroad" raised the theory of sonnō (revere the emperor), the focal expression of the spirit of nationalism, to the level of a guiding principle for the "overthrow of feudal society," there were a number of stages to be traversed.

The menace from the foreign powers had already become a problem in the Meiwa (1764–72) and An'ei (1772–81) eras, seventy or eighty years before Perry's arrival. The threat came initially from the north. In 1771 a Russian ship was stranded in Awa (Shikoku); in 1778 Russian merchants landed on Kunashiri Island in the Kuriles and asked the Matsumae han for commercial relations. In 1792 a Russian envoy, Laxman, arrived at Nemuro in Hokkaido with some shipwrecked Japanese sailors and submitted a formal request to enter into commercial relations. It was also during this year that Hayashi Shihei (1738–93) was imprisoned for publishing his *Sangoku tsūran zusetsu* [An illustrated survey of three nations] and *Kaikoku heidan* [Military talks for a maritime nation]. During these years intelligent and informed people began to discuss the Russian problem. These men asked the entire nation to concern itself with the foreign menace and the problem of defending the northern frontiers. This movement for coastal defense or *kaibōron* was simply the first step in the emergence of a premodern nationalism. In his *Sangoku tsūran zusetsu*, Hayashi Shihei asked that the entire nation become familiar with the geography of the three lands, Korea, the Ryukyus, and Hokkaido, which are near Japan and directly affect her defenses. "These three countries are located near our country," he wrote. "They are in fact our neighbors. The people of our country, irrespective of status or occupation, must know the geography of these three countries." In his *Kaikoku heidan*, he asserted: "The most urgent aspect of Japan's military preparations is the necessity of learning the way to stop foreign enemies." He stressed that Japan was a maritime country and gave details as to the international situation and ways of coping with it.

[3] Tokutomi Iichirō: *Yoshida Shōin* (Tokyo, 1908), p. 87.

Another noteworthy work of this period is *Hokuchi kigen* [Words of warning about the northern regions], written by Ōhara Kokingo in 1797. "Foreign foes," he wrote, "are enemies of the entire country, not just of one *han*. Thus it is necessary to exhaust the intellectual faculties of the entire country" in formulating plans for the defense of the country. He therefore argued that men of ability from among "those who earn a living in the cities and those hidden in the mountains" should be ferreted out and utilized, and that in matters of strategy, tactics, and matériel, the secrecy by which the "feudal lords greedily further their own interests and conceal valuable information from others and hinder its diffusion to others" must be abandoned and everything opened to all the han. It is necessary, he held, to make certain that "everyone is equal and no one is inferior to others" in military arts. This is the first sign of the process that was to lead to the end of vertical status distinctions and horizontal regional divisions as a response to the call for state defenses against foreign powers.

Once the Kansei era (1789–1801) had passed and the Bunka (1804–18) and Bunsei (1818–30) eras arrived, the foreign menace was no longer merely a probability, but had become a harsh reality. In 1806 the Russians, denied their request for commercial relations, invaded Sakhalin and Etorofu in the Kuriles. In 1808 the English frigate *Phaeton* forced its way into Nagasaki. Now the Russians in the north were joined by the British in the south. The pleas for coastal defense became more urgent in tone. *Kyokuron jiji fūji* [A secret memorial on the urgency of current affairs] by Koga Seiri (1750–1817) clearly reflects this attitude; it is a ten-point argument for a reinforcement of the inner structure of the country. Seiri's main motive in writing it was his anger at the lack of interest in national defense pervading society from top to bottom. "*Today powerful barbarians, running about in a wild manner, and great nations menace us. The conflagration has already started. Many incompetent and useless subjects hold official positions and draw stipends. The peasants are no longer loyal.* The sickness has advanced to a critical stage. . . . This subject has submitted these ten points driven by an uncontainable anger." According to Seiri:

Some men have lost their stipends for earnestly suggesting that it is not wise for the government to open our borders to foreigners. Some men have been arrested for writing books calling attention to the barbarian menace in the outlying regions. . . . If the affairs of the outlying regions are discussed in the streets of the cities, the participants are arrested and imprisoned. The men who have been punished in this manner form an endless line. Subjects who are aware of errors in calculations and mistakes in planning are afraid of speaking up. . . . When those above meet disaster, those below remain indifferent as if they knew nothing about it. . . . When those below suffer hardships, those above haughtily ignore it. . . . Those above and those below are divided in this manner. Once trouble starts [the entire society] will dissolve and collapse.

Like the three monkeys who hear no evil, see no evil, and speak no evil, the nation as a whole was indifferent and this indifference was the natural product of the bakufu's policies, which strictly prohibited all political criticism, even in private discussion. So Seiri placed at the top of his list of suggestions for the country's defense the need "to permit open discussions and prevent wisdom from being stifled." The call for coastal defense thus started with the demand that the entire nation concern itself with the foreign threat, and gradually came to locate the core of the problem inside society itself.

In addition, from this period on, the structural contradictions of Tokugawa society became more and more acute, and the serious economic difficulties confronting the ruling class made Sadanobu's Kansei Reforms necessary. As a result, heavier taxes were imposed on the peasantry, adding to their hardships, plagued as they had been by famines and floods since the Tenmei era (1781–89). The effect was disastrous to the farm communities. The practice of infanticide grew more widespread, and the number of uprisings (ikki) and riots increased throughout the country. Since the society contained within it these serious social problems, it was no longer sufficient to attempt to meet the foreign menace simply by increasing military facilities or devising piecemeal political measures. And the existing financial policies of the bakufu and the han made it difficult to strengthen military forces. As a result, a trend of thought emerged which sought to deal with the international threat by first securing domestic economic stability and then strengthening the country's defenses on this basis. The earlier argument for defense of the coastal regions was therefore transformed into the call for *fukoku kyōhei,* or "enriching the nation and strengthening the military." Of course, the earlier advocates of coastal defense had been aware of the relationship between domestic economic problems and foreign policy and had considered such measures as returning the samurai to their fiefs and the colonization of Hokkaido. But their primary concern had been the technical aspects of national defense.[4] Now, however, solving the domestic economic problems was made the central element of the solution to the international crisis. And it was more or less realized that these difficulties were not the product of mistakes in specific policies or the negligence of certain individuals; they were deeply rooted in the Tokugawa social structure itself, as a comparison of Japanese and European conditions revealed. Consequently, the solution was to be sought, not in the introduction of isolated measures, but in a considerable institutional transformation. In order to make such a transformation possible it was essential to centralize political power. This meant the abandonment of the daimyo system, both in terms of its content and of its function as a driving force, and the formulation of a state system with centralized, absolutist overtones. This was the picture that developed in the minds of the advocates of the fukoku kyōhei policy. As the end of Tokugawa rule approached, this theory was heatedly debated, and in combination with the sonnō-jōi theory, it became a factor in the closing phase of premodern nationalism.

II

Honda Toshiaki and Satō Nobuhiro were the most significant of the systematic proponents of a theory of fukoku kyōhei ("enriching the nation and strengthening the military") with such a centralizing and absolutist cast. The ideas of *"dai Nippon koku"* (the great Japanese nation [Toshiaki]) or *"kōkoku"* (the imperial country [Nobuhiro]) form a constant background to their theories of elabo-

---

[4] For example, of the sixteen volumes of the *Kaikoku heidan,* fifteen are devoted to national defense in the narrow sense and only the last is devoted to the topic "On Increasing Food and Soldiers."

rate institutional reform. They were no longer concerned with separate regional or han interests. The idea of the imperial country complemented, and in turn was complemented by, the awareness of the world fostered by Dutch Learning, and can thus be seen to have been completely emancipated from the Chinese notion of *chunghua*, "the Middle Kingdom," or "the Celestial Empire." Both Toshiaki and Nobuhiro began by recognizing that the East had fallen behind the West. "It is the custom of the Western nations," wrote Toshiaki in *Keizai hōgen*, "to consider a wise policy of overseas expansion as the most important of their national problems. This system fully satisfies the task of infinitely increasing the wealth of one's nation. *Such a practice does not as yet exist in the countries of the Orient*. This is indeed regrettable." And Nobuhiro observed in *Seiyō rekkokushi-ryaku*: "There is nothing that compares with shipping and commerce to enhance greatly a state's interests. Unfortunately, the peoples of the Orient concern themselves only with the preservation of their own nations, pursue temporary pleasures and wallow in excessive luxury, while neglecting to plan for the future. . . . Internally and externally they are in extreme poverty, and their sickness is serious. They have already allowed two young nations, Russia and England, to become the leaders of the world. How sad! How sad!"

Hence their theory of national defense was opposed to a conservative policy of national seclusion, favored positive defensive measures such as foreign trade and the colonization of overseas areas, and culminated in Nobuhiro's *udai kondō* ("fusion of the entire world"), that is, international unification. At a time when the policy of national seclusion was still firmly entrenched, they advocated strengthening the country by "overseas shipping and trade" (Toshiaki). Rejecting the traditional contempt for commerce, they proposed to "increase production and develop industries" by means of state control of industrial production and commerce. By such a policy they hoped to transform Japan into "the richest and strongest nation of the world" (Toshiaki) or "the supreme nation of the world" (Nobuhiro). These notions clearly indicate that their basic theories were far in advance of their age and, in effect, utopian in nature. (Of course, the two differed in the content of their thought, but here I am merely concerned with the shared aspects of their fukoku kyōhei theories.) What about the points that reveal the absolutist character of the institutions they proposed to introduce? The historical role of the absolutism that preceded the modern nation-state was to unify and centralize the multiple authorities of feudalism. As the supreme ruler monopolized political legitimacy, the so-called *pouvoirs intermédiaires* (intermediary powers) were dissolved, and a homogeneous, equalized nation under the jurisdiction of a single national law emerged. Further, by what Max Weber called the differentiation of the *Verwaltungsstab* (administrative staff) from the *Verwaltungsmittel* (means of administration), the modern bureaucracy and army were formed.

In Toshiaki's and Nobuhiro's fukoku kyōhei proposals there is clearly, but very incompletely, a tendency toward the maximum possible integration of the multiple political authorities, thus dissolving the intermediary powers that stood between the "national ruler" or prince on the one hand, and "the myriads of the people" on the other. In *Keisei hisaku* Toshiaki explained what he expected to achieve with the establishment of institutions to deal with what he called the "four urgent needs":[5]

> If we recapture the ancient fame that the great Japanese nation enjoyed as a military power, gradually establish and perfect various enterprises, establish an eastern capital in Ezo (Hokkaido), a central capital in Edo, and a southern capital in Osaka, and have the [shogun] conduct the affairs of government by rotating his seat of government among these three places, Japan will surely become *the world's wealthiest and strongest nation*. . . . All this depends on the way of doing things. There are no special reasons behind it. If the way of doing things is good, heroes and great men will quickly come to the fore and will act as the hands and legs [of the shogun] and serve with the utmost loyalty. Then the gold and silver of the land will naturally flow [to the shogun] and he will be able to use them as he pleases. *The entire population* will endeavor to serve the ruler loyally, and confidence will prevail throughout the land. Since the entire population will unite in supporting the existing institutions, no one will turn against the national government, and hence there will be few criminals.

[5] Gunpowder, metals, shipping, and colonization. (Translator's note.)

For Japan to become "the world's richest and strongest nation" on the one hand implied on the other the entire nation (strictly speaking the entire nation with the unique exception of the supreme ruler) becoming one unit and submitting inwardly to the new order. According to Toshiaki, the result of leaving shipping and commerce in the hands of the merchants had been the emergence of wealthy merchants and an impoverishment of the "two classes," the samurai and the peasantry, unlike any time since the foundation of Japan. "Unless the ruler controls [the merchants] under such circumstances, the two classes will give vent to their bitterness, accumulated grievances, and anger, and an impossible situation may arise."[6] He issued this warning not because he favored the feudal suppression of the merchants, a policy founded on a disdain for commerce itself, but because he believed that if the rich merchants developed into strong intermediary powers between the ruler and the people, it would disrupt the homogeneity of the people and jeopardize the ruler's chances of unifying the nation. Toshiaki saw the ruler as someone transcending all classes, samurai, peasants, and merchants.

In Satō Nobuhiro's famous three-department, six-ministry, eight-group system of suitō (social control), formulated as the first stage in his astounding policy of "fusing the world" and converting "the entire world into (Japanese) counties and prefectures,"[7] the traditional classes of samurai, peasants, artisans, and merchants were to be completely dissolved, and then the "myriad people" divided into the eight groups engaged in plant cultivation, forestry, mining, manufacture, trade, hired labor, shipping, and fishing, and assigned to the six ministries. As in Toshiaki's plan, here too the status of the samurai class under the sole ruler was to be no different from that of the other social classes; each was to be no more than an element of the "myriad people." The daimyo's fiefs were to be retained, but within a limit of two hundred thousand koku, under the jurisdiction of governers appointed by the supreme ruler. On the other hand, even merchants could be appointed to high government posts such as commissionerships

---

[6] *Keizai hisaku.*
[7] *Udai kondō hisaku.*

(*bugyō*). The ultimate object of Nobuhiro's basic social reforms was thus to enable the sovereign "to manipulate the entire country of Japan as if it were his hands and feet." And the establishment of this kind of absolute authority in the country was a necessary prerequisite for overseas expansion: "How can there be time to conquer other countries if the management of one's own country poses difficulties?"[8] Another notable feature of this state based on social control was the establishment of the imperial residence in Edo and the consolidation of the neighboring regions under the authority of officials and soldiers directly controlled by the ruler. Toshiaki also imagined the establishment of a bureaucratic system utilizing men of ability in the state to be established in Kamchatka after its colonization. These features can be regarded as partial replicas of the structure of a modern state.

What kind of ruler was the absolutist colonial empire of Toshiaki and Nobuhiro to have? The unification of the multiple powers necessarily raises this question. Nobuhiro's use of such words as *kōkyo* (imperial court) implies that the supreme authority of his huge Japanese nation was to be more than a military despot but embody traditional and divine elements as well. Moreover, this design for an ideal state was stimulated by serious threats from abroad. Hence Nobuhiro had to find a spiritual basis for national existence in the historical traditions of his own nation. Thus the theory of fukoku kyōhei ("enrich the nation and strengthen the military") itself gave birth to a theory of sonnō, or reverence for the emperor. In my investigation of the development of premodern nationalism, I have now come to its final stage.

III

Recalling in his later years the sonnō-jōi movement, the most significant socio-political movement of the Bakumatsu period, Ōkuma Shigenobu[9] remarked:

In this situation it came to be believed that the nation would be in danger if it remained divided under feudalism. It is said that when

[8] Ibid.
[9] Ōkuma (1838–1922) was the founder of the Constitutional Reform Party, prime minister twice, and the founder of Waseda University. (Translator's note.)

a man is desperate he appeals to Heaven, but there was nowhere to appeal to at this time. The menacing forces were already on our doorstep. In this situation, the Imperial Court with its unbroken lineage from time immemorial came to the fore. It became the basis for Japan's unification. It had already become clear, as civilization advanced, that military rule or feudal rule would not do. So the time was ripe for unification, but without the proper impetus seven hundred years of feudal rule would not have collapsed. . . . As civilization advanced, there were voices in favor of the preservation of political legitimacy in the Confucian sense [*taigi meibun*], but they were faint. Faced with a national crisis, the belief that the fragmented nation must be unified to cope with the national crisis swept the country. This produced the anti-foreign and royalist factions. These two forces joined hands and produced the *sonnō-jōi* movement. This soon became a great national movement.[10]

Ōkuma's words suggest the broad outlines of the role played by the sonnō-jōi theory as the final phase of premodern nationalism, but when we inquire into the specific content of this "great national movement," we discover that currents extremely diverse in motive and tendency coexisted and intermingled in the sonnō-jōi movement; it is not susceptible to simple schematization. For instance, the jōi theory ("repel the barbarians") is often mechanically conceived as opposed to the *kaikokuron* ("theory of opening the country"), but this confuses the theory of *sakoku* or national seclusion with the jōi theory. In reality the most ardent advocates of jōi were often aggressive kaikoku supporters too (e.g., Sakuma Zōzan, Yoshida Shōin, Ōkuni Takamasa). On the other hand, there were men who apparently supported opening the country but whose fundamental inner tendency was toward a very conservative seclusionism. They were forced by circumstances to accept the opening of the country against their true inclinations.[11] Even when sonnō ("revere the emperor") became a meaningful political slogan in the Bakumatsu period, it did not necessarily imply opposing or overthrowing the bakufu, not to speak of over-

[10] *Nihon no seitō* in *Meiji kensei keizai-shi-ron* [Treatises on Meiji constitutional and economic history], ed. Kokka Gakkai (Tokyo, 1919), p. 102.

[11] For instance, the adherence to the Cabinet's policy of opening the country by the Tairō (Great Councilor) Ii Naosuke was of this nature. Cf. *Fukuō jiden* [Autobiography of Fukuzawa Yukichi] (Iwanami edition), p. 175.

throwing feudalism; there were innumerable nuances in the extent of the revolutionary character of its assertions, from revering the emperor and respecting the bakufu via *kōbu gattai* (uniting the imperial court and the bakufu) to revering the emperor and overthrowing the bakufu.

What is important then is not the subjective use made of the terms jōi and sonnō, but their objective significance. Only a concrete analysis of this theoretical current, ascertaining *by which social class and from what social standpoint* in the complex political conditions of this period these assertions were made, will reveal its full historical significance. We shall then understand why the sonnō-jōi movement cannot be directly linked with theses of modern nationalism such as national unification and national independence. For example, class interest was often plainly at work in determining the feudal lords' jōi posture. They feared that their political privileges would be undermined as closer international ties were formed. This has already been mentioned in passing. In this respect the visible result was opposition to the bakufu's timorous willingness to open Japanese ports, but the two positions had much in common when it came to a matter of fundamental motives. Hence the following remarks of Rutherford Alcock, the British minister in Japan during this period, cannot simply be dismissed as a foreigner's prejudices:

> The Rulers have just sufficient knowledge and intelligence to see and understand that the enlightenment, intellectually and morally, of the mass of the population must lead inevitably to fundamental changes, the first of which would be the destruction of their jealous, restrictive, and feudal tenure of power. Hence the persistent and implacable hostility with which all the more powerful Princes and Daimios regard the establishment of foreign relations and the extension of commerce, notwithstanding the fact that the pecuniary interests of many as producers might be furthered by foreign trade.[12]

In a memorial submitted to the Council of Elders on April 12, 1857, Matsudaira, lord of Shimōsa, wrote: "At present the military class has been exhausted and it seems that power has passed

---

[12] R. Alcock, op. cit., II, pp. 249–50, also 211–12.

to the merchant class. *If on top of this, trade is made freer, the merchants will surely increase their profits even more, and the samurai's authority will decline still further.*" These statements of Alcock and Matsudaira together reveal the essence of the feudal version of the jōi position.

It is interesting to note that although Alcock detected the weakness of this antiforeignism when its purpose was to protect the privileges of the ruling class, he urged the Western powers to move cautiously (while taking a firm stand) so as not to turn this into a mass movement by "rousing a latent fanaticism of patriotic feeling which no doubt exists in the Japanese character."[13] The sonnō-jōi movement may well have been one of the forces that saved Japan from being colonized or partially colonized in this period—not the feudal lords' version of it, but rather "the young students' (*shosei*) sonnō-jōi theory."[14] On the whole, the feudal lords' jōi theory fused with the proimperial, probakufu movement and the effort to unite the imperial court and the bakufu (kōbu gattai), while the young students' sonnō-jōi movement joined forces with those who opposed the bakufu and favored its overthrow. From the standpoint of sonnō-jōi thought, Bakumatsu history is the process whereby leadership gradually passed from the former to the latter. Sonnō-jōi was not simply an intellectual or theoretical movement; it was also a political creed inseparable from political action. The task of tracing the complete course of its development therefore belongs to the realm of political history. Here I shall restrict myself to an examination of those aspects that are organized according to relatively theoretical criteria and trace the change in emphasis noted above, by contrasting the positions of the later Mito school, where the first and most significant expressions of sonnō-jōi sentiments can be found, and those of Yoshida Shōin as a typical example of the student advocates of sonnō-jōi.

The work that presented the later Mito school's position on sonnō-jōi in a most systematic fashion was Aizawa Seishisai's *Shinron* [New proposals]. Written against the background of the turbulent conditions of the period in which the bakufu issued its decree of 1825 calling for the expulsion of all foreign vessels approaching Japanese shores, it consists of five sections: National Polity, Gen-

---

[13] Ibid., p. 222.
[14] Marquis Ōkuma: *Sekijitsu dan.*

eral Conditions, Conditions in Foreign Countries, Defense, and Long-Range Planning. A well-organized thesis, it begins with the sanctity of the *kokutai* or national polity, turns to the world situation and the policy of Asian conquest adopted by the Western powers, and ends by discussing the defense of Japan against these powers, both from the point of view of immediate measures and from that of long-term strategy. Seishisai's work made a profound impression on the intellectual world of the Bakumatsu period. For a time it was even regarded as the bible of the Bakumatsu shishi or "men of high purpose." It is precisely this bible of the sonnō-jōi movement that clearly reveals the premodern character of sonnō-jōi nationalism. Underlying Seishisai's doctrine of sonnō-jōi was a basic distrust of the subjugated common classes and a fear that they might acquire foreign support to undermine the feudal political system. This distrust and fear were based upon his belief that the people were stupid (*gumin*). "Many among the people of the country are stupid, only a few are superior," he remarked. "Once the hearts of the stupid begin to lose their balance, it is impossible to govern the country in a stable manner. The reason the Sages established strict punishment for insurgents who spread false doctrines is because they despised those who mislead the stupid people."[15]

Seishisai criticized the fukoku kyōhei theory as follows:

Theorists say that to defend the border regions it is essential to enrich the nation and strengthen the military. At present the barbarians are seeking to take advantage of the fact that the people have no guiding principles and are covertly seducing them in the border regions to capture their allegiance. When the people transfer their loyalty to the barbarians, the nation will fall into the possession of the latter without military conflict. Thus the rich and the strong will no longer belong to us. They will simply supply troops and food to the enemy furtively. After exhausting ourselves in thinking and planning to enrich and strengthen the nation, we will find that it will all be turned over to the invading armies. What a sad state of affairs.[16]

[15] *Shinron,* Book II.
[16] Ibid., Book I.

He warned against Dutch Learning: "When in the future the crafty barbarians take advantage of this [Dutch Learning] and *mislead the stupid people,* it will be impossible to prevent them from behaving like lowly beasts. The result will be widespread injury and extensive contamination. We must plan carefully to prevent this from occurring."[17] Both these statements are based on exactly the same logic—or rather psychology.

While on the one hand, he praised the "wise calculations and clever planning" in Ieyasu's establishment of feudal government because he made "the people ignorant, the entire country weak, and the former hero earnestly obedient to his orders," on the other hand, he recognized that this policy was responsible for Japan's weakness in the international crisis of his own time: "Keeping the people ignorant and the military weak is a clever way to govern, but basically it is to the advantage of the government only. Where there are advantages, defects inevitably follow. It is then necessary to correct the situation." Thus, he recognized the limitations of the policy of keeping the people ignorant. He therefore advocated a limited decentralization of power, specifically a system of peasant soldiery, so that "the entire energy of the country can be utilized" against the foreign enemy (here we can see the irrepressible logic inherent in nationalism). But if the state system of national defense developed in his *Shinron* (in his own words, "the invincible project") were ever realized, it followed that "the people must be made dependent on it but not informed about it."[18]

This belief in the stupidity of the people was not confined to the *Shinron;* it was an overt and covert accompaniment to the entire later Mito school. In his *Kaiten shishi* [History of poems that have transformed the world], Fujita Tōko (1806–55) described the slow decline of the antique spirit of military valor and remarked that when the custody of military values passed from the aristocracy to the military class "the best was destroyed while the next best remained." However, given that "peace has prevailed for many years and . . . [people] vacillate and lack perception," if the "next best" elements fail, "*evil people and cunning barbarians* will rise and

---

[17] Ibid.
[18] Ibid., Book IV.

seek to take over. Is it not a frightening thought?" Evil people at home and cunning barbarians from abroad are put on the same plane as enemies. The famous thesis in the *Shinron* claims that "when heroic men inspire the land their only fear is that the people may fail to act. When ordinary men seek to get by with makeshift arrangements, their only fear is that the people may act." Even Yoshida Shōin, who criticized the *Shinron* as "false and empty discussions" and "empty words on paper," singled out this paragraph as "containing something that touches on the crux of the matter."

But it would appear that, unlike modern nationalism, the sonnō-jōi movement of the later Mito school (including the *Shinron*) tended to "fear that the people may act" rather than endeavoring to defend the nation against the foreign foes in cooperation with the people. "It is stated in the classics," wrote Fujita Tōko in *Kōdō-kan kijutsugi*, "that superior men who work with their minds [*kokoro*] govern the people, and men who work with their bodies are governed by others. In effect, the lower a person's status, the more he has to work with his body. The higher a person's status, the more he has to work with his mind." Given such a rigid definition of rulers and ruled, he asked: "Who is responsible for the fact that the state of our nation is growing more dangerous every day? Is not the sole cause the fact that those who govern have neglected their duties?" In other words, he expected only the rulers, defined as above, to bear the responsibility during the national crisis. It is not difficult to imagine the exact nature of the royalist movement that fused with this kind of antiforeign movement. Not only did it not clash with the feudal hierarchy of estates; it supported that hierarchy.

I pointed out in chapter 2 of this part that Seishisai's sonnō position always went hand in hand with a probakufu position. The same is fundamentally true of both Fujita Yūkoku and his son Tōko. In their view the emperor occupied the highest place in the hierarchy of lord and subject relations in the feudal system. According to Seishisai in *Tekiihen*, for the subject "obedience to his lord means obedience to the laws of the Bakufu. This is the way he reveres the Emperor and fulfills his obligations to the Imperial ancestors." In other words, obedience to one's immediate lord is the concrete application of one's royalism. In the same way, from the ruler's point of view, "if the Bakufu reveres the Imperial Family, the feudal lords will respect the Bakufu. If the feudal lords respect the Bakufu, the ministers and high officials will respect the feudal lords. As a result high and low will support one another and the entire nation will cooperate. Is it not imperative that distinctions of name and status [*meibun*] be properly and strictly preserved?" said Fujita Yūkoku in *Seimeiron*. The proper maintenance of distinctions of "name and status" meant in effect the preservation of the hierarchical order of superiors and inferiors. It did not mean that the myriad people were to pledge their loyalty to one prince, directly and as equals.

This investigation has unmistakably revealed that the Mito school produced its theoretical formulation of the sonnō-jōi position from the feudal lords' standpoint. Of course, the real influence of the Mito school extended much more widely and it seems to have provided the theoretical basis for all the sonnō-jōi movements, including lower-class samurai or *sōmō* ("grass-roots") movements. One reason for this was that the idea of a national polity was here for the first time linked to concrete exigencies, and the doctrines of sonnō and fukoku kyōhei forcefully presented as an inseparable whole. Because they were appropriate to the dark trends of the times, the people did not probe into the concrete content of the doctrines of sonnō-jōi and fukoku kyōhei but were drawn to them as political slogans. Second, the political conflict between Nariaki, the central figure of the Mito school, and the ministers of the bakufu, while not involving the core of the bakufu-han system, was seen as a major clash because of the unique position of the Mito han as a *shinpan* or a domain held by a branch family of the Tokugawa. The Mito han thus came to be regarded as the rallying point for all the ill-defined movements for the destruction of the status quo. But when we trace the ideological genealogy of the sonnō and jōi movements, we find that the Mito school version represented the movement as a whole only during the 1850s. The earlier antiforeignism, whose object had been to drive off all foreign ships by force, was no longer realistic once treaties had been signed with the foreign powers. Once, late in their lives, Nariaki and Seishisai had come round to supporting the opening of the country, the split in the sonnō-jōi movement came out into the open. The original position of the Mito school was inherited by men like Shimazu Hisamitsu (1817–87) of Satsuma han, and began to come into serious conflict with an extremist branch of the movement. The first to expound this extremism theoretically was none other than Yoshida Shōin.

While the sonnō-jōi doctrine of Aizawa Seishisai and the two Fujitas was completely formed in the second quarter of the nineteenth century, Shōin's version only came to full maturity after Perry's arrival. The concrete results can be seen in the memorial that he submitted to the Edo estate of his han, Chōshū, after viewing firsthand the American warships anchored off Uraga. The most urgent problem of the day, he argued, was the need to eliminate feudal and regional particularism and to make it the whole nation's duty to the emperor to defend the country in the grave international crisis that would take place in six months' time when Perry returned. He headed his memorial *Taigi*, or "Cardinal Principle," and stated:

All the land under heaven is royal land, and all the coast lines are [inhabited by] royal subjects. . . . However, a deplorable vulgar theory prevails today. It is said that "Edo belongs to the Bakufu so it is the duty of the *hatamoto* [immediate retainers of the bakufu], the *fudai* [daimyo with hereditary ties to the bakufu], and the *gokamon* [the *han* belonging to the Tokugawa family] to assist it. The lords of the many *han* should concern themselves with their own domains. They need not exert themselves on behalf of Edo." Alas! these men not only do not know how to respect the Bakufu, they are ignorant of the cardinal principle of the world. Of course the feudal lords should value their own domains. But the land under heaven belongs to the Imperial Court. The nation belongs to the nation as a whole. It is not the private property of the Bakufu. Therefore, if any part of the land is desecrated by the foreign barbarians, the Bakufu must lead all the feudal lords of the land and avenge the dishonor inflicted on the entire nation. This is the way to ease the Imperial mind. In these critical times, how can the people of the entire heaven and earth not exert their utmost efforts?[19]

[19] *Yoshida Shōin zenshū* [Collected works of Yoshida Shōin], Popular Edition by Yamaguchi-ken Kyōiku-kai, 12 vols. (Tokyo, 1938), I, pp. 298–99.

At the same time, Shōin complained that "the custom of making bold remonstrances to the lord has vanished of late," and asked that "the verbal channels be opened." "Generally speaking," he maintained, "when an important matter is to be acted on, the policy agreed upon by public discussion should be adopted. This is a most important political matter."[20] In other words, he realized that national unity was seriously impeded not only by horizontal, regional exclusiveness but also by the vertical exclusiveness of estates.

In a Chinese poem composed at about the same time, Shōin expressed what can be regarded as a summary of his thought:

The Americans have come with a message making demands.
The nation's safety is now at stake.
In the entire heaven and earth everyone is a royal subject and all the land is royal land.
We must all join forces to repel the crafty barbarians.
At present it seems that high and low are all enjoying good government.
But law and order are declining.
Most serious is the stifling of wise opinions.
The custom of the prince personally attending the assembly of the ministers and listening to political discussions has long been abandoned.
High officials remain indolent and unconcerned.
Lesser subjects are preoccupied with schemes to make money.
The hearts of subjects outside the government are filled with pent-up anger.
Subjects in the government do nothing but flatter and fawn.
Only when these faults have been completely removed will we be ready for national defense.

He also called for a free discussion of the pros and cons of domestic and foreign policies.[21] All this suggests the aspects of the problems of his age that concerned him.

On the other hand, as the statement quoted earlier ("Alas! these men not only do not know how to respect the Bakufu . . .")

---

[20] Ibid., p. 300.
[21] Ibid., pp. 311–12.

shows, at this time his attitude regarding the relationship between the imperial court and the bakufu had not gone beyond the Mito school policy of respect for both emperor and bakufu. Although he was very angry when the bakufu "bowed its head, bated its breath, and agreed to whatever was asked regarding intercourse and commerce,"[22] and concluded the Treaty of Amity with Perry, in a letter he wrote from Noyama prison in March, 1855, to his friend Gesshō (1817–58), a Buddhist monk, he disagreed with the latter's proposal to overthrow the bakufu. "It is impossible to ask the Emperor's permission to attack the Bakufu," he wrote. "Brothers may argue at home but must defend the home against intruders from outside. There are formidable foes abroad. This is not the time to have a domestic squabble. Our sole task is to join hands with the feudal lords, admonish the Bakufu, and together devise long-range plans to build a powerful nation."[23] That is, he believed that the imperial and bakufu forces should join hands to unite the nation (kōbu gattai). In June, 1858, however, when Ii Naosuke (1816–60), the senior minister of the bakufu, signed the commercial treaty with Townsend Harris without imperial approval, Shōin changed his position completely:

Clearly the designs of the Americans are inimical to the Land of the Gods. It has been proven that the words of the American envoy lead to dishonor for the Land of the Gods. For this reason, the Emperor in extreme anger issued a decree severing relations with the American envoy. The Bakufu was obliged to obey, reverently and in haste. But it did not do so. It behaved with arrogance and complacency. It made flattery of the Americans the highest policy of the land. It gave no thought to the national danger, neglected to reflect upon the national dishonor, and failed to obey the Imperial decree. This is the crime committed by the Shogun. Heaven and earth will not tolerate it. All the gods and men are incensed. It is proper to destroy and kill in accordance with the basic principle of justice. No mercy need be shown.[24]

At last, then, his sonnō-jōi doctrine became a movement to overthrow the bakufu.

[22] Ibid., p. 353 (Yūshūroku).
[23] Ibid., IV, p. 25 (Noyama-goku bunkō).
[24] Ibid., V, p. 192 (Taigi o gisu, a memorial to the han, July 12).

Soon afterwards, the so-called great persecution of Ansei[25] began, and Shōin himself was imprisoned for the second time for
plotting to ambush Manabe Akikatsu, a member of the Council of
Elders (*rōjū*). From this time forward, Shōin's thought became
more and more radical. Initially he expected the antibakufu daimyo to provide the active leadership in overthrowing the bakufu.
Soon he concluded: "At present there are 260 daimyo but they
have all led a life of luxury and are unconcerned about the affairs
of the nation and the state. They are only concerned about themselves and their families and curry favor with the shifting times."[26]
As a result, he placed his hope in the *sōmō no shishi*, the "men of
high purpose from the grass roots," and the *tenka no rōnin*, the
"lordless samurai of the land." At about the same time Umeda
Unpin (1816–59) also wrote: "I know that the daimyo of today
are incompetent. They are as a whole childish and ignorant, and
are also without wealth and militarily weak. When one day there
is a national crisis, they only fear the loss of the independence of
their own domains. How could they serve the Emperor and concern themselves about the foreign menace?. . . But there is a saga-
cious Emperor above. The Imperial authority shines more brightly
each day. After a thousand years' eclipse, it is about to recapture
its ancient position. All men of purpose! How can you fail to work
towards this end?"[27]

These statements show that the sonnō-jōi movement had defini-
tively gone beyond the stage of the Mito school. It was no longer
content just to reaffirm the feudal hierarchy. On April 7, 1859,
Shōin wrote:

> As long as the Tokugawa government exists the extension of Ameri-
> can, Russian, English, and French control will know no bounds. It
> is indeed a matter of grave concern. Fortunately there is a wise
> Emperor above, who is deeply concerned about the situation. But
> the moth-eaten ways of the court nobility are even worse than the
> pernicious ways of the Bakufu. All they can do is to say that "it would
> pollute the Land of the Gods to permit the foreign barbarians to

[25] Great Councilor Ii Naosuke's policy of punishing men who opposed his policies
in the Ansei era (1854–60). (Translator's note.)
[26] *Yoshida Shōin zenshū*, V, pp. 251–52 (*Jiseiron*).
[27] Letter to Kusaka Yoshisuke.

approach the country." None are capable of realizing the grand designs and foresight of the ancients. For this reason nothing gets accomplished. As for the lords of the *han,* they can only flatter the Shogun and have no suggestions of their own. When the Shogun surrenders to the foreign barbarians they have no other choice but to surrender also. How can any red-blooded person bear to see our great Japan, which has remained independent and unconquered for three thousand years, suddenly become enslaved by other powers? Until a Napoleon emerges in our midst to champion our freedom, our inner agony will not cease.[28]

This was the harsh reality as he saw it. There was no one among the bakufu, the daimyo, the court nobility, among all the members of the ruling class, capable of assuming the responsibility of preserving Japan's freedom and independence against the foreign powers. This realization led him to conclude that "the doctrine of *sonnō-jōi* cannot possibly be put into effect unless the world [that is, the whole of Japan] of today is completely transformed."[29] "The world of today is like an old, decaying house. This is obvious to everyone. I believe that if this house were blown down by a great wind, and we were to rebuild it by replacing the rotten pillars, discarding worn-out rafters, and adding new wood, it would become a beautiful building. . . . But because of this [the need for major renovation] it will not be easy to put into effect the doctrines of *sonnō-jōi.*"[30] Clearly he was not interested in preserving the existing political and social structures but rather favored "the complete transformation of the world of today" as the solution to all Japan's problems. Of course, Shōin himself had no concrete idea what this "complete transformation of the world" would entail. He had a vague premonition that it would lead to a single ruler governing the entire population (ikkun banmin), and he went to his execution calmly, leaving behind these words:

The four seas all belong to the King [the Emperor].
A myriad people all worship the sun.
Return to the Emperor without questioning,

[28] *Yoshida Shōin zenshū,* IX, p. 326 (Letter to Kitayama Ansei).
[29] Ibid., p. 330 (Letter to Okabe Tomitarō, April 9).
[30] Ibid., VI, p. 122 (*Shien ni tsugu*).

And expound the doctrine of *sonnō-jōi* everywhere.[31]

We can justifiably conclude that with Shōin the sonnō-jōi movement was carried as far as it could go within its historical limitations.

IV

The general survey I have made of the intellectual currents of
premodern nationalism reveal that, despite the diversity of their
intellectual content, certain inner tendencies can be seen running
through the entire movement. As the pluralist segmentation of
feudal society demonstrated its impotence when confronted by the
foreign powers, the demand for national unity in the interests of
the nation's independence took two forms in the realm of domestic
policy. One was a demand for the concentration of power in the
hands of the state; the other was a call for its distribution throughout the nation. In the earlier debates on coastal defense, I noted
that the condemnation of horizontal regional particularism and
the call for nationwide involvement were inextricably bound up
with the demand for a relaxation of vertical estate distinctions and
the opening of a channel of articulation between the people and
the government. This theoretical connection led straight to the
sonnō-jōi doctrine. As long as the autonomous existence of intermediary powers impeded the inward union of state and nation,
the nationalism that was to overcome these intermediary powers
sought to concretize itself in what can be called a dialectical process of unification, simultaneously embodying these two elements:
centralization and extension.

This tendency toward political centralization advanced decisively toward an absolutist system in the doctrine of fukoku kyōhei (enrich the nation and strengthen the military). The search
for an agent in whom this centralized political authority could
ultimately be lodged brought the doctrine of sonnō (revere the
emperor) to the political forefront. I have also noted how the
sonnō-jōi movement gradually extended its search for social lead-

---

[31] Ibid., XI, p. 191 (*Tōkōzen nikki*, May 19).

ership from the feudal rulers to the people, who were expected to
"rise with determination from the grass roots." This is an expression of the same historical movement that produced the demand
among the intellectuals of the Bakumatsu period for "public discussion and the voicing of public opinion." In this respect Abe
Masahiro's[32] behavior on Perry's arrival can be regarded as an
indication of the dissolution of the intermediary powers along two
lines, one toward centralization around a supreme authority and
the other toward the extension of authority among the people.
Unable to make any decision, Masahiro consulted the imperial
court on the one hand, and on the other asked for the opinions of
the daimyo and other officials, requesting them to "express your
opinions freely without reservation, for even if they are disagree-
able no offense will be taken." In this respect Masahiro's action had
a greater significance than he had intended and can be interpreted
as a historical symbol for the dynamics of nationalism.

Did these two currents of premodern nationalist thought develop equally? Certainly not. It is easy to see the current that took
the dominant position from beginning to end was political centralization. Faced with the external crisis, the most urgent necessity was the unification of the divided feudal political forces, and
the reinforcement of the national defenses by the establishment of
a powerful central government capable of "manipulating the entire country of Japan as if it were its hands and feet" (Nobuhiro).
Stabilization of national life and the development of industrial
enterprises were proposed as the preconditions for this. On the
other hand, the movement to arouse political awareness among
wider and wider sections of society so as to stir the nation out of its
previous state of passive dependence and irresponsibility toward
the political order, and mobilize all its forces politically, was rather
amorphous; and although it was expounded as an integral part of
the move for centralization, it barely managed to keep pace with
it, its tempo being much slower. Its proposals grew steadily in
concreteness, beginning with the request for the opening of channels of articulation between the people and the ruler, a semi-
Oriental concept, followed by demands for the relaxation of status

---

[32] 1819–57, a member of the Council of Elders (rōjū). (Translator's note.)

barriers, the utilization of men of ability from the lower classes, and open public discussions and the voicing of public opinion. But the demand for the extension of political authority lower in the society was always blocked at a line of demarcation that could not be crossed.

When it came to the critical question of who was ultimately responsible for national independence, the public at large outside the feudal ruling class was, as the Mito school reveals in typical fashion, excluded from the discussions. Abstractly speaking, it might be true that "from the feudal lords at the top down to the high officials, samurai, and common people, we must all be of one mind and combine our efforts" (Shōin),[33] and that "the entire nation of Japan is to be regarded as a single family" (Hashimoto Sanai).[34] But no one went deep enough into the social factors that made a general political mobilization of the nation impossible in practice. Shōin, searching for a driving force for the sonnō-jōi movement, looked lower and lower in the society for it, from the bakufu, to the feudal lords, to their retainers, and to the ronin. But his last hope was the sōmō no shishi, the "men of high purpose from the grass roots," all of whom were, of course, samurai. He did not look any lower.[35] What is noteworthy here is that it was this inability of premodern nationalist thought to extend itself broadly into the society that made possible the tenacious survival of feudal intermediary powers and thus prevented elements favoring centralization from gaining complete success.

The centralization of political power so as to increase production, develop industries, and strengthen military defenses, which

[33] *Yoshida Shōin zenshū,* I, pp. 553–55.

[34] *Hashimoto Keigaku zenshū* [Collected works of Hashimoto Keigaku], 2 vols. (Tokyo, 1943), I, p. 555 (Letter to Murata Ujihisa, November 28). (Hashimoto Sanai [1834–59] was scholar and physician of the Bakumatsu period who played an active political role and fell victim to the Ansei purges. Translator's note.)

[35] In a letter written to Nomura Yasushi on March 26, 1859, Shōin stated: "Under the present circumstances, neither the feudal lords nor the court nobility can be relied on. Only the people of the grass roots remain. But they, too, lack the power for leadership. *Might there not be an extraordinary scheme to travel around the nation and take advantage of the situation when a peasant rising occurs?*" (*Yoshida Shōin zenshū,* IX, p. 291). This clearly illustrates the impatience and despair he felt toward the end of his life. That he hit upon the idea of utilizing the energy of peasant uprisings shows his perceptivity, but he still intended merely to "take advantage of the situation"; he did not regard these uprisings as revolutionary agencies in themselves.

was more or less favored by all the advocates of the fukoku kyōhei doctrine whether they proposed foreign trade and colonization (Nobuhiro, Toshiaki, Zōzan, and Hoashi Banri)[36] or the establishment of a peasant soldiery (Shihei, Yūkoku, Seishisai, and Tōko), was something that went beyond the political and economic self-sufficiency of the feudal domains, but it did not envision their destruction. This remained the case whether the centralized political power was conceived as falling to the imperial court or to the bakufu. Even when the sonnō doctrine ("revere the emperor") changed from sonnō keibaku ("revere the emperor and respect the bakufu") to kōbu gattai (the union of the two) and finally tōbaku ("overthrow the bakufu"), many advocates of sonnō-jōi had no intention of lifting a finger against the independent authority of the han. This point of view was expressed by Maki Yasuomi,[37] who believed that the good policy was "to serve the feudal lords in order to accomplish things," while the bad policy was "for righteously motivated individuals to take direct action." Only in Shō-in's thought in its final phase can we detect a vague indication of a premonition of the fact that a fundamental change in the entire system would be necessary to preserve the vrijdom of Japan against the foreign powers. In short, both in their efforts to extend their ideas among the people and to centralize political power, the fukoku kyōhei movement as well as the sonnō-jōi movement came to a halt at the last historical iron barrier of the feudal structure. This accurately reveals the limitation common to all these nationalistic theories. This is the fundamental reason why I have called these kinds of nationalism premodern. The unique features of the intellectual development I have described up to this point correspond exactly to the basic direction of the actual course of political unification in Bakumatsu Japan.

As I have already pointed out, the political force that was to solve the domestic disunity and anarchic chaos produced when the arrival of foreign vessels sapped the bakufu's authority was not to arise from the common people. As is well known, the political

---

[36] Hoashi Banri (1778–1852) was a Confucian scholar as well as a student of mathematics and Dutch. He was known as one of the three greatest scholars of his day. (Translator's note.)

[37] Maki Yasuomi (1813–64) was a disciple of Aizawa Seishisai and an extremist advocate of sonnō-jōi. (Translator's note.)

reforms of the Restoration of Imperial Rule (Ōseifukkō) were put into effect under the leadership of extremist court nobles, lower-class samurai, and some elements from the upper strata of the common people, while the feudal ruling class was in process of disintegration. And the political pattern that emerged immediately after the liquidation of the bakufu was an alliance of the most powerful han under the leadership of the imperial court. This was the immediate concrete result of the movement for public discussion and the voicing of public opinion. Of course, this government cannot be regarded as a mere continuation or variation of the feudal, pluralistic political pattern. To preserve Japan's national independence in the face of the ever-present pressure of the Western powers, the fulfillment of the policy of enriching the nation and strengthening the military by *seirei no kiitsu* or centralization of political forces was a matter of the utmost urgency. Actually, the modernization of the military forces and the "increase of production and development of industries," advocated by the various thinkers I have discussed, had already been implemented to some extent by the bakufu itself before its downfall. And the powerful han of southwestern Japan, which constituted the government of the Restoration, were particularly advanced in these fields. So in their final stage, the feudal powers themselves had to rely on non-feudal, modern industry and technology to ensure their survival.

As the end of the Tokugawa period approached, then, the need to establish an absolutist system became a matter of general concern, for both the court and the bakufu. The question of leadership was the only issue in dispute. This being so, there was no possibility of the survival of a purely feudal hierarchical and decentralized system. Nevertheless, the fact that the liquidation of the pouvoirs intermédiaires was carried out without the active participation of the popular classes, and, moreover, by the very elements that constituted those intermediate powers, had a decisive effect on the character of the Meiji innovations intended to give rise to a modern nation-state. In the continuing presence of external pressures, what Fukuzawa Yukichi called "the implantation of the concept 'nation' in the minds of the people of the entire country" now became the urgent task of the Meiji thinkers.

BIBLIOGRAPHY

Works in English

Akamatsu, Paul. *Meiji, 1868*. New York: Harper & Row, 1974.

Anesaki, Masaharu. *History of Japanese Religion*. Tokyo and Rutland, Vt.: Tuttle, 1963.

Beasley, W. G. *The Meiji Restoration*. Stanford: Stanford University Press, 1972.

Bellah, Robert N. *Tokugawa Religion: The Values of Pre-industrial Japan*. Glencoe, Ill.: Free Press, 1957.

Blacker, Carmen. *The Japanese Enlightenment*. New York: Cambridge University Press, 1964.

Borton, Hugh. *Peasant Uprisings in Japan of the Tokugawa Period*. 2d ed. New York: Paragon Reprint Corp., 1968.

Chan, Wing-tsit. *A Source Book of Chinese Philosophy*. Princeton, N.J.: Princeton University Press, 1963.

Chang, Carsun. *The Development of Neo-Confucian Thought*. New York: Bookman Associates, 1957.

Chikamatsu, Monzaemon. *The Major Plays of Chikamatsu*. Translated by Donald Keene. New York: Columbia University Press, 1961.

Craig, Albert M. *Choshu in the Meiji Restoration*. Cambridge, Mass.: Harvard University Press, 1961.

————, and Shively, Donald H. *Personality in Japanese History*. Berkeley: University of California Press, 1970.

Dore, Ronald P. *Education in Tokugawa Japan*. Berkeley: University of California Press, 1965.

Dumoulin, Heinrich, tr. "Kamo Mabuchi: Kokuikō." *Monumenta Nipponica*, II, 1 (1939).

Earl, David M. *Emperor and Nation in Japan: Political Thinkers of the Tokugawa Period*. Seattle: University of Washington Press, 1964.

Fung Yu-lan. *A History of Chinese Philosophy*. Translated by Derk Bodde. 2 vols. Princeton, N.J.: Princeton University Press, 1952–53.

Hall, John W. *Tanuma Okitsugu, 1719–1788: Forerunner of Modern Japan*. Princeton, N.J.: Princeton University Press, 1968.

————, and Jansen, Marius B., eds. *Studies in the Institutional History of Early Modern Japan*. Princeton, N.J.: Princeton University Press, 1968.

Harootunian, Harry D. *Toward Restoration*. Berkeley: University of California Press, 1970.

Havens, Thomas R. H. *Nishi Amane*. Princeton, N.J.: Princeton University Press, 1970.

Hibbett, Howard. *The Floating World in Japanese Fiction*. New York: Grove Press, 1960.

Holtom, Daniel C. *The National Faith of Japan: A Study in Modern Shinto*. New York: Dutton, 1938.

Honjo Eijiro. *Economic Theory and History of Japan in the Tokugawa Period*. Tokyo: Maruzen, 1943.

Ihara, Saikaku. *The Japanese Family Storehouse*. Cambridge, England: Cambridge University Press, 1959.

———. *The Life of an Amorous Woman and Other Writings*. Translated by Ivan Morris. Norfolk, Conn.: Laughlin, 1963.

Jansen, Marius B., ed. *Changing Japanese Attitudes Toward Modernization*. Princeton, N.J.: Princeton University Press, 1965.

———. *Sakamoto Ryōma and the Meiji Restoration*. Princeton, N.J.: Princeton University Press, 1961.

Keene, Donald. *The Japanese Discovery of Europe, 1720–1830*. Stanford: Stanford University Press, 1969.

Kitagawa, Joseph M. *Religion in Japanese History*. New York: Columbia University Press, 1966.

Kumazawa, Banzan. "Daigaku Wakumon: A Discussion of Public Questions in the Light of the Great Learning." Translated by Galen M. Fisher. *Transactions of the Asiatic Society of Japan* (2nd series), 16 (1938), 259–346.

Lidin, Olof G. *Life of Ogyu Sorai*. Lund, Sweden: Student Litteratur, 1973.

Lloyd, Arthur. "Historical Development of the Shushi Philosophy in Japan." *Transactions of the Asiatic Society of Japan*, 34, pt. 4 (1906).

Matsumoto Shigeru. *Motoori Norinaga*. Cambridge, Mass.: Harvard University Press, 1970.

McEwan, J. R. *The Political Writings of Ogyū Sorai*. Cambridge, England: Cambridge University Press, 1962.

Muraoka, Tsunetsugu. *Studies in Shinto Thought*. Translated by D. M. Brown and J. T. Araki. Tokyo: Japanese Committee for UNESCO, 1964.

Norman, E. H. "Andō Shōeki and the Anatomy of Japanese Feudalism." *Transactions of the Asiatic Society of Japan* (3d series), 2 (1949).

Passin, Herbert. *Society and Education in Japan*. New York: Bureau of Publications, Teachers' College and East Asian Institute, Columbia University, 1965.

Pittau, Joseph. *Political Thought in Early Meiji Japan, 1868–1889*. Cambridge, Mass.: Harvard University Press, 1967.

Sadler, A. L. *The Maker of Modern Japan: The Life of Tokugawa Ieyasu*. New York: Norton, 1941.

Sansom, Sir George B. *A History of Japan, 1615–1867.* Stanford: Stanford University Press, 1963.

———. *The Western World and Japan.* New York: Knopf, 1950.

Satow, Sir Ernest M. *A Diplomat in Japan.* London: Seeley Service, 1921.

Sheldon, Charles D. *The Rise of the Merchant Class in Tokugawa Japan, 1600–1868.* Locust Valley, N.Y.: Association for Asian Studies, 1958.

Smith, Neil Skene. "An Introduction to Some Japanese Economic Writings of the 18th Century." *Transactions of the Asiatic Society of Japan* (2nd series), 11 (1934), 32–105.

Spae, Joseph J. *Itō Jinsai. Monumenta Serica,* Monograph 12. Peking, 1948.

Straelen, Henricus van. *Yoshida Shoin.* Leiden: E. J. Brill, 1952.

Totman, Conrad D. *Politics in the Tokugawa Bakufu.* Cambridge, Mass.: Harvard University Press, 1967.

Tsunoda, Ryusaku, de Bary, Wm. Theodore, and Keene, Donald, eds. *Sources of Japanese Tradition.* New York: Columbia University Press, 1958.

Webb, Herschel. *The Japanese Imperial Institution in the Tokugawa Period.* New York: Columbia University Press, 1968.

Zachert, Herbert. "Social Changes During the Tokugawa Period." *Transactions of the Asiatic Society of Japan* (2nd series), 17 (1938).

Works in Japanese

Aoki Kōji. *Hyakushō ikki no nenjiteki kenkyu* (A chronological study of peasant uprisings). Tokyo: Shinseisha, 1966.

Bitō Masahide. *Nihon hōkenshisōshi kenkyū* (Study of the history of Japanese feudal thought). Tokyo: Aoki Shoten, 1961.

Furushima Toshio. *Nihon hōken nōgyō-shi* (History of Japanese agriculture in the feudal period). Tokyo: Shikai Shobō, 1941.

Haga Noboru. *Bakumatsu kokugaku no tenkai* (Development of kokugaku at the end of the Tokugawa period). Tokyo: Hanawa Shobō, 1963.

Hani Gorō. *Nihon ni okeru kindai shisō no zentei* (The background to modern Japanese thought). Tokyo: Iwanami, 1949.

Hirose Yutaka. *Yoshida Shōin no kenkyū* (A study of Yoshida Shōin). Tokyo: Tōkyō Musashi Shoin, 1931.

Honjō Eijirō. *Nihon keizaishisōshi kenkyū* (Study of the history of Japanese economic thought). Tokyo: Nihon Hyōronsha, 1942.

Hori Takao. *Yamaga Sokō.* Tokyo: Yoshikawa Kōbunkan, 1959.

Ienaga Saburō. *Nihon dōtokushisōshi* (History of Japanese moral thought). Tokyo: Iwanami, 1951.

Imanaka Kanji. *Soraigaku no kisoteki kenkyū* (Basic study of Sorai's philosophy). Tokyo: Yoshikawa Kōbunkan, 1966.

Inoue Minoru. *Kamo Mabuchi no gakumon* (The scholarship of Kamo Mabuchi). Tokyo: Yagi Shoten, 1943.

Inoue Tadashi. *Kaibara Ekken*. Tokyo: Yoshikawa Kōbunkan, 1963.

Inoue Tetsujirō. *Nihon kogakuha no tetsugaku* (The philosophy of the Japanese school of ancient learning). Tokyo: Fuzanbō, 1902.

―――. *Nihon shushigakuha no tetsugaku* (The philosophy of the Japanese Chu Hsi school). Tokyo: Fuzanbō, 1902.

―――. *Nihon yōmeigakuha no tetsugaku* (The philosophy of the Japanese Wang Yang-ming school). Tokyo: Fuzanbō, 1900.

Ishida Ichirō. *Chōnin bunka—Genroku, Bunka, Bunsei jidai no bunka ni tuite* (Townsmen's culture—the culture of the Genroku, Bunka, Bunsei periods). Tokyo: Shibundō, 1961.

―――. *Itō Jinsai*. Tokyo: Yoshikawa Kōbunkan, 1960.

Itō Tasaburō. *Nihon kinseishi (2): Kyōhō–Bunka–Bunsei* (History of early modern Japan, 2: From Kyōhō to Bunka-Bunsei periods). Yūhikaku Zensho Series. Tokyo: Yuhikaku, 1952.

―――. *Kokugaku no shiteki kōsatsu* (Historical observations on kokugaku). Tokyo: Ōokayama Shoten, 1932.

Iwabashi Junsei. *Sorai Kenkyū* (A study of Sorai). Tokyo: Seki Shoin, 1934.

Kikuchi Kenjirō. *Mito-gaku ronsō* (Studies of the Mito school). Tokyo: Seibundō Shinkōsha, 1943.

Kitajima Masamoto. *Edo jidai* (Edo period). Tokyo: Iwanami, 1958.

―――. *Edo bakufu no kenryoku kōzō* (The power structure of the Edo bakufu). Tokyo: Iwanami, 1964.

Kokushō Iwao. *Hyakushō ikki no kenkyū* (A study of peasant uprisings). Tokyo: Iwanami, 1929.

―――. *Hyakushō ikki no kenkyū, zoku-hen* (A study of peasant uprisings: a sequel). Kyoto: Mineruba, 1959.

Kōno Shōzō. *Kokugaku no kenkyū* (A study of kokugaku). Tokyo: Ōokayama Shoten, 1932.

Kurita Motoji. *Edo Jidai, I* (Edo period), in *Sōgō Nihonshi Taikei* (Comprehensive Japanese history). Tokyo: Naigai Shoseki, 1927.

Maezawa Engetsu. *Dazai Shundai*. Tokyo: Shūzanbō, 1920.

Matsumoto Sannosuke. *Kokugaku seiji shisō no kenkyū* (Study of the political thinking of kokugaku). Tokyo: Yūhikaku, 1957.

Mikami Sanji. *Edo Jidai-shi* (History of the Edo period). 2 vols. Tokyo: Fuzanbō, 1943.

―――. *Sonnōron hattatsushi* (History of the development of the theory of sonnō). Tokyo: Fuzanbō, 1941.

Morimoto Junichi. *Tōyō seijishisōshi kenkyū* (A study of Oriental political thought). Tokyo: Miraisha, 1967.

Muraoka Tsunetsugu. *Motoori Norinaga*. Tokyo: Keiseisha, 1911.

―――. *Nihon shisōshi kenkyū* (Studies in the history of Japanese thought). 4 vols. Tokyo: Iwanami, 1930–49.

————. *Motoori Norinaga to Hirata Atsutane.* Tokyo: Sōbunsha, 1957.

Nagata Hiroshi. *Nihon hōken ideorogi* (Japanese feudal ideology). Tokyo: Hakuyōsha, 1947.

————. *Nihon tetsugakushisōshi* (A history of Japanese philosophical thought). Tokyo: Mikasa Shobō, 1938.

Nakamura Kichiji. *Nihon keizaishi-gaisetsu* (Outline of Japanese economic history). Tokyo: Nihon Hyōronsha, 1941.

Nakamura Kōya. *Genroku oyobi Kyōhō-jidai ni okeru keizaishiso no kenkyū* (Study of the economic thought of the Genroku and Kyōhō periods). Tokyo: Kokumin Bunka Kenkyūkai, 1927.

Naramoto Tatsuya, ed. *Kinsei Nihon shisōshi kenkyū* (Studies in early modern Japanese intellectual history). Tokyo: Kawade Shobō, 1965.

————. *Nihon hōken shakaishi-ron* (Historical treatises on Japanese feudal society). Tokyo: Kōtō Shoin, 1948.

————. *Nihon no shisōka* (The thinkers of Japan). Tokyo: Mainichi Shinbunsha, 1954.

————. *Yoshida Shōin.* Tokyo: Iwanami, 1955.

Nihon Keizai Kenkyūjo, ed. *Kinsei Nihon no sandai kaikaku* (Three great reforms in early modern Japan). Tokyo: Ryūginsha, 1944.

Nomura Kentarō. *Ogyū Sorai.* Tokyo: Sanseidō, 1937.

————. *Tokugawa-jidai no keizai-shisō* (Economic thought of the Tokugawa period). Tokyo: Nihon Hyōronsha, 1939.

Numata Jirō. *Yōgaku denrai no rekishi* (History of the advent of Western learning). Tokyo: Shibundō, 1960.

Ōkubo Tadashi. *Edo jidai no kokugaku* (Kokugaku in the Edo period). Tokyo: Shibundō, 1963.

Sagara Tōru. *Kinsei no jyukyō shisō* (Premodern Confucian thought). Tokyo: Hanawa Shobō, 1966.

————. *Kinsei Nihon jukyō undō no keifu* (Genealogy of the Confucian movement of early modern Japan). Tokyo: Kōbundō, 1955.

Saito Ryūzō. *Genroku sesōshi* (Record of Genroku social conditions). Tokyo: Hakubunkan, 1905.

Tahara Tsuguo. *Motoori Norinaga.* Tokyo: Kodansha, 1968.

————. *Tokugawa shisōshi kenkyū* (Study of the history of Tokugawa thought). Tokyo: Miraisha, 1967.

Takeoka Katsuya. *Kinseishi no hatten to kokugakusha no undō* (The development of early modern history and the kokugakusha movement). Tokyo: Shibundō, 1927.

Takeuchi Yoshio. *Sōgaku no yurai oyobi sono tokushusei* (The origins and uniqueness of the Sung School). Tokyo: Iwanami, 1934.

Takigawa Masujirō. *Nihon Shakai-shi* (Social history of Japan). Tokyo: Tōkō Shoin, 1929.

Tatsui Matsunosuke. *Edo jidai, II* (Edo period), in *Sōgō Nihonshi taikei* (Comprehensive history of Japan). Tokyo: Naigai Shoseki, 1926.

Tokugawa-kō Keisō Nanajū-nen Shukuga Kinenkai, ed. *Kinsei Nihon no jugaku* (Confucianism of early modern Japan). Tokyo: Iwanami, 1939.

Tsuchiya Takao. *Hōkenshakai hōkai-katei no kenkyū* (Study of the process of decline of feudal society). Tokyo: Kōbundō Shobō, 1927.

———. *Kinsei Nihon hōken shakai no shiteki bunseki* (Historical analysis of feudal society of early modern Japan). Tokyo: Ochanomizu Shobō, 1949.

Tsuda Sōkichi. *Bungaku ni arawaretaru kokuminshisō no kenkyū* (A study of Japanese thought as manifested in literature). 4 vols. Tokyo: Iwanami, 1951–55.

———. *Nihon no shintō* (Japanese Shinto). Tokyo: Iwanami, 1949.

Tsuji Tatsuya. *Kyōhō kaikaku no kenkyū* (Study of the Kyōhō reform). Tokyo: Sōbunsha, 1963.

Watanabe Daitō. *Andō Shōeki to Shizen Shineidō* (Andō Shōeki and Shizen Shineidō). Tokyo: Mokuseisha Shoin, 1930.

Watsuji Tetsurō. *Nihon rinri shisōshi* (A history of Japanese ethical thought). 2 vols. Tokyo: Iwanami, 1952.

———. *Sonnō shisō to sono dentō* (The ideology of sonnō and its tradition). Tokyo: Iwanami, 1944.

Yoshida Tōgo. *Tokugawa seikyōkō.* (A study of Tokugawa government and philosophy). Tokyo: Fuzanbō, 1893–94.

* This bibliography, prepared by the translator, is suggested for background reading and is not a bibliography of the sources used by the author.

INDEX

Abe Masahiro: 364
agemai (presentation rice): 121
Aizawa Seishisai: 366; on "barbarians," 304; on commoners, 354–355; on Emperor and bakufu, 304–305; and natural order, 305–306; and *sonnō jōi*, 353–358
Akō warriors: 71–72, 103–104
Alcock, Rutherford: 352, 353
Amaterasu O-mikami: 156
Amenomori Hōshū: 9
Ancient Learning (Confucian school): 17, 65–68 *passim*, 202
Ancient Way (*kodō*): 155, 175, 264, 265, 270
Andō Shōeki: 189, 249 *passim*, 274; on Confucian concepts, 257; on early Confucians, 253–254; on "direct cultivation," 256; on *gosei*, 259–260; on ideal society, 261–262; on peasants, 252–253; on sages, 254–255; on samurai, 253; on Taoists, 258
Andō Tōya: 136, 138
Ansai. SEE Yamazaki Ansai
Ansei, great persecution of: 361
anti-feudal consciousness: 191–192
Aquinas, Thomas: 234
Arai Hakuseki: 121, 123, 178, 247
Ashiwake-obune [A little boat weaving through the reeds]: 167
Autobiography in Exile (haisho zanpitsu): 40 n. 41, 43

Baba Tatsui: 313
Bankoku sōwa [Anecdotes from myriad nations]: 240, 247
Banzan. SEE Kumazawa Banzan
Barker, Ernest: 233
Bendō [On distinguishing the Way]: 67, 75, 110, 210, 212
Bendō kaihei [Unmasking Sorai's Bendō]: 282

Bendōsho [Discourse on distinguishing the Way]: 145, 172
Benmei [On distinguishing terms]: 67, 75, 104, 242
Bitō Nishū: 242
Book of Changes (I Ching): 21, 196–197
Book of Rites (Li Chi): 24, 197
Buddhism: and Sung Philosophy, 13
Buke Hatto (Laws governing the military households): 10 n.14, n.15, 39, 244 n.7
Bunkai zakki [Miscellaneous essays]: 101
bunmei kaika (enlightenment and civilization): 311
Bunmeiron no gairyaku [Outline of civilization]: 315
Burke, Edmund: 317

Calvin, John: 234–235
Catherine II: 276
ch'eng (sincerity): 198
Ch'eng I-ch'uan: 19
Ch'eng Ming-tao: 19
ch'i (Ether): 21 *passim*, 52–53, 62–63, 197
Chikamatsu Monzaemon: 115, 124, 329 n.3
Chimeiki [An account of knowing one's destiny]: 302
Chinese poems (*shi*): Sorai on, 108
ching (seriousness): 13, 13 n.22, 24, 44, 64
Ching chai chen [Admonitions on reverence and abstention]: 38
Chin-ssu lu [Reflections on things at hand]: 199–200
Chirizukadan [Discourses from a dust heap]: 285
chokkō (direct cultivation): 253, 256

375